Twilight of the Idols and
Nietzsche's Late Philosophy

Also available from Bloomsbury

Nietzsche's 'Ecce Homo' and the Revaluation of All Values, by Thomas H. Brobjer
Joy and Laughter in Nietzsche's Philosophy, edited by Paul E. Kirkland and Michael J. McNeal
Nietzsche's Renewal of Ancient Ethics, by Neil Durrant
'The Gift' in Nietzsche's Zarathustra, by Emilio Corriero
The Parallel Philosophies of Sartre and Nietzsche, by Nik Farrell Fox

Twilight of the Idols and Nietzsche's Late Philosophy

Toward a Revaluation of Values

Thomas H. Brobjer

BLOOMSBURY ACADEMIC
LONDON • NEW YORK • OXFORD • NEW DELHI • SYDNEY

BLOOMSBURY ACADEMIC
Bloomsbury Publishing Plc
50 Bedford Square, London, WC1B 3DP, UK
1385 Broadway, New York, NY 10018, USA
29 Earlsfort Terrace, Dublin 2, Ireland

BLOOMSBURY, BLOOMSBURY ACADEMIC and the Diana logo are trademarks of
Bloomsbury Publishing Plc

First published in Great Britain 2023
This paperback edition published 2024

Copyright © Thomas H. Brobjer, 2023

Thomas H. Brobjer has asserted his right under the Copyright, Designs and Patents Act, 1988, to be identified as Author of this work.

Series design by Charlotte Daniels
Cover image: Aare, Switzerland (© Dan Schleusser / Unsplash)

All rights reserved. No part of this publication may be reproduced or transmitted in any form or by any means, electronic or mechanical, including photocopying, recording, or any information storage or retrieval system, without prior permission in writing from the publishers.

Bloomsbury Publishing Plc does not have any control over, or responsibility for, any third-party websites referred to or in this book. All internet addresses given in this book were correct at the time of going to press. The author and publisher regret any inconvenience caused if addresses have changed or sites have ceased to exist, but can accept no responsibility for any such changes.

A catalogue record for this book is available from the British Library.

A catalog record for this book is available from the Library of Congress.

Library of Congress Control Number: 2023939549.

ISBN: HB: 978-1-3503-2940-9
PB: 978-1-3503-2944-7
ePDF: 978-1-3503-2941-6
eBook: 978-1-3503-2942-3

Typeset by Deanta Global Publishing Services, Chennai, India

To find out more about our authors and books visit www.bloomsbury.com and sign up for our newsletters.

To Laura and Miranda

Contents

List of illustrations		viii
1	Introduction: The purpose of *Twilight of the Idols*	1
2	How has *Twilight of the Idols* been read, understood and used?	11
3	The genesis, chronology and composition of the *Twilight of the Idols* and the *Revaluation of All Values*	27
4	Sources to and influences on *Twilight of the Idols*	37
5	Reading *Twilight of the Idols* as relating to Nietzsche's *Revaluation of All Values*	53
	5.1 General consequences and observations	53
	5.2 Title, subtitle, foreword and the aphorisms (chapter 1)	55
	5.3 The philosophy-critical chapters (2, 3 and 4)	67
	5.4 The morality- and religion-critical chapters (6, 5 and 7)	72
	5.5 The old preface and its critique of the Germans and their educational system (8)	84
	5.6 The long miscellaneous chapter on aesthetics, writers, artists and others (9)	85
	5.7 The last chapter on antiquity and the Dionysian (10)	109
	5.8 The epilogue: The hammer speaks	112
	5.9 References to the *Revaluation of All Values* in *Götzen-Dämmerung*	117
	5.10 Some conclusions	118
6	What is not included in *Twilight of the Idols*: Or what is it a 'summary' of?	125
7	The role and place of the idea of eternal recurrence in *Twilight of the Idols*	145
8	The role of psychology, reason and instinct in *Twilight of the Idols*	165
9	The critique of Christianity in *Twilight of the Idols* and its relation to *The Antichrist*	177
10	Conclusion and summary	189
Appendix: Tables summarizing aspects of *Twilight of the Idols*		193
Notes		201
Bibliography		241
Index		245

Illustrations

Figures

5.1   A schema to illustrate Nietzsche's physiological and psychological approach to art and aesthetics   90

Tables

3.1   The Evolution of the Planned Title of Nietzsche's *magnum opus*, from Autumn 1881 to December 1888   32
3.2   Planned Chapter Titles for Nietzsche's Hauptwerk from Earlier in 1888, Here Classified and Organized according to the Book Divisions from September to November 1888   34
5.1   Summary of Nietzsche's Views on Aesthetics in *Götzen-Dämmerung*   94
5.2   Summary of the Contents of the Late (4–13 October 1888) Added Sections, 32–44, to the Chapter 'Expeditions of an Untimely Man'   97
9.1   Summary of the Critique of Religion and Christianity in *Götzen-Dämmerung*   179
9.2   The Relation between *Götzen-Dämmerung* and *Der Antichrist* (as the First Volume of the *Umwerthung aller Werthe*)   180
A.1   Chapters, Thematic Listing and the Chronology of the Chapters of *Götzen-Dämmerung*   194
A.2   Summary of Themes in *Götzen-Dämmerung*   195
A.3   Summary of Nietzsche's Critique and Affirmation in *Götzen-Dämmerung*   196
A.4   Pointers in *Götzen-Dämmerung* to the *Umwerthung aller Werthe*   197
A.5   The Presence of (and Pointers to) the Idea of Eternal Recurrence in *Götzen-Dämmerung*   199

1

Introduction

The purpose of *Twilight of the Idols*

1.1 Introduction 1
1.2 How has *Götzen-Dämmerung* been regarded? 2
1.3 The relation of *Götzen-Dämmerung* to Nietzsche's planned *magnum opus* (*Hauptwerk*) 3
1.4 Is *Götzen-Dämmerung* a summary of Nietzsche's philosophy? 6

1.1 Introduction

Why did Nietzsche write *Twilight of the Idols* (*Götzen-Dämmerung*) in the autumn of 1888? What was his purpose? What are we meant to get out of reading it? What is its relation to Nietzsche's late philosophy and to his other late books? In particular, what is its relation to his work on the never completed *Hauptwerk* in four volumes that he had been working on since circa 1884 and which was at the time of writing *Götzen-Dämmerung* coming to a crescendo?

Götzen-Dämmerung is short, well and clearly written, full of interesting thoughts, radical, polemical, humorous and profound, but at the same time a book which it is difficult to get a grasp of. According to Nietzsche himself, it contains an extract and summary of his late philosophy, and as such merits full attention. If one were to read only one work by Nietzsche, this is surely in most cases the best candidate. It is true that Nietzsche himself would perhaps have argued for *Also sprach Zarathustra* – and there is much to warrant such a view, but that work is much longer, and more importantly, it is a very different sort of work, poetical and metaphorical, which makes the interpretation of it far from obvious, complex and problematic. Of his other books from 1888, *Ecce homo* and *Der Fall Wagner* contain much less philosophy,[1] and *Der Antichrist* is focused almost exclusively on critique of Christianity.

A large number of introductions and summaries of Nietzsche's philosophy have been written. To a large extent this has been unnecessary, for Nietzsche, unlike most great philosophers, himself wrote an introduction and 'summary' of his philosophy in writing *Götzen-Dämmerung* – he calls it 'this *vade mecum* to my philosophy' and 'this book is my philosophy *in nuce* [in a nutshell]'.[2] If one wants quickly to get a grasp of Nietzsche's (critical) philosophy this is probably what one should best read instead of accounts in the secondary literature. However, no work is perfect, and *Götzen-Dämmerung* is not a perfect summary of Nietzsche's philosophy. This present study aims to relate the work to Nietzsche's late philosophy, to show the limitations of *Götzen-Dämmerung* as a summary, but also how to get the most out of it by relating it to his unfinished *magnum opus*, the planned and only partially fulfilled four-volume *Revaluation of All Values* (*Umwerthung aller Werthe*).

1.2 How has *Götzen-Dämmerung* been regarded?

As we will see in the next chapter, there have been essentially two ways of reading and regarding *Götzen-Dämmerung*.

A) Most readers and commentators have read and regarded it as an independent and isolated book, the way one regards most books.
B) The perhaps best and most influential Nietzsche scholar, Mazzino Montinari (who also edited the standard critical German edition of Nietzsche's works, KSA and KGW), has argued that it should be regarded as a twin work to *Der Antichrist*, and that these two works together constituted the end and result of Nietzsche's plans for a *magnum opus* (*Hauptwerk*) called *The Will to Power* (*Der Wille zur Macht*), and as such they also constitute the end of Nietzsche's philosophical activity. Thereafter, nothing philosophical was written, only his 'autobiography', poems and compilations. This view has been immensely influential in German and Italian Nietzsche research, and also influenced much of the best Anglo-American writing on Nietzsche. However, this goes against almost everything Nietzsche says about both *Götzen-Dämmerung* and his planned *Hauptwerk* (as we will see later in this study).

I want to suggest and argue for a third alternative of how to read and regard *Götzen-Dämmerung*.

C) Nietzsche did not give up on the idea of writing a four-volume *Hauptwerk* at the end of August or beginning of September 1888 (he only changed its title from *Der Wille zur Macht* to *Umwerthung aller Werthe*, which previously had been the subtitle), and although he wrote *Götzen-Dämmerung* and *Der Antichrist* in part during the same time, and in part utilizing the same very extensive set of notes, they nonetheless are and were regarded as two very different sorts of works by him; *Götzen-Dämmerung* as briefly summarizing or giving extracts about his critical philosophy and, as such, was meant to be preparatory for, and to tempt readers to the *Umwerthung aller Werthe*, while *Der Antichrist* constituted the first volume of that work, the *Umwerthung aller Werthe*. They are also stylistically different; *Götzen-Dämmerung* contains a wide variety of styles and touches on many different themes and questions, while *Der Antichrist* is a closely argued (but also strongly polemical) focused study or treatise of only one theme, Christianity. Throughout the period of writing these books (August and September 1888) he certainly planned to write three further volumes of the *Umwerthung aller Werthe* (and it seems as if he continued to intend to do so until at least the end of December).³ Such a view has consequences for how we interpret and read *Götzen-Dämmerung* as well as how we understand Nietzsche's late philosophy generally, as I will show in the following.

An alternative way to pose the question of the purpose of *Götzen-Dämmerung* is to ask how this book should be regarded:

(i) As a resting place from the work on *Umwerthung aller Werthe* (this is how he presents it in the foreword to *Götzen-Dämmerung*, in the prologue to *Ecce homo* and in several letters).

Or as a straightforward presentation of his philosophy, which divides into two alternatives:

(ii) As a summary of his (complete, both critical and affirmative) philosophy, because he had arrived at the end of his philosophy. This is the view of M. Montinari and seems to have become the standard view today. However, this view, as I argue in the next chapter and in Chapter 6, runs into insurmountable problems. So much of what is obviously part of Nietzsche's philosophy is missing from it, including in particular, his own affirmative philosophemes.

(iii) As an extract and summary of his (critical) philosophy for the purpose of preparing the reader for the next step, the *Umwerthung aller Werthe*. This seems to be how Nietzsche presents the book when he reviews it in *Ecce homo*:

> Anyone who wants to get a quick idea of how topsy-turvy everything was before I came along should make a start with this work. What the title page calls *idol* is quite simply what till now has been called 'truth'. *Twilight of the Idols* – in plain words: the old truth is coming to an end ... [...] It has in it the profligacy of an all-too-rich autumn: you trip over truths, you even trample some to death – there are too many of them. ... But what you lay your hands on is nothing still doubtful, rather decisions.⁴

I aim to show that a combination of (i) and (iii) is the one which is closest to Nietzsche's own claims, and also seems to constitute the best description of its purpose.

1.3 The relation of *Götzen-Dämmerung* to Nietzsche's planned *magnum opus* (*Hauptwerk*)

That *Götzen-Dämmerung* was written in the shadow of his projected *Hauptwerk* is visible in the title, preface, general contents, the original last sentence of the book ('Expeditions of an Untimely Man', 51) and the actual last sentence of the book. Until the very end, the proofreading stage of the manuscript, Nietzsche had a different and much less belligerent title for the work: *Müßiggang eines Psychologen* (*The Idle Hours of a Psychologist* or *The Relaxation of a Psychologist*, compare (i) earlier), implying, as he also states in the preface, that he here takes a pause from the difficult task of writing his *Hauptwerk* – for the purpose of summarizing his critical philosophy and thus to show the mistaken nature of much of philosophy, morality and religion, and thus for the need for a revaluation of values. The subtitle to the new title, 'or How to Philosophize with the Hammer', is somewhat misleading and its primary meaning has not been understood by most commentators and readers.[5] As one can see from Nietzsche's notebooks, the hammer is for him a symbol for the idea of eternal recurrence, and the title thus first and foremost means: 'how to philosophize from the perspective of the idea of eternal recurrence'.[6] The subtitle is in part misleading since he does not explicitly discuss the idea of eternal recurrence in the book (since he saves that for the planned fourth book of the *Hauptwerk*). However, Nietzsche felt that his thought from 1881 onwards had been shaped by this idea and implicitly it colours almost all of the work, so the subtitle is perhaps not inappropriate (apart from the fact that very few of his readers could have been able to realize the primary meaning of it – at least until he published his *Umwerthung aller Werthe* or the content of his notebooks had been published).

In the foreword to *Götzen-Dämmerung* Nietzsche explicitly says that he is working on his *Hauptwerk*, at this late stage entitled *Revaluation of All Values*:

> To stay cheerful when involved in a gloomy and exceedingly responsible business is no inconsiderable art: yet what could be more necessary than cheerfulness? Nothing succeeds in which high spirits play no part. Only excess of strength is proof of strength. – A *revaluation of all values* [or *Revaluation of All Values*], this question-mark so black, so huge it casts a shadow over him who sets it up – such a destiny of a task compels one every instant to run out into the sunshine so as to shake off a seriousness grown all too oppressive. Every expedient for doing so is justified, every 'occasion' a joyful occasion. Above all, *war*. War has always been the grand sagacity of every spirit which has grown too inward and too profound.[7]

Furthermore, he ends the short preface by explicitly stating that he had just finished the first volume of the *Hauptwerk*, that is, *Der Antichrist*: 'Turin, 30 September 1888, on the day the first book of the *Revaluation of All Values* was completed'.

The contents of *Götzen-Dämmerung* are highly interesting and (unlike the case for *Jenseits von Gut und Böse* and *Zur Genealogie der Moral*) he allowed himself to use material and notes which he had set aside for his *Hauptwerk* in writing it. He nonetheless – intentionally – avoided many of the themes he planned to cover in his *Hauptwerk*, such as eternal recurrence and nihilism, as we will discuss in Chapter 6. Other topics, such as the physiology of aesthetics, higher human beings, the revaluation of all values and *amor fati*, he only alluded to. In fact, he states this explicitly in the title of the longest chapter (constituting the whole second half of the book when he wrote it), with the term 'Streifzüge', 'Streifzüge eines Unzeitgemässen', which can be translated as 'Expeditions of an Untimely Man', or 'Reconnaissance Raids of an Untimely Man', or, in a less military and more intellectual sense 'Short Outlines of an Untimely Man['s Views]'. What we are given here is thus 'reconnaissance raids' or 'short outlines' of his philosophy – some of which he intended to treat more fully later. We should thus not be surprised if several of the topics he planned to discuss in *Umwerthung aller Werthe* are also touched upon here, such as, for example, the physiology of art, nihilism, eternal recurrence and will to power. The penultimate sentence of the chapter also ends with the words: 'my ambition is to say in ten sentences what everyone else says in a book – what everyone else does *not* say in a book . . .' (section 51). This is his philosophy in a *nutshell*, that is, extremely condensed.[8] Themes being mentioned here do not preclude them being treated more fully in his coming work.

The last sentence of the book (with the exception of the quotation from *Also sprach Zarathustra* placed on separate pages at the end) – with references to revaluation of all values (the title of his *Hauptwerk*), Dionysus and eternal recurrence – points forward to his coming *Hauptwerk* (just as the end of *Die fröhliche Wissenschaft* promised *Also sprach Zarathustra*): 'the *Birth of Tragedy* was my first revaluation of all values: with that I again plant myself in the soil out of which I draw all that I will and *can* – I, the last disciple of the philosopher Dionysus – I, the teacher of the eternal recurrence . . .'. This pointing forward to his coming *Hauptwerk* is still more obvious at the end of the penultimate chapter of the book, 'Expeditions of an Untimely Man', which was originally meant to constitute the end of the book:[9] 'I have given mankind the most profound book it possesses, my *Zarathustra*: I shall shortly give it the most independent one –'. This, of course, refers to his *Hauptwerk*, which he planned to publish within one or two years.

That *Götzen-Dämmerung* did not constitute the end of Nietzsche's intention to philosophize (as Montinari and others after him have argued) is clear from letters in which Nietzsche speaks of the book as preparatory and preparing the way for his *Hauptwerk*. In letters written immediately after having finished the manuscript, he states that 'the book [*Götzen-Dämmerung*] can serve the purpose of *initiating* and *whetting the appetite* for my *Umwerthung der Werthe* (which first book is almost completed)'.[10] Two days later he writes:

> My publisher already has *another* manuscript, which is a very stringent and subtle expression of my whole *philosophical heterodoxy* – hidden behind much gracefulness and mischief. It is called *Müssiggang eines Psychologen*. In the last analysis, *both these works* [*Der Fall Wagner* and *Götzen-Dämmerung*] are only recuperations in the midst of an immeasurably difficult and decisive task which, *when it is understood*, will split humanity into two halves. Its aim and meaning is, in four words: the *revaluation of all values*.[11]

Nietzsche regarded the *Umwerthung aller Werthe* as much more important than *Götzen-Dämmerung* (and all his other books since *Zarathustra*). Even during the first week of September 1888, when he must have worked very intensively on *Götzen-Dämmerung* (he sent off the cleanly written manuscript to his publisher on 7 September), not only does he not mention it, he instead in his letters speaks of and refers to the work on the *Umwerthung aller Werthe*.

The very fact that we have so little information about when and for how long Nietzsche worked on *Götzen-Dämmerung* reflects that in August and until 7 September, when he sent the finished manuscript to his publisher, what he speaks about in his letters is his work on the *Hauptwerk*, not *Götzen-Dämmerung*. We cannot assume that he during the first week of September worked hard and with much inspiration *only* on *Götzen-Dämmerung*. He must at least *also* have worked on the *Hauptwerk* then, for we know that he wrote the first foreword to *Der Antichrist* or the complete four-volume *Umwerthung aller Werthe* on 3 September. His statement in letters shows that he was much more engaged in the work on the *Hauptwerk* than in the work on *Götzen-Dämmerung* even during the first week of September. And yet, almost all commentators have almost completely concentrated on *Götzen-Dämmerung* and ignored that which Nietzsche regarded as much more important, the *Hauptwerk*. They have thus also ignored the relation between *Götzen-Dämmerung* and the *Hauptwerk*.

In December 1888, just weeks before his mental collapse, after having just received the first copies of the printed book, printed on or near 25 November, he refers to it as: 'in relation to that which it prepares, almost a piece of fate'[12] and on a postcard to his publisher Naumann, 20 December 1888, he refers to *Götzen-Dämmerung* as 'short and in the highest degree preparatory'.[13] And that for which it was meant to be preparatory was his forthcoming *Hauptwerk*.

Nietzsche's planned *Hauptwerk* is thus very present in *Götzen-Dämmerung*. This profoundly affected what *Götzen-Dämmerung* contains, and also the things excluded from it, as well as its overall purpose. The task of this study is to elaborate on *Götzen-Dämmerung* and its relation to the *Hauptwerk* and examine the consequences of this close entanglement for our understanding of *Götzen-Dämmerung* and his late philosophy.

1.4 Is *Götzen-Dämmerung* a summary of Nietzsche's philosophy?

Does *Götzen-Dämmerung* constitute, as Nietzsche repeatedly claims, a summary of his philosophy? What sort of summary is it? Is it an adequate summary? Is it a summary of his complete philosophy, or of his late philosophy or of something else?

It seems as if all commentators have accepted Nietzsche's own description and words about *Götzen-Dämmerung* as containing a 'summary' of his philosophy.[14] To quote just one recent example, Andreas Urs Sommer, one of the best Nietzsche scholars and the author of a highly valuable and useful philological commentary to *Götzen-Dämmerung* writes: 'GD is carefully composed and gives a good overview of N's philosophical life-themes.'[15]

If it is an extract and summary of his philosophy, why are several important themes missing? And even more significant, why are several of his most celebrated ideas and philosophemes, such as his idea of eternal recurrence (and *amor fati*), his *Übermensch*, his will to power, his perspectivism, his analysis of nihilism, completely or almost completely absent in it?

Many commentators and readers have drawn the natural conclusion that their absence show that he no longer held fast to these ideas and views. However, at least for some of them, like his will to power, his critique of nihilism and his idea of eternal recurrence, this seems hard to argue convincingly since they are in fact present, although less emphasized than one would perhaps expect if *Götzen-Dämmerung* were to be a summary of his philosophy. Furthermore, these themes are very present in his notes from this time.

To me, although I count *Götzen-Dämmerung* as perhaps his best book, there seem to be three fields or themes for which it is not correct to describe it as a 'summary'. The work was composed so quickly, and consists essentially of a number of thematic essays or treatises, that it can perhaps adequately be described as an extract of (part of) Nietzsche's mature philosophy, but not really a summary of it. When we compare it with his earlier writings, with, for example, *Die fröhliche Wissenschaft*, including the fifth book from 1887 and with *Jenseits von Gut und Böse* we can observe:

(i) The very thematic nature of the texts of the more philosophical first half of *Götzen-Dämmerung* prevents it from containing the wealth of perspectives and different attempts and approaches that characterize so much of these earlier books.

(ii) Furthermore, some major fields of interest seem to be missing or only vaguely present in it, such as Nietzsche's discussions of epistemology, his existentialism, the continual discussion of the relationship between culture and philosophy and so on.

(iii) But most obviously lacking are many of Nietzsche's own most celebrated ideas such as his idea of eternal recurrence (mentioned earlier), *amor fati*, his *Übermensch* (or expressed differently, his view of higher humans and of law-givers), his will to power, his perspectivism, his analysis of nihilism, of pessimism of strength, order of rank, of great style, slave- and master morality and so on.

The first two of these categories, (i) and (ii), may simply be the necessary side-effect of any summary – being much shorter, it simply cannot contain everything. However, even so, some awareness of the second point (the absence of much of Nietzsche's epistemology and existentialism) is necessary for a correct appreciation of *Götzen-Dämmerung*. The third point, though, constitutes an important, and I believe conscious, omission on Nietzsche's part, which requires an explanation.

The answer, I believe, is that *Götzen-Dämmerung* contains an extract and summary of only part of his philosophy, of his *critical* philosophy, that is, that which would be needed to follow his arguments in the first three planned volumes of *Umwerthung aller Werthe*, while his own affirmative philosophy is, on the whole, not present. This affirmative philosophy was to be presented in the fourth volume, entitled, *Dionysos* or *Dionysos philosophos*. This is in line with Nietzsche's own claims in *Ecce homo*. After having reviewed and discussed all of his books up until and including *Also sprach Zarathustra* – the latter work which Nietzsche emphasized enormously in *Ecce homo* – he summarizes his task and work for the coming years:

> The task for the years that now followed was marked out as strictly as possible. Now that the yes-saying part of my task was solved it was the turn of the no-saying, *no-doing* half: the revaluation of previous values itself, the great war [the work relating to the first three volumes of the *Umwerthung aller Werthe*] – the conjuring up of a day of decision [. . .] *in destroying*.[16]

A plausible interpretation of what Nietzsche here describes is his work on his *Hauptwerk*, and what he for several years had referred to as his main task. This does thus *not* refer to the actual books we possess – *Jenseits von Gut und Böse, Zur Genealogie der Moral* and *Der Fall Wagner* (*Der Antichrist* was not published when he wrote *Ecce homo*) – but to the *Umwerthung aller Werthe*. This may seem strange to a reader of today – for we expect him to speak of *Jenseits von Gut und Böse* and the other books we possess – but we need to remember that he regarded *Ecce homo* as a preface to the *Umwerthung aller Werthe*, which he expected to publish in the near future. This is also consistent with that he worked much more on the *Hauptwerk* during these years than on the actual books he published. The actual books he wrote during this time, 1886–8, *Jenseits von Gut und Böse, Zur Genealogie der Moral, Der Fall Wagner* and *Götzen-Dämmerung* are instead described as 'fish-hooks' and as a way to find people with kinship to or sympathy for his philosophical project:

> Included here is the slow look around for related people, for those who from strength would lend me a hand *in destroying*. – From then on all my writings are fish-hooks: perhaps I am as good as anyone at fishing? . . . . If nothing was *caught*, then I am not to blame. *There weren't any fish*[17]

These four actual and published books are then reviewed in *Ecce homo* on less than a page each,[18] with an emphasis that they are not so very important in comparison to his main task, the *Umwerthung aller Werthe*.[19] *Jenseits von Gut und Böse* is described as a 'recuperation', *Zur Genealogie der Moral* as containing 'three *preliminary* works of a psychologist towards a revaluation of all values' (my italics), *Götzen-Dämmerung* is also referred to as a recuperation, and as short and 'the product of so few days that I hesitate to say how many', and he further says that he *touches* on many themes in it, 'there are too many of them', and in the review of *Der Fall Wagner* he says that something else (i.e. the *Umwerthung aller Werthe*) is of greater importance: 'Ultimately my task's purpose and path contains an attack on a more subtle "unknown", not easily guessed by anyone else – oh, I have still to expose "unknowns" quite different from a Cagliostro of music [i.e. Wagner]',[20] and he ends the review by referring to the *Umwerthung aller Werthe* which will be published 'roughly two years' after *Der Fall Wagner*, and by claiming that he is 'carrying the destiny of humanity on his shoulders',[21] which obviously refers to the *Umwerthung aller Werthe*.

It follows from this that, according to Nietzsche, the books *Jenseits von Gut und Böse, Zur Genealogie der Moral, Der Fall Wagner* and also *Götzen-Dämmerung* do not contain his most important thoughts, but mostly more timely critique of values and thought. In particular, they do not primarily contain Nietzsche's own affirmative philosophy (which only shines through occasionally). Specifically, *Götzen-Dämmerung* does not then contain an extract of Nietzsche's whole philosophy, but primarily of his critical philosophy. That would explain the absence of much of his own affirmative philosophy and many of his own philosophemes. He is likely not to have rejected them but simply saving them for later, for the *Umwerthung aller Werthe*.

Götzen-Dämmerung is primarily *critical* – its purpose is first and foremost to present a critique of accepted views (of an overemphasis of reason and its consequences, of pessimism, of metaphysics, of morality, of Christianity and of our view of aesthetics). Occasionally throughout the book he presents or suggests alternatives to this, but the *emphasis* is on critique (see Table A.3 in the appendix). Only in the last chapter, added late, does the affirmative predominate – with such 'affirmative' themes as the tragic, ancient Greek culture, the Dionysian and eternal recurrence.[22]

The appendix to this study gives a number of tables summarizing different aspects of *Götzen-Dämmerung*. Of special interest to the reader, for following the arguments and discussions in this work, may be that the first table lists the chapters and thus the table of contents of *Götzen-Dämmerung*. The same table also lists the chronology of the manuscript, that is what was included in the manuscript when he sent it to his publisher, on 7 September 1888, and information about the changes and additions he made to it thereafter (see Table A1 in the appendix). The second table gives a chapter-by-chapter summary of the main themes of the book (Table A2), while the third summarizes Nietzsche's critique and affirmations in it (Table A3). The fourth table gives pointers in *Twilight of the Idols* to the *Revaluation of All Values* (Table A4) and the fifth table lists references to the idea of eternal recurrence in *Twilight of the Idols* (Table A5).

I use the translations of Hollingdale for *Götzen-Dämmerung* and *Der Antichrist*, Duncan Large for *Ecce homo* and Kaufmann's for *Jenseits von Gut und Böse* and *Zur Genealogie der Moral*, unless otherwise stated. Translations from notes and letters are my own, if not otherwise stated.

2

How has *Twilight of the Idols* been read, understood and used?

2.1 Introduction   11
2.2 German-language accounts of *Götzen-Dämmerung*   12
2.3 English-language discussions of *Götzen-Dämmerung*   18

2.1 Introduction

Nietzsche describes *Götzen-Dämmerung* as an extract of his philosophy, as a summary of his philosophical heresy and as a handbook for his philosophy, as we have seen earlier. In the following examination of how the book has been dealt with in the secondary literature, we will especially keep our eyes open to discover what has been said about it in regard to three questions:

(i) Since Nietzsche claims that *Götzen-Dämmerung* is a summary or extract of his philosophy, how has it been used as such?
(ii) Has this claim of it as a summary been examined and questioned, in particular, as to in what ways is it correct and in what ways it perhaps is not correct?
(iii) Considering how explicitly Nietzsche relates *Götzen-Dämmerung* to his *Hauptwerk* (which he worked on at the same time), especially in the foreword and at the end of the text, how has this relation been treated?

One would expect commentators and biographers to show an especial interest in a short work described by its author as a summary of his views: 'It is a complete introduction to my philosophy.'[1] It ought to be possible to use such a summary to resolve or clarify countless questions regarding the meaning or status of many aspects of Nietzsche's often obscure philosophy. It would also seem tempting to relate it to his earlier books and perhaps using it to explicitly summarize his philosophy. That, however, has not been done. Instead it appears to me as if some of the most important aspects of *Götzen-Dämmerung* have largely been either misunderstood or ignored.

When we examine how *Götzen-Dämmerung* has been used and interpreted, it appears as if, with but a very few exceptions, it has been merely superficially treated, in spite of Nietzsche's description of it.

2.2 German-language accounts of *Götzen-Dämmerung*

The best and most authoritative Nietzsche biography in German, that of Curt Paul Janz, *Friedrich Nietzsche: Biographie*, three volumes (1978, second revised edition 1993), covering about 1,500 pages, expends less than two pages on *Götzen-Dämmerung*, and almost all of that are quotations from Nietzsche's letters about the book, and a short account of the history and development of the manuscript and the first edition of the book. Janz's only general statement regarding it is his last words, where he even suggests that Nietzsche did not take it and the problems it deals with very seriously (in contrast to the previous book on Wagner):[2]

> In contrast to 'The Case of Wagner' this 'Twilight of the Idols' is really put together with a light hand and in a few days, simply put together from his store of notes as a *Hors d'oevre* of his philosophy: at least that is how Nietzsche views its effect. For detailed work and early drafts as was the case with 'The Case of Wagner', which was of fundamental importance to him, he had no time, for he had now finally pulled himself together to take on his 'magnum opus', the 'Revaluation of All Values'.[3]

As we can see, Janz mentions the *Umwerthung aller Werthe*, but only as an explanation of why *Götzen-Dämmerung* was written so quickly and with such little preparatory work and attention directed at it – since Nietzsche wanted to begin working on his *Hauptwerk*, a project that, Janz claims, failed from the very start.[4] Janz's short account makes it possible, perhaps even probable, that the purpose and contents of *Götzen-Dämmerung* would have been affected by Nietzsche's plans for the *Umwerthung aller Werthe*, but he does not mention or discuss this possibility.

Another important modern biography of Nietzsche is Werner Ross' *Der ängsliche Adler* (1980), in which *Götzen-Dämmerung* is not dealt with more extensively or in any more detail than in Janz's. However, the treatment is nonetheless very different. Ross, like Janz, says little about it, makes essentially no paraphrase of its contents (except the foreword) and presents no quotations, but makes a number of minor comments, in particular, he too regards it as a 'Hors-d'oeuvre aus seinen Schriften und Gedanken' and shows by several examples that he finds little new in it; the chapter 'Socrates as Problem' is like Nietzsche's treatment of him in *Die Geburt der Tragödie*, the chapter 'Morality as Anti-Nature' contains nothing new in comparison with *Jenseits von Gut und Böse*, 'What the Germans Lack' just repeats his old battle against the German lack of spirituality and culture, 'Expeditions of an Untimely Man', even reuses the word untimely (from his earlier writings) and merely presents his old hostilities (with a couple of new ones added).[5] However, Ross also strongly emphasizes its relation to the *Umwerthung aller Werthe* in that Nietzsche in the book alludes to the figure of Dionysos (in a manner similar to how he had introduced Zarathustra at the end of *Die fröhliche Wissenschaft*) and it is thus used to announce the coming of his *Hauptwerk*, but by which Ross means merely the first volume, *Der Antichrist*.[6]

Rüdiger Safranski, in his *Nietzsche: Biographie seines Denkens* (2000), a work which, unlike the two better ones by Janz and Ross, has been translated into English and many other languages, treats Nietzsche's writings from 1888 but scantily, mostly together, all at once, and he does so without enthusiasm. 'The last works, which were quickly produced one after another, "The Case of Wagner", "Twilight of the Idol", "Antichrist" and "Ecce Homo" develop no new thoughts any longer, but instead makes the already known coarsened or exaggerated' (p. 318). He briefly lists the general philosophical contents of these late books in a manner which may contain some general truth, but at least for the case of *Götzen-Dämmerung* (which, after all, is the most philosophical of these late texts) is far from correct or adequate.

> The thoughts, which stand at the centre of the last works, are, one would not expect it otherwise, the will to power in a double version, as grand politics and as individual art of living, the critique of the morality, which is full of resentment and the praise of the Dionysian life as transcendence of the nihilistic superficiality and depression. There is little that is surprising here. (p. 318)

Safranski says almost nothing about *Götzen-Dämmerung* specifically, in spite of its importance as a sort of summary of Nietzsche's critical philosophy. It is only briefly mentioned twice. On the first occasion, Safranski characterizes Nietzsche's style and manner of writing in 1888, and then also interprets the meaning of the hammer of *Götzen-Dämmerung*, in the form of a synthesis of the two most common views (compare my discussion of the meaning of the hammer in Section 5.2 of this book):

> It is now time to speak clearly, perhaps even to speak over-clearly [. . .] The double meaning is meant: a very small hammar and a hammer, testing and crushing, diagnosis and powerful therapy. (p. 318)

The other is a few pages later when he discusses (and misunderstands) Nietzsche's response to Louis Jacolliot's edition of 'The Laws of Manu', and makes a faulty, misdirected and misrepresenting quotation from the chapter 'The "Improvers" of Mankind' where Nietzsche discusses this.[7] Safranski thus claims that it contains nothing new, but otherwise says so little that he does not even mention it as a sort of summary, and says nothing about its relation to the *Hauptwerk*.

To examine one further example of the German discussion for the purpose of seeing how *Götzen-Dämmerung* has been viewed and whether its contents have been related to his overall philosophy and to the project of *Umwerthung aller Werthe*, we can go to Josef Rattner's *Nietzsche: Leben – Werk – Wirkung* (2000). Rattner expends four and a half pages on *Götzen-Dämmerung*, mostly by extensive quoting and paraphrasing, with some discussion but little analysis.[8] Interestingly, although giving a fairly detailed paraphrase of the whole book, he avoids completely precisely the only theme Safranski chose to refer to, Nietzsche's relation to and view of the Laws of Manu. The account makes no general characterization of the book, apart from saying that it contains an overview of the most important themes of Nietzsche's philosophy, and completely ignores the relevance of the *Umwerthung aller Werthe* for *Götzen-Dämmerung*.[9] He explains the hammer of the subtitle, as reflecting that the book contains many polemics.

Mazzino Montinari has written a short important, insightful and influential article about *Götzen-Dämmerung*, emphasizing that both *Götzen-Dämmerung* and *Der Antichrist* were written and put together from notes originally written for the *Der Wille zur Macht*.[10] However, Montinari's interpretation, and what can be described as the standard interpretation of *Götzen-Dämmerung*, at least in the German-speaking world, leads to three problematic consequences:

(i) A strange and extremely compressed chronology for the writing of *Götzen-Dämmerung*. Montinari argues that *Götzen-Dämmerung* arose only after Nietzsche gave up on the *Der Wille zur Macht*, sometimes after 26 August 1888, when Nietzsche wrote his last outline for that work – and according to which he then organized and gave new titles to a large number of older notes.[11] This process is likely to have taken at the very least a couple of days, and thus *Götzen-Dämmerung* is regarded as having been essentially composed and written during the first week of September (while at the same time Nietzsche seems to also have worked hard on *Der Antichrist*) for he sends off the manuscript of *Götzen-Dämmerung* to his publisher on 7 September.

(ii) Due to the fact that *Götzen-Dämmerung* and *Der Antichrist* arose from essentially the same set of earlier notes (written for *Der Wille zur Macht*), Montinari regards the two works as closely intertwined, and he writes: 'That *Götzen-Dämmerung* should be regarded as a sort of "twin work" to *Der Antichrist* has already been emphasized above'[12] – in contrast to Nietzsche's own description of these works, one as a recuperation and relaxation from the work on the *Hauptwerk*, and the other, *Der Antichrist*, as volume one of the *Hauptwerk*.

We can also note that the set of earlier notes from which Nietzsche created *Götzen-Dämmerung* and *Der Antichrist* he had been working on for several years, and they were written for a four-volume main work, and could and did result in two works, *Götzen-Dämmerung* and *Der Antichrist*, which are twin works in some senses, but very different in others, including having very separate contents.

(iii) Montinari argues that out of Nietzsche's extensive work on the *Hauptwerk*, *Der Wille zur Macht*, resulted *Götzen-Dämmerung* and *Der Antichrist*: the rest is merely the remains.[13] Nietzsche had nothing more philosophically relevant to say. He was finished with everything.

Montinari continues by claiming that when writing *Der Antichrist* it constituted the first book of *Umwerthung aller Werthe*, but later, in the middle of November 1888 Nietzsche came to regard it as the complete *Umwerthung aller Werthe*, and thus, he concludes: 'The Turiner catastrophe came when Nietzsche literally was finished with everything'.[14]

These consequences are problematic since they go counter to Nietzsche's own statements as well as counter to common sense. They imply that *Götzen-Dämmerung* was composed and written in an extremely short time (much shorter even than that which Nietzsche himself refers to). They are problematic in that Montinari emphasizes *Götzen-Dämmerung* and *Der Antichrist* as twin works, while Nietzsche seems to regard them as very different (one as part of the *Umwerthung aller Werthe*, the other as not – and he treats them very differently in *Ecce homo*). Finally, Montinari's view that Nietzsche at the age of forty-four was 'finished with everything' seems, in general, unlikely, and in severe conflict with Nietzsche's hard work and sense of purpose since several years to produce a *magnum opus*. That Nietzsche felt far from finished as a philosopher as late as in September 1888 – that is after he had finished *Götzen-Dämmerung* and had written about half of *Der Antichrist* – is plainly expressed in two letters from that month, where he speaks of his need for suitable living conditions 'for a number of years' for the purpose of completing 'the most important work of my life', which is a reference to the *Umwerthung aller Werthe*.[15] Furthermore, he considered *In media vita* ('In the Middle of Life') as a possible title or subtitle to *Ecce homo*, which he wrote after *Götzen-Dämmerung* and *Der Antichrist*, showing that he did not regard himself as being near the end of his creative life. Nietzsche, at the age of 44, did not know that he would mentally collapse, and did not regard himself as finished with everything!

Montinari's text is somewhat ambivalent (and coloured by his justified severe critique of and hostility towards the compilation *Der Wille zur Macht*, edited by Elisabeth Förster-Nietzsche). Most contemporary Nietzsche scholarship and research (since Montinari's critical Nietzsche edition, KSA and KGW, from *c.* 1975) has avoided and ignored to take into account Nietzsche's intention to write a *Hauptwerk* – in spite of the fact that this intention and work strongly coloured not only Nietzsche's notes but also all of his published books after *Also sprach Zarathustra*. In the Anglo-Saxon world, this has been even more the case – less, perhaps, out of ideological reasons, but because there has been a stronger emphasis on the published books (all in good translations) than on the notes and letters (which mostly have not been translated into English). The result has been that also here one has ignored how Nietzsche's plans and work on a *Hauptwerk* has *affected also the contents and arguments of his published books.*

My interpretation may only differ from Montinari's in minor points and in regard to nuances in general, but here it has major consequences. Where Montinari argues that Nietzsche gave up on *Der Wille zur Macht* and regards it as very significant that both *Götzen-Dämmerung* and *Der Antichrist* arose from the notes for this project, I see Nietzsche's work on a *Hauptwerk* as something continual, from 1884 (and even earlier) until at least December 1888 (Nietzsche collapsed mentally on the 3 January 1889), with over sixty different outlines for its contents, and with about eight major stages of development.[16] What Montinari sees as giving up on the project, I regard as merely going from one of these several stages to another. That Nietzsche used notes from his work on the *Hauptwerk* for *Der Antichrist* is as it should be (although much of it was not just composed of earlier notes, but created and written in September). That Nietzsche used notes from his work on the *Hauptwerk*, but in a different manner, selecting disparate already almost-finished mini essays for about half of *Götzen-Dämmerung* is relevant, but does not warrant the far-reaching conclusions Montinari draws from it.

According to my interpretation, other conclusions should be drawn.

(i) During the second half of August 1888, Nietzsche was certainly working intensively on writing notes and texts for his *Hauptwerk*. We have no definite evidence that he worked on anything else, either as expressed in his letters or in his notes from this time. However, it is nevertheless possible that he worked both on the *Hauptwerk* and on a 'preparatory' text for it (i.e. what was to become *Götzen-Dämmerung*) which we know was the case during the first week of September. Two arguments in favour of such a scenario are:
1. Simply the time to compose *and* write a legible manuscript for the printer of the full book seems to require more than a week's time, however, inspired Nietzsche may have been. This is especially true since we know that Nietzsche during this first week of September also worked on *Umwerthung aller Werthe*. He was even so engaged in it that he wrote a long preface to it on 3 September, implying that he was much more engaged in that work than the work on *Götzen-Dämmerung*, which is not mentioned in any letter from the time of writing it.[17]
2. Perhaps even more important is Nietzsche's own statement in the middle of September that he had written *Götzen-Dämmerung* in twenty days. This suggests that he worked on it from about the middle of August to 7 or 9 September:

    > Only since last summer am I standing on *my* feet – and only since then do I know *how infinitely valuable* this Sils is for me. – I have for my way of life no other criteria than the measure of my power to work. Last summer I wrote a publishable version of the three treatises of the 'Genealogy' in less than a month; in this I have finished the 'psychological Relaxation' [i.e. *Götzen-Dämmerung*] in 20 days.[18]

(ii) Although Montinari's point that *Götzen-Dämmerung* and *Der Antichrist* arose out of essentially the same set of notes is an important observation, repeated by most German and Italian commentators, the conclusion that the two books therefore should be regarded as a sort of 'twin' publications is not a necessary one, and seems not to have been the view of Nietzsche. When we examine Nietzsche's statements regarding *Götzen-Dämmerung*, he, on the contrary, seems to separate *Götzen-Dämmerung* from *Der Antichrist* in every possible way: in form and appearance of the books (where Nietzsche insisted that *Götzen-Dämmerung* should be given the same appearance as *Der Fall Wagner*, while *Der Antichrist* was to be given a new appearance), on insisting on an adequate time between the two books *Götzen-Dämmerung* and *Der Antichrist*, in the nature of the books (with *Götzen-Dämmerung* as a cheerful and unsystematic book while *Der Antichrist* as extremely serious and much more focused and systematic) and by claiming that *Götzen-Dämmerung* (and *Der Fall Wagner*) were merely relaxations from the much more serious and difficult work of writing the *Umwerthung aller Werthe*, of which *Der Antichrist* constituted the first volume. In conclusion, although arisen from essentially the same set of notes, Nietzsche regarded *Der Antichrist* as part of his main task, while *Götzen-Dämmerung* was seen rather as preparatory for it, and was written so as to make the project comprehensible and tempting for potential readers. Rather than connecting *Götzen-Dämmerung* to *Der Antichrist*, Nietzsche instead refers to *Götzen-Dämmerung* and *Der Fall Wagner* as twin works.[19] Montinari's interpretation leads to a down-playing of the importance of *Der Antichrist* and the *Umwerthung aller Werthe* project, while Nietzsche's words rather emphasize its importance.

(iii) What is relevant when discussing Nietzsche's late books (in our case, in particular *Götzen-Dämmerung*) and his late philosophy is his views and intentions *when* he wrote these last books, *Götzen-Dämmerung*, *Der Antichrist* and *Ecce homo* – that is, before the middle of November 1888 – and then Nietzsche had very definite plans for a *Hauptwerk* and felt very far from being philosophically finished – and this affected the writing of those late books and his late notes and letters. If Nietzsche later, near 20 November 1888, shortly before his mental collapse, gave up on the four-volume project as Montinari argues (but I have argued that the case is more complex than Montinari here assumes and that Nietzsche kept referring to the *Hauptwerk* as an unfinished four-volume work until late in December),[20] that is a question which does not concern Nietzsche's last books – and since we hardly have any philosophical notes from that time (from after the end of November) is a question of very little philosophical relevance. It is merely a biographical question, and impossible to distinguish and disentangle from his mental collapse in early January 1889.

Two short but high-quality accounts of *Götzen-Dämmerung*, written by two of the very best Nietzsche scholars, can be found in the *Nietzsche-Handbuch* (Stuttgart, Weimar, 2000), 130–2, and in the *Nietzsche-Lexikon* (Darmstadt, 2009), 111–13. In the former, written by Marco Brusotti, *Götzen-Dämmerung* is twice referred to, following Nietzsche's words, as a summary, without comment or qualifications. Nothing is said about its relation to Nietzsche's *Hauptwerk*, except that it is implied that he gave up that project, and *Götzen-Dämmerung* (and *Der Antichrist*) is what resulted from it. The hammer is interpreted as being both destructive and diagnostic.[21]

Andreas Urs Sommer, who has written the text on *Götzen-Dämmerung* in the *Nietzsche-Lexikon*, states that the text was in large part written in September 1888, and emphasizes with both Nietzsche's and in his own words that it constitutes a summary of Nietzsche's philosophy:

> N. regarded GD as 'a complete total introduction' to his thought [. . .] GD is carefully composed and gives a good overview of N's philosophical life-themes.[22]

He emphasizes the hammer of the subtitle as destructive, diagnostic and also as a 'Prägehammer' used to stamp the value on coins and metal. He briefly, but correctly to my mind, states that *Götzen-Dämmerung* was meant as an associated work to the four-volume *Umwerthung aller Werthe,* for the purpose of presenting his philosophy *in nuce*: '*Umwerthung aller Werthe* in vier Büchern vorsah, zu der GD ein Beiwerk sein sollte, um seine Philosophie *in nuce* darzustellen' (p. 111). On the other hand, while discussing the last chapter and the last sentence (except the epilogue), with its reference to Nietzsche as the teacher of eternal recurrence, Sommer writes: 'The eternal recurrence is not otherwise present in GD and plays in Nietzsche's late work anyhow only a marginal role' (p. 113). This may be true for the surface or explicit level of Nietzsche's published books, but clearly it is much more important than that would suggest (as shown by even this example – by that it is not just mentioned, but is how Nietzsche *defines* himself in the last sentence of the book: 'I, the teacher of eternal recurrence . . . '). See also my discussion in Chapter 7.

Andreas Urs Sommer has thereafter greatly expanded and deepened his treatment of *Götzen-Dämmerung* by writing an immensely useful and often profound extensive commentary to the work of about 380 dense pages in *Nietzsche-Kommentar: Band 6/1. Der Fall Wagner und* Götzen-Dämmerung (Walter de Gruyter, 2012).[23]

My argument is that we need to be aware of Nietzsche's plans and work on a *Hauptwerk* when we analyse the contents of Nietzsche's late books – and what is excluded from them. This requires a very thorough reading of these books and the late notes. We ought to examine his late books, with awareness that he had more to say. Traces of that can be found in his books (as I will show for the case of *Götzen-Dämmerung*), more can be found in his late notes, but the full extent of Nietzsche's intended philosophy of the future and the revaluation of all values we will never know for he collapsed before he had completed it.[24] Perhaps some of us need also to attempt to think *beyond* Nietzsche, on the consequences of revaluating values and on the possibility and consequences of a total affirmation or acceptance of reality.

2.3 English-language discussions of *Götzen-Dämmerung*

There is no obvious standard biography of Nietzsche in English. The probably most influential ones are R. J. Hollingdale's *Nietzsche: The Man and His Philosophy* (1965, reprinted with additions 1999), Ronald Hayman's *Nietzsche: A Critical Life* (1980), Curtis Cate's *Friedrich Nietzsche* (2002) and the one by Julian Young, *A Philosophical Biography: Friedrich Nietzsche* (Cambridge, 2010).

Hollingdale discusses *Götzen-Dämmerung* in a chapter entitled 'The Year 1888', pp. 193–216, in which he deals with all four major books of that year, giving most space to *Der Fall Wagner*. *Götzen-Dämmerung* is treated on four pages (mainly by giving a selection of quotations, with very limited discussion). No general characterization of the book is given, but Hollingdale makes a few general statements in regard to all four books from 1888. He praises the style and the brevity of them, but adds, to my mind the problematic statement: 'The philosophical content of these last works is a repetition in brief and uncompromising form of the views Nietzsche has held from *Human, All Too Human* onwards'.[25] Although in line with Nietzsche's description of it as a summary (but surely as a summary of the late Nietzsche's thought), it seems to ignore the importance of Nietzsche's first book, *Die Geburt der Tragödie*, clearly important for the second and last chapter and seems to overemphasize the continuity of his thought by referring to that work from 1878. Nietzsche's more detailed and severe critique of morality and religion, for example, only began in *Morgonröthe*, and many important affirmative tenets of his thought only emerge in *Also sprach Zarathustra* or thereafter.[26] I will later (at the end of Chapter 5 and in Chapter 6) discuss to what extent *Götzen-Dämmerung* can be regarded as a summary of the contents of Nietzsche's earlier books, or whether it rather is a summary of his work on the *Hauptwerk* (which only in part overlap with what he had earlier published).

Hayman spends only three pages, 321–3, on *Götzen-Dämmerung*, all of which consists of an unsystematic paraphrase and short quotations. He seems to make no general judgement or description of the book at all. Nor does he refer to it, or discuss or question it, as a summary or extract of Nietzsche's philosophy. Futhermore, there is no discussion that the contents of the book need to be interpreted also in relation to Nietzsche's plans for and work on his *Hauptwerk*.

Cate spends about four pages on *Götzen-Dämmerung*, generally giving a rather idiosyncratic paraphrase of the contents (but ignoring the last chapter and the epilogue).[27] Like Hayman, he makes no general judgement or characterization of it at all, and does not relate it to the *Umwerthung aller Werthe*.

In Julian Young's massive and in many ways excellent, profound and thought-provoking biography and discussion of all of Nietzsche's books, *Götzen-Dämmerung* is dealt with on thirteen pages (497–509, which is significantly more than he gives to *Der Antichrist* and *Ecce homo*, not surprising since *Götzen-Dämmerung* contains more philosophy) in chapter 24, simply entitled '1888'. After a short introduction, he presents nine questions which according to him 'receive decisive answers' in the text. The brief introduction is informative,[28] and Young clearly appreciates the book, calling it brilliant, graceful in style, possessing no pre-echoes of the approaching madness ('unlike its successors'), light in style, but *not* in content. From the perspective of the present study, we can take note of two points. First, that Young is aware that *Götzen-Dämmerung* can serve, as he quotes Nietzsche's letter to Gast, September 1888, 'to "whet the appetite" for the masterwork', that is, for the *Umwerthung aller Werthe*. However, Young does not discuss what this means or implies, and never refers to the *Hauptwerk* in his analysis of the book, and how it may have affected what Nietzsche wrote and how we are to read the book. (However, in the later chapter 26, 'The Rise and Fall of *The Will to Power*', he deals more extensively with the *Hauptwerk*, but then without relating it to *Götzen-Dämmerung*.) Second, he quotes Nietzsche's statements that *Götzen-Dämmerung* is a 'summary' and 'a complete introduction' to his philosophy, and comments: 'which indeed it is'. He is thus not aware of the limitations of that description. Both these factors lead to errors, weaknesses and important omissions (or misunderstandings) in Young's arguments and expositions of the book in his otherwise valuable analysis. However, the study is not a commentary to *Götzen-Dämmerung*, and much of it constitutes textual interpretation, skillful paraphrasing and analyses which are relatively independent of these main perspectives and approaches.

The first question Young poses to the text is: 'What is the Nature of Reality?' and he uses a brief analysis of the 'Fabel' chapter (Chapter 4) to answer it. His conclusion that Nietzsche affirms the 'apparent world' as the only one is similar to mine (given in Chapter 5), but with three differences. Young fails to see that the sixth section is not only the last and final section but that it also points forward (to the *Umwerthung aller Werthe* project, with references to 'Midday' and to the philosophy of Zarathustra). Second, not commented on by Young, it seems to me that Nietzsche implies that what he and his philosophy will be doing is drawing *consequences* of the death of metaphysics (and of God). These consequences are not drawn in this 'Fabel' chapter or in this book, but I think there are reasons to believe that he meant to deal more extensively on this theme in the *Umwerthung aller Werthe*. Third, by assuming that *Götzen-Dämmerung* is a valid summary of Nietzsche's late philosophy, and since there is no discussion of will to power in relation to forces and the physical world, Young draws the conclusion that Nietzsche had given up on that view (expressed in *Jenseits von Gut und Böse* and in many late notes). It seems to me clear that Nietzsche had not rejected the concept of will to power as such and as a psychological drive and explanatory concept (he refers to it in *Götzen-Dämmerung*, and in the later books *Der Antichrist* and *Ecce homo*, as well as in many late notes), but it is possible that he no longer affirms it as a drive behind also inorganic change. However, it is dubious if its absence in this respect in *Götzen-Dämmerung* is sufficient to justify such a conclusion. I will discuss this question more extensively in Chapter 6.

In answering the second question, 'What is Freedom?', Young discusses the end of chapter 6 ('Four Errors'), but without noting the strong presence of the idea of eternal recurrence at the end of that chapter (which is very relevant for his continued discussion). Young formulates the third and fourth questions as 'What is Happiness?' and 'Why Is Willing the Eternal Return "Dionysian"?'. He concludes for the third question that 'Perfect happiness is the ability to will the eternal return' (p. 501), and eternal recurrence is also the theme of the fourth answer, based mainly on a discussion of the last chapter ('What I Owe the Ancients'). I agree and sympathize with his views and arguments in these two sections, but find him inconsistent and silent on a pertinent point regarding eternal recurrence. Inconsistent, in that he previously discarded will to power as relating to physical forces and nature, since Nietzsche, although mentioning will to power four times, does not seem to relate it to the physical world. Now, however, although eternal recurrence is only mentioned once or twice explicitly in *Götzen-Dämmerung* (and *amor fati* never), he makes them into pivotal concepts of Nietzsche's late philosophy. I agree with Young's view that they are pivotal, but find that he is silent when he ought to discuss and perhaps explain the reasons why these pivotal concepts are so apparently absent in *Götzen-Dämmerung*, after having accepted that the book constitutes a summary of Nietzsche's philosophy. The answers to the rest of the nine questions are interesting but do not directly say anything about the overall nature or interpretation of *Götzen-Dämmerung*.[29]

Sue Prideaux, in her readable but non-philosophical book about Nietzsche's life, *I Am Dynamite* (2018) has, strangely enough, almost nothing to say about *Götzen-Dämmerung*, which she treats on less than two pages, 302–4, of which more than half are quotations from the first chapter of aphorisms.

Perhaps introductions and commentaries to *Götzen-Dämmerung* contain more explicit elaborations on its nature and purpose, as well as discussions of its relation to the *Umwerthung aller Werthe*, and the consequences of this for the use and interpretation of the book?

Walter Kaufmann has been the most influential Nietzsche scholar in the Anglo-Saxon world. His introduction to his translation of *Götzen-Dämmerung* from 1954 (bound together with several other texts in *The Portable Nietzsche*, The Viking Press, New York) is extremely brief (two pages) and he is thus unable to go beyond the commonplace, except in pointing it out as a summary: 'Compared to such fireworks [as *Der Antichrist* and *Ecce homo*], *Twilight of the Idols* is relatively calm and sane, except for its title; and none of his other works contains an equally comprehensive summary of his philosophy and psychology.' Kaufmann dislikes the title and claims that the hammer does not signify a sledgehammer. 'The preface, however, from which the image is derived as an afterthought, explains: idols "are here touched with a hammer as with a tuning fork"'.

R. J. Hollingdale's ten-page introduction to his own translation of *Götzen-Dämmerung* and *Der Antichrist*, from 1968, with many later editions (*Penguin Classics*), consists, with a few exceptions, of a well-written and thought-provoking general essay on Nietzsche, and therefore does not give much information on, nor does it present an interpretation of specifically *Götzen-Dämmerung*. However, the edition also contains eight one-to-two page thematic discussions of Nietzsche's views on logic, metaphysics, epistemology and so on placed at the end of the book. This section – very much in the spirit of Nietzsche's claim that the book contains an extract of his philosophy – is introduced with the words: 'However, in *Twilight of the Idols*, what the reader has is a *compendium* of Nietzsche's philosophy and some help in using it is called for' (p. 16). These are good and useful, but again refer to the whole of Nietzsche's thought (and are very short), and do not give us any interpretations regarding specifically *Götzen-Dämmerung*. The *Umwerthung aller Werthe* is mentioned in regard to *Der Antichrist*, but nothing is said about the relation between *Götzen-Dämmerung* and it.

For editions of the *Penguin Classics* translation of *Götzen-Dämmerung* from 1990 and later, Hollingdale's introduction has been exchanged for one by Michael Tanner. In it Tanner uses *Ecce homo* to understand *Götzen-Dämmerung*, but uses the older version of the *Ecce homo* text (before the revision of the critical edition KSA and KGW in the 1970s). He regards the tone of *Götzen-Dämmerung* as 'strident, even shrill' and regards it as primarily critical. He views it as a summary, as 'a lightning tour of his whole philosophy' (p. 8) and strongly emphasizes the critique of Christianity in *Götzen-Dämmerung*, and thus closely connects it with *Der Antichrist*. He writes about *Götzen-Dämmerung*:

> There can't be any question that at each point he is preparing the ground for his final attack on Christianity. It is – the whole brief book – very much a matter of *reculer pour mieux sauter*. And although, reading *The Anti-Christ* immediately afterwards, one has a strong sense of more of the same. (p. 14)

Using the older version of Nietzsche's late texts and belonging to the pre-critical tradition of understanding Nietzsche, it is perhaps not surprising that he regards *Der Antichrist* as 'actually intended to be the first instalment of his *Revaluation of All Values*, which was itself to be in four parts' (p. 14). However, this insight does not seem to have affected his analysis and discussion of either *Götzen-Dämmerung* or *Der Antichrist*.

Duncan Large has written a thirty-page rich and insightful introductory essay to his own excellent translation for the *Oxford World's Classics* (1998). He accepts the 'standard' view of *Götzen-Dämmerung*, and assumes that it was written extremely quickly, between 26 August and 3 September, and also that it constitutes a summary of Nietzsche's thought, without questioning or qualifying it.

> Nietzsche himself intended *Twilight* to serve as a short introduction to the whole of his philosophy, and consequently it is also the most synoptic of his books [. . .] and recommends itself as giving the best single-volume overview of Nietzsche's mature philosophical themes and styles [. . .] a text which was intended, on one level at least, to be a kind of primer in his philosophy [. . .] a catechism.[30]

Duncan Large is one of the few commentators who is well aware that *Götzen-Dämmerung* was intended as a prelude to the *Umwerthung aller Werthe* – but after having said that (p. xv), it is not used in the analysis and discussion of the work.

Looking up Nietzsche's *Götzen-Dämmerung* in the English-language *Wikipedia* (February 2022, it has hardly changed at all, and not in any essentials in terms of interpretation, over the past ten years) one is given a short, third of a page, introduction and three pages paraphrase and quotations, with some little interpretation and comments of some of the chapters. The introduction strongly emphasizes it as a short introduction to Nietzsche, and states, correctly, that in it the revaluation (which they call 'transvaluation') of all values is claimed to be Nietzsche's most important project (referring to the philosophical project, the planned four-volume literary project is not mentioned).

> He felt that he needed a text that would serve as a short introduction to his work [. . .] The book states the transvaluation of all values as Nietzsche's final and most important project.

However, no more is said or done about the revaluation. The reason they give for why Nietzsche needed or wanted a short introduction to his work is erroneous, because 'his fame and popularity were spreading both inside and outside Germany', while what he actually says, that he wrote it as a relaxation, and for the sake of preparing his readers for the coming *Hauptwerk*, is not mentioned.[31]

Strangely enough, the introduction to the translation of Nietzsche's *Götzen-Dämmerung* in the Cambridge University Press series, edited by Aaron Ridley and Judith Norman (2005), xxvii–xxix, contains almost no information relevant for an interpretation of *Götzen-Dämmerung*.

In the very brief, seven lines discussion of 'Twilight of the Idols, The' in Douglas Burnham's *The Nietzsche Dictionary* (2015) he simply states: '*Twilight* is often seen as a useful and concise summation of N's late thought' (p. 329). I agree that this is often claimed or said of it, but it seems rarely to be used as such.

Bernd Magnus has written one of the relatively few English-language papers dedicated exclusively to *Götzen-Dämmerung*, the essay 'The Deification of the Commonplace: Twilight of the Idol', in *Reading Nietzsche*, ed. R. Solomon and K. Higgins (1988), 152–81. In this study he reads Nietzsche 'as a therapeutic philosopher', and makes a number of points with which I am in many ways sympathetic. However, for the purpose of examining and understanding, not Nietzsche's overall philosophy, but specifically what he says in *Götzen-Dämmerung*, the essay is problematic and has serious drawbacks due to its vague and subjective interpretations. Magnus claims that 'I do not commit Nietzsche to any final substantive, first-order generalizations' (p. 154), and instead Nietzsche 'becomes Nietzsche-as-read-by-x-on-occasion-y' (p. 155), and later in the text he reaffirms this hyper-relativistic view by referring to 'the perspective I have brought to bear on it today' (p. 177). Such extreme scepticism and relativism in regard to understanding and interpretation seem to me misguided and 'nihilistic'.

On only a few pages does he actually discuss *Götzen-Dämmerung*. He interprets the hammer of the title as diagnostic rather than destructive (but without giving any new arguments) and affirms the view that the book constitutes a summary or an extract of Nietzsche's philosophy. Thereafter he says little about *Götzen-Dämmerung*, or at least equally much or more about *Zur Genealogie der Moral*, *Der Antichrist* and *Also sprach Zarathustra*. Although having accepted *Götzen-Dämmerung* as a summary, he almost without motivation speaks primarily of themes which have little overt room in it: the *Übermensch*, eternal recurrence, *amor fati* and perspectivism. There is no discussion why these, for Magnus, so important ideas or themes are basically absent from *Götzen-Dämmerung*, the 'summary' of his philosophy.

Magnus does not say anything about the relation of *Götzen-Dämmerung* to the *Umwerthung aller Werthe* project explicitly, but implicitly he says much. He, counter Nietzsche's own words in the foreword and elsewhere, completely rejects the idea of a *Hauptwerk* and simply assumes that Nietzsche's notes are 'dustbin manuscripts' (p. 161; and in the connecting footnote 23, Nietzsche's notes are dismissed as 'discarded'). This is counter all evidence. It is surely true that some notes were 'discarded' (and Nietzsche often crossed out such notes in his notebooks), but for many notes this was obviously not the case, since he organized, structured, re-wrote and re-worked them and even copied many notes into new notebooks for his work on the *Hauptwerk*.

David Thatcher has written an interesting and valuable article, 'A Diagnosis of Idols', in *Nietzsche-Studien* 14 (1985), 250–68, devoted exclusively to the title and subtitle of *Götzen-Dämmerung*. I agree with Thatcher that one of the primary senses of the hammer in the subtitle (and in the work as a whole) is that of a diagnostic hammer – and believe that his paper advanced the understanding of the title and the book when it was published in 1985. Nonetheless, today his paper must be seen as having several weaknesses. (i) He fails to realize the importance of Nietzsche's whole *Hauptwerk* project, and thus also of the hammer as eternal recurrence (which I will argue for in Section 5.2 as follows).[32] (ii) He seems not to comment at all on, and interpret, the optimistic tone of the main title, *Götzen-Dämmerung*, as that 'the old truth is coming to an end' (*Ecce homo*, 'GD', 1). In my view this is a reference to the soon-to-be published *Umwerthung aller Werthe*, which would have resulted in an extended exposure and severe critique of those old idols. (iii) Oddly and problematically enough for his interpretation, he claims that 'the hammer in "Der Hammer redet" is *not* the same as that of the subtitle or foreword'.[33] Considering that the word 'hammer' only occurs in the subtitle, foreword and epilogue, this seems a very serious drawback with this interpretation. (iv) Thatcher too strongly emphasizes a unique meaning of the symbol hammer – and forgets that one and the same hammer can serve and be used for many different tasks, and also to symbolize more than one thing. He seems to me, in particular, to underemphasize its role as destructive[34] – which is surely one of the primary senses Nietzsche refers to when he writes to Gast, 27 September 1888 in reference to this new title and subtitle: 'The meaning of the words, are, after all, also self-evident'. (v) Thatcher himself admits that there are two further flaws with his interpretation, as I discuss as follows in connection to examining the meaning of the title and subtitle in Section 5.2. Nonetheless, this paper constitutes the best available discussion and interpretation of the title of *Götzen-Dämmerung*.

A recent discussion of *Götzen-Dämmerung* is Carol Diethe's text 'Twilight of the Idols' in *A Companion to Friedrich Nietzsche*, edited by Paul Bishop (2012), 315–38. Her discussion is strongly biographically oriented, and is a useful and valuable introduction to the work, especially in its emphasis on the importance of psychology for the late Nietzsche. However, she, like virtually all other commentators, admits that Nietzsche during the past year had been working hard on his *Hauptwerk* – 'Nietzsche had set aside the year 1888 for classifying his notes for *The Will to Power*, often – though not always – subtitled the *Revaluation of All Values* (*Umwerthung aller Werte*)' (p. 317, compare also pages 315, 319 and 330) – but believes that Nietzsche gave up on that project, and therefore does not discuss the relation between *Götzen-Dämmerung* and that *Hauptwerk* and their respective contents. She instead concludes that he used some material from it for *Götzen-Dämmerung*: 'Having relinquished the struggle to expand the material for *The Will to Power*, his immediate task was to redirect some of it into a shorter, light-hearted introduction to his philosophy' (317). Instead of regarding the *Umwerthung aller Werthe* as a direct continuation of the *Der Wille zur Macht*, she thus argues that the whole *Der Wille zur Macht* project collapsed, some of its contents were used for *Götzen-Dämmerung* and that the *Umwerthung aller Werthe* was a *new* project.[35] She does not discuss what contents of *Der Wille zur Macht* were used for *Götzen-Dämmerung*, why and what happened to the rest of the material (the great majority) – where I argue that the reason for the book was to prepare the reader for his coming *Hauptwerk* (the *Umwerthung aller Werthe*) – which continued to remain his *Hauptwerk* project. Furthermore, if *Götzen-Dämmerung* was not only a summary of Nietzsche's philosophy but also what remained of the *Der Wille zur Macht* project – that he had been working intensively on for several years – it ought to be worthy of greater attention and more in-depth analysis than is suggested by Diethe.

Diethe accepts *Götzen-Dämmerung* as a summary – 'Nietzsche's claim to have fashioned *Twilight of the Idols* into a summary of his philosophy is valid' (p. 322),[36] although she in the next paragraph notes that any mention of the *Übermensch* 'is completely lacking', that eternal recurrence is only mentioned once and that 'Nietzsche's central insight of the will to power is implicit rather than explicit' (p. 323) in the book. The revaluation of all values, as a philosophical theme and literary project, is not mentioned at all by her. I cannot find that she in any way uses (or discusses) in what way *Götzen-Dämmerung* is a summary, and her slight dislike of the book and somewhat dismissive comments seem rather to suggest that it is not particularly important.

The rest of her text constitutes a paraphrase and discussion of each of the ten chapters, 'there being no overall pattern for the work as a whole' (p. 325).[37] It thus seems to me that Diethe under-emphasizes the importance of *Götzen-Dämmerung* – stressing that it was written in a hurry (like almost all of Nietzsche's books) and lacking any overall scheme (also like many of Nietzsche's other books) – instead of realizing that it to a large extent consists of excerpts from his work on the *Hauptwerk* (which he had been working on for several years) and that this *increases* its importance, although perhaps making it lack a unifying thesis. Even more important is that it points at and prepares the readers for – hinting at the planned further contents of – the *Hauptwerk Umwerthung aller Werthe*.

Summary: In most of the serious discussions of *Götzen-Dämmerung* it is regarded – following Nietzsche's own words – as a sort of summary of his philosophy, but very few of the commentators, if any, explicitly use it in any such manner, and, more importantly, none of them question, qualify or discuss what it means and in what sense it is correct and in what it is not correct to regard it as a summary.

The fact that so few, if any, commentators or biographers *use* it as a summary seems to suggest that it does not work well as such. My basic answer to that is that it, after all, is not a summary, but rather a collection of extracts of his philosophy – not so much of what he had discussed in his previous books (although it overlaps with that) but extracts of what he planned to present as his philosophy in the near future, in his *Hauptwerk*. Extracts mostly of its critique, but in the last chapter also of his affirmative philosophy (tragedy, Dionysos, ancient values, eternal recurrence, affirmation of life and reality).

In spite of the fact that it is strongly and explicitly stated in the foreword of the book, we have not found any biographer or commentator who recognizes and discusses the pivotal role of the *Umwerthung aller Werthe* for the writing, and the understanding, of *Götzen-Dämmerung*. And yet, such recognition is just a first step to extract from this book what Nietzsche put into it. The second step is to examine how this should affect our reading of *Götzen-Dämmerung*. The third step is to examine what Nietzsche did *not* present and discuss in the book, precisely due to its relation to the, as he expected, soon-to-be-published *Umwerthung aller Werthe* (discussed in Chapter 6). Furthermore, a fourth step would be to examine if perhaps *Götzen-Dämmerung* can be used to shed some light on the philosophical project and on the planned four-volume work with which it is so closely intertwined, and about which we know so little since only the first volume was written before he collapsed, and that the rest of the project in modern times has been ignored.

Without awareness of the relation between *Götzen-Dämmerung* and the *Umwerthung aller Werthe* the whole book is likely to be misunderstood. After all, the purpose of the book was to prepare the reader for the coming *Hauptwerk*, and it is only as preparatory to the *Umwerthung aller Werthe* that Nietzsche can adequately describe it as an extract or summary of his critical philosophy. What it summarizes or gives excerpts from is not his whole philosophy but some of the critical contents of his planned future *Hauptwerk*. It does not summarize his affirmative philosophy, which, after all, is what we expect of a summary; that is only hinted at in the book, mostly in the last chapter, added as an afterthought.

3

The genesis, chronology and composition of the *Twilight of the Idols* and the *Revaluation of All Values*

3.1 Introduction 27
3.2 The genesis and chronology of *Götzen-Dämmerung* 27
3.3 What sort of notes is *Götzen-Dämmerung* constructed from? 29
3.4 History of Nietzsche's work on a Hauptwerk, at the end called *Revaluation of All Values* 31

3.1 Introduction

Relatively little is known about the genesis and chronology of *Twilight of the Idols*. The first time we hear of the work is when Nietzsche sends the finished manuscript to his publisher on 7 (or 9) September 1888, although he will make a few additions later. However, a careful reading of Nietzsche's letters and notes[1] makes it possible to get a better conception of how it evolved.

Another question related to chronology and composition is the difficult and vague question of to what extent *Götzen-Dämmerung* was written *ab initio* or to what extent was it based on previous work and notes. Furthermore, to the extent that it was based on earlier notes – is it possible to say whether these notes belong to the large set of notes written for his *Hauptwerk*, or to more spurious notes not directly related to the *Umwerthung aller Werthe*?

Since *Götzen-Dämmerung* was written in the shadow of his work on the *Umwerthung aller Werthe*, and its main purpose was even to be preparatory for this larger work, we will in the last section summarize the history and development of that major project.

3.2 The genesis and chronology of *Götzen-Dämmerung*

Nietzsche had since at least 1884 been working on a *magnum opus* or *Hauptwerk*. During July of 1887 he wrote *Zur Genealogie der Moral* but had before then, and with increasing intensity thereafter, worked on writing notes for that *Hauptwerk* (at the same time as he read the proofs to *Zur Genealogie der Moral*). During the spring of

1888, while in Turin, he took another pause from this work and wrote most of the short pamphlet *Der Fall Wagner*. However, he kept on making revisions of that work, and adding postscripts, while at the same time reading the proofs of that work (together with Peter Gast, at another location) until about 12 August.[2] On 24 August he made the last revision of the epilogue of that work (which was printed and finished and he received it in his hand on 15 September). During this time, and especially during the summer, he also continued working on the *Hauptwerk*.

It is likely that this work on the *Revaluation of All Values* intensified at about the middle of August, when he was finished with *Der Fall Wagner*. At that time he also seems to have decided that yet another work was needed to prepare and initiate readers for his coming *Hauptwerk* – as well as needing it to encourage himself due to the difficulty of re-evaluating values and writing the *Hauptwerk* (as he says in the foreword to *Götzen-Dämmerung* and in letters).

When we examine Nietzsche's letters we can see the following (possible) early references to *Götzen-Dämmerung*: There are no explicit references to *Götzen-Dämmerung* in his letters before 7 September when he sends his finished manuscript to his publisher. However, from the letters it is clear that Nietzsche was working hard and with inspiration during the period from the middle of August until and including the first week of September, presumably on both the *Umwerthung aller Werthe* and on *Götzen-Dämmerung*. We also possess a letter from 14 September, to Overbeck, where Nietzsche claims that he only worked on *Götzen-Dämmerung* for 20 days.[3] It would thus seem reasonable to assume that he worked on *Götzen-Dämmerung* from about the middle of August 1888 (when he had finished working on *Der Fall Wagner*) until 7 or 9 September, when he sends off the completed manuscript (a few additions were made later). Thereafter he continued to work hard on *Der Antichrist*, but also occasionally making additions to *Götzen-Dämmerung* until the middle of October. *Der Antichrist* was finished on 30 September (as stated in the foreword to *Götzen-Dämmerung*).

The situation regarding a detailed dating of *Götzen-Dämmerung* is little improved by examining Nietzsche's notes from this period. There are relatively few notes extant from the whole second half of 1888, and in our case, for the period early August until the middle of September there are very few extant notes indeed. Only some of the notes in the two sections 18 and 19 of KSA 13 are relevant (these sections do not consist of notebooks, but of loose pages in folders). The former consists of seventeen notes (eight pages), 18[1–17], dated by the editor as July–August, with the last note dated by Nietzsche as 26 August, and the latter, consisting of eleven notes (eight pages), 19[1–11], dated by the editor as September 1888, in which the seventh note is dated by Nietzsche as early September. However, without further information, the exact dating and the reliability of the dating of these notes remain uncertain – therefore of little use to us here (but see the following).

The critical edition of Nietzsche's writings, KSA and KGW, attempts to be *almost* complete, but exclude from publication most of Nietzsche's mundane personal notes (e.g. lists of things to do, what to buy and where to travel)[4] and texts which Montinari judged as 'Vorstufen', that is early versions of published texts (some of which are included in the commentary volume KSA 14).[5] There seems to exist a number of such 'Vorstufen' relating to *Götzen-Dämmerung*, *Der Antichrist* and the *Umwerthung aller*

Werthe which have not been published. Most important is an apparently 'finished' *Druckmanuskript* (manuscript ready to be given to the printer) from the end of August and early September 1888 in which the first part of *Der Antichrist* is intermixed with the *Götzen-Dämmerung*-manuscript. Montinari refers to this on several occasions, but never gives any references where it can be found or about its size and so on.[6] Apparently this manuscript contains texts of the essays listed in note KSA 13, 19[4],[7] without a title, but almost certainly referring to a plan to publish excerpts of his philosophy (that which becomes *Müßiggang eines Psychologen* and later *Götzen-Dämmerung*), since such titles are listed immediately above this listing on the same sheet of paper.

1. Wir Hyperboreer.
2. Das Problem des Sokrates.
3. Die Vernunft in der Philosophie.
4. Wie die wahre Welt endlich zur Fabel wurde.
5. Moral als Widernatur.
6. Die vier großen Irrthümer.
7. Für uns – wider uns.
8. Begriff einer Décadence-Religion.
9. Buddhismus und Christenthum.
10. Aus meiner Aesthetik.
11. Unter Künstlern und Schriftstellern.
12. Sprüche und Pfeile.

Since this manuscript with excerpts apparently began in the middle of August 1888 it did not then imply a giving up on the plans for a *Hauptwerk* in four volumes (although the excerpts themselves were largely extracted from finished material for that work or earlier versions of that work), for Nietzsche continued to list plans for that work thereafter, 26 August and several times in early September. Apparently Nietzsche realized that four of these essays (1 and 7–9) could be regarded as belonging together and could constitute the beginning of the first volume of the *Hauptwerk*, thus consisting of a critique of Christianity (rather than his earlier plan, when the first volume mostly consisted of a critique of philosophy and nihilism, which now was moved to the second volume).

3.3 What sort of notes is *Götzen-Dämmerung* constructed from?

For our question of the importance of Nietzsche's planned *Hauptwerk* for understanding *Götzen-Dämmerung*, and thus also for the relation between these two works, the question of to what extent *Götzen-Dämmerung* (and *Der Antichrist*) was created out of or from the notes for that *Hauptwerk* is relevant. The best Nietzsche scholar for questions relating to Nietzsche's notes and texts, Mazzino Montinari has claimed that: 'It consisted of nothing but notes which originally were written for the *Wille zur Macht*'.[8]

This statement seems to me largely true, at least in the sense that it is much more true for *Götzen-Dämmerung* than for *Der Fall Wagner*, as well as than for *Jenseits von Gut und Böse* and *Zur Genealogie der Moral* (for these books Nietzsche mostly avoided using notes planned to be used for his *Hauptwerk*). However, it is difficult to determine the extent of how correct this statement is – for at least four reasons:

(i) It is often not clear what should be regarded as earlier versions and notes preparatory for the final text of *Götzen-Dämmerung* (a significant part of the text has probably been written directly by Nietzsche, without utilizing earlier specific notes – sometimes such earlier notes can perhaps nonetheless be identified, but often this is not the case).

(ii) Part of Nietzsche's notes have not been published – this is especially true for texts which Montinari regarded as 'Vorstufen', early versions of texts which eventually (in a similar form) were included in his books (some of which is included in the commentary volume KSA 14). However, for the task we are dealing with here, such earlier versions are likely to be relevant. Much of this has been published in the volumes of KGW IX, but these are difficult to use until completed and until the commentary texts are also published, and so far the contents of the relevant folders of KSA 13, sections 18 and 19, have not been published in facsimile.

(iii) It is likely that some of Nietzsche's notes (including early versions of texts which were of little relevance to him after the books were finished) are missing. The extent of such missing material is not known (but we have very few notes from the second half of 1888).

(iv) Most importantly, it is often difficult to distinguish among Nietzsche's extant notes which were designated to be used for the *Umwerthung aller Werthe* and which should be regarded as other sorts of notes. For many of them there probably was no such clear distinction and demarcation even in Nietzsche's own mind. Nonetheless, there exists a fairly large set of notes which obviously was intended to be used for the *Hauptwerk* when he wrote them down, and furthermore, there are a fairly large number of individual notes which Nietzsche added titles to, where it is obvious that they too were meant for the *Hauptwerk*. This is especially true for most of the notes listed in three large notebooks, W II 1, W II 2 and W II 3, published in KSA 12, 9[1–190], 10[1–206] and KSA 13, 11[1–138] respectively,[9] and also for many notes in the notebook W II 4, KSA 13, 14[1–227], used during April and May 1888.

When we examine the origin of the texts for chapters 2–7 in *Götzen-Dämmerung*, from the Socrates chapter to 'The "Improvers" of Mankind', it seems not definite but possible that these notes come from the material for the *Hauptwerk*. A much stronger argument for that these chapters originally were conceived as part of the *Hauptwerk* is that all of these chapter titles (or similar titles) occur in the listing of chapters to be included in the *Hauptwerk*.

Chapter 8, 'What the Germans Lack', began as the foreword to *Götzen-Dämmerung*, and seems less directly to emanate from the notes for the *Hauptwerk* (and is not obviously mentioned among the planned chapters for that work).

The last one, chapter 10, 'What I Owe to the Ancients', was added to *Götzen-Dämmerung* long after the rest of the text, *c.* 16 October, and as the title suggests, has its origin in the first draft for *Ecce homo*. The reason that he added it, was that he felt that *Götzen-Dämmerung* could not be without references to 'the *Dionysos-morality*? It struck me that this set of concepts at no price should be missing from this *vade mecum* to my philosophy.'[10]

The situation for the long originally last chapter 9, 'Expeditions of an Untimely Man', which constitutes about half the book, is different. Nietzsche treats it as different,[11] it is different in style, it is mostly more miscellaneous and timely in nature (as also suggested by its title), and it does not appear among listings of chapters for the *Hauptwerk*.[12] It thus seems less related to work on the *Hauptwerk*, but even so about a third of the notes from which it is composed appear to have been part of work for the *Hauptwerk*.

3.4 History of Nietzsche's work on a Hauptwerk, at the end called *Revaluation of All Values*

To make the relation between *Götzen-Dämmerung* and the planned *Umwerthung aller Werthe* more distinct, let us briefly look at Nietzsche's plans to write a *Hauptwerk*, and thereafter discuss the planned contents of these four volumes in 1888.

There are a very large number of drafts of titles for this *Hauptwerk* project in Nietzsche's notebooks, far more than for any other projected or realized book. Already this can illustrate the extent to which Nietzsche planned and worked on this *Hauptwerk* for many years. Nietzsche used the word *Hauptwerk* more than half a dozen times for referring to this project, but most frequently he referred to it by means of the different planned titles and other more indirect means, including as his 'major task' and the 'purpose' of his life. On the whole, there is significant consistency between the different drafts, and in several instances it is a previous subtitle that has become the main title. There are good reasons to regard these different titles as referring to essentially the same planned *Hauptwerk*, see Table 3.1.

The evidence for this intention to write a *Hauptwerk* can, apart from in the notebooks, be seen in his published works and in his letters.

Nietzsche had, as stated earlier, had plans for such a four-volume *magnum opus* since 1884, and had written a large number of notes and preliminary tables of contents for it. When Nietzsche in September 1888 wrote *Der Antichrist* as the first volume, this meant that he then decided to move all or almost all the material relating to religion and Christianity into the first book (earlier this material had been divided into several volumes, with most of it in book 2), and this, of course, also affected the contents of the other books. For the period after his decision that *Der Antichrist* would constitute the first book, we possess seven listings of the planned names of the volumes of *Umwerthung aller Werthe*[13] – and these are all consistent with one another[14] but they are less detailed than many of the earlier ones, in particular, they contain no listing of chapter titles. However, using the consistent divisions into four books after that *Der Antichrist* was decided upon, we can go back to the more detailed divisions from earlier in 1888 and

Table 3.1 The Evolution of the Planned Title of Nietzsche's *magnum opus*, from Autumn 1881 to December 1888. © Thomas H. Brobjer.

Autumn 1881–Summer 1885	August 1885–August 1888	September–December 1888
Three to five books (but mostly four)	Consisting of four books	Four books
Many different titles	Consistent title	Consistent title (earlier subtitle)
Not called *Hauptwerk*, but	Called *Hauptwerk*	Called *Hauptwerk*
For example 'Haupt-Bau' (from 1884)		
Die neue Rangordnung Die ewige Wiederkunft Philosophie des ewigen Wiederkunft Mittag und Ewigkeit Die Unschuld des Werdens Dionysos Philosopie der Zukunft	Der Wille zur Macht	Umwerthung aller Werthe
The New Order of Rank The Eternal Recurrence Philosophy of Eternal Recurrence Midday and Eternity The Innocence of Becoming Dionysus Philosophy of the Future	The Will to Power	Revaluation of All Values

classify these chapter titles according to these new book divisions. It turns out that this is relatively straight forward using the three most detailed chapter divisions.[15] This information is presented in Table 3.2, and gives us a reasonably detailed view of Nietzsche's plans for the three remaining volumes of the *Umwerthung aller Werthe*.

The standard, but to my mind far too narrow and limited, view of Nietzsche's work on a *Hauptwerk* with the title *Der Wille zur Macht* is that he began it in August–September 1885, from which time we have the first draft of a title with that name: 'The Will to Power: Attempt at a New Explanation of All Events'.[16] At the latest by the summer of 1886, the subtitle was changed to 'Attempt at a Revaluation of All Values',[17] which then continued as subtitle until the end of the project. He announces the four-volume *Der Wille zur Macht* project as a work in progress on the cover of *Jenseits von Gut und Böse*.[18] This project then lasts for three years, until shortly after 26 August 1888, on which day he wrote his last draft, a very detailed draft, of the planned contents for this work.[19] Thereafter he returned to several of his older notebooks, added chapter and section titles to notes in them, that is, structured old notes according to this plan. One or two weeks later, in early September, Nietzsche instead wrote (what most likely was) his first draft for the four-volume work entitled *Umwerthung aller Werthe*, and this is thereafter followed by another six drafts for that work.[20]

The *Umwerthung aller Werthe* is generally either not referred to at all in the secondary literature when discussing the *Der Wille zur Macht* project, or not related to it and regarded as a separate project. *Der Wille zur Macht* is thus frequently regarded as a project lasting three years, from August 1885 to the end of August 1888. *Götzen-Dämmerung* was written exactly at this time of transition or rather, according to this view, at the time when he decided to end or gave up on this major project (at the end of August and the first week of September).

However, to me, the most convincing interpretation is that *Umwerthung aller Werthe* is simply a continuation of *Der Wille zur Macht* (which itself was a continuation of an earlier version of a work on a *Hauptwerk*), where simply the subtitle is made into the main title.²¹ Nietzsche actually refers to the *Hauptwerk* as *Umwerthung aller Werthe* several times already during the three-year period from August 1885 to August 1888 (see the following discussion). According to my interpretation, Nietzsche does not end the project, and if there was a transition (in a deeper sense than just the change of title) in going from *Der Wille zur Macht* to *Umwerthung aller Werthe*, that seems to me to be a very minor transition. Furthermore, nothing in his letters from these weeks suggests any major change in regard to either Nietzsche's mood or his work and feeling in regard to the *Hauptwerk*.²² If he had just given up the major work and what he had regarded as his purpose of life, even the purpose for staying alive, for the past four years or more, this ought to have been visible. On the contrary, Nietzsche continues to speak of his 'task' in several letters after this, as well as in *Götzen-Dämmerung* and in other late books.

However, even if we limit ourselves to examining the title of this planned *Hauptwerk* during the period August 1885 to August 1888, things are not quite as simple as the standard view and Montinari argues. All the references to the *Hauptwerk* during these three years, in which the main title of the four-volume work is explicitly given, use the title *Der Wille zur Macht*, with three or four exceptions, which all use *Umwerthung aller Werthe* already before September 1888.

Let us examine these exceptions. We have a dated draft, from March 1887, with the planned title of the four volumes of his *Hauptwerk*, where part of the main title is missing – only the words 'All Values' remain, followed by a listing of the titles of the four volumes.²³ This could be the remains of either the full title and subtitle of *Der Wille zur Macht*, or possibly simply the title *Umwerthung aller Werthe*.²⁴ The former alternative is the more likely, but the latter cannot be completely excluded.²⁵

In two letters, both from 13 February 1888, Nietzsche refers to his *Hauptwerk* as *Umwerthung aller Werthe*.²⁶ This could mean that he from this time began to vacillate about the main title. For this view argues that many notes obviously listing the contents or titles of the *Hauptwerk* are given no title at all (perhaps because he had become uncertain about the title), in particular the notes KSA 13, 12[1 and 2] which lists twelve chapter titles divided into four volumes, and lists to which volume the 374 notes belong. On the other hand, he sometimes refers to his books by their subtitles, so this need not necessarily imply that he had changed the title. However, if that is the case, it certainly reflects how easy and what little change is implied by going from changing the title of *Der Wille zur Macht* to instead using its subtitle *Umwerthung aller Werthe*. It is thus difficult to know for certain what these two references to the *Hauptwerk* as *Umwerthung aller Werthe* implies about the main title of it.

The fourth reference to his *Hauptwerk* during this period as *Umwerthung aller Werthe* is definitely referring to the *Hauptwerk* with this title, but although written in a notebook used in early 1888, this specific note was probably added later and although difficult to date, it was perhaps most likely written in or near September 1888, that is, after he had already changed the title. In the notebook 'W II 3', the contents published as KSA 13, 11[1–417], covering 200 pages, which he used for working on his *Hauptwerk*,

Table 3.2 Planned Chapter Titles for Nietzsche's Hauptwerk from Earlier in 1888, Here Classified and Organized according to the Book Divisions from September to November 1888. © Thomas H. Brobjer.

Umwerthung aller Werthe September–November 1888	Table of contents from early 1888 KSA 13, 12[2]	Table of contents from May or June of 1888 KSA 13, 16[51]	Table of contents from 26 August 1888 KSA 13, 18[17]
Book 1 of *Umwerthung aller Werthe* *The Anti-Christ: Attempt at a Critique of Christianity*	Critique of the Christian ideals	The *religious* man as typical décadent The pagan in religion	The homines religiosi Thoughts about Christianity
Book 2 of *Umwerthung aller Werthe* *The Free Spirit: Critique of Philosophy as a Nihilistic Movement*	Nihilism, considered to its final conclusion The 'will to truth'	The *true* and the apparent world The *philosopher* as typical décadent Science against philosophy *Nihilism* [and its *opposite*]	The psychology of errors The value of truth and error The will to truth The metaphysicians To the history of European nihilism
Book 3 of *Umwerthung aller Werthe* *The Immoralist: Critique of Morality as the Most Dangerous Kind of Lack of Knowledge*	The origin of ideals How virtue becomes victorious Herd-instincts Morality as the Circe of the philosophers Psychology of the 'will to power'	The *good* human being as typical décadent	The good and the improvers
Book 4 of *Umwerthung aller Werthe* *Dionysos: The Philosophy of Eternal Recurrence*	Life-prescriptions for us The 'eternal recurrence' The great politics	The will to power as life: Peak of the historical self-consciousness The will to power: as discipline	The *principle of life*: "Order of rank" The two ways The eternal recurrence
Eternal recurrence The type of the lawgiver			

the title *Der Wille zur Macht* is only mentioned twice, on the very last pages.[27] However, on the otherwise empty page 157, Nietzsche has written a large title and listed the titles of the four volumes of the work *Umwerthung aller Werthe*, and drawn a square around it.[28] If this addition was made after 26 August, as seems likely, it, of course, does not reflect vacillation in regard to the title before that date, but it does clearly indicate *the continuity of this project*. *Umwerthung aller Werthe* was now (probably from early September) the main title to which these 374 numbered notes belonged previously under the title *Der Wille zur Macht*.

One final example, relevant here, although not referring to the title *Umwerthung aller Werthe*, is that several of the seven listings or table of contents in the notebook W II 7a (KSA 13, 16[1–89], used by Nietzsche during the end of April until the end of June or early July) have much similarity to that of the *Umwerthung aller Werthe* from early September onwards.[29] In particular, the note KSA 13, 16[70], probably written at the end of June, is similar to the book divisions of the *Umwerthung aller Werthe* as most of them looked in September and thereafter:

> Worum es sich handelt?
> das religiöse Mißverständniß.
> das moralische Mißverständniß.
> das philosophische Mißverständniß.
> das aesthetische Mißverständniß.

The first three themes here correspond to the first three volumes of the *Umwerthung aller Werthe*. The fourth theme, about aesthetics, is oddly enough missing in all plans for the *Umwerthung aller Werthe* (from September and later). However, there are so very few notes from that period that it seems to me much more likely that this is merely an omission, and that Nietzsche planned to discuss such questions in one of the remaining volumes.[30] The fourth volume, mostly called *Dionysos* or *Dionysos philosophos*, is not mentioned in the note,[31] but the first three volumes are described in a very similar manner in several notes from September 1888 and later, which also contain a description of the planned fourth volume.

Revaluation of All Values

Book 1: *The Antichrist*.
Book 2: *The Misosopher*.
Book 3: *The Immoralist*.
Book 4: *Dionysos*.
Revaluation of All Values.[32]

We have seen that there was a remarkable consistency in both of the titles and the planned contents of Nietzsche's work on a *Hauptwerk* consisting of four volumes from 1884 to late 1888.

4

Sources to and influences on *Twilight of the Idols*

4.1 Introduction   37
4.2 General and philosophical sources to *Götzen-Dämmerung*   38
4.3 Reading of books relating to science and 'reality'   40
4.4 Reading in and about psychology and physiology   41
4.5 Sources to the chapter 'The "Improvers" of Mankind'   43
4.6 Sources to the chapter 'What the Germans Lack'   45
4.7 The place and role of British philosophy and thinkers in *Götzen-Dämmerung*   46

4.1 Introduction

In this chapter we will examine different aspects of the sources to *Götzen-Dämmerung*. The book is very condensed – Nietzsche calls it 'my philosophy in a nutshell' – and thus its relation to his knowledge and reading is often not apparent. In particular, it is easy to regard his comments about the many thinkers and authors he refers to as merely ignorant and prejudiced. Whether they are prejudiced or not I will not resolve, but I hope to show that for almost all the persons referred to in the book Nietzsche had rather extensive knowledge. What he attempts to do is summarize his interpretation of what they stand for, and in this sense use them as signposts and points of reference.

There is probably no book (except *Also sprach Zarathustra*) by Nietzsche in which his reading plays such an apparently limited and hidden role as is the case of *Götzen-Dämmerung*. This is mostly due to the nature of the book as a sort of concentrated compilation, 'summary' or as a collection of a number of very brief excerpts of his philosophy (which he had worked on for a fairly long time). This means, especially for the first half of the book, that Nietzsche made few extended discussions or longer examination of themes. We thus do not see him enter into any extensive 'dialogues' with other thinkers by means of discussing their texts. Almost all specific recent reading he had done is likely to have, at most, coloured only some specific and limited argumentation or view.

It follows from the above that a full discussion of the relevance and importance of Nietzsche's knowledge and reading for *Götzen-Dämmerung* would require a more detailed examination and discussion, not suitable for this more interpretative and thesis-driven study which concentrates on *Götzen-Dämmerung*'s relation to the planned *Hauptwerk*. Furthermore, much of the late Nietzsche's reading and its importance is not well examined and many of the books he read have not been examined. Thus, much of what I say here will be preliminary and merely point at possible sources and influences (positive as well as negative ones), with few definite conclusions. However, an awareness of Nietzsche's reading before *Götzen-Dämmerung* helps us to better understand the general context in which this work was written.

This is very different from *Der Antichrist*, the first volume of his *Umwerthung aller Werthe*, which is a much more focused work, and for which Nietzsche read a number of specific texts and books, which he uses (but sometimes hidden, without naming them) and in many cases goes into dialogue with.

Nonetheless, Nietzsche's knowledge and reading play an important role also for *Götzen-Dämmerung*, and for the last chapters an essential role. The long chapter, 'Expeditions of an Untimely Man', cannot be fully understood without knowledge about Nietzsche's extensive reading (without that it is almost inevitable that many of his statements there are viewed as merely ignorant and prejudiced). To a large extent this chapter consists of Nietzsche's responses to reading.[1] The last chapter, 'What I Owe to the Ancients', is strongly coloured and inspired by his reading of ancient philosophers and writers, and about them, even if much of it goes back to earlier reading.

Also for parts of the first half of the book, especially the chapter 'The "Improvers" of Mankind', specific reading is of significant importance for understanding the text.

Although written (or written and put together from earlier fairly complete notes) very quickly, there are a number of important sources which has formed and shaped the text of *Götzen-Dämmerung*. These sources, the result of Nietzsche's reading of different texts, primarily in 1888, but also a few years before that, can be divided into two categories: those of major importance, which have helped shape the whole book or the chapter in which it appears, and more minor reading, which has shaped particular arguments and specific sections or statements.[2] This is true for texts read during the last few years before the writing of *Götzen-Dämmerung*. The third kind of sources, which I will include in the second category, are more general reading or texts read earlier or mostly earlier, such as Schopenhauer, Goethe and Plato, which is likely to have influenced the text.

4.2 General and philosophical sources to *Götzen-Dämmerung*

During Nietzsche's last three active years, from 1886 to 1888, he read fewer philosophical books than during the earlier parts of the 1880s. This was in part due to the fact that he was increasingly influenced by non-philosophical sources, such as literature, literary criticism, studies of Christianity, and biographies, and in part due to the related fact that he had found his own philosophical position and thus had less need for further philosophical reading and influences.[3]

His main object of interest during the years 1886–8 was an attempt to work out a revaluation of all values, and, related to that, an increasingly harsh critique of Christianity (Christianity in a broad sense, including much of philosophy and psychology). For his critique of Christianity and Christian values, his reading of Tolstoy, Dostoyevsky, Wellhausen, Lippert, Jacolliot, Strauss, Renan, Janssen and the Bible was more relevant and influential than any reading of 'purely' philosophical texts, and all of these texts influenced, or was used in, the writing of *Der Antichrist*. He also became increasingly engaged in psychology and physiology and read a fairly large number of texts in these fields. He came to regard psychology, rather than philosophy and metaphysical philosophy, as the road to the solution of the major philosophical problems (as we will discuss in Chapter 8).

However, even during these last three years he read a number of texts which perhaps can be regarded as primarily philosophical (although it is difficult to distinguish between philosophy and psychology in the nineteenth century). This is especially true for the year 1887. Equally important is that he continued to re-read texts and authors whom he had been reading for a long time, such as Schopenhauer, Mill, perhaps Hartmann,[4] Montaigne and Pascal.

The most important philosophical reading of this period, as expected, consisted of texts relating to Christianity: Guyau, Pascal and Simplicius (together with a large number of historical, psychological and other non-philosophical texts on this theme). This reading was primarily important for the writing of *Der Antichrist*, but also of some relevance for the writing of *Götzen-Dämmerung*, considering that he wrote these two books more or less at the same time, and that critique of Christianity is a fairly major theme also in *Götzen-Dämmerung*, as discussed in Chapter 9.

In 1887, Nietzsche also read the philosopher and sociologist Alfred Fouillée's *La science sociale contemporaine*, xiii+424 pages.[5] In this work there are continual references to Spencer, Mill, contemporary French philosophy and different theories about society, rights and justice. In several notes from the autumn of 1887 Nietzsche criticized Fouillée (and Guyau),[6] and it seems likely that several of the late Nietzsche's statements about sociology, sociologists and society referred to Fouillée (and Guyau) and to what he learned from reading this book.[7]

Nietzsche's rereading of Pascal in 1887, when he was increasingly engaged in a battle against Christian values, caused him to regard Pascal more and more as an example of how Christianity can corrupt even the most supreme and honest of men. However, the two brief references to Pascal in *Götzen-Dämmerung* ('The Four Great Errors', 6 and 'Expeditions', 9) are really side-effects while discussing psychology. Nietzsche goes further back in history and blames Plato:

The *counterfeit* of everything factual by means of morality is everywhere to be seen; wretched psychology; the philosopher reduced to a 'country parson' – and of all this *Plato is the cause*! *he remains* the greatest misfortune of *Europe*![8]

In 1887 Nietzsche also read and heavily annotated Émile Gebhart's *Etudes méridionales* (1887), which contains a chapter on Machiavelli. It is probable that it was this reading, possibly together with a reading of *The Prince* in a French translation during the 1880s,[9] which led Nietzsche to praise Machiavelli highly in *Götzen-Dämmerung*.[10]

The most intensive 'purely' philosophical reading Nietzsche seems to have done in these last three years he did in the library of Chur in May and early June 1887, and shortly thereafter, during the summer of 1887. In Chur Nietzsche read, apart from the British historian Buckle (referred to in section 44 of 'Expeditions of an Untimely Man') and other non-philosophical texts, two volumes of Kuno Fischer's *Geschichte der neuern Philosophie*, the volumes about Spinoza and Kant. He excerpted extensively from both these volumes.[11] This is likely to have reinforced Nietzsche's views of them, and his statement regarding them in *Götzen-Dämmerung* (even if not new in comparison to what he had written earlier). This reading may well have worked as a stimulus for Nietzsche to refer to Spinoza, here in a highly critical vein: 'Nothing is less Greek than the conceptual cobwebspinning of a hermit, *amor intellectualis dei* [intellectual love of God] in the manner of Spinoza.' (GD, 'Expeditions of an Untimely Man', 23) and 'Thus they acquired their stupendous concept "God". . . . The last, thinnest, emptiest is placed as the first, as the cause in itself, as *ens realissimum* [the most real being]. . . . That mankind should have taken seriously the brainsick fancies of morbid cobweb-spinners! – And it has paid dearly for doing so! . . . ' (GD, 'Reason in Philosophy', 4).[12] However, we should be aware that Nietzsche earlier, when he first read about him in the same Kuno Fischer's work in 1881, felt a close kinship with him.

During the autumn of 1887 or the winter of 1887–8 Nietzsche read and annotated the Comtean E. de Roberty's account of the history of philosophy *L'ancienne et la nouvelle philosophie: Essai sur les lois générales du développement de la philosophie* (Paris, 1887). It is not known if and how this possibly affected *Götzen-Dämmerung*, but it is possible that it could have affected or worked as a stimulus, especially in the writing of the chapter 'How the 'Real World' at last Became a Myth' which deals with the history of philosophy, and where positivism is mentioned.

In 1888, Nietzsche's most productive year, during which he wrote six books, he read of philosophical relevance Victor Brochard's *Les sceptiques grecs* (Paris, 1887), which inspired Nietzsche's positive statements about the sophists in *Götzen-Dämmerung*,[13] and he reread Schopenhauer and possibly Hartmann's *Philosophie des Unbewussten*. He also read or reread several books about religion, including Renan's *Vie de Jésus* (which this time he extensively excerpted), which helped to shape a number of Nietzsche's statements regarding the historical development of the concept of God, the Old Testament prophets, the psychology of Jesus and the social psychology of the early Christian community in *The Antichrist*.[14]

4.3 Reading of books relating to science and 'reality'

Considering the strong emphasis on reality and realism in *Götzen-Dämmerung*, it is relevant to mention some of the books relating to science and reality that he read in the later 1880s.

In the later 1880s Nietzsche reread and worked through several books that he had first read in 1880–1. The most important of these were: Roux's *The Struggle of the*

Parts in the Organism, Vogt's *Force*, Semper's *The Natural Conditions of Existence as they Affect Animal Life* and Espinas's *Animal Societies*. Nietzsche's copies of all four books, all of them read in German, are annotated throughout.[15]

The Anglo-German anti-Darwinist biologist W. H. Rolph's *Biologische Probleme, zugleich als Versuch zur Entwicklung einer rationellen Ethik* (*Biological Problems, also an Attempt at an Elaboration of a Rational Ethics*, 1884), was a significant influence on his understanding of Darwinism and evolutionary ethics, as well as on his conception of the will to power. The probably most important reading relating to science, reality, philosophy of nature and epistemology was C. v. Nägeli's *Mechanisch-physiologische Theorie der Abstammungslehre* (*Mechanico-Physiological Theory of Descent*) (München, Leipzig, 1884), which Nietzsche acquired in 1886. This is primarily a natural scientific work, important for its critique of Darwinism, but it also contains a lengthy appendix containing several philosophical essays, heavily annotated by Nietzsche,[16] but it is difficult to know for certain how much this reading influenced the contents of *Götzen-Dämmerung*. Nietzsche annotated his copy of this massive book extensively and toyed with some of Nägeli's ideas in his notebooks.[17]

Other relevant books about science and 'reality', but overlapping with the titles covering psychology and physiology dealt with in the next section, which Nietzsche read during this period include the following. In 1884, in addition to Rolph's book, Nietzsche also read Francis Galton's *Inquiries into Human Faculty and its Development* (1883) and an article entitled 'Heredity' by H. W. Holland in the *Atlantic Monthly* about Galton. In April 1886 Overbeck sent Nietzsche a copy of *Vitalismus und Mechanismus* (1886), the inaugural lecture of the new professor of physiology at Basel, Gustav von Bunge, a leading vitalist. Nietzsche annotated almost every page of this short text. Finally, Nietzsche also purchased Joseph Delboeuf's *La matière brute et la matière vivante* (1887), but it is unclear whether he actually read it or not (his copy of the book contains no annotations, but that is sometimes true for books we know he read).

4.4 Reading in and about psychology and physiology

The title of *Twilight of the Idols* was actually to have been *Müßiggang eines Psychologen* (*The Idle Hours of a Psychologist* or *A Psychologist's Leisure* or *The Idleness of a Psychologist*), in part reflecting that Nietzsche in the 1880s came to increasingly emphasize the importance of psychology, which we will discuss in Chapter 8. With this interest came also an extensive reading of books in the fields of psychology (and physiology). To these books belong a number written by literary authors such as Stendhal, Dostoyevsky,[18] Tolstoy[19] and Strindberg.[20] Others, such as Montaigne and Pascal, could also be included in this category. Biographical and cultural studies by, for example, the brothers Goncourts, Galiani, Bourget and Lefebvre were also of importance for Nietzsche's understanding of man and psychology.

Nietzsche also read a number of textbooks and more specialist psychological studies. The Danish philosopher Harald Höffding's *Psychologie in Umrissen auf Grundlage der Erfahrung* [*Outlines of Psychology on the Basis of Experience*] (Leipzig, 1887), 463 pages, is probably the most heavily annotated book Nietzsche read during this period, with annotations on almost every page.[21] The book contains discussions of psychology, including accounts of classical and contemporary philosophers' discussions of psychology. Höffding especially emphasized British and German views. The contents of this book influenced Nietzsche and found its way into *Zur Genealogie der Moral* (1887) on several instances, both in terms of several smaller examples and the use of specific concepts, and in larger themes such as the content of 'English' philosophy and psychology and the psychology of forgetting.[22] Only one of the specifically identified 'Lesefruchte' relates to *Götzen-Dämmerung*, but there are likely to exist many more, especially in the chapter 'The Four Great Errors', and as background to much of his whole discussion of psychology.

The book by Henri Joly, *Psychologie des grands hommes* [*Psychology of Great Men*] (Paris, 1883), 280 pages,[23] which Nietzsche read in 1887 (also annotated, but to a lesser degree) discusses great men and geniuses and their dependence on the environment and heritage – themes Nietzsche discusses in *Twilight of the Idols* – including the theories of Darwin, Galton and W. James. Further studies of Nietzsche's reading of Joly need to be done to determine if and how this reading influenced him.

Nietzsche also read the future Nobel laureate Charles Richet's *L'homme et l'intelligence: Fragments de physiologie et de psychologie* (Paris, 1884), in 1884 and 1887, and his copy of the book is lightly annotated, and his *Essai de psychologie générale* (Paris, 1887), which also is present in his library, but their relevance for *Götzen-Dämmerung* have not been examined.[24]

Nietzsche's reading of the three specialist physiological works by Alexandre Herzen, *Le cervau et l'activité cérébrale au point de vue psycho-physiologie* [*The Brain and Cerebral Activity from a Psycho-Physiological Viewpoint*] (Paris, 1887), and Charles Féré, *Sensation et mouvment* (Paris, 1887) and *Dégénérescence et criminalité: Essai physiologique* (Paris, 1888), all played a role for the writing of *Götzen-Dämmerung*.[25] All three of these works played a role in the expansion of his extraordinary range of medicalized vocabulary in the late 1880s and in the elaboration of his concept of *décadence*. The latter work is also relevant for his discussions of Socrates and of criminals in *Götzen-Dämmerung*.

Nietzsche's library also contains several books dealing with psychology and physiology, which it is likely that Nietzsche read during his late period, but for which we have no definite knowledge of when, or even if, he read them. This is true for the following works; Henry Houssaye *Les hommes et les idées* (Paris, 1886), 392 pages, A. Krauss *Die Psychologie des Verbrechens: Ein Beitrag zur Erfahrungsseelenkunde* [*The Psychology of Crime*] (Tübingen, 1884), 421 pages, F. Paulhan, *Les phénomènes affectifs et les lois de leur apparition: Essai de psychologie générale* (Paris, 1887), 163 pages. Nietzsche also possessed and had read, in French translations, two works by the English philosopher and psychologist, James Sully (1842–1923), who was an adherent of the associationist school of psychology and held views similar to those of Alexander Bain (by whom Nietzsche also had read several books). The books by Sully he possessed and had annotated are *Le pessimisme (histoire et critique)* (Paris, 1882) [*Pessimism: A History and a Criticism*], 452 pages[26] – pessimism is a major theme in *Götzen-Dämmerung* – and *Les illusions des sens et de l'esprit* (Paris, 1883) [*Illusions: A Psychological Study*], 264 pages,[27] both containing extensive discussions of psychology and physiology.

Another interesting work which it is not known when Nietzsche read – but since his copy contains annotations and comments throughout, it is clear that he did read it – is the professor of pathology in Vienna, S. Stricker's *Physiologie des Rechts* (Wien, 1884), x+144 pages. The study strongly emphasizes power as the motive of men, and the source of law and justice, and further emphasizes a close connection between thinking, willingness and knowledge with muscular activity. The strong emphasis of power and the human desire to maximize their power in general and as a source of law is likely to have influenced Nietzsche's continued thinking about his 'will to power'.[28] Stricker, like Nietzsche, is naturalistic and critical of religion in his arguments and denies the possibility of free will (e.g. pages 21–3, annotated by Nietzsche). It seems likely that the reading of this book was an important background for Nietzsche's genealogical and naturalistic critique of social and moral phenomena, including law, in *On the Genealogy of Morals* and probably also as background for *Götzen-Dämmerung*.

Another, in some ways related study, is the French anthropologist Charles Letourneau's *Physiologie des passions* (Paris, 1868), 232 pages, which also is in Nietzsche's library, containing no annotations, but two dog-ears (which Nietzsche frequently used to mark interesting pages or the extent of his reading). It is not known if and when Nietzsche read this work, but he lists the name Letourneau and the title of the book during the winter of 1884–5, probably as part of a list of books to buy and read.[29]

There are several further books relating to psychology and physiology in Nietzsche's private library, but for most of them it is not known if and when he read them.[30]

I have here not dealt with the fairly large number of medical books (and related studies) which Nietzsche primarily read for the sake of his own health. Some of these, such as, for example, L. Löwenfeld's *Die moderne Behandlung der Nervenschwäche (Neurasthenie), der Hysterie und verwandter Leiden* (Wiesbaden, 1887), are likely to also have affected his broader thought.[31]

Important for *Götzen-Dämmerung* (and all the books from 1888) is Nietzsche's use of the concept of decadence – which he almost always used in the French form *décadence*, since he picked it up from French literary critics, although his reading of French physiological texts, especially Herzen and Féré, were also of great importance. He began to use the concept after his reading of Paul Bourget's *Essais de psychologie contemporaine* (Paris, 1883), which he read in the winter of 1883–4,[32] but used it only rarely until the autumn of 1887. Apart from Bourget, Nietzsche's frequent use of the concept of *décadence* may have derived from his extensive reading of other French literary critics,[33] and from his reading of contemporary physiological and medical literature, especially Herzen and Féré (mentioned earlier). In his published works he began to use the term only in 1888, when it became a major *Leitmotif* in the book *Der Fall Wagner*. Thereafter, he used it frequently in *Götzen-Dämmerung, Der Antichrist* and *Ecce homo*.

4.5 Sources to the chapter 'The "Improvers" of Mankind'

The purpose of the chapter 'The "Improvers" of Mankind' is a continued critique of morality from the previous two chapters. He does this by discussing two main ethical alternatives; taming and breeding: 'Both the *taming* of the beast man and the *breeding* of a certain species of man has been called 'improvement': only these zoological *termini* express realities' (section 2). The two most obvious sources for this chapter are the Bible (and other sources of Christian morality), in general well known to Nietzsche and his readers, and the much less well-known source for Nietzsche's knowledge of the Laws of Manu. It is therefore the latter which it is relevant to discuss in this section.

The Manu whom Nietzsche seemingly praises is in the mythology of India the first man and the legendary author of an important Sanskrit code of law, the *Manu-smrti*. This code of law, or lawbook, is one of the most authoritative books of the Hindu code in India. In its present form it dates back to about the first century BC. The book contains twelve chapters dealing with such themes as initiation, marriage, hospitality, dietary restrictions, pollution, the conduct of women and the law of kings. Its influence has been monumental, and it has provided justification and a practical morality for the Hindu Caste system.

The direct reason that Nietzsche discusses Manu and the society and laws of Manu is his reading of Louis Jacolliot's *Les legislateurs religieux: Manou-Moise-Mahomet* (Paris, 1876) which is a 480-page translation of a version of the *Manu-smrti*. The French titles are somewhat misleading for it refers to a series of books which Jacolliot planned to write, each only dealing with one religious legislator – thus, this work is only a translation of the Laws of Manu, with some commentaries in footnotes (Moses and Mohammed are dealt with in separate books).

Nietzsche read the work in May 1888 and his copy of the book, with fairly extensive annotations, is still in his library. The reading resulted in a large number of notes,[34] discussions of Manu in *Twilight of the Idols* and in *The Antichrist* (sections 55–8), discussion of it in a letter to Gast and in annotations in Nietzsche's copy of the book (in the form of underlinings, marginal lines and a few minor corrections of spelling throughout).[35]

Jacolliot's book is essentially a translation of one version of the Laws of Manu with occasional discussions and comments in the brief preface and in footnotes. Annemarie Etter has examined and discussed the reliability of Jacolliot's text and has characterized him as someone who knew India well but his work as pseudo-scientific.[36] Jacolliot was an India-fanatic who believed that all of human culture literally had its origin in India, everything from Greek and Roman Law to weights. He also believed that most peoples were originally Indians, like Arabs, Semitics, Babylonians and so on. He combined this belief with anti-Semitism, but also with a still stronger anti-Christianism, especially directed against Catholicism. The reading of this book may have influenced Nietzsche's decision to write *The Antichrist*, which he had not planned before May 1888, but in general Nietzsche probably was very little influenced by the comments in the footnotes.

It is not known when Nietzsche acquired Jacolliot's book, but a possible stimulus could come from Nietzsche's reading in 1884 of the article 'Maenadism in Religion' by Elizabeth Robins in the *Atlantic Monthly*.[37] She there writes: 'There was, unfortunately, no Louis Jacolliot in ancient times to watch unseen the sacred midnight revels, and then give a gloving description of them to the unilluminated' (p. 498).

4.6 Sources to the chapter 'What the Germans Lack'

In the first seven short chapters of *Götzen-Dämmerung* few specific thinkers are mentioned, and among those mentioned (here as well as in the last chapter) ancient Greeks are most prevalent and almost the only ones who are appreciated and praised. As a professor of classical literature and thought this is perhaps not altogether surprising, and his knowledge of them was, of course, extensive.

In the eighth chapter, 'What the Germans Lack', he briefly mentions a number of Germans (as well as Napoleon): Bismarck, Strauss, Goethe, Wagner, Hegel, Heine, Schopenhauer, Burckhardt and Kant. Nietzsche had fairly detailed knowledge of all of these persons and had read them, and about them, extensively. This is least true for Bismarck and Hegel, both of whom were immensely influential and written about in contemporary texts (and in the news). Nietzsche had read texts by both of them earlier in life and would have read extensively about them, but his knowledge of them may nonetheless not necessarily be much above that of an educated German at this time.

The young and early Nietzsche knew David Strauss well, and had read him, including his *magnum opus Das Leben Jesu*, and at that time been influenced by it, but later turned against him and wrote his second book against Strauss' last book *Der alte und der neue Glaube* (1872), and what Nietzsche regarded as superficial German culture. Thereafter Nietzsche was not much concerned with him.

Goethe, Wagner, Heine, Schopenhauer and Burckhardt Nietzsche knew well, and had read extensively. Nietzsche knew Wagner and Burckhardt personally. The (cultural) historian Burckhardt had been Nietzsche's colleague in Basel (and to whom Nietzsche almost always sent the first copy of his new books, although he after *Also sprach Zarathustra* no longer received any response), and he had closely read several of Burckhardt's books (and his library contains three of them).

Napoleon (who is also referred to in the next long chapter, sections 44, 45, 48 and 49) is one of the persons Nietzsche most frequently refers to affirmatively. We should notice that it is less the general and 'statesman' Napoleon he refers to than his character and personality. His reading about Napoleon was extensive.

Nietzsche may have read less Kant than expected to be the case by a nineteenth-century German philosopher, perhaps only the third *Critique* early in life (but possibly also a few other works), but his reading about Kant was extensive. Most relevant for *Götzen-Dämmerung* is, as we have seen earlier in this chapter, that he read and excerpted Kuno Fischer's extensive and massive study of Kant in the library in Chur during the early summer of 1887.

Schopenhauer is almost certainly not only the philosopher but also the author Nietzsche read most and was most influenced by. He had been a dedicated Schopenhauerian for ten years, c. 1865–75, but continued to read him frequently also after this.

Nietzsche liked and had read fairly much Heinrich Heine, but his two references to him (and Hegel) in *Götzen-Dämmerung* are merely general.

Nietzsche had throughout his life read much Goethe, and Goethe is the person he most frequently and most consistently praises in all of his published books. Goethe is almost certainly the most important person, the most important 'signpost' in *Götzen-Dämmerung* (a 'signpost' to a healthy life and attitude to life), and the long chapter 'Expeditions of an Untimely Man', which was meant to end the book, ends with sections 48–51, with a crescendo of praise of Goethe – both as a real person and as a symbol of human greatness according to Nietzsche.

4.7 The place and role of British philosophy and thinkers in *Götzen-Dämmerung*

There are good reasons to assume that Nietzsche regarded the first seven chapters (and the last, written and added later), as the most important ones, as constituting extracts from his work on his *Hauptwerk* entitled *Revaluation of All Values*. The first observation to be made in regard to British philosophy is the almost complete absence of explicit references to 'England' and the 'English' (i.e. British) philosophers and thinkers in these chapters.[38]

However, when we examine the content of what he says about philosophy and morality in these eight chapters, there seems to be room for what can be called British philosophy. He speaks about empiricism, naturalism and positivism especially in chapters 2–4, affirmatively, and, perhaps not surprisingly, negatively, in regard to utilitarianism in chapters 5–7 (but without actually naming it).

Almost all of Nietzsche's explicit references to 'English' philosophy and to British thinkers occur in the chapter 'Expeditions of an Untimely Man'. There he refers to seven British (and one American thinker, R. W. Emerson),[39] all of them used as signposts or symbols, or sometimes as examples, mostly of what he disapproves of. English thinkers and culture are used in the late books almost exclusively negatively.[40] How is this to be resolved with his at least partial support for empiricism, naturalism and positivism in these works?

Regarding empiricism, naturalism and positivism, which also play a major role also in *Der Antichrist* and *Ecce homo*, Nietzsche does not himself explicitly connect them to British or 'English' thought. This is not due to lack of knowledge. Nietzsche knew and had even studied Mill and Spencer, had read Bacon, Locke, Hume and Alexander Bain, who all broadly stand in or close to these traditions, and he knew from secondary literature much about British thought generally. We do not know why he does not do so – but a plausible hypothesis is that it is due to three connected reasons:

(i) Nietzsche probably felt that his own possible affiliation to empiricism, naturalism and positivism differed significantly from what perhaps can be regarded as the 'English' conception (as he would have encountered it). He did not emphasize utility, unlike so many English thinkers (Bacon and many followers); he did not, like Locke (and several others), assume man to be extensively changeable and beginning as a 'blank slate', but believed in a granite human nature,[41] which in *Götzen-Dämmerung* (and the other 1888 books) is most visible in his emphasis on that some are fundamentally healthy while others are unhealthy or decadent), and also associated this with them representing ascending or descending forms of life. Unlike most empiricists and positivists (who were less concerned with the philosophy of value), Nietzsche strongly emphasized the importance of value and values. Nietzsche also stressed such aspects as status and power (rather than utility). He probably also regarded British thought as too passive, too reactive and based on a search for equilibrium – in human life, in psychology (association-psychology à la Locke and Hartley), in biology (Darwin, Spencer, Malthus and Huxley) and even in physics (mechanistic views). Against this Nietzsche emphasizes a strong sense of dynamism and activism (most visible in his praise of Heraclitus, and in his concept of will to power). He seems also to object to British democracy and its political culture. This seems not primarily to be a rejection of democracy (as it is usually interpreted as, although it includes this, for his favourite cultural entities, such as France and ancient Athens, were at least in part also democratic). His objection is probably more against the belief that with reason (or common sense) and reform, life can be substantially improved, whereas he emphasized *amor fati*, and saw life as merely becoming more shallow and comfortable by such means.

(ii) He regarded much of British thought as superficial, and had explicitly rejected it (especially in *Jenseits von Gut und Böse*, 1886, and in the early parts of the first essay of *Zur Genealogie der Moral*, 1887), and is unlikely to want to use it to signal or symbolize his own position.

(iii) The one thing which he explicitly criticizes the English for in *Götzen-Dämmerung* is their agnosticism, that many of them are free-thinkers, but without sufficient courage, honesty and depth to see and draw the reasonable and necessary consequences of their denial of, or scepticism about, the existence of God. In fact, according to him they often draw the *opposite* conclusion – that we must still firmer hold on to Christian values and morality (GD, 'Streifzüge', 5 and 12), a view that Nietzsche, of course, completely rejects.

I will briefly discuss Nietzsche's view of 'English' thinkers in thematic order: three philosophers or thinkers, Mill, Spencer and Carlyle; two biologists, Darwin and Malthus (but Spencer could fit here as well); one historian, Buckle (but Carlyle can equally well be seen as a historian as a philosopher, a romantic historian generally holding the opposite position to that of Buckle); and one radical, agnostic intellectual, George Eliot. My main point will be to show that Nietzsche was not ignorant about them (and this is likewise true for most other persons he refers to in *Götzen-Dämmerung*), although it may appear thus, and to help the reader realize what they symbolized for Nietzsche.[42]

John Stuart Mill (1806–73)

It is easy to assume that Nietzsche's knowledge of Mill was superficial and very limited. In *Götzen-Dämmerung* his only reference to him is: '*My impossibles.* [. . .] – *John Stuart Mill*: or offensive clarity' (GD, 'Expeditions of an Untimely Man', 1). The reasons for such an assumption are the few references to Mill in Nietzsche's published works, only four, and the fact that these few references seem to imply a quick rejection of Mill rather than a close knowledge and analysis. However, Nietzsche's knowledge of Mill was far from superficial and limited. He had read much of Mill, and read it with great attention, some of it at least twice, in 1880 and in 1887, and he had read much about Mill. Nietzsche possessed five out of totally twelve volumes of the German translation of Mill's collected works.[43] He has made extensive annotations in many of the texts, with an average of several annotations per page. In some texts there are up to twenty annotations per page, with many 'nota bene', exclamation marks and occasional words. Perhaps surprisingly, his comments in the margin of his Mill books are more positive than critical, with annotations such as 'ja' and 'Gut'. We also know that he, probably in 1879, attempted to acquire Mill's *Autobiography* in German translation, and only failed to do so because it has sold out (he may instead have read it in libraries, but we have no evidence of that).[44] There is a copy of *The Subjection of Women* in Elisabeth Förster-Nietzsche's library today, with a few annotations. This copy probably belonged to and was read by Nietzsche (who seems to refer to this work in some notes).

What Nietzsche does with his *ad hominem* statements in regard to Mill is to point out that he and Mill and are two very different types of thinkers. Since knowledge and evaluations essentially always are comparisons, what he does is compare himself with Mill, obviously from his own perspective. Mill is diagnosed as a superficial thinker with Christian and egalitarian values.

Herbert Spencer (1820–1903)

Nietzsche often refers to Spencer, all in all almost fifty times, almost always highly critically. However, Nietzsche originally seems to have sought knowledge and texts by Spencer with positive expectations, and we know that he carefully read at least two of his books. In three letters from August 1877 he tells how he has met professor Robertson, the editor of the philosophical journal *Mind*, to which 'all the greatest men of England contribute, Darwin, [. . .] Spencer Tylor'. Two years later, in a letter to his publisher Schmeitzner, Nietzsche recommends him to have Spencer's *The Data of Ethics* translated into German and published.[45] Schmeitzner writes to the English publishers but it turns out that the book had already been translated and published in Germany. Nietzsche then asks him to acquire the book for him. This seems to have been done. Nietzsche then closely reads *Die Thatsachen der Ethik* during 1880 and 1881 (i.e. at the same time as his extensive reading of several volumes of Mill's collected works). Nietzsche also possessed and read Spencer's *Einleitung in das Studium der Sociologie* (in two parts, 1875) probably during the autumn of 1883.[46]

Nietzsche is more willing to discuss ideas in regard to Spencer than he was when referring to Mill. This is reflected in his relatively frequent statements in his notes: 'against Spencer', before, during or after discussing certain ideas and values. Most of the statements are related to morality, and Nietzsche mostly regards and treats Spencer as a moral philosopher.

Nietzsche's discussion of Spencer's ideas deals with many different topics, but most importantly are the three themes: altruism, the genealogy or origin of morality and utility, especially that the good is identical with the useful. In *Götzen-Dämmerung* it is the first of these themes that he comments on in his single reference to Spencer. As with all of Spencer's ideas Nietzsche refers to, he regards these as erroneous. Altruism he denies outright. Likewise with the view that usefulness is identical with good. This is also a major reason for his critique of Spencer's view on the origin of morality. Other themes in Nietzsche's critique of Spencer are his Darwinism (e.g. his belief that natural selection always leads to the best results), his emphasis on happiness and comfort (Nietzsche even uses the English word 'comfort' on a few occasions), his belief in equality, his view of human nature as passive and reactive, that is, adaptive (rather than Nietzsche's more active will to power) and his emphasis on consequentialism in ethics (while Nietzsche claims that the full consequences of actions are unknown and unknowable). Nietzsche regards Spencer as a utilitarian[47] and he is associated with some of its most fundamental ideas: happiness, utility, consequences of acts and altruism.

Thomas Carlyle (1795–1881)

Carlyle is the British thinker, after Shakespeare, Byron and Spencer, whom Nietzsche most frequently refers to, and yet we have no certain knowledge of a single work by him that Nietzsche had read. However, since Nietzsche so frequently refers to or discusses Carlyle, he must have had some knowledge and reason for doing so. It is possible that he had read Carlyle's *On Heroes, Hero Worship and the Heroic in History* before 1881 and he certainly had read H. Taine's seventy-five-page account of Carlyle in his *Geschichte des englischen Literatur* in 1880–1 (or possibly 1884). When Nietzsche, in *Twilight of the Idols* claims that he has 'read the life of Thomas Carlyle,'[48] he is probably referring to Taine's account, although it is possible that he also had read other accounts of him.

Henry Thomas Buckle (1821–62)

The most interesting of Nietzsche's relations to the great British historians is that to Henry Thomas Buckle, together with Hume (whom he however does not mention in *Götzen-Dämmerung*). He read at least two works by him, and in one of these, Buckle's *Essays*, he made annotations. He thereafter judged Buckle to be one of his 'strongest antagonists' and in a late note he explained why this is so.

In 1880 Nietzsche possessed and read a copy of É. Littré *La science au point de vue philosophique* (Paris, 1876). This study contains a long essay on Buckle entitled 'De l'histoire de la civilisation en Angleterre, par Buckle', pages 478–521. Nietzsche has annotated seven pages in this essay (and only in one other of the essays), signifying interest in Buckle.

Nietzsche's earliest first-hand encounter with Buckle seems to have been in the following year, 1881, at least he then ordered a copy of Buckle's *Essays* (Leipzig and Heidelberg, 1867) from his publisher and also received it.[49] The book, of 151 pages, contains three essays, an anonymous biographical sketch of Buckle, an essay on Mill's *On Liberty* and an essay on the influence of women on the progress of science.

Nietzsche's copy is still in his library and contains annotations only in the by far longest essay about Mill.

Nietzsche's second and more fundamental encounter with Buckle occurred in Chur during the spring of 1887, where he waited for the temperature and weather to be such that he could continue to the higher altitude Sils-Maria. While there he used the local library intensively, including reading Buckle, as he told Peter Gast in a letter:

> The library in Chur, circa 20 000 volumes, gives me this and that which teaches me new things. I saw, for the first time, the famous book by Buckle, 'History of Civilisation in England' – and fantastically! it turned out that B[uckle] is one of my greatest antagonists. Incidently, it is almost unbelievable how much E. Dühring is dependent on the crude value-judgements of this democrat in historical things.[50]

It is the reading that Nietzsche made in Chur, and the value-judgements he then formed, which lie behind his future critique of Buckle. This critique is expressed for the first time in *On the Genealogy of Morals*, written during the autumn of the same year.

> With regard to a moral genealogy this seems to me a *fundamental* insight; that it has been arrived at so late is the fault of the retarding influence exercised by the democratic prejudice in the modern world toward all questions of origin. And this is so even in the apparently quite objective domain of natural science and physiology, as I shall merely hint here. But what mischief this prejudice is capable of doing, especially to morality and history, once it has been unbridled to the point of hatred is shown by the notorious case of Buckle; here the *plebeianism* of the modern spirit, which is of English origin, erupted once again on its native soil, as violently as a mud volcano and with that salty, noisy, vulgar eloquence with which all volcanoes have spoken hitherto.[51]

About half a year later, Nietzsche intended to include Buckle in a list of authors and thinkers who are 'completely compromised' and whom he dismisses in *Twilight of the Idols*, 'Expeditions of an Untimely Man', 1, under the title 'My Impossibles', although Buckle was in the end not included in the final version.[52] Buckle is instead dismissed in section 44 of the same chapter:

> The Englishman has only two possible ways of coming to terms with the genius and 'great man': either the *democratic* way in the manner of Buckle or the *religious* way in the manner of Carlyle. ('Expeditions of an Untimely Man', 44)

The fundamental reason for Nietzsche's rejection of Buckle is here not completely clear, and it is easy for the modern reader to dismiss Nietzsche's dismissal of Buckle as merely due to prejudice, and anti-English and anti-democratic prejudice at that. However, Nietzsche does have good and firm grounds for rejecting Buckle's (and Carlyle's) view of great men. Carlyle believes in great men, and values them because of what they do or the effect they have (it is what a man does which determines if he is great or not). Buckle denies that great men have great effects – effects are instead due to climate, soil and other material causes – and thus believes that he has shown that there are no great men. Both Buckle and Carlyle emphasize that it is the effects, or the consequences of deeds that matter – that is, they assume a broad form of consequential ethics or utilitarianism, which Nietzsche sees, not without some justification, as typically English.[53] Nietzsche's position, which is much more related to ancient ethics or an ethics of virtue,[54] claims that great men exist – although in a less idealistic manner than Carlyle – but that the greatness has nothing to do with acts or consequences, but is an inherent aspect of his character. Put differently, for Nietzsche, human greatness is the most fundamental value or the starting point, equivalent to 'goodness' (or 'rightness') in deontological ethics and utility or pleasure in utilitarian ethics. Not principles, but persons, but character, is the determining criterion of value for Nietzsche.

George Eliot [Mary Ann Evans] (1819–80)

Nietzsche's only published reference to George Eliot is the harsh condemnation in *Twilight of the Idols*, 'Expeditions of an Untimely Man', 5, where he regards her as moralistic and typically English, with all the negative associations that has for him in 1888.

> G. Eliot. – They have got rid of the Christian God, and now feel obliged to cling all the more firmly to Christian morality: that is *English* consistency, let us not blame it on little bluestocking *a la* Eliot. In England, in response to every little emancipation from theology one has to reassert one's position in a fear-inspiring manner as a moral fanatic. That is the *penance* one pays there. [. . .] For the Englishman morality is not yet a problem...

In part, this probably refers to that George Eliot had translated David Friedrich Strauss' *Das Leben Jesu* into English, and the discussion around this.

Several of the negative statements about women elsewhere in *Götzen-Dämmerung* are also, at least partially, done with Eliot in mind, for example, aphorisms 20, 27 and 28 in the first chapter 'Maxims and Arrows' and in section 27 in 'Expeditions of an Untimely Man' although this is not visible in the public versions.[55] Is it possible to determine the reasons for Nietzsche's critique and hostility, and the sources for it, what Nietzsche had read by her and perhaps about her?

The earliest knowledge we have of Nietzsche's encounter with Eliot is that Elisabeth read *Middlemarch* in his company during the autumn of 1879. It seems likely that she also read, at least part of it to him, for she usually read aloud for him. Elisabeth seems to have liked and read much Eliot. Nietzsche's library contains two works by Eliot, *Die Mühle am Fluss* and *Middlemarch*, but it is not known if and when he read them. H. Taine, in his study of English literature, *Geschichte des englischen Literatur*, which Nietzsche read carefully in 1880 and 1884, has essentially nothing about Eliot in.

In the autumn of 1884 Nietzsche met frequently for about a month's time, the feminist author Helene Druscowitz, who had written about and was enthusiastic about Eliot. Nietzsche was later greatly disappointed by her, and she wrote a negative review of one of his books. The association of Eliot with an active feminist may have influenced Nietzsche's anti-feminist hostility towards her.

There are thereafter no references to Eliot until 1887 and 1888, when there are five, which are all hostile. In a note entitled '*Among moralists*' from the autumn of 1887, probably intended to be part of a continuation or second volume of On the Genealogy of Morals, Nietzsche wrote: 'The great moral philosophers. Morality as the un-doing of the philosophers so far'. There follows a list of twenty-four names, three of them British and placed on the same line: 'Carlyle. G. Eliot. H. Spencer'.[56] Eliot's name in the list is somewhat surprising, but it shows that Nietzsche primarily saw her as a moralist and that he knew enough about her to plan to deal with her more extensively.

In a letter to Peter Gast, 24 November 1887, Nietzsche criticizes Rousseau and claims that there exists a whole family of Rousseaus (which, to him, essentially means romantics, moralists and sentimentalists):

> The fact that Rousseau was among the first admirers of Gluck makes one think; to me, at least, everything that Rousseau valued is a little questionable, likewise everyone who has valued *him* (there is a whole Rousseau family; Schiller belongs to it, Kant also, to some extent; in France, George Sand, even Sainte-Beuve; in England Eliot and so on). Anyone who needs 'moral dignity' *faute de mieux* has numbered among Rousseau's admirers, down to our own favourite Dühring, who even has the good taste to present himself in his autobiography as the *Rousseau of the nineteenth century*. (Notice how a person stands vis-à-vis Voltaire and Rousseau: it makes the profoundest difference whether he agrees with the former or with the latter. Voltaire's enemies, for example, Victor Hugo, all the romantics – even the sophisticated romantics, like the Goncourt brothers – are all gracious toward the masked plebeian Rousseau; I suspect that there is a certain amount of plebeian rancour at the basis of romanticism . . .)

This view later also enters *Twilight of the Idols*, 'Expeditions of an Untimely Man', sections 5 and especially 6 (which primarily deals with George Sand).

In 1887 Nietzsche had seen Eliot primarily as an English moralist, in 1888 the point of gravity shifts somewhat and he now mainly critically emphasizes her as a (failed) woman.

> Behind all the moralistic scribbling of these country females, by G. Eliot, I always hear the excited voice of all female literary debutants: 'je me verrai, je me lirai, je m'extasierai et je dirai: Possible, que j'aie eu tant d'esprit? . . .'[57]

This and related notes give rise to several aphorisms in *Twilight of the Idols* – 20, 27 and 28 in section 'Maxims and arrows' and 27 in 'Expeditions of an Untimely Man'.

It has not been possible to determine with certainty what Nietzsche had read by George Eliot, but the fact that he discusses and criticizes her so relatively much, makes it likely that he had read, apart from *Adam Bede* (that his mother read to him during the winter 1879–80), the two books by her that he possessed: *Die Mühle am Fluss* (1861), bought and bound in December 1878 and *Middlemarch*, 4 vols. (1872–3).

5

Reading *Twilight of the Idols* as relating to Nietzsche's *Revaluation of All Values*

5.1	General consequences and observations	53
5.2	Title, subtitle, foreword and the aphorisms (chapter 1)	55
5.3	The philosophy-critical chapters (2, 3 and 4)	67
5.4	The morality- and religion-critical chapters (6, 5 and 7)	72
5.5	The old preface and its critique of the Germans and their educational system (8)	84
5.6	The long miscellaneous chapter on aesthetics, writers, artists and others (9)	85
5.7	The last chapter on antiquity and the Dionysian (10)	109
5.8	The epilogue: The hammer speaks	112
5.9	References to the *Revaluation of All Values* in *Götzen-Dämmerung*	117
5.10	Some conclusions	118

5.1 General consequences and observations

As we have seen earlier, *Götzen-Dämmerung* has not been read and interpreted in a manner which takes account of its relation to the *Umwerthung aller Werthe* project which Nietzsche was then working on, and had been for several years. That will be done in this chapter. This lack of taking Nietzsche's work on a *Hauptwerk* seriously, in spite of its obvious presence in the foreword to *Götzen-Dämmerung* (and elsewhere in the book) as well as in his notes and letters from this time, may seem surprising. It is probably primarily due to the fact that no such work was published (with the exception of *Der Antichrist*, but its publication was delayed until 1895 and could obviously not be considered to constitute the whole of that planned work),[1] and the general belief that Nietzsche later gave up on writing it.[2] Another reason is that the question actually did cause much debate and controversy in the first half of the twentieth century, and the winners then seem to have been those that rejected the often exaggerated views of the importance of the projected *magnum opus* and the belief that it would be possible to almost fully reconstruct the content of that work (which some commentators then hoped to find among the notes). This has led to a strong scepsis to talk about a *Hauptwerk* in Nietzsche research. This sceptical attitude has been greatly reinforced by the to a large extent justified hostility to Elizabeth Förster-Nietzsche's selection of Nietzsche's notes published under the title *Der Wille zur Macht*, which many at first took as a representation of that *Hauptwerk*.

However, today, with a definite knowledge that no such work was completed by Nietzsche (the last three volumes of the planned four) and with all the notes available,[3] there is no reason to continue to ignore this strong and persistent intention on Nietzsche's part. Instead we should examine the extent and the consequences of this intention. In the case of *Götzen-Dämmerung*, I will argue that this lack of attention on the relevance of that planned *Hauptwerk* has led to a misreading of the book, both in what it contains and what is left out of it. Another consequence concerns Nietzsche's late notes. Many have assumed and argued, like Bernd Magnus, discussed in Chapter 2, that the notes must be regarded as discarded material (as 'dustbin manuscripts'),[4] but although that is obviously true for some late notes, it cannot be denied that a large part of the extant notes from *c*. 1885–8 Nietzsche collected, systematized, edited and kept as material for future work.[5] That is, Nietzsche's notes were far from discarded, but rather saved and organized to be used as working material mainly for the planned *Hauptwerk*.

There exist specific references in *Götzen-Dämmerung* to the *Umwerthung aller Werthe*, both explicit and implicit ones, as we will see later. Much more frequent are pointers to that work or in that direction. *Götzen-Dämmerung* is full of 'Gedankenstriche' (thought dashes), ellipses and open questions. These occur almost everywhere in the text, and many sections and chapters also end with them. Most of them signify to the reader to continue the line of thought himself or herself. But some of these seem also to be pointers to the planned continued discussion of the theme in the *Umwerthung aller Werthe*.[6] I will show how Nietzsche continually in *Götzen-Dämmerung* refers to and points towards the *Umwerthung aller Werthe*, a work which he regarded as much more important and comprehensive than *Götzen-Dämmerung*.[7]

Nietzsche seems in a letter to Overbeck, 14 September 1888, to divide *Götzen-Dämmerung* into two major parts, the first (consisting of the first six chapters and, presumably, the last one, which, however, had then not yet been written and added to the manuscript) where he summarizes his philosophical heresy, and the second (the chapter on the Germans and his expeditions of an untimely man) where he is much more timely:

> A second manuscript [apart from *Der Fall Wagner*], completely ready to be printed, is furthermore already in the hands of Herrn C. G. Naumann [Nietzsche's publisher]. However, we will leave that lying for some time. It is called '*A Psychologist's Idleness*' and is for me very valuable since it expresses in the shortest possible form (perhaps also in the most high-spirited) my *essential philosophical heterodoxy*. In the rest it is very 'timely': I express my 'politeness' about all sorts of thinkers and artists in present-day Europe – not included in that, is that in it the Germans will straight to their faces be told unrelenting truths *in puncto* spirit, taste and *depth*.

This letter can help us better understand the structure of *Götzen-Dämmerung* – as consisting of three parts (but where the third part was added to it after this letter was written). The first part, consisting of the first seven chapters, which can in some ways be regarded as a summary or extract of his work on the *Hauptwerk*, especially of the first three critical volumes. The second part, originally consisting of the latter half of the book, chapters 8 and 9, which is more 'timely' and consists of more miscellaneous and timely reflections. To this a third shorter part, in the form of chapter 10 and the epilogue, was added late in the printing process, which has its origin as a part of the first draft of *Ecce homo*, and which must be regarded as belonging to the more extract-oriented part of the book, but which more explicitly announces Nietzsche's own affirmative philosophy (and is thus related to the planned fourth volume of the *Hauptwerk*).

5.2 Title, subtitle, foreword and the aphorisms (chapter 1)

The main title

The title of *Götzen-Dämmerung, Twilight of the Idols: How to Philosophize with the Hammer* is very catchy and effective, but what does it mean, and does it communicate to us something about how one best reads this book? However, before discussing this final title, we should be aware that the work actually had three different titles: a working title (actually several, but with much similarity), a definite title and a final title, which took the place of the definite one late in the proofreading stage. These three titles are in regard to content and the message they transmit very different, informative, mild and humble, and warlike and proud, respectively.

The first, which I have called a working title, but which perhaps is better described as mere drafts for the title, exists in four versions, all with essentially the same subtitle, but with two alternatives for the main title: 'Thoughts for the Day after Tomorrow' or '*Multum in parvo*' ['Much in Little'], both with the subtitle 'My Philosophy in Extract'.[8] The first main title points to the future (and is probably also a pointer at the coming *Umwerthung aller Werthe*, just as was the case of the subtitle of *Jenseits von Gut und Böse*, 'Prelude to a Philosophy of the Future'), while the second and the subtitle inform us that the book contains an extract of Nietzsche's philosophy. This is in several respects correct and is consistent with how he describes the book in letters after he had finished it (although he there does not actually use the word 'extract'). In many ways, '*Gedanken für Übermorgen*: Meine Philosophie im Auszug' is a beautiful, effective and informative title, and would have suited the work well. However, Nietzsche instead decided for a different title, 'Müssiggang eines Psychologen' ['A Psychologist's Leisure' or 'The Idleness of a Psychologist' or 'A Psychologist's Leisurely Stroll'], without a subtitle (in contrast to all his other titles, which have subtitles). This title indicates the importance of psychology for Nietzsche, but the 'Leisure' is surely both too humble and misleading for prospective readers. The reason for this title is surely that Nietzsche here refers to it from his own perspective – he must here not work hard at realizing and drawing conclusions regarding his new philosophy as was the case with the *Umwerthung aller Werthe*, but here merely select some excerpts from that part of the work that he basically had finished.[9] It seems to me, unlike many other commentators, that Peter Gast was correct in criticizing this title, as he did in a letter to Nietzsche, 20 September 1888 where he argues that it is too humble.[10] By 27 September Nietzsche had changed the title to the final one.[11]

The critique of Wagner suggested in the final title – with its *Götzen-Dämmerung* instead of *Götterdämmerung* (*twilight of the idols* instead of *twilight of the gods*) is, however, as suggested by the letter, only of minor importance. He had just written a whole book on Wagner, *Der Fall Wagner*, and when he, a few months later, on 17 December 1888, wrote in a draft of a letter to Jean Bourdeau, for the purpose of trying to get him to translate the book into French, he suggested the title *Götzen-Hammer* (*Marteau des Idoles*) – *Hammar for Idols* or *Idol-Hammar* – instead, which increases the importance of the hammer and makes the pun on Wagner's work completely disappear.

The double nature of the two titles of this book, the very mild 'A Psychologist's Leisure' and the warlike *Twilight of the Idols* reflect the book's undefined and double relation to the *Umwerthung aller Werthe* project. It is both 'outside' the project – as a relaxation and leisure for Nietzsche himself (and in this sense the original title 'A Psychologist's Leisure' fits) – and 'a part' of it – for readers of it, as an extract of the difficult and fundamental work on a revaluation of all values (and in this sense the final title fits) – and it was also to serve as a preparation and stimulus for the *Hauptwerk*. The two titles also reflect that *Götzen-Dämmerung* is both 'untimely' and 'timely'; it both deals with the great untimely questions concerning all of human history (chapters 1–7 and 10) and those merely reflecting the (German) present (chapters 8 and 9, constituting about half the book). This is also how he describes the book in *Ecce homo*, that it 'touches' 'not just *eternal* idols, but also the most recent of all'.[12]

The primary meaning of the final title is an optimistic one, that the old idols, the old ideals and 'truths', are on the way out – also confirmed in *Ecce homo* where he writes: '*Twilight of the Idols* – in plain words: the old truth is coming to an end . . . '.[13] The reason for this optimism is probably in part that Nietzsche felt certain that he would soon publish the work which would expose and make more detailed critique of these 'idols' – which would make it indecent to hold fast to them in the future. The title, just as already the subtitle of *Jenseits von Gut und Böse* did, thus proclaims the coming of the *Umwerthung aller Werthe*, which Nietzsche was convinced that he would shortly publish.[14] This is also why he proclaims the finishing of the first book of that work in the foreword.

The subtitle

The subtitle to *Götzen-Dämmerung* is *Wie man mit dem Hammer philosophirt*, *How to Philosophize with the Hammer*.[15] This is an effective slogan which has caught the imagination of many, but what does 'to philosophize with the hammer' mean? Or more specifically, what did Nietzsche mean when he used the expression? I will show that 'hammer' was an important metaphor for Nietzsche, that it means something different and much more specific than has hitherto been assumed and thus that the interpretation of the subtitle to *Götzen-Dämmerung* is an essential part of correctly understanding this work.

The almost certainly most common and most 'obvious' interpretation of 'to philosophize with the hammer' is that the reference is to iconoclastic philosophizing which – possibly for the sake of new alternatives – destroys all or much of that which stands. This 'self-evident' interpretation seems to be confirmed by Nietzsche's words in the foreword that the book is a '*grand declaration of war*', by his claim in *Ecce homo* that there exists nothing 'more overthrowing – more wicked' and by the sentence 'There is no reality, no "ideality" which is not touched on in this writing (– touched on: what a cautious euphemism! . . .)'.[16] This is probably also the only meaning which is consistent with Nietzsche's claim in the letter to Gast, 27 September 1888, where he says that the sense of the title, apart from being the theme of the short foreword, is also 'an sich errathbar', self-evident.[17]

However, contrary to this interpretation are Nietzsche's words in the foreword to *Götzen-Dämmerung* where the meaning seems rather to be a *diagnostic* one of determining if the 'idols', the truths and ideals, are hollow or not:[18]

> *to sound out idols* [. . .] For once to pose questions here with a *hammer* and perhaps to receive for answer that famous hollow sound which speaks of inflated bowels – what a delight for one who has ears behind his ears – for an old psychologist and pied piper like me, in presence of whom precisely that which would like to stay silent *has to become audible* . . . [. . .] and as regards the sounding-out of idols, this time they are not idols of the age but *eternal* idols which are here touched with the hammer as with a tuning fork.[19]

Especially Walter Kaufmann has used this to insist that the hammer is not a sledgehammer but a tuning fork.[20] In a long, detailed, learned and in many respects excellent paper David Thatcher has further strengthened the interpretation of the hammer as a diagnostic hammer – not this time as a tuning fork but as a medical percussion hammer.[21] He gives several good arguments for this interpretation but cannot explain away two inconsistencies.[22] First, there is an inherent incompatibility, which Thatcher well recognizes, between the tuning fork, which Nietzsche refers to as a simile in the foreword, which produces sound while a hammer (including a percussion hammer) elicits it. Thatcher is forced to conclude that Nietzsche had made a bad simile with his use of the tuning fork.[23] This is problematic since the reference to 'as a tuning fork' is one of the most definite pieces of information we have in favour of this interpretation. Second, the title of the book – *Götzen-Dämmerung* – with its allusion to *Götterdämmerung* (the-end-of-the-world-catastrophe according to Germanic and Scandinavian mythology), and his words in *Ecce homo*, clearly suggests destruction rather than mere diagnosis.

Both these major suggestions, the hammer as destructive and as diagnostic, find support in the foreword, and in Nietzsche's letter where he says that he created the title out of the foreword and that its meaning is reflected in it.[24]

Nonetheless, other relevant candidates for, or relevant associations to the hammer are also possible. A strong candidate is the sculptor's hammer – a simile which Nietzsche used in *Also sprach Zarathustra* and then again in *Jenseits von Gut und Böse*:

> If one could observe the strangely painful, equally coarse and refined comedy of European Christianity with the derisive and impartial eye of an Epicurean god, I should think one would never cease marvelling and laughing; does it not actually seem that some single will has ruled over Europe for eighteen centuries in order to make a *sublime abortion* of man? He, however, who, with opposite requirements (no longer Epicurean) and with some divine hammer in his hand, could approach this almost voluntary degeneration and stunting of mankind, as exemplified in the European Christian (Pascal, for instance), would he not have to cry aloud with rage, pity, and horror: 'Oh, you bunglers, presumptuous pitiful bunglers, what have you done! Was that a work for your hands? How you have hacked and botched my finest stone! What have you presumed to do!' – I should say that Christianity has hitherto been the most portentous of presumptions. Men, not great enough, nor hard enough, to be entitled as artists to take part in fashioning *man*; men, not sufficiently strong and far-sighted to *allow*, with sublime self-constraint, the obvious law of the thousandfold failures and perishings to prevail; men, not sufficiently noble to see the radically different grades of rank and intervals of rank that separate man from man: – *such* men, with their 'equality before God,' have hitherto swayed the destiny of Europe. (JGB, 64)

I would like to suggest that several senses of the word 'hammer', including the more constructive builder's, minting hammer,[25] judge's hammer and sculpture's hammer have a role in Nietzsche's metaphor of philosophizing with the hammer, with special emphasis on the destructive hammer and the diagnostic hammer (the two alternatives most clearly suitable to the title, subtitle, foreword and what Nietzsche says in *Ecce homo*). After all, a hammer (almost any hammer) can be used for many different purposes.

However, the most fundamental sense of the expression is another – one which simultaneously is constructive, destructive and diagnostic – and one which is important for our interpretation of *Götzen-Dämmerung* – *the hammer and the 'Götzen-Hammer' represents the idea of eternal recurrence*.[26] To philosophize with the hammer is to philosophize from the perspective of the eternal recurrence. That, in its turn, means to philosophize from the perspective of having accepted and affirmed (*amor fati*) reality as it is (a major theme in *Götzen-Dämmerung*) – without metaphysics, without moralizing, without external purposes and goals (without God), without wishing oneself and the world to be different and changed, neither in the present nor in the past and not in the future.

That this is the case is shown in many of Nietzsche's notes. This means that this sense, Nietzsche's own primary sense, would not be available to readers of *Götzen-Dämmerung* when it first was published, planned to occur in early 1889. At that stage, it would be the interpretations we have discussed earlier which would be available (just as it has been for us, since that *Hauptwerk* was never published). However, Nietzsche's notes make it clear that this sense would become apparent *after* he had published the *Umwerthung aller Werthe* one or two years later,[27] where the hammer (and eternal recurrence) was planned to play a prominent role in the fourth volume, according to several notes even in its very title.[28] This is thus again – as we will see many instances of throughout this study – an example of how Nietzsche in *Götzen-Dämmerung* points forward to his coming *Umwerthung aller Werthe*.[29]

The hammer occurs as a symbol for eternal recurrence for the first time in a note from 1883: 'The most difficult knowledge as hammer'.[30] He repeats this statement a year later,[31] but it is not yet clear what this 'most difficult' thought or knowledge is, although there are good reasons to assume that he refers to the idea of the eternal recurrence. However, shortly thereafter it is explicitly stated in one of the first drafts for his *Hauptwerk*, at that time entitled '*Die ewige Wiederkunft*', where he describes the end of this planned work with the words: 'The teaching of the eternal recurrence as *hammer* in the hands of the *most powerful* humans, – – –'.[32] Immediately thereafter, in another draft of that work, the last part of it is simply described as: 'The Hammer and the Great Midday' (which both are symbols for the eternal recurrence).[33] This sense is then repeated several times, although not as clearly, during the second half of 1884.[34] In the spring and early summer of 1885, the hammer again occurs at the end of several drafts of what is almost certainly early versions of Nietzsche's *Hauptwerk*, then most frequently called '*Midday and Eternity*' (i.e. again with allusions to eternal recurrence). In these drafts, the last part of the book or work is simply entitled 'The Hammer' (with and without italics), and twice modified as 'The *Hammer* – a danger, by which mankind can break to pieces' and 'The Hammer (or Dionysos)'.[35] Nietzsche thereafter continues to use the hammer as a symbol for his idea of eternal recurrence in a number of notes.

By the summer of 1886, the plans for the *Hauptwerk* has become more stable and definite, always consisting of four volumes, now with the main title *Der Wille zur Macht*, and *Umwerthung aller Werthe* as subtitle, and he will soon announce it as a work in progress on the cover of *Jenseits von Gut und Böse*. The hammer from now on becomes either the title of or part of the description of the fourth volume in a number of notes:[36]

> **Der Wille zur Macht**.
> *Versuch*
> *einer Umwerthung aller Werthe.*
> In vier Büchern.
> Erstes Buch: die Gefahr der Gefahren [. . .]
> Zweites Buch: Kritik der Werthe (der Logik usw.
> Drittes Buch: das Problem des Gesetzgebers [. . .]
> Viertes Buch: der Hammer
>   ihr Mittel zu ihrer Aufgabe
> Sils-Maria, Sommer 1886[37]

The first book, entitled 'The Danger of Dangers', was meant to deal with the problem of nihilism (which he regards as a necessary consequence of our present values), as is visible in these and other related notes. This remained the case in almost all drafts until Nietzsche decided to instead begin the work with 'an attempt at a critique of Christianity' (i.e. *Der Antichrist*), after which nihilism became a major theme of the second volume instead.

Another, closely related draft of the four volumes of the *Hauptwerk* lists the following titles:

1. The Danger of Dangers
2. Critique of Morality
3. We Reversed Ones
4. The Hammer.[38]

This is the *only* metaphor in which he uses the word 'hammer' from then on, until, and including, when he constructs the new title of *Götzen-Dämmerung* (and thereafter there is no further reference to hammer). The last four instances before the construction of the title for *Götzen-Dämmerung* are the following:[39]

'The Eternal Recurrence as Hammer'

'4. The Reverse Ones / Their Hammer, "the Teaching of the Recurrence"'

'IV The Teaching of the Recurrence. As Hammer'

'The Hammer: The Teaching of the Eternal Recurrence'

Note that in all four of these notes, as in many of the earlier ones, the hammer is furthermore associated with the most important, the fourth and last book of the planned *Hauptwerk*, in which Nietzsche was to discuss eternal recurrence. Furthermore, this fact alone illustrates the continuity of his conception of the *Hauptwerk*, even when it has different titles (but there are also many other indications that this is the case).

Every English translation of the subtitle I have seen renders it as 'How to Philosophize with *a* Hammer' – although the correct rendering of the original German is – 'How to Philosophize with *the* Hammer'. I believe Nietzsche used the determinate form 'the Hammer' because it was a specific sort of hammer he had in mind (the eternal recurrence), while the determinate form has been avoided in all English translations for precisely this reason – without an awareness of what sort of specific hammer Nietzsche is referring to, it makes no sense to use *the* hammer – because we are unable to satisfactorily answer the then almost unavoidable question 'what hammer?'

This illustrates the importance of understanding the hammer as a specific sort of hammer – not just any hammer. The problem with all suggested interpretations of the meaning of the hammer (except eternal recurrence) is that although often good and relevant, none of them suit *all* of Nietzsche's contrary statements about and allusions to the hammer sufficiently well to justify the use of the expression '*the* hammer'. However, if Nietzsche was thinking of eternal recurrence as the hammer (as the notes show) then he *must* use the determinate form – and all the other possible associations with the term 'hammer' are secondary, but at the same time a windfall – and it is a matter of little importance if these allusions are not completely consistent.

The interpretation which I have discussed earlier has the additional advantage that with it the title of the book is connected with its final sentence: 'I, the teacher of eternal recurrence . . . ' and with the epilogue entitled 'The Hammer Speaks', which is a quotation from the end of the third book of *Also sprach Zarathustra*, which abounds with references and allusions to eternal recurrence (this 'Zarathustra's fundamental thought', *Ecce homo*, 'Za', 1). Still more important, it places the focus on one of the late Nietzsche's most important and original thoughts which he uses as a sort of touchingstone or criteria. I will discuss the presence and importance of the idea of eternal recurrence in *Götzen-Dämmerung* in Chapter 7 (and show that it echoes throughout the text although there are almost no explicit references to it).

Further, the understanding of the hammer as a metaphor for the eternal recurrence is simultaneously consistent with several of the previous interpretations of the hammer – it is destructive, diagnostic and constructive.[40] It is destructive in the sense that, according to Nietzsche's belief, the thought of the eternal recurrence will crush those too weak to sustain the thought (he seems to regard it in this sense as an extreme form of pessimism or nihilism).[41] Expressed differently, it will crush those too weak to live without an external goal or *telos*. It is diagnostic in the sense in which Nietzsche introduces the idea in *Die fröhliche Wissenschaft*, 341, that is, the eternal recurrence is really a diagnostic idea or conception to test and measure our ability to affirm our life and the world. In a note from immediately after he discovered the idea of eternal recurrence, Nietzsche writes: 'The question to ask by everything you wish: "is this what I want to do innumerable times?" is the *greatest* weight',[42] and in another 'to live in a manner such that we want to live again and *thus* to live in eternity! – Our task comes to us in every moment'.[43] Or expressed differently, eternal recurrence is used diagnostically when we examine whether ideals (idols) aid us in affirming ourselves and reality or inhibit and prevent such affirmation. Finally, it is constructive in the sense that a philosophy based on the eternal recurrence liberates us from every form of metaphysical *telos* and ideal so that we instead can create our own ideals (our Yes and Nos) and our own goals.[44]

The foreword

The short foreword strongly emphasizes the close connection – but also the difference – between *Götzen-Dämmerung* and his *Umwerthung aller Werthe* project. It makes acute the question of how *Götzen-Dämmerung* is to be related to that other, for Nietzsche, more important work – but being so brief, in combination with Nietzsche's own ambivalence about its role, means that it fails to fully answer that question.

The foreword consists of three shorter paragraphs. Most of the first paragraph concerns the relation between the two works, and *Götzen-Dämmerung* is described as cheerful and as an escape from the work on that more serious and difficult task.[45] This is basically repeated at the beginning of the third paragraph (where the book is described as a convalescence and a relaxation, with reference to the old title). The foreword also ends by announcing that the first book of the *Revaluation of All Values* has just been completed.

The rest of the foreword, about half of it, describes *Götzen-Dämmerung*. In the first two paragraphs it is described as two different forms of recuperation: first, as, by implication, a war, and second, as a testing or a sounding-out of idols. In the third paragraph, *Götzen-Dämmerung* is again referred to as a recuperation and a sunspot by means of being a declaration of war and by sounding-out idols. (However, at the end of that paragraph, one can wonder if he has not forgotten himself and is really speaking about the first book of the *Revaluation of All Values*, *Der Antichrist*, which he also announces at the very end:

> this time they are not idols of the age but *eternal* idols which are here touched with the hammer as with a tuning fork – there are no more ancient idols in existence.... Also none more hollow.... That does not prevent their being the *most believed in*; and they are not, especially in the most eminent case, called idols....)

Nietzsche is here emphasizing the sounding-out of *eternal* idols (and even the most eminent one, God), while in the older foreword, which became the chapter 'What the Germans Lack', there is a strong emphasis on *timely* idols. This is the same ambivalence we saw in regard to the title (not altogether surprising for the titles and the foreword are closely related.) When Nietzsche comes back to *Götzen-Dämmerung* a few months later and reviews it in *Ecce homo*, he states more clearly that it contains a critique of both kinds of idols: 'Not just *eternal* idols, but also the most recent of all'. This ambivalence as to if *Götzen-Dämmerung* should be regarded as part of the *Umwerthung aller Werthe* project (as a summary) or as primarily a recuperation from it – whether it represents philosophizing with the hammer or should be seen as the leisure of a psychologist – is still present in the prologue to *Ecce homo*. When Nietzsche first wrote it on his birthday, 15 October 1888, he described what he had produced during the last quarter of the year: 'The first book of the *Umwerthung aller Werthe*, [...] *Götzen-Dämmerung*, my attempt to philosophize with the hammer'. However, when he corrects the proofs of *Ecce homo*, dated by Nietzsche as 'Turin, 18 Dec. 1888' and signed with the words: '*ready to print*. N.' ('*druckfertig*. N.'), he changes the association of *Götzen-Dämmerung* again to: 'The first book of the *Umwerthung aller Werthe*, [...], and as recuperation, *Götzen-Dämmerung*'. This ambivalence continues in the text of *Ecce homo*, where about half of the space allotted to discussing *Götzen-Dämmerung* is actually about the first book of the *Umwerthung aller Werthe*, that is *Der Antichrist*.

Nietzsche seems thus to say that the book is a recuperation (as he also says in several letters) by means of being a challenge to fight ('a great declaration of war') and by sounding-out ideals and 'truths'. Both of these senses can be seen as preparatory for, as whetting the appetite for, as being initiatory for the *Revaluation of All Values* – which was to constitute the actual war against the false idols and values.

The fact that this foreword announces the completion, not of *Götzen-Dämmerung*, but of another text, the first volume of the *Revaluation of All Values*, that is, *Der Antichrist*, strongly suggests that Nietzsche regarded *Götzen-Dämmerung* as a prelude to the *Umwerthung aller Werthe* (as he also explicitly says in several letters).

The first chapter of aphorisms

Nietzsche was a skilful writer of aphorisms, and it was a form of writing he very much appreciated and valued. In the last section, 51, of the chapter 'Expeditions of an Untimely

Man' he says about the writing of aphorisms: 'To create things upon which time tries its teeth in vain; in form and in *substance* to strive after a little immortality – I have never been modest enough to demand less of myself. The aphorism, the apophthegm, in which I am the first master among Germans, are the form of "eternity"'. Nietzsche had included sections of short aphorisms in many of his books since *Menschliches, Allzumenschliches* (1878). It is likely that he also planned to have sections of aphorisms in his *Hauptwerk*. We know, for example, that in his last plan for a table of contents for the *Hauptwerk* while it was still called *Der Wille zur Macht*, from 26 August 1888,[46] had a section of aphorisms, between the third and fourth books, called 'Psychologen-Kurzweil' with the meaning of something like 'Entertainment for Psychologists' or 'Diversions for Psychologists'. Many of the aphorisms of the first chapter of *Götzen-Dämmerung* probably come from those which also may have been used in that section, and even the original title of *Götzen-Dämmerung*, 'The Idle Hours of a Psychologist' or 'A Psychologist's Leisure' [*Müssiggang eines Psychologen*] may well have its origin from this section.

It seems to me likely that the main reason for the presence of sections of aphorisms in Nietzsche's works, and in particular of this first chapter of *Götzen-Dämmerung*, was less because he wanted to get a particular message across than it is related to his 'existentialism', to his wish to engage and activate the reader.

It belongs to the nature of aphorisms that they can be interpreted in many ways, and many of the forty-four aphorisms in the first chapter 'Maxims and Arrows' can be associated with different aspects of Nietzsche's *Hauptwerk* and his project of making a revaluation of all values. I will here only comment on a few of the most relevant ones.

The first aphorism is clearly related to the original title of the work. The second seems to have a meaning related to Nietzsche's own experience (as is the case for many of them), a general sense and one related to his view of the nature of values.

2. Even the bravest of us rarely has the courage for what he really *knows*...

Nietzsche uses versions of this expression in several letters. We there see that the expression not only refers to his own general experience but that it specifically relates to his attempt at developing his philosophy and writing in connection with working on his *Hauptwerk*. In a letter to Overbeck, 12 February 1887, Nietzsche speaks of the philosophical problems which weigh him down: 'And such problems! If only I had the courage to *think* through everything that I know...'. He writes in a similar vein, while working hard on his *Hauptwerk* during the winter of 1887–8, for example, to Georg Brandes, 2 December 1887: 'I possess in me a suspicion against dialectics, even against giving reasons. It seems to me to depend more on *courage*, on the degree of one's courage, *what* a person is ready to accept as "true" or not *yet*... (I only rarely have the courage to that which I really know)'. In a draft to a letter to his mother, 29 January 1888, he writes: 'I am so happy that I again can work: or expressed differently, that my spirit again had the *courage* to the task in which service I have lived'. Finally, with a direct reference to his work on the *Hauptwerk*, he writes to Peter Gast, 13 February 1888: 'I have finished the first version of my 'Attempt at a Revaluation': it was, all in all, a torture, also, I do not at all yet have the courage for it. I will make it better in ten years time.'

An early version of the aphorism can be found among Nietzsche's notebooks:

> Even the bravest one among us does not have enough courage for that which he really *knows* . . . Thus, where one stops, or not *yet* stops, where one judges 'here is the truth' reflects the degree and strength of his courage; more, at least, than any subtlety or bluntness of eye or spirit.[47]

In a broader sense, one of the background assumptions behind Nietzsche's view of values is that there are basically only two sets, our present values which, on the whole, are false, decadent and unnatural, and the revalued values which are life-affirming and more natural. Nietzsche regarded our present values as already revalued once, away from an earlier set of healthier values (which is, for example, visible in the chapters on Socrates and the last chapter). Already by the first occurrence of the word 'revaluation' and of the concept 'revaluation of all values' in Nietzsche's published writings, *Jenseits von Gut und Böse* 46, he clearly sets up a dichotomy and claims that a revaluation has already occurred. The dichotomy is between freedom, pride and self-confidence on the one side and enslavement, self-mockery and self-mutilation on the other, where the latter is associated with Christianity. Then Nietzsche states: 'the paradoxical formula "god on the cross" [. . .] promised a revaluation of all the values of antiquity', that is, a dichotomy between ancient and Christian values is constructed. Thus, in this first occurrence the revaluation referred to is the earlier and *negative* one from antiquity to Christianity. The second reference, and most of his later references, to the concept, in *Jenseits von Gut und Böse* 203, now refers to a positive revaluation:

> whither must *we* direct our hopes? Towards *new philosophers*, we have no other choice; towards spirits strong and original enough to make a start on antithetical evaluations and to revalue and reverse 'eternal values' [. . .] a revaluation of values under whose novel pressure and hammer a conscience would be steeled, a heart transformed to brass, so that it might endure the weight of such a responsibility.[48]

Nietzsche's revaluation is thus a second revaluation, and constitutes an attempt to return to those healthier and more natural sets of values. The theme that which is more natural is also better will be a recurrent theme throughout *Götzen-Dämmerung*, and the more natural is related to healthier values. However, since we have been raised and educated among decadent values we often lack the courage for that which is more natural (for that which we really know).

3. To live alone one must be an animal or a god – says Aristotle. There is yet a third case: one must be both – a *philosopher*.

An important aspect of Nietzsche's revaluation of values is a Heraclitian affirmation of apparently opposite values – not the average of such values, but both of them – affirming our 'higher' selves, through sublimation (see the main theme of the beginning of the chapter 'Morality as Anti-Nature') *and* our animal or Dionysian selves. During the autumn of 1887 he had expressed the similar thought in an interesting manner:

Man is *beast* [*Unthier*] and *over-animal* [*Überthier*], the higher man is monster [*Unmensch*] and overman [*Übermensch*]: thus it belongs together. With every human growth into greatness and height, he also grows deeper and more terrible: one should not want the one, without the other – or better: the more thoroughly one wants the one, the more thoroughly one actually fulfills the other.[49]

Compare also the closely related aphorism 6: 'It is by being "natural" that one best recovers from one's unnaturalness, from one's spirituality . . .'. This is not a critique of spirituality, but a reformulation of aphorism 3, that we need *both* the 'natural' (the animal, the primitive) and the higher and sublimated.

    7. Which is it? is man only God's mistake or God only man's mistake? –

Nietzsche's answer to this question is obvious (but that is not the case with all the questions posed in the aphorisms), but he also wants the reader to answer or respond. The whole first book of the *Umwerthung aller Werthe*, *The Anti-Christ: Attempt at a Critique of Christianity*, is an answer to it and explains why he finds God and Christianity so life- and world-denying.

    12. If we possess our *why* of life we can put up with almost any *how*. [. . .]

Nietzsche uses this to criticize utilitarianism, but we will also see that this relates to the last aphorism, his idea of eternal recurrence and to the *Umwerthung aller Werthe* project. Having a purpose and a goal, *creating* a purpose and a goal, is of profound importance for man according to Nietzsche.

    26. I mistrust all systematizers and avoid them. The will to a system is a lack of integrity.

This is surely true for Nietzsche. He also rebelled against Kant and the German romantic philosophers who attempted to build philosophical systems. In a note written in August 1888, Nietzsche relates this to his own writing.

> I mistrust all systematizers and avoid them. The will to a system is, at least for us thinkers, something which compromises, a form of our immorality. – Perhaps one can guess, with a glance behind this book, what systematizer I myself only with effort have avoided. . . .[50]

It is not certain if this note – with its reference to 'this book' – was written with reference to *Götzen-Dämmerung* or to his *Hauptwerk* (the latter is the more probable). Nietzsche wrote in many different styles, and did not hesitate to use poetry, metaphors, polemics, paradox, humour, irony and so on in his writings. Some of his books are essayistic, some aphoristic and some are written more in the style of treatises, most are mixtures of these, and none more so than *Götzen-Dämmerung*. But with 'systematizers' Nietzsche is not primarily referring to style. What he is objecting to is the same that we will see in the first six mini-treatises of this book – an overemphasis of reason – where 'reason' (systematic reason, deductive reason, rationalism) rather than reality (complex empirical reality) determines the thought and the text.

However, there is a risk that this aphorism is misunderstood or its meaning exaggerated. Frequently, it is referred to explain and justify that Nietzsche was not a systematic philosopher. This is correct in a general sense, but it does not mean that he had no system at all, or that he could or would not deal with questions systematically. The best examples of the latter are the three essays of *Zur Genealogie der Moral*, which book he even calls 'my touchstone for what belongs to me'.[51] Furthermore, as we can see in the last quoted text earlier (and in the texts referred to in the footnote as similar to it), Nietzsche admits that he only with difficulty manages to avoid being systematic. There can be no doubt that Nietzsche had planned to write the *Umwerthung aller Werthe* in a more systematic manner than his other books, akin to these essays in *Zur Genealogie der Moral*.[52] Already in 1883 he speaks of wanting to construct something more 'theoretical', thereafter he refers to his *Hauptwerk* as a 'conceptio',[53] as '*a coherent construction of thought*',[54] 'my conception as a whole',[55] that he will perform a 'working through of my "philosophy"',[56] 'work through a scheme, with which I have outlined my "philosophy"',[57] 'work through my complete system of thought'[58] and in September 1888 he refers to its 'very strict and earnest character'.[59] That those descriptions are accurate and also were fulfilled is confirmed by the first volume, *Der Antichrist*, which is written as a sort of treatise.

> 36. Whether we immoralists do virtue any *harm*? [. . .] Moral: one must shoot at morals.

Nietzsche had started calling himself an immoralist in *Jenseits von Gut und Böse* (1886), but that expression was already then a pointer to full books or chapters that he planned to write.[60] Eventually, *The Immoralist* became the title of the planned third volume of his *Hauptwerk*, and his references to it thereafter are also to that work.

The last aphorism, although this may not be obvious at first, is a direct pointer at the *Umwerthung aller Werthe*.

> 44. Formula of my happiness: a Yes, a No, a straight line, a *goal* . . .

That very same words are used as the last sentence of the first section of *Der Antichrist*, and this section is not only the first section of the first volume of the *Umwerthung aller Werthe*, but it (together with the following six sections) were originally written as a preface to the whole *Umwerthung aller Werthe* project and describe the effect of the revaluation of all values.[61] Its meaning, related to aphorism 12 discussed earlier, relates to having a 'why', a meaning, with one's life.[62] As an aphorism that is not completely clear, but in the first section of *Der Antichrist* it is clarified and discussed at greater length.

> We have discovered happiness, we know the road, we have found the exit out of whole millennia of labyrinth. Who *else* has found it? [. . .] We were brave enough,

we spared neither ourselves nor others: but for long we did not know *where* to apply our courage. We became gloomy, we were called fatalists. *Our* fatality – was the plenitude, the tension, the blocking-up of our forces. We thirsted for lightning and action, of all things we kept ourselves furthest from the happiness of the weaklings, from 'resignation' . . . There was a thunderstorm in our air, the nature which we are grew dark – *for we had no road*. Formula of our happiness: a Yes, a No, a straight line, a *goal* . . .

This seems in Nietzsche's case both generally to refer to having a goal, a meaning, a purpose (a 'why'), but also to the more specific goal of having 'found the exit out of whole millennia of labyrinth', that is, to the revaluation of all values.

The same sense is also visible in one of his drafts for the *Hauptwerk* from this time, where he characterizes the last chapter, entitled '*We Hyperboreans*' in this manner:

Nothing but absolute positions e.g. *happiness*!! e.g. history
enormous pleasure and triumph at the end, *to have nothing but definite yeses and nos* . . . Liberation from *uncertainty*!⁶³

This seems also to be how Nietzsche uses a similar statement in *Also sprach Zarathustra*. III, 11. 'On the Spirit of Heaviness', 3: 'All-contentment, which knows how to taste everything: that is not the best of taste! I respect the rebellious selective tongues and stomachs, that have learned to say "I" and "Yes" and "No".'

Another, compatible way to read this aphorism is to regard the emphasis on 'a Yes, a No' and so on as being the opposite of nihilism (lacking a yes and a no, lacking values and thus goals). Nihilism is not a theme dealt with explicitly in *Götzen-Dämmerung* (nor in *Der Antichrist*), but was to have been a major theme in *Umwerthung aller Werthe*, especially in its second volume.⁶⁴

5.3 The philosophy-critical chapters (2, 3 and 4)

The second volume of *Umwerthung aller Werthe*, with the planned title *The Free Spirit: Critique of Philosophy as a Nihilistic Movement*, was meant to present a critique of philosophy. Some drafts of chapter titles from 1888 which were meant to deal with this theme in the *Hauptwerk* are:⁶⁵

(a) *Nihilism, considered to its final conclusion*
(b) *The 'will to truth'*
(c) The true and the apparent world
(d) The philosopher as typical décadent
(e) Science against philosophy
(f) *Nihilism* [and its *opposite*]
(g) The value of truth and error
(h) The will to truth

(i) The metaphysicians
(j) The history of European nihilism

We can note that for two of these planned chapters, (c) and (d), there seems to be a fairly large overlap with the three chapters of this part of *Götzen-Dämmerung*:

2. The Problem of Socrates
3. 'Reason' in Philosophy
4. How the 'Real World' at last Became a Myth

In fact, the chapter 'The Problem of Socrates' has its origin in 'The philosopher as typical décadent', and the two chapters "Reason' in Philosophy' and 'How the 'Real World' at last Became a Myth' in 'The true and the apparent world'.

Three general interpretations are possible:

(i) Nietzsche selected and used the material for these three chapters from his work on the *Hauptwerk*, which thus *as a whole* was pre-empted. (This is approximately the view of Montinari, and of most studies of Nietzsche.)
(ii) Nietzsche selected and used this material from his work on the *Hauptwerk*, and thus these specific chapters (or themes) were pre-empted, but other chapters and themes were to be dealt with in the second volume of *Umwerthung aller Werthe*.
(iii) Nietzsche selected and used this material from his work on the *Hauptwerk* as an extract of and teaser for that work – these themes were not meant to be pre-empted, only briefly presented, and much more could and was planned to be said of them and other related themes in the second volume of *Umwerthung aller Werthe*.

I would argue for a combination of the second and the third interpretation as the one closest to Nietzsche's intentions. Since I interpret Nietzsche's work on writing a *Hauptwerk* between 1884 and 1888 as a continuous project,[66] what was at most in part pre-empted was one version of that work (actually better seen as small parts of several versions of that work). One is then left with the latter two interpretations. It is probably true that some parts of these themes or chapters were pre-empted – especially the planned 'The true and the apparent world' – but Nietzsche's view of *Götzen-Dämmerung* as an extract, summary, *vade mecum* and as leading and tempting readers on to his *Hauptwerk* suggests rather that what he saw himself doing in *Götzen-Dämmerung* was a quick and sketchy treatment of these themes, which would not prevent him from treating them again, in a somewhat different and more systematic manner in his *Umwerthung aller Werthe*. That certainly seems to be the case with his critique of Christianity present in *Götzen-Dämmerung*, which did not prevent him from repeating and/or continuing and expanding on that theme in the first volume, *Der Antichrist*. The fact that he introduces the seventh chapter of *Götzen-Dämmerung* with the words: 'A first example, merely as an introduction' also suggests it, at least for that chapter. His general description of *Götzen-Dämmerung* in *Ecce homo* as containing 'an all-too-rich autumn: you trip over truths, you even trample some to death – there are too many of them' and that in it many themes are merely 'touched on' also suggests that here we are given many examples of new truths, but a more detailed treatment and discussion will be presented in *Umwerthung aller Werthe*. A brief treatment of a theme in *Götzen-Dämmerung* would thus not necessarily prevent further discussions of it in the *Umwerthung aller Werthe*.

However, even more obvious than the potential overlap of these three chapters of *Götzen-Dämmerung* with some of the 1888 drafts for chapters of the *Hauptwerk* is that in this philosophical-critical area, Nietzsche considered or planned to deal with many themes *not* discussed in *Götzen-Dämmerung* in the *Umwerthung aller Werthe*. Such themes as, for example, nihilism, the will to truth, the relation between science and philosophy and the value of truth and error. We can, in particular, note that these three philosophy-critical chapters in *Götzen-Dämmerung* do not seem to pre-empt or overlap significantly with the last plan of the *Hauptwerk* from before he wrote *Der Antichrist*.[67]

The first real chapter of *Götzen-Dämmerung*, 'The Problem of Socrates', contains a severe critique of the whole Western philosophical tradition of emphasizing the rational (dialectics – i.e. persuasive rational definitions and arguments) and the conscious above tradition, culture and the subconscious (the instinctual). We are not told how a society and a philosophy which emphasizes the opposite (like Nietzsche's own) would look like and function – possibly he intended to describe that in the fourth book of *Umwerthung aller Werthe*. However, we can get a first small indication of it by examining Nietzsche's view of pre-Socratic Greece and the manner of thought and the philosophy from that time which he briefly mentions in this chapter.[68] Nietzsche further expands on this theme in the last, tenth chapter.

Nietzsche claims that Socrates and the greatest names in our philosophical tradition stand in a 'negative relation to life'. Judgements concerning the value of life can never be true – 'they possess value only as symptoms'. Those who have felt and argued for that life is without value are decadents. Socrates was a decadent. This is reinforced by physiological arguments. Socrates and the others thought they needed 'rationality at any cost' to control and conquer their instincts, which were in anarchy. 'As long as life is *ascending*, happiness and instinct are one' (section 11). Socrates wanted to die.[69]

In this chapter, Nietzsche points out that an overemphasis of reason leads to pessimism and life denial, in that it goes against what is natural, against our instincts and the subconscious. Nietzsche regards pessimism as a subgroup of nihilism, but the extensive theme of nihilism is not discussed explicitly in this chapter (nor in the whole book), although it was planned to constitute a major theme of the second volume of *Umwerthung aller Werthe*. This alone is enough to show that Nietzsche had much more to say than that which is present in *Götzen-Dämmerung* and *Der Antichrist* (where nihilism also is not discussed).

What Nietzsche does in this introductory chapter is to show that Socrates, by many regarded as the father of Western philosophy, was a decadent, that already with him began the use of reason *against* the senses, the body and the instincts – which will be the main theme in the following two chapters. Here it is discussed in relation to one specific person (although Nietzsche makes clear that Socrates was not alone but merely represents a general trend in Athens). In the next two chapters, this rationalism is regarded as a fundamental tendency of Western thought.

The fact that Nietzsche is not critical of reason as such but only of a wrong use of reason and of an overemphasis of reason is visible in that he on several occasions refers to 'reason' with quotation marks around it, and also by his repeated references to reason in a neutral or positive sense, such as, for example, 'this corruption of reason' ('The Four Great Errors', 1) and 'the great original sin of reason, *immoral unreason*' ('The Four Great Errors', 2). Likewise, Nietzsche is not hostile to logic as such, as can be seen by his references to it as necessary in the chapter 'What the Germans Lack', 7.

Much of the critique of Socrates echoes what Nietzsche had written already in his first book, *Die Geburt der Tragödie* (1872). It seems as if he became particularly interested in this book in the late 1880s (perhaps in part due to his newfound interest in Dionysos and the tragic).[70] He wrote a new preface to the book in 1886, and in the first half of 1888, he worked through the book and wrote down a large number of notes with reflections and thoughts on it.[71] Some of this work led to chapters two and ten of *Götzen-Dämmerung*, and to the review of the book in *Ecce homo* (which is longer and more thorough than any other with the exception of *Also sprach Zarathustra*).

The chapter "'Reason' in Philosophy' continues Nietzsche's critique of an overemphasis of the rational. In it he briefly mentions three related fundamental misconceptions and mistakes in our philosophical tradition which is a consequence of that emphasis of 'reason'.

(i) Over-emphasizing 'reason' and logic leads to a denial of change and becoming. Such thinkers are very likely to lack historical sense, and thus to falsify reality.[72]
(ii) Placing reason, logic and the conscious before the instincts and the subconscious leads necessarily to a rejection of the body and the senses.[73]
    Nietzsche here, as elsewhere, criticizes being and affirms becoming and praises the senses – apparently placing himself near the sensationalist, the empiricist, the naturalist tradition and against the rationalist one.
(iii) Emphasizing reason, language and logic leads philosophers to mistake the last for the first – believing that the most abstract concepts (e.g. Plato's 'ideas' or the Christian God) to be the most real and true.

Especially in section 5, Nietzsche summarizes his own views – against reason, logic and language – which views 'unity, identity, duration, substance, cause, materiality, being' as simplifications and errors. Reason and 'the metaphysics of language' fool us into everywhere seeing deed and doer (instead of regarding it as a continuous and ever-evolving whole), into believing will to be a cause and so on, while today we know that 'will' is just a word. Nietzsche here also points forward to the chapter 'The Four Great Errors', where some of these themes reoccur.

This whole manner of traditional thought leads to a two-world view – a logical abstraction is created as the 'real' world while the world of change and of our senses is denigrated into being regarded as a merely 'apparent' world. This construction of a rationalistic 'real' world is, according to Nietzsche, done out of a rejection of and hostility to our present, actual world.

In the last few sentences Nietzsche points out that the tragic artist is not a pessimist but affirms reality, 'he is Dionysian'.

The chapter 'How the 'Real World' at last Became a Myth' summarizes the history of how we have become liberated from the error of the two-world metaphysical view in six brief sections. Julian Young describes it well in his *Friedrich Nietzsche: A Philosophical Biography*:

> This is not only the most brilliant *A Very Short History of Western Philosophy* ever written but also, save for the first stage, autobiography. It recounts Nietzsche's own passage from the Christianity of his boyhood, via a Kantian-Schopenhauerian 'true' world, to positivism, and from there to the naturalism of his mature philosophy.[74]

The fifth section and stage represent to Nietzsche the most advanced contemporary philosophical position, where one has rejected the notion of a 'real world' (as useless, as refuted). The sixth stage represents Nietzsche's going beyond the contemporary position by considering the *consequences* of the rejection of the 'real world' (or, expressed in an alternative manner, the consequences of the death of God). This is not elaborated on in the book – because he was going to deal with it in the *Umwerthung aller Werthe*, especially in the fourth book (usually entitled *Dionysos* or *Dionysos philosophos*, but sometimes entitled *The Great Midday* [*Der grosse Mittag*]). He ends this section and this chapter with what is probably a reference to the fourth volume of the *Umwerthung aller Werthe*: 'Midday; moment of the shortest shadow; end of the longest error; zenith of mankind; INCIPIT ZARATHUSTRA' [here begins Zarathustra].[75]

This sixth section has attracted much attention, especially the apparently paradoxical statement: '6. We have abolished the real world: what world is left? The apparent world perhaps? . . . But no! *with the real world we have also abolished the apparent world!*'. It is unfortunately common to refer to this apparently paradoxical end to show that Nietzsche rejected both the 'real' and the 'apparent' world (or for some other mysterious interpretation),[76] but that is a mistaken view. Nietzsche denies the 'apparent' world only *as* apparent, which he clearly shows in the previous chapter, where he writes 'The "apparent" world is the only one: the "real" world has only been *lyingly added* . . . ' (section 2) and 'The grounds upon which "this" world has been designated as apparent establish rather its reality' (6). He spells it out even more explicitly in the foreword to *Ecce homo*: 'Reality has been robbed of its value, its sense, its truthfulness insofar as an ideal world was *faked up* . . . The "real" and the "apparent world" – in plain words: the *fake* world and reality' (*Ecce homo*, Foreword, 2). Also in *Der Antichrist*, 10, he clarifies the situation: 'One had made of reality an "appearance"; one had made a completely *fabricated* world, that of being, into reality'.

Concluding and ending with that Nietzsche affirms the apparent world as the only one, as, for example, Young does,[77] is in a sense correct, but ignores the important further implications present in the text of section 6. This is perhaps best seen by comparing with Nietzsche's parallel critique of Christianity. It is not sufficient for Nietzsche for us simply to admit that there exists no God,[78] this is just the beginning (but also a terribly dangerous phase of potential nihilism).[79] What we need to do is to draw the *consequences* of the death of God (or of the disappearance of metaphysics), and realize that that fundamentally affects many of our values and conceptions of the world, including the meaning of life. Some of these consequences were probably meant to be discussed in the *Umwerthung aller Werthe*. We need to learn not to pray or wish the world to be different, but to praise it as it is.[80]

The end of the text, with the reference to 'Midday', 'moment of the shortest shadow' and 'zenith of mankind', and 'INCIPIT ZARATHUSTRA' hints at, and serves to tempt the reader towards his *Umwerthung aller Werthe*.[81] The fact that Nietzsche here writes: 'Here begins Zarathustra' signifies that we have now (with the sixth section) come to Nietzsche's affirmative philosophy.[82] This affirmative philosophy is presented poetically in *Also sprach Zarathustra* and was going to be discussed more philosophically in the fourth volume of *Umwerthung aller Werthe*. That Nietzsche is alluding to the fourth volume of the *Umwerthung aller Werthe* is visible, apart from the reference to the philosophy of Zarathustra, by his use of the word 'Midday'. Nietzsche had started using 'midday' (or noon-day) or 'the great midday', and associating it with eternity, as a symbol for the highest awareness of mankind (probably including an awareness of eternal recurrence) already in 1881, shortly after having 'discovered' the idea of eternal recurrence and at the same time as he began conceiving *Also sprach Zarathustra*.[83] By the time of writing *Ecce homo*, he writes about it: 'into that *great noon-day*, when the most select dedicate themselves to the greatest of all tasks' (*Ecce homo*, 'GT', 4) and 'My task, that of preparing the way for a moment of highest self-contemplation on humanity's part, *a great noon-day* when it will look back and look ahead [. . .] and for the first time ask the question "why?" "what for?" *as a whole*' (*Ecce homo*, 'M', 2). He frequently used the terms 'midday' or 'noon-day' in drafts for titles for books already in the early 1880s, and in the later 1880s often for the fourth volume of the *Hauptwerk*.[84] In fact, two notes written while he was working on *Götzen-Dämmerung*, show that he then planned to entitle the fourth volume of the *Hauptwerk*, then called *Der Wille zur Macht*, thus: '**Fourth Book**: *The Great Midday*'.[85] This book is further divided into three chapters, of which the last one is called 'The Eternal Recurrence'. In the other shorter note, is listed under the title '*The Great Midday*', the words: 'why 'Zarathustra'?', followed by: '*The great selfovercoming of morality*'.[86] Also the expressions 'zenith of mankind' and 'shortest shadow' serve the same purpose: Nietzsche is here again pointing at and referring to his coming *Hauptwerk*.

5.4 The morality- and religion-critical chapters (6, 5 and 7)

The planned third volume of *Umwerthung aller Werthe*, with the title: *The Immoralist: Critique of Morality as the Most Dangerous Kind of Lack of Knowledge*, was meant to deal with morality and related problems. Some of the drafts of chapter titles in Nietzsche's notebooks from 1888 which were meant to deal with these themes are:[87]

The origin of ideals
How virtue becomes victorious
Herd-instincts

Morality as the Circe of the philosophers
Psychology of the 'will to power'
The *good* human being as typical décadent
The will to power as life
The will to power as discipline
The psychology of errors
The good and the improvers

The three morality-critical chapters of *Götzen-Dämmerung* seem to be closely related to some of these themes (especially to the fourth and the last two of these planned chapters):

5. Morality as Anti-Nature
6. The Four Great Errors
7. The 'Improvers' of Mankind (Originally entitled 'The Background of Morality')[88]

We can again see from the planned chapter titles that Nietzsche in the planned *Hauptwerk* intended to discuss many themes and questions not discussed in *Götzen-Dämmerung*, such as the origin of ideals, how virtue becomes victorious, herd-instinct,[89] the good human being (a critique of the morally 'good'), the psychology of the will to power and possibly several other themes related to will to power. Contrary to the case with the philosophy-critical chapters, two of the three morality-critical chapters in *Götzen-Dämmerung* seem to, at least in part, overlap with the planned content of the last draft of the *Hauptwerk* before he wrote *Der Antichrist*. However, the overlap is far from complete. There are many notes for the chapter 'The good and the improvers', as well as references in his published books,[90] which show that unlike the case in the corresponding chapter in *Götzen-Dämmerung*, it was meant to extensively discuss and criticize not only the 'improvers', but in particular 'the good'.

We can observe that Nietzsche was able to write *Götzen-Dämmerung* extremely quickly since it was in large parts based on notes and plans that he had been working on for more than a year. There is an obvious overlap with material originally intended for his *Hauptwerk* (in contrast to all his earlier post *Also sprach Zarathustra* books which are not based on notes for the *Hauptwerk*). However, that does not mean that that material became pre-empted with the writing of *Götzen-Dämmerung*. What *Götzen-Dämmerung* gives are extracts from that greater work, what it yields are meant to give an initiation to the coming work.

In the sixth chapter of *Götzen-Dämmerung*, 'The Four Great Errors', Nietzsche continues to present critique of the foundations of rationalistic thought, and here adds four further fundamental errors (to the three already mentioned earlier; denial of change and history; denial of the senses and believing that the most abstract is also the most true) which has determined much of our thought the past two or two and a half thousand years.[91]

The four errors, which, according to Nietzsche, all relate to and constitute the foundation of much of practical philosophy, of morality and religion, are:[92]

(i) The error of mistaking cause for consequences (sections 1–2)
(ii) The error of false causality (3)
(iii) The error of imaginary causality (4–6)
(iv) The error of free will (7)

The title of the chapter, 'The Four Great Errors', can be seen as an abbreviation of the statement: The four great errors on which the whole of religion and morality is based. Nietzsche specifically claims that 'every proposition formulated by religion and morality' is based on the first error. Every religion and morality claims 'Do this and this, refrain from this and this – and you will be happy! Otherwise . . . '. Nietzsche takes this to be such an obvious characterization of religion and morality that he does not elaborate on it. He instead presents his own alternative – which surely he planned to elaborate on in his *Umwerthung aller Werthe*, he refers to it as a '*first* example' of his revaluation:

> In my mouth this formula is converted into its reverse – *first* example of my 'revaluation of all values': a well-constituted human being, a 'happy one', *must* perform certain actions and instinctively shrinks from other actions, he transports the order of which he is the physiological representative into his relations with other human beings and with things. In a formula: his virtue is the *consequence* of his happiness [. . .] Every error, of whatever kind, is a consequence of degeneration of instinct, disgregation of will: one has thereby virtually defined the *bad*. Everything *good* is instinct – and consequently easy, necessary, free. ('The Four Great Errors', 2)

This is a radical view, where Nietzsche goes much further in accepting and affirming 'reality', without needing to change it, than most readers also in the twenty-first century would accept.

In discussing the second error – that of belief in 'false causality' – that is, believing in the consequences of accepting the 'information' or 'evidence' of conscious 'inner facts' – such as willing, conscious motives, responsibility, the mind as cause and also the ego as cause – as true. This led to a whole world of false causality, which we no longer can believe in, but which is so typical of all religious and moral thought. Nietzsche here, in an extremely compressed form, questions much of traditional psychology, and just as he earlier did with the two-world error, he claims that modern psychology has realized this error ('meanwhile we have thought better'), but not yet drawn the consequences of it. Those consequences are not drawn or discussed in this section but briefly touched on later in the chapter. It seems to me likely that a new psychology, based on the will to power instead of conscious 'inner facts', and the consequences of this for our conception of life, religion and morality was going to be one important theme for his *Umwerthung aller Werthe*, as is suggested by, for example, the proposed chapter title 'Psychology of the "will to power"'.

In discussing the third kind of error – the belief in 'imaginary causality' – Nietzsche reduces much of philosophy to psychology, which in turn is reduced to physiology. He shows how wrong we can be about causality in dreams, and claims that we do the same also when awake. We feel uncomfortable when we do not have or know the causes for how we feel – and therefore seek causes – not the true causes, but those which most quickly and convincingly satisfy our need to explain how we feel. In section six he gives a number of examples of such thought, such as that a physiological discomfort can be explained as due to having committed a sin.

The fourth error – believing in 'free will' – is an old theme for Nietzsche, but one which is suitable and relevant here (although it can be seen as merely the consequences of the error of imaginary causes, but with a distinct separate history and development, and one which even the most advanced thinkers have difficulty leaving behind them). He explains why it arose – that theologians wanted to make man accountable (and there is evidence to support this view in intellectual history): 'Men were thought of as "free" so that they could become *guilty*: consequently, every action *had* to be thought of as willed, the origin of every action as lying in the consciousness (– whereby the most *fundamental* falsification *in psychologicis* was made into the very principle of psychology) . . . ' ('The Four Great Errors', 7). Nietzsche's denial of free will does not, perhaps counter our expectations, imply determinism, at least not according to Nietzsche himself. In *Der Antichrist*, 15, he denies both free and unfree will: 'Nothing but imaginary *causes* ("God", "soul", "ego", "spirit", "free will" – or "unfree will")'. He expands and discusses this in a long note planned for the *Umwerthung aller Werthe*, with the title 'For the Struggle against Determinism'.[93] He ends this seventh section by pointing at the third book of the *Umwerthung aller Werthe*, with the planned title *The Immoralist*, by stating: 'we immoralists especially are trying with all our might to remove the concept of guilt and the concept of punishment from the world'.

One of the themes of the fourth book of *Umwerthung aller Werthe* is likely to have been to show what a world and a philosophy completely without religion and morality (and also without guilt and the concept of punishment) would look like.[94] Nietzsche's most obvious answer to this is related to the idea of eternal recurrence and the total affirmation associated to it (see the discussion in Chapter 7).

The last, eighth, section points even more clearly towards his *Umwerthung aller Werthe* and his own affirmative alternative. He begins it by asking: 'What alone can *our* teaching be?' and answers:

> That no one *gives* a human being his qualities: not God, not society, not his parents or ancestors, not *he himself* [. . .] *No one* is accountable for existing at all, or for being constituted as he is, or for living in the circumstances and surroundings in which he lives. The fatality of his nature cannot be disentangled from the fatality of all that which has been and will be. He is *not* the result of a special design, a will, a purpose [. . .] One is necessary, one is a piece of fate, one belongs to the whole, one *is* in the whole – there exists nothing which could judge, measure, compare, condemn our being, for that would be to judge, measure, compare, condemn the whole . . . *But nothing exists apart from the whole!*

What he is describing here, *is* the kernel of his idea of eternal recurrence although that term does not occur. Essential to that idea is the acceptance of oneself as a piece of fate connected to everything else in the universe. This emphasis on fate and fatality here is continued in the last section of the next chapter and in the epilogue.

Another closely related theme also related to a philosophy without guilt, punishment and revenge and constituting one of Nietzsche's affirmative philosophemes is the 'innocence of becoming' mentioned in the last two sections of this chapter: 'One has deprived becoming of its innocence if being in this or that state is traced back to will, to intentions, to accountable acts' (chapter 6, section 7) and 'That no one is any longer made accountable [. . .] thus alone is the *innocence* of becoming restored . . . ' (section 8). This concept is closely related to the idea of eternal recurrence (see the discussion in Section 7.4).[95]

The major fundamental changes that Nietzsche suggests in this chapter are:

(i) Rather than 'happiness is the result of good deeds', Nietzsche claims that 'the happy person' (a well-constituted human being) necessarily performs 'virtuous' deeds. He seems here to go so far as to claim that the best definition or characterization of a good deed is that it is what a well-constituted person does, that is, he places the person before any abstract definition of deeds or goodness.
(ii) Rather than the old psychology and conception of human thought (which believes in conscious 'inner facts' like willing, responsibility, the mind and the ego as cause) Nietzsche suggests a new psychology based on physiology, the unconscious and will to power.
(iii) Nietzsche's discussion of the third error – the belief in 'imaginary causality' – does perhaps not lead to any 'revaluation', but rather to a different and more profound manner of understanding human thought and psychology. The 'imaginary causality' is based on human needs and thus strongly anthropomorphic. Nietzsche suggests a more scientific and less anthropomorphic approach.
(iv) Against the concepts of responsibility, guilt and punishment associated with free will, Nietzsche suggests (the revaluation of) a world free of these concepts (which he calls the innocence of existence).

This together would lead to a completely new conception of our relation to the world, and especially the traditional conceptions of religion and morality would be impossible.

In the fifth chapter, 'Morality as Anti-Nature', Nietzsche claims that moral and religious thought have always wanted to exterminate the passions (e.g. sensuality, enmity etc.). 'But to attack the passions at their roots means to attack life at its roots: the practice of the Church is *hostile to life* . . . ' (first section). He counters this with an approach which instead attempts to spiritualize, beautify or deify passions or desires. He gives three examples of such a procedure: the spirituality of sensuality is called love, the spirituality of enmity lacks a good name but consists in the realization of the value of having enemies, and the spirituality of inner enmity, that is the acceptance and affirmation of inner struggle and war: 'One is *fruitful* only at the cost of being rich in contradiction; one remains *young* only on condition the soul does not relax, does not long for peace' (section 3). This is thus the opposite inner goal to that of most religious and moral men, who strive precisely for 'peace of soul'. However,

Nietzsche adds, 'peace of soul' is often a misunderstanding for something else, not religious or moral, but psychological or physiological, such as a good digestion. He gives at the end of the third section several examples of such states and situations which often are understood as 'peace of soul'. Thereafter he had originally written at the end of the section: 'Revaluation of All Values',[96] probably referring to his attitude of spiritualization of the passions and desires rather than to their destruction, and to the affirmation of inner and outer struggle rather than the search for peace of soul. This would also have been yet another pointer to the coming work with that title, *Revaluation of All Values*, in which he was likely to deal more extensively on these themes (which he also did already in the first volume, *Der Antichrist*, for example in sections 16 and 29, with the concept of 'peace of soul'). However, he eventually crossed out these three words, and instead realized that perhaps this work too (as he later wrote in the foreword) was 'a relaxation' or 'a recuperation' from something else that he ought to be working on, the *Umwerthung aller Werthe*. He therefore wrote: '*The Idle Hours of a Psychologist*: also a form of 'peace of soul' . . . '. However, when he at the end of September changed the title of the book, he again needed to reformulate it – and this time, although the meaning is the same, it is somewhat obscured: '*Twilight of the Idols*: who knows? Perhaps that too is only a kind of "peace of soul" . . . '.[97] The main purpose of this last sentence is again to inform the reader that he is working on something more difficult and more important (as he had stated in the foreword).

The second part of the chapter 'Morality as Anti-Nature', sections 4–6, was actually written first and as a separate piece. In this part he claims that virtually every morality that has hitherto been taught has been anti-natural – has condemned the instinct of life. Morality as it has been understood hitherto has been a denial of life, an imperative: Perish! Against this, Nietzsche proposes a '*healthy* morality', a morality which is natural and which is dominated by an instinct of life. He says no more about it here, in the fourth section, but returns to it in the last, sixth, section. Before that, he again, as in the Socrates chapter, claims that it is not possible to determine the value of life. On the contrary, when we establish values, it is life itself that evaluates through us. Our morals and values are really only symptoms. But how is it then possible, he asks, that almost all morality is so life-denying. It is because it is the value judgement 'of declining, debilitated, weary, condemned life' (section 5).

In the last section, Nietzsche here, as in several of the other chapters, again hints at his own solution and view, which is an affirmation of the plurality of life and life forms. The moralist makes himself ridiculous by claiming that man should be different. According to Nietzsche (and he here almost repeats what he also said at the end of the chapter 'The Four Great Errors'): 'the individual is, in his future and in his past, a piece of fate, one law more, one necessity more for everything that is and everything that will be. To say to him 'change yourself' means to demand that everything should change, even in the past. . . . ' (section 6). Nietzsche concludes – basically presenting his thesis of eternal recurrence and *amor fati*, but without using these words: 'We others, we immoralists, have on the contrary opened wide our hearts to every kind of understanding, comprehension, *approval*. We do not readily deny, we seek our honour in *affirming*'.

The section and the chapter ends by Nietzsche pointing towards the *Umwerthung aller Werthe* and claiming that there is after all an advantage with priests and virtuous men – implicitly referring to those who can spiritualize enmity (and thus reconnecting to his claims in the first part of the chapter) – '*what* advantage? – But we ourselves, we immoralists, are the answer to that . . .' (end of section 6).

With this statement, and as a consequence of the sublimation ethics, another aspect of Nietzsche's own new morality becomes apparent. Where modern morality is primarily concerned with how we should act in particular situations, Nietzsche's view is instead more akin to ancient ethics, which instead emphasized the answer to the question 'how should one be?', 'what sort of person should I be?' or 'what sort of character-traits and virtues should one affirm?'. Nietzsche's view of morality is thus less concerned with rules and behaviour, but instead with character, traits and virtues – more akin to an ethics of virtue. This is, for example, visible in his frequent use of *ad hominem* arguments (see especially the beginning of the chapter 'Expeditions of an Untimely Man' and my discussion of it there) and the importance of *exemplum* (see especially the praise of Goethe at the end of that chapter).[98]

Nietzsche thus suggests two fundamental changes in this chapter:

(i) Rather than exterminate the passions, we should accept and spiritualize them (and he gives three examples; love, the value of having enemies, and the value of inner tension).
(ii) Against anti-natural morality (virtually every morality hitherto) instead healthy morality – which is naturalistic and dominated by an instinct of life.

In the last chapter which explicitly deals with morality, 7, 'The "Improvers" of Mankind', he draws the conclusion from the two preceding chapters and claims that moral and religious judgements are based upon 'realities which do not exist'. Morality is only a '*misinterpretation*' of the world and '*there are no moral facts whatever*' (section 1).[99] However, morality is not without information (as the non-cognitivists and the value-nihilists claim) but as a symptom, as semiotics, it can reveal much about cultures and the inner worlds of those who 'did not *know* enough to "understand"' themselves. Morality is merely sign-language, merely symptomatology' (1).

In contrast to tradition and almost every earlier thinker, Nietzsche demands that philosophers 'place themselves *beyond* good and evil – that they have the illusion of moral judgement *beneath* them' (1). This is a difficult demand, and possibly Nietzsche had much more to say about it. Nietzsche has just claimed that it is possible to have a natural, life-affirming morality – but philosophers need to see also this as merely a set of symptoms (albeit of much healthier constitutions). In the next, and last four sections of this chapter, he will show that every means to make mankind moral hitherto has been *immoral*, by discussing two different fundamental ways to 'improve' man, by means of taming and by means of breeding.

For the thesis of the present study, it is signifying how Nietzsche presents this short treatise in the first sentence: 'A first example, merely as an introduction' (section 2), and that which it is introductory to was meant to follow in the *Umwerthung aller Werthe*.[100] Thereafter this short treatise begins. This shows that Nietzsche did not feel that he had fully covered this theme (and by implication other themes) in this book – on the contrary, here they are treated only provisionally – there are good reasons to assume that he would have returned to this or related themes in the *Umwerthung aller Werthe* – as he also did in *Der Antichrist*, as we will see, and he also had extensive notes on the theme of 'the good' and 'the improvers' allocated to the third volume, *The Immoralist*.

He begins by presenting Christianity as a morality of taming in the second section and in the third the Laws of Manu are treated as a morality of breeding.[101] That Nietzsche rejects Christianity and a morality of taming is obvious. His relation to Manu and a morality of breeding is less obvious. Nietzsche often refers to breeding (*Züchtung*), although the interpretation of this is complicated by the fact that the German word can mean both physiological and biological breeding, as well as spiritual or cultural breeding or development (*Bildung*). When he writes: 'These regulations [those of Manu's Laws] are instructive enough: in them we find for once *Aryan* humanity, quite pure, quite primordial – we learn that the concept "pure blood" is the opposite of a harmless concept [...] Christianity [...] represents the *reaction* against that morality of breeding, of race, of privilege' (4), it can appear as if Nietzsche affirms the one and rejects the other. However, Nietzsche was highly sceptical of any discussion of 'Aryan' – and what he writes is probably part of a provocation aimed at late nineteenth-century German reader.[102] In the fourth section the morality of taming and of breeding are compared to one another (chiefly in terms of Christianity's relation to Manu): Manu as a morality of 'pure blood'[103] (and of breeding, race and privilege) and Christianity as a morality of revenge and resentment. In the fifth and last section, he summarizes that both of them are 'in the means they employ to attain their ends entirely worthy of one another' and he draws the conclusion that '*every* means hitherto employed with the intention of making mankind moral has been thoroughly *immoral*'.

The whole discussion of the Laws of Manu and the morality of breeding, as well as the discussion of the holy lie (*pius fraus*) cannot be interpreted as pre-empting this theme. On the contrary, his discussion in this chapter should perhaps rather be regarded as preparatory to the longer treatment he gives these themes in *Der Antichrist*, 55–8. After having established that priests and theologians lie (section 55), he treats in the three following sections a question which had not been raised in *Götzen-Dämmerung* (but alluded to): are all lies equally bad? The first sentences of sections 56 and 58 address this question: 'Ultimately the point is to what *end* a lie is told' and 'It does indeed make a difference for what purpose one lies: whether one preserves with a lie or *destroys* with it', respectively.

The main trust of the chapter 'The "Improvers" of Mankind' is against morality. But beyond or behind morality two realities exists – it is either of a taming nature or of a breeding one.[104] Nietzsche exemplifies the former with Christianity and the latter with the Laws of Manu. It seems very probably that in the choice between the two alternatives, Nietzsche would choose the latter[105] – but, in fact, although he speaks better of breeding than taming, he here does not actually choose one or the other. Instead, he not only emphasizes their differences (where he seems to favour breeding), but also their similarity (where he rejects both). In the title of this chapter in *Twilight of the Idols* the word 'Improvers' has been placed in quotation marks – implying a scepsis to *both* alternatives. He begins the chapter with a critique of morality which is aimed at *both* alternatives and in the last section he writes: 'The morality of *breeding* and the morality of *taming* are, in the means they employ to attain their ends, entirely worthy of one another' (5). The chapter ends with an explicit critique of both Manu and Christianity, and in emphasizing an 'inconsistency', or paradox, which they both share: 'Neither Manu nor Plato, neither Confucius nor the Jewish and Christian teachers, ever doubted their *right* to tell lies. Nor did they doubt their possession of *other rights*. . . . Expressed in a formula one might say: *every* means hitherto employed with the intention of making mankind moral has been thoroughly *immoral*.' (5). Nietzsche does not choose one alternative; he rejects both.

In the letter to Gast where he speaks of his reading of Jacolliot (discussed in Section 4.5), he refers to the Laws of Manu as 'a priestly code of morality based on the Veda'.[106] In *Ecce homo*, 'Zarathustra', 6, written immediately after *Götzen-Dämmerung* and *Der Antichrist*, Nietzsche says: 'the poets of the Veda are priests and are not even worthy to unloose the latchet of the shoes of a Zarathustra', showing that the Laws of Manu were no way close to Nietzsche's ideal.

That the view expressed by Nietzsche in *Götzen-Dämmerung* and *Der Antichrist* concerning Manu does not constitute Nietzsche's ideal is most clearly seen in the notes which he wrote while reading Jacolliot, and thereafter, on this theme, and which constitute the material out of which the content of these sections has grown.[107] The context and the rhetoric in these notes are not as clearly determined by the intention of constructing a contrast to Christianity as is the case in the finished published texts in *Götzen-Dämmerung* and *Der Antichrist*, and it is therefore easier there to see Nietzsche's views and values (which is often the case with his notes).

In the note KSA 13, 14[195] Nietzsche constructs a scheme of five religions and places Manu, Islam and the Old Testament in the same group. Nietzsche held these as higher than Christianity, but few would believe that they constitute his ideal. In the long note, KSA 13, 14[199], with the title 'The Origin of Morality', Nietzsche critically discusses how the priests make themselves into the highest caste, that which he on several occasions claims to be typical of the spirit of Manu.

Most distinctly, three notes from early 1888 have variants of 'A Critique of Manu' as title.[108] In these notes the Laws of Manu are strongly criticized for being built on a lie, for the fact that they only use obedience and punishment as means, for only using metaphysical motivations (the 'beyond') and for making people and society numb and dumb. In the first of these notes he writes: '*Nature* is reduced down to morality: a state of human punishment: there are no natural effects – the cause is the Brahman. [. . .] It is a school *which blunts the intellect* [. . .] Including the *in-breeding* within the castes . . .. Here nature, method, history, art, science – is lacking'. This note is immediately followed by one in which Nietzsche claims that the spirit of the priest is worse in the book of Manu than anywhere else.[109] In the second of these notes, Nietzsche among other things writes: 'For this purpose the whole life is set in the perspective of a beyond, so that it in the most horrible manner is seen as *rich in consequences* . . .', that is in imaginary consequences.

In many other notes from this time the Laws of Manu are also criticized for similar reasons.[110] In KSA 13, 15[44] with the title 'The Reversal of the Order of Rank', Nietzsche claims that 'among us', the opposite of what was characteristic of the society of Manu would be the case: 'the pious counterfeiters, the priests, will among us become tschandala [...] we are proud that we no longer need to be liars, slanderers, or belong to those who arouse distrust of life ...'. Immediately after this note comes the third note with critique of Manu in the title – 'Toward a Critique of the Lawbook of Manu' – and it contains hash expressions like: 'The whole book rests on the holy lie: [...] – we [there] find a sort of human being, the *priestly sort*, which regards itself as norm, as peak, as the highest expression of man: from themselves they take their view of "improving"'. This note ends with the already quoted words: 'the *Aryan influence* [i.e. the pattern of the Laws of Manu] has ruined the whole world ...'.[111]

What is then the reason why Nietzsche expresses himself in the published text of *Götzen-Dämmerung* (as well as in *Der Antichrist*) in such a manner that it can be misunderstood as his ideal? The main reason, as I see it, is that the purpose here is to make the contrast with Christianity as strong as possible. Furthermore, his aim is to make the reader 'realize' that even the Laws of Manu – about which he in *Twilight of the Idols* had said: 'perhaps there is nothing which outrages our feelings more than *these* protective measures of Indian morality' – is, nonetheless, higher and more humane than Christianity (but we are so used to this that we do not normally see it).

Already in the early Socrates chapter, section 11, he had stated: 'the entire morality of improvement, the Christian included, has been a misunderstanding ...'.

Nietzsche makes one further statement in this short fifth section, which I take to be a pointer at the coming *Umwerthung aller Werthe*: 'This is the great, the *uncanny* problem which I have pursued furthest: the psychology of the "improvers" of mankind. A small and really rather modest fact, that of so-called *pia fraus* [pious fraud], gave me my first access to this problem.'[112] As we have seen earlier, Nietzsche's notes for the *Umwerthung aller Werthe* contain several drafts of chapters with 'Improvers' in the title, for example: 'The Good and the Improvers'.[113]

Having thus rejected both the taming and the breeding sort of 'improving' of man, sort of morality, what is Nietzsche's own alternative? This is not stated in this provisional account, but from the two previous chapters two or three alternatives present themselves:

(i) A total denial of morality as false, fictitious, generally life-denying and as we have seen in this chapter, also as necessarily immoral. Nietzsche seems to suggest this solution in the first section of the chapter with his demand that philosophers should place themselves beyond good and evil as well as in the previous chapter which argued that morality is based on fundamental errors. It seems not unlikely that Nietzsche intended to elaborate on what this means and the consequences of this in the last two volumes of *Umwerthung aller Werthe*. Some of the prospective chapter titles (although written down before *Götzen-Dämmerung* was written) seem to suggest such an elaboration: 'Morality as the Circe of the philosophers' and perhaps 'The will to power as life' and '*The principle of life: "Order of rank"*'.
(ii) However, another alternative seems also plausible, most clearly suggested in the chapter 'Morality as Anti-Nature', emphasizing the possibility of a healthy, life-affirming morality based on spiritualization (*Vergeistigung*) and sublimation of desires and passions.

(iii) There is perhaps also a third alternative which Nietzsche interestingly enough does not mention in *Götzen-Dämmerung*, but which he in the epilogue to *Der Fall Wagner* (written just before or during the work on *Götzen-Dämmerung*) calls a 'noble' and a 'master' morality (and exemplifies by Roman, pagan, classical and Renaissance morality), representing that which has 'turned out well, of *ascending* life, of the will to power as the principle of life'. This morality is characterized by that it affirms (whereas conventional and Christian morality denies, negates, set limits and inhibits rather than inspires), 'transfigures' and 'beautifies'.

> Noble morality, master morality, conversely, is rooted in a triumphant Yes said to *oneself* – it is self-affirmation, self-glorification of life; it also requires sublime symbols and practices, but only because 'its heart is too full'. All of *beautiful*, all of *great* art belongs here: the essence of both is gratitude.

Shortly after this text in the epilogue of *Der Fall Wagner*, Nietzsche adds one of the very few footnotes he writes to his own texts, and there emphasizes the importance of this category:

> The opposition between '*noble* morality' and 'Christian morality' was first explained in my *Genealogie der Moral*: perhaps there is no more decisive turning point in the history of our understanding of religion and morality. This book, my touchstone for what belongs to me, has the good fortune of being accessible only to the most high-minded and severe spirits: the *rest* lack ears for it.[114]

Nietzsche has examined and elaborated quite extensively on this sort of morality earlier, for, as he says, he had dealt with it not only in the first essay of *Zur Genealogie der Moral*, but also in the last chapter of *Jenseits von Gut und Böse*. That this noble or master morality is not even mentioned in *Götzen-Dämmerung* is surprising, and shows that the book was far from a complete summary and handbook of his philosophy.[115] Claims that we can conclude that Nietzsche had given up on it, since it is absent from *Götzen-Dämmerung*, is as unreasonable as this assumption is for most of his other concepts and philosophemes not mentioned in *Götzen-Dämmerung* (for this reason alone), since he added the epilogue to *Der Fall Wagner* while writing *Götzen-Dämmerung*.[116]

These three possible interpretations of Nietzsche's views of morality and ethics have been used and emphasized in different ways in the secondary literature. By far the most common view (also especially in more popular representations of Nietzsche's thought) is the first one, Nietzsche as the destroyer of morality, of *all* morality. The problem with this view is that it ignores Nietzsche's affirmative morality (both the 'natural morality' mentioned in *Götzen-Dämmerung* and the 'noble morality' discussed in *Zur Genealogie der Moral*) and that it tends to lead to interpretations of Nietzsche as a nihilistic thinker, rather than as an opponent of nihilism. The second interpretation, morality as a sublimation process, has unfortunately rarely been seen, taken into account and discussed (I discuss it further in Sections 8.3 and 8.4). The third interpretation, Nietzsche as affirming 'noble' morality, in contrast to 'slave' and 'Christian' morality, seems to be avoided by many interpreters, except by those who actively reject and criticize Nietzsche.

We can conclude that *Götzen-Dämmerung* does not constitute a summary of Nietzsche's view of morality, but does present three good example studies of how he relates to and analyses morality. Furthermore, we can also conclude that Nietzsche was not finished with morality by having published *Götzen-Dämmerung*. On the contrary, we know that he planned to write the third volume of the *Umwerthung aller Werthe* on morality after having finished *Götzen-Dämmerung*. Even if Nietzsche would not have gone beyond what he had already discussed here – but there are good reasons to assume that he would, both in his critique of morality, compare, for example, his critique of the morality of unselfing oneself, '*Entselbstungsmoral*', which he does not even mention in *Götzen-Dämmerung*, but refers to in *Der Antichrist* and *Ecce homo*,[117] and in his constructive view of morality by relating ethics to such affirmative concepts as tragedy, the Dionysian, eternal recurrence and *amor fati* – he could say and clarify much by simply discussing how these affirmative alternatives relate to one another. I believe that a good case can be made for that the second alternative (ethics based on spiritualization or sublimation) and the third (affirmative or master morality) are just different versions of basically the same morality, and that can be combined with the first alternative (rejection of conventional morality as false). I am not aware that Nietzsche has discussed this explicitly, but he could probably argue that conventional morality fundamentally is based on false premises and is thus fictitious, but the sublimation alternative (natural morality), could perhaps be regarded not so much as a morality, but as a medical, psychological and physiological approach to the development and health of human beings.

In fact, Nietzsche does argue for, or perhaps only point at, the second solution (sublimation), without necessarily rejecting the first, in *Götzen-Dämmerung* itself, but in different, less philosophical contexts. In the next chapter, 'What the Germans Lack', he will argue for the importance and value of *Bildung* (self-education and development, at least in part based on sublimation) and the thereupon following chapter, 'Expeditions of an Untimely Man', ends with three sections praising Goethe, as Nietzsche's ideal form of life, as someone who has precisely succeeded in creating himself by means of sublimation.

This ends the more philosophical first half of *Götzen-Dämmerung*, consisting of six shorter essays or treatises (or five and a summary, the fifth, 'myth', chapter). What follows in the second half is mostly very different, first a 'timely' (as opposed to untimely) critique of the Germans and their educational system, thereafter the longest chapter by far, consisting of long 'aphorisms', or rather short mini-essays, dealing primarily with timely aesthetic themes. Thereafter, the last chapter, originally written in relation to *Ecce homo*, and thus being rather autobiographical in content, but is otherwise more similar to the first six chapters.

Nietzsche regarded the *Umwerthung aller Werthe* as a very serious work, dealing with the fundamental questions of humanity, and meant it to be more structured and systematic than his earlier works (as we also can see that it was, since this is true for *Der Antichrist*).[118] One would therefore expect much less overlap (than to that of the first half) between these 'timely' chapters and that work, also so different in style.

A good case can be made for that the late added sections 32–37 of the long 'Expeditions' chapter really belongs to, or are closely akin to, these more thematic short treatises, with a title like 'The Immoralist Speaks' (Nietzsche's title of the first of these), or more descriptively 'The Immoralist Speaks of Real and Ideal Values'.

The reader may well jump to Section 5.6 and read them now, but in the end I have decided to stay close to Nietzsche's plans for the placements of the contents (but since these were added late, when proofreading was well under way, he really had little choice about where to place them) so they will be discussed in Section 5.5.

5.5 The old preface and its critique of the Germans and their educational system (8)

The eighth chapter, 'What the Germans Lack', began, but then in a different form, as the preface to the book, and deals with questions and ideals ('idols') that are timely rather than 'eternal' and untimely. Most of it consists of a critique of Germany and the Germans since the unification in 1870–1,[119] but frequently he extends his critique much further backwards in time. The timely ideals that are touched upon here are especially the German people and state (German nationalism), German politics and the German educational system. In the process of doing this, he will also claim that the goal of the state is culture and *Bildung*, not politics or the state itself, and he elaborates on what he regards as the contents and goals of good education.[120]

In the first section Nietzsche points out that the Germans have become too political and nationalistic: 'politics devours all seriousness for really intellectual things'. In the second, he claims that the German decline is due primarily to three narcotics: alcohol, Christianity and German music. In the third and fourth sections – transferring the discussion from politics to culture and education – he says that 'fundamentally, it is something quite different which appals me: how German seriousness, German profundity, German *passion* in spiritual things is more and more on the decline'. Culture and the state 'are antagonists' – the main thing is culture, and 'German culture is declining'. The last three sections (5–7) then deal exclusively with 'noble culture' and Nietzsche's affirmative view on education and *Bildung*. He gives two reasons why German education has declined. (1) There are no longer any superior educators (except rare exceptions such as Jakob Burckhardt). (2) Higher education has been made too democratic and includes too many, which prevents it from being a privilege and of high quality. In the next two sections he presents and describes what is needed – to learn to see, to think and to speak and write. He ends the chapter by stating that thinking, speaking and writing are forms of dancing, and need to be learnt in a manner similar to how one learns dancing (so that it becomes instinctual).

As stated earlier, we would not expect this chapter to point at or refer to the coming *Hauptwerk* in any more specific sense, for that its themes are too timely. The only explicit reference to the *Umwerthung aller Werthe* is at the end of the third section, where Nietzsche reminds the reader that this book is only a resting place from the seriousness of writing that *Hauptwerk* (as he had also said in the foreword and in the third section of 'Morality as Anti-Nature'): *'Götzen-Dämmerung*: ah, who today could grasp *from how profound a seriousness* a hermit is here relaxing!' (3). There is also one further much more indirect one, at the beginning of the sixth section, where he says that his nature is *affirmative* (Nietzsche's italics) and only deals with contradictions when compelled to. As stated earlier, the affirmative appears to have been planned to constitute the core of the fourth volume of *Umwerthung aller Werthe* and closely relates to eternal recurrence and other Nietzschean concepts.

The late added sections 38–44 of the next long chapter, mostly about modernity, could have been treated as a short treatise with a possible title of the kind: 'Modern and Anti-Modern [Aristocratic] Values and Ideals,' could be regarded as belonging to or as being closely related to the present chapter. However, they are discussed later in the next subchapter, where Nietzsche placed them.

5.6 The long miscellaneous chapter on aesthetics, writers, artists and others (9)

The ninth chapter, 'Expeditions of an Untimely Man', is by far the longest one, and different in style and argument from the rest of the book, especially in regard to the first six treatise-like chapters (after the chapter of aphorisms). The title of this chapter (constituting the whole second half of the book when he wrote it), 'Streifzüge eines Unzeitgemässen', indicates how preliminary and far from being one or several treatises it is. The word '*Streifzüge*' in the title can be translated as 'forays', 'expeditions', 'incursions', 'reconnaissance raids' or, in a less military and more intellectual sense 'short outlines' or 'excursions'. It is probably not unreasonable to regard the title as a shortened form of 'Timely Expeditions of an Untimely Man' or 'Timely and Aesthetic Excursions of an Untimely Man'. Nietzsche writes in a letter to Overbeck, 14 September 1888 – before he had rewritten the foreword and instead added it as chapter 8 ('What the Germans Lack'), and before he had added the last chapter and the epilogue, and before he had added sections 32–44 to this then last chapter, which then constituted the second half of the book – that the first half of the *Götzen-Dämmerung* manuscript constitutes a very brief representation of his essential difference from conventional philosophy: '[It] is for me very valuable since it expresses in the shortest possible (perhaps also in the most high-spirited) form my *essential philosophical heterodoxy*', while the second half is much more 'timely':

> In the rest it is very 'timely': I express my 'politeness' about all sorts of thinkers and artists in present-day Europe – not included in that, is that in it the Germans will straight to their faces be told unrelenting truths *in puncto* spirit, taste and depth.

The chapter consists of fifty-one sections, many of them rather 'timely' or 'modern' discussions of artists and writers, and questions relating to Nietzsche's aesthetics. However, some of them deal with more miscellaneous themes. The chapter was originally shorter, consisting of thirty-eight sections, to which Nietzsche added thirteen further ones in instalments during the first half of October.

This chapter primarily represents Nietzsche's last view on questions concerning aesthetics. He had originally divided these sections into two main parts:

1–18: 'Among Artists and Authors'
19–31 and 45–51 (the original sections 19–38): 'From My Aesthetics'.

Among the first group, sections 8–11, originally had the separate title: 'About the Physiology of Art', and also sections 19–20 are related to this theme. These sections, together with sections 7 and 24, are those which most directly concern Nietzsche's view of aesthetics.

The late added sections 32–44, constituting a little more than a third of the chapter, however, do not deal with aesthetics at all; in them Nietzsche discusses ethics, society and modernity.

They fall into three groups:

32–7: These deal with morality and seem to originally have been written for the third volume of the *Umwerthung aller Werthe*, with the title *The Immoralist*.
38–9: These deal with modernity and were taken from another clean-written section consisting of six shorter sections, entitled: 'Modernity / *Vade mecum* of One Belonging to the Future'.
40–4: These seem not to have any definite or common origin.

Perhaps somewhat surprisingly it seems as if Nietzsche did not really worry about where the thirteen late added sections would be placed, as long as it was not too early and not at the very end. Perhaps about ten sections from the end, he suggests to his publisher Naumann, in a letter from 4 October 1888, when he sends in the first of these additions, and he thus seems to let Naumann decide their exact position.[121]

Aesthetics can be regarded as the main theme of this chapter, even if half of the original thirty-eight sections do not primarily deal with aesthetics, but discuss other themes and questions. This discussion of other than aesthetic questions is true for sections 14–18, 25–31 and 45–51 (although 27, 30 and 47 deal with art) – as well as for the added sections 32–44). The contents of many of these are often well suited to the original title of *Götzen-Dämmerung*, consisting as many of them do, of psychological observations and reflections.

In general, the concentration on aesthetic questions is most obvious and focused at the early parts of the two main divisions (1–18 and 19–51), sections 1–13 and 19–24. The former group (1–13) consists mainly of rather idiosyncratic literary critique, except sections 7–11 which are wider and more far-reaching in scoop.

The divisions and preliminary titles discussed so far have been Nietzsche's own. An alternative (but similar and related) way to divide these fifty-one sections into groups (done by me) could be:

1–6 and 12–13: Literary critique
7–11: The morality, psychology and aesthetics of artists ('The Physiology of Art')
14–18: Psychological observations
19–24: Thoughts about aesthetics
25–31: Psychological observations and thoughts (not generally focused on aesthetics)
32–7: Thoughts about morality and values (added late)
38–43: Thoughts about modernity and society (added late)
44–8: The great human and society. Biological determinism
48–51: Goethe as concrete ideal and *exemplum*
51: The original end of the whole book

A brief commentary to the general contents of this chapter

The contents of this chapter are very miscellaneous, and in that sense it reminds one of Nietzsche's 'middle' aphoristic works, such as *Morgonröthe* and *Die fröhliche Wissenschaft*. Many themes and questions are touched on, but with the possible exception of aesthetics, none are dealt with in any detail.

Many of the first sections, especially 1–6 and 12–13, deal with romanticism and its after-effect. Nietzsche does not here explicitly discuss his view and interpretation of romanticism but had done so recently, in the fifth book of *Die fröhliche Wissenschaft*, section 370 (1887), and to fully understand his arguments in *Götzen-Dämmerung* one needs to know his view of romanticism. There he writes:

> *What is romanticism?* – Every art, every philosophy may be viewed as a remedy and an aid in the service of growing and struggling life; they always presuppose suffering and sufferers. But there are two kinds of sufferers: first, those who suffer from the *over-fullness of life* – they want a Dionysian art and likewise a tragic view of life, a tragic insight – and then those who suffer from the *impoverishment of life* and seek rest, stillness, calm seas, redemption from themselves through art and knowledge, or intoxication, convulsions, anaesthesia, and madness. All romanticism in art and insight corresponds to the dual needs of the latter type [. . .] Regarding all aesthetic values I now avail myself of this main distinction: I ask in every instance, 'is it hunger or superabundance that has here become creative?'[122]

Very noticeable in these sections is Nietzsche's rather subjective critique of other persons – rather than responding directly to their actual writing or arguments. This is a theme and question which I will address in the next section.

As we have seen earlier, the first eighteen sections can be divided into three parts. Sections 1–6 and 12–13 present Nietzsche's response to mainly contemporary writers and thinkers, sections 7–11 contain a more theoretical discussion of art and aesthetics (including the physiology of art discussed as follows) and sections 14–18 consist of more miscellaneous psychological themes.

In the first group twenty-three persons are mentioned, whereof eight authors and thirteen thinkers (and only two of them artists, the musicians Liszt and Offenbach, in spite of the original title 'Among Artists and Authors'). Many of them he classified as romantics, or post-romantics, and regarded as influenced by Rousseau. Nietzsche had, as it seems (with a few uncertain cases) read texts by all of them rather extensively, in many cases also extensively about them – much more than his brief dismissal of them would suggest.[123]

Those briefly mentioned in the first section under the title '*My impossibles*' are probably primarily referred to in regard to their styles, while those discussed later are considered in a broader context. Only a single one of them, the last one, Ralph Waldo Emerson, is discussed in the affirmative.[124]

The last sentence of this chapter was originally meant to end the book, and he does it with a reference to his soon-to-be-published *Umwerthung aller Werthe*: 'I have given mankind the most profound book it possesses, my *Zarathustra*: I shall shortly give it the most independent' (section 51). That this refers to the *Umwerthung aller Werthe* in four volumes is clear from the context (and from the preface of *Götzen-Dämmerung*), and also from his letter to Meta von Salis, 7 September 1888, the very day when he finished the *Götzen-Dämmerung* manuscript: 'In the next years, I will decide to have my *Revaluation of All Values* published, the most independent book that exists . . . Not without great hesitation! *The first* book is, for example, called *the Antichrist*'.

Nietzsche's *ad hominem* approach and method

Throughout *Götzen-Dämmerung*, but especially at the beginning of this chapter, Nietzsche continually and frequently uses *ad hominem* arguments. Sometimes in a very provocative and dismissive manner: '*Carlyle*: or pessimism as indigestion [. . .] *Zola*: or 'delight in stinking' [. . .] *Sainte-Beuve*. – Nothing masculine in him'[125] but at other times more suggestively as when he discusses Kant's 'categorical imperative' and asks what sort of man would make such a claim. These and many other instances can be regarded as *argumentum ad hominem*, which can be defined as: 'an irrelevant or malicious appeal to personal circumstances; it consists in diverting an argument from sound facts and reasons to the personality of one's opponent, competitor or critic.'[126] Nietzsche frequently uses such arguments. Sometimes he uses them as an indicator or sign to clarify where he stands – these are my 'friends' and those are my 'enemies' or 'opposites'. At other times, he uses persons as examples – because in the final analysis what really matters to him is what sort of person one is. That is, Nietzsche uses persons, examples and *ad hominem* arguments because he does not accept philosophy as an essentially abstract field of inquiry – this is, after all, one of his main themes in *Götzen-Dämmerung*.

What Nietzsche does can hence be regarded as diagnoses of persons rather than as analyses of arguments. This seems not to be an aberration, but is, in fact, consistent with his view of ethics, psychology and philosophy.[127] When Nietzsche here expounds his opinions of different thinkers and men in short disconnected statements this is not idle prejudice. He is, in fact, here expressing his morality, his values, more clearly than at almost any other time. He is here illuminating not ideas or principles but the kinds of men (character or personality) which he finds worthy of veneration and numerous examples of the opposite to this. This is true, not only when he is discussing the highest forms, for example, Goethe in sections 49–51 and the lowest forms, for example, Rousseau in section 48, but also in all the numerous short *ad hominem* (positive and negative) statements which the chapter is filled with.

The purpose of philosophy should according to Nietzsche be the production of 'new Platos' as he says early in his development, or 'new philosophers' as he says later.[128]

Nietzsche's views on art and aesthetics in *Götzen-Dämmerung*

Much of Nietzsche's writings, from *Die Geburt der Tragödie* until *Der Fall Wagner* can be regarded as a philosophy of art, and this was obviously a field of much concern to him. It is to my mind surprising that he did not discuss and 'summarize' (or give an extract concerning) his view on art in the first (more important) half of *Götzen-Dämmerung*. The most likely reason he does not do this is that he had just finished his previous book, *Der Fall Wagner* (he read the proofs and made additions to it until August 1888), which deals extensively with art, especially music, but primarily with contemporary '*décadent*' art, not with healthy art, not life-affirming art.

Much of Nietzsche's whole approach as a philosopher and cultural critic is that of a psychologist. His writings abound with psychological observations, investigations, occasionally with advice and prescriptions, and with analysis of more complex phenomena in terms of psychology (vanity, cruelty, resentment etc.). The most important aspect of his genealogical method is to search in history and human psychology for the original (or at least earlier) psychological causes as he, for example, does with asceticism in *Zur Genealogie der Moral*.[129] His critique of earlier philosophers is often based on their simplistic psychological assumptions, and in *Ecce homo* he says: 'The fact that from my writings there speaks a *psychologist* beyond compare, this is perhaps the first insight a good reader achieves – a reader such as I deserve' ('Why I Write Such Good Books', 5).

A picture or schema that can help to conceptualize Nietzsche's psychological approach to aesthetics, and the difference between Nietzsche's approach and that of most other philosophers, is to divide the field of investigation into four levels of psychological abstraction (see Figure 5.1). Each of these levels can be associated with respectively physiology, psychology, social psychology (or sociology or general culture) and lastly metaphysics or idealism. All four levels belong to the field of aesthetics, but normally the focus for the last two hundred years has been on the third level, although for idealists and romantics the emphasis have often been on the fourth level. The first and most fundamental level consists of the physiological (and unconscious) responses to different colours, shapes and so on. According to Nietzsche we have more perceptions than we have senses (and therefore we are unaware of much of our surroundings). We have senses only for those perceptions:

> with which we have to concern ourselves in order to preserve ourselves. *Consciousness is present only to the extent that consciousness is useful.* It cannot be

Levels		
4. Idealism	'The beautiful in itself' Metaphysical aesthetics Platonism	Absolute and objective beauty
	↑↓	
3. Society or social psychology	Conventional, traditional, social and communicative level of aesthetics	Social and traditional aesthetics
	↑↓	
2. Psychology	Subjective or existential aesthetic values	Psychological responses to objects as beautiful and ugly, etc.
	↑↓	
1. Physiology	Physiological drives	Physiological responses to objects, etc.

Figure 5.1 A schema to illustrate Nietzsche's physiological and psychological approach to art and aesthetics. © Thomas H. Brobjer.

> doubted that *all sense perceptions are permeated with value judgements* (useful and harmful – consequently, pleasant or unpleasant). Each individual colour is also for us an expression of value [. . .] Thus insects also react differently to different colours: some like this colour, some that; e.g. ants.[130]

The second-level consists of our subjective, and still partly unconscious, responses to, for example, an object. Here, more drives and responses are involved, including conscious ones (e.g. thinking) and semiconscious ones (e.g. habits and emotions). One can say that this level corresponds to our psychological aesthetic response to an object. The third level consists of the social or communicable aspect of an aesthetic perception, and hence is closely related to language and consciousness.[131] This level is the focus of most modern discussion of aesthetics and requires a certain amount of abstraction and conceptualization.[132] The fourth level consists of higher degrees of abstraction, reaching up into 'the idea of the beautiful' and 'the beautiful in itself' and so on. We can note that for each step upwards, the degree of generalization and abstraction increases and the degree of the existential, individual and subjective experience decreases.

These four levels are, of course, ideal types and not separable or independent of one another. According to Nietzsche, the main moment of influence is from the first physiological level and upwards, through sublimation, socialization (including language) and abstraction, but strong counter-currents also exist. The two lowest levels can perhaps be described as constituting important parts of character or personality.

The third, sociological, level corresponds to everyday experience which is at least partly conscious and communicable and hence to a sort of common-sense level.

The aim for Socrates and Plato – and much of the romantic and idealistic tradition – was clearly in the direction of the fourth level, towards an increased level of abstraction. Nietzsche, however, rejects the fourth level as 'higher swindle' and not being content with the sociological or the common-sense level ('merely decorative culture') his aim is clearly downwards, to the psychological, and sometimes even the physiological responses to an aesthetic object. Nietzsche comments on his downward intention and ability:

> If there is anything in which I am ahead of all psychologists, it is that my eye is sharper for that most difficult and caprious kind of *backward inference* in which the most mistakes are made: the backward inference from the work to the maker, from the deed to the doer, from the ideal to him who *needs* it, from every way of thinking and valuing to the *want* behind it that prompts it.[133]

Most of Nietzsche's analysis goes from the general cultural level towards the psychological, and more rarely beyond to the physiological level. However, Nietzsche is convinced that physiology is of outmost importance, which he expresses on many occasions. For example, in the epilogue of *Der Fall Wagner*, written immediately before *Götzen-Dämmerung*, he states:

> In its measure of strength every age also possesses a measure for what virtues are permitted and forbidden to it. Either it has the virtues of *ascending* life: then it will resist from the profoundest depths the virtues of declining life. Or the age itself represents declining life: then it also requires the virtues of decline, then it hates everything that justifies itself solely out of abundance, out of the overflowing riches of strength. Aesthetics is tied indissolubly to these biological presuppositions: there is an aesthetics of *décadence*, and there is a *classical* aesthetics.

He immediately afterwards explicitly rejects the highest level in our schema by adding: 'the "beautiful in itself" is a figment of the imagination, like all of idealism'.

He makes plans to write a chapter in the *Hauptwerk*, and writes draft versions for parts of it, entitled *The Physiology of Aesthetics* as we will discuss in the next section.[134]

One outstanding example of how Nietzsche not only goes from the common sense or sociological level towards the two levels that correspond to character but also takes his most ultimate aesthetic criterion from these levels (and more from the physiological than the psychological one) is: 'Regarding all aesthetic values I now avail myself of this main distinction: I ask in every instance "is it hunger or superabundance that has here become creative?"'[135]

We can see, in the first sections of 'Expeditions of an Untimely Man' that Nietzsche's approach while discussing writers and thinkers, is to make diagnoses rather than discussing texts or arguments, and this means that he focuses his attention on the first and second levels of our schema, often referring to physiology in his diagnoses: 'Renan [...] Catholic and prist in one's bowels!' (2), the *Imitation Christi* (which Nietzsche had read and admired as an adolescent) 'I cannot hold in my hand without experiencing a physiological resistance' (4), Carlyle's writings is the 'interpretation of dyspepsia' (12) and so on.

The three strongest aesthetic claims he makes in *Götzen-Dämmerung* – that all (good) art emanates from the physiological state of euphoria or intoxication [*Rausch*] (8), that his influential twin concepts of the Apollinian and the Dionysian are forms of euphoria (10) and that aesthetic responses are anthropocentric (9, 19–20)– all emphasize the lowest, physiological, level.

Especially the emphasis on euphoria shows how Nietzsche begins from the lowest level and can explain why he attempted to construct a physiology of art.

Nietzsche's views of drives and impulses, especially on controlling them, may at first seem contradictory. On several instances in *Götzen-Dämmerung* he emphasizes the importance of being able to control them. For example, in the chapter 'What the Germans Lack', 6, he speaks of the things which we should learn through education, and one of them is seeing:

> Learning to *see* – habituating the eye to repose, to patience, to letting things come to it; learning to defer judgement, to investigate and comprehend the individual case in all its aspects. This is the *first* preliminary schooling of spirituality: *not* to react immediately to a stimulus, but to have the restraining, stock-taking instincts in one's control. [. . .] the essence of it is precisely *not* to 'will', the *ability* to defer decision. All unspirituality, all vulgarity, is due to the incapacity to resist a stimulus – one *has* to react, one obeys every impulse. In many instances, such a compulsion is already morbidity, decline, a symptom of exhaustion.

And he criticizes those who are unable to control their impulses: 'weakness of will, more precisely the inability *not* to react to a stimulus, is itself merely another form of degeneration'.[136] Primitive life may to many of us appear to merely and unavoidably respond to stimuli, but that is not the view of Nietzsche.[137] Nonetheless, even for Nietzsche it is necessary to show how it is possible to inhibit and/or control direct responses to stimuli. With the aid of the schema in Figure 5.1 and the *downward* directed movements and arrows, we can realize that a 'higher' level, in this case the psychological level, can 'learn' to, or be conditioned to, at least temporarily, inhibit and control such immediate reactions.

However, Nietzsche also argues that in the Dionysian state one is unwilling and unable to control one's impulses:

> In the Dionysian state [. . .] The essential thing remains the facility of the metamorphosis, the incapacity *not* to react [. . .] It is impossible for the Dionysian man not to understand any suggestion of whatever kind, he ignores no signal from the emotions [. . .] he is continually transforming himself.[138]

This is probably not a contradiction due to Nietzsche, but one due to the nature of the 'two cultures', the difference between art and science. In art, Nietzsche favours the Dionysian, creativity and euphoria, but in philosophy and science, he favours realism (see the discussion in Chapter 8). In section 7 Nietzsche seems to recognize this difference and dichotomy when he criticizes 'realism' in art and literature:

> [For the artist] To study 'from nature' seems to me a bad sign: it betrays subjection, weakness, fatalism – this lying in the dust before *petits faits* is unworthy of a *complete* artist. Seeing *what is* – that pertains to a different species of spirit, the *anti-artistic*, the prosaic. One has to know *who* one is . . . (GD, Expeditions, 7)

The last sentence seems to suggest that one is either a thinker or an artist. It might to many readers appear that 'the *anti-artistic*, the prosaic' represents a lower state of being according to Nietzsche, but that that is not necessarily the case is shown at the end of the chapter where he praises Goethe (who was both an artist and a scientist), and claims that he strove for was 'reckless realism, reverence of everything factual' (50).[139] Nietzsche seems never to have fully resolved the relationship between the two 'cultures', except perhaps in his description of Goethe, who manages to be supreme in both. However, in general, he seems to suggest that it is not some average position, but that we need to affirm both, sometimes being mainly the one, at other times, mainly the other. But we are also not all equals and the same, so some are fundamentally more artists while others are more thinkers.

This schema, Figure 5.1, can in similar ways be used to conceptualize the psychological and physiological direction of Nietzsche's thought in many other fields of enquiry, for example, ethics, epistemology and ontology and to illuminate his critique of, for example, religion and culture.[140]

We can summarize Nietzsche's view of art and aesthetics in *Götzen-Dämmerung* in Table 5.1.

Nietzsche's plans for and attempt to construct a physiology of art

In Nietzsche's notes from 1886 onwards, there are extensive discussions of 'physiological' aspects of art and aesthetics. He was clearly planning to write something on this theme in his *Hauptwerk*. This is confirmed by the fact that he had promised to discuss a physiology of aesthetics or a physiology of art in two of his published books before *Götzen-Dämmerung*. While discussing the importance of sensuality for Schopenhauer's view of beauty in *On the Genealogy of Morals* he adds a comment in parenthesis: 'I shall return to this point on another occasion, in connection with the still more delicate problems of the *physiology of aesthetics*, which is practically untouched and unexplored so far.'[141] In his next published work, *Der Fall Wagner* he again explicitly refers to the content of his coming 'Hauptwerk': 'I shall have an opportunity (in a chapter of my main work [*meines Hauptwerks*], entitled "Toward a Physiology of Art") to show in more detail how this over-all change of art into histrionics is no less an expression of physiological degeneration [. . .].'[142]

What happened to the promised theme and chapter dealing with physiology of art? Apparently it was never published, but can we, from his notes on this theme, say something about what he had intended it to contain? Or, has it been published? Should

Table 5.1 Summary of Nietzsche's Views on Aesthetics in *Götzen-Dämmerung*

'Bad' Art or Aesthetics	'Good' Art or Aesthetics
Art created out of suffering or for sufferers (out of 'hunger')	Art created out of the over-fullness of life (out of 'superabundance')
Life-denying art	Life-affirming art
Aesthetics of decline	Aesthetics of ascending life (classical aesthetics)
Judges art from the perspective of the viewer	Judges art from the perspective of the artist
The 'anti-artisticality of instinct' – which impoverishes. [Naturalism and realism]	Euphoria necessary for art ('the feeling of plenitude and increased energy'). Idealizing: 'one gives to things, one *compels* them to take, one rapes them'. 'The man in this condition transforms things until they mirror his power – until they are reflections of his perfection. This *compulsion* to transform into the perfect is – art.'
Art without euphoria. (Realism?)	Apollinian and Dionysian euphoria. Two different forms of euphoria, for vision and for the whole physiology, respectively.
Cold, multi-coloured wallpaper style. Mosaic, 'put together', restless, flashy.	Grand style. Associated with the highest feeling for power. Power which distains to please, which reposes in *itself*.
Beautiful and ugly are anthropocentric judgements: Ugly is degenerate man, and that which reminds us of degeneration.	Beautiful and ugly are anthropocentric judgements: Beauty is man's pleasure in man.
Examples:	
Romantic art	Tragic and Dionysian art
Realism and naturalism	Expressionism.[a]
Christian art	Pagan art
Flaubert, those inspired by Rousseau	Goethe
Carlyle, G. Sand, G. Eliot, et al	Emerson

[a] *Götzen-Dämmerung*, 'Expeditions of an Untimely Man', 7.
© Thomas H. Brobjer

the chapter 'Expeditions of an Untimely Man' (or parts of it, especially sections 8–11 and 19–20) be regarded as Nietzsche's account of his physiology of art? If not, why was it not published? Did he give up on the idea of developing a physiology of art? There are few philosophical notes from September 1888 and onwards, but in these, discussions of art are all but completely absent. Is this a further consequence of that Nietzsche gave up on the idea? Are we able to follow this idea in his writings?

The theme of the physiology of art must be regarded as a radicalization and a subgroup of Nietzsche's general philosophy of art.[143]

Nietzsche's notes abound with thoughts, analyses and reflections on art. However, the expression 'physiology of art' only occurs for the first time as late as in four notes written in May or June 1888,[144] where it was definitely intended as the title of one of the chapters of his *Hauptwerk*.[145] It also occurs in the last detailed outline of this *Hauptwerk*, written on 26 August 1888.[146] In all of these notes, the expression 'physiology of art' is listed as a chapter title of the *Hauptwerk*, but there is no description of its content. Furthermore, in all of these it is the *only* chapter which judging from the title was meant to deal with questions of art and aesthetics.[147] However, there are also other drafts for the *Hauptwerk* from near this time, which contain other chapters obviously dealing with art.[148] There are only two longer notes, both of them with 'Towards a Physiology of Art' as title, in which the content of that planned chapter is explicitly discussed.[149] However, we need also to be aware of the fact that art, artists and aesthetics are discussed in very many other notes and some of these are also obviously relevant here.

The last and the most important of these two notes, KSA 13, 17[9], from May–June 1888, begins with the title 'Towards a Physiology of Art'. This indicates that Nietzsche regarded this as an important and major theme (as also suggested by the earlier published references to it). This note, of two printed pages, lists eighteen themes which obviously belong to the question of the physiology of art.[150]

Towards a Physiology of Art

1. Euphoria as a prerequisite: causes of euphoria [or intoxication].
2. Typical symptoms of euphoria
3. The *feeling* of force and plenitude in euphoria: its effect of *idealizing*
4. The actual *increase* of force: its actual *making more beautiful*. Consideration: to what extent is our value 'beautiful' completely *anthropocentric*: [based] on biological prerequisites of growth and progress. The increase of force, e.g. by the *dance* of the sexes. The sickliness in euphoria; the physiological danger of art –
5. The Apollonian, the Dionysian . . . Fundamental types: more extensive, compared with our specialized arts
6. Question: Where architecture belongs
7. The work of the artistic ability in ordinary life, its practice tonic: the reverse for the ugly
8. The question of epidemics, and being contagious
9. Problem of 'health' and 'hysteria' – Genius = Neurosis
10. Art as suggestion, as a manner of communication, as an inventive area of the induction phyco-motrice [induction phyco-motrice]
11. The non-artistic states: objectivity, madness of wanting to mirror everything [Spiegelwuth], neutrality. The impoverished *will*; loss of capital
12. The non-artistic states: abstractness. The impoverished *senses*.
13. The non-artistic states: Emaciating, impoverishing, emptying, – will to nothing. Christian, Buddhist, nihilist. The impoverished *body*.
14. The non-artistic states: Idiosyncrasy (– that of the *weak*, of the *average*). The fear of the senses, of power, of euphoria (instinct of those *inferior* in life)
15. How is *tragic* art possible?
16. The type of the romantic: ambivalent. Its consequence is 'naturalism' . . .
17. Problem of the *actor* – the 'dishonesty', the typical force of transformation as *character flaw* . . . the lack of shame, the clown, the satyr, the Buffo, the Gil Blas, the actor, who acts the artist . . .
18. Art as *euphoria*, from a medical point of view: Amnesty. Tonic complete and partial impotence

Nietzsche's discussion of art and aesthetics in the most focused sections of this chapter, 'Expeditions', sections 8–11, which originally stood under the title 'Physiology of Art', must, in comparison to note KSA 13, 17[9] and other notes and plans, be regarded as very sketchy and incomplete. The only themes he briefly discusses are the importance of ecstasy, euphoria or intoxication (*Rausch*), the Apollinian and the Dionysian, and very briefly the role of architecture. These sections (based on parts 1–6 of the note) end with associating the feeling of power and will to power with grand style, which is not mentioned in the note, but is a major theme in the late Nietzsche's aesthetics.

If we add, as seems justified, sections 19–20 of the chapter 'Expeditions', there is also a discussion of the beautiful and the ugly in terms of biology or physiology (as in part 4 of the note); they represent, respectively, human perfection and human decline, and are also related to will to power.

More work ought to be done on Nietzsche's late aesthetics and plans of writing a chapter on the physiology of art, but I have to leave this theme here.

The late added sections, 32–44, on morality and society

As stated at the beginning of this section, 5.6, the late added sections 32–44, constituting a little more than a third of the chapter, are unlike most of the rest of the chapter and do not deal with aesthetics at all. In them Nietzsche instead discusses ethics, society and modernity.

They can be divided into two main groups:

32–7: These deal with morality and seem to originally have been written for the third volume of the *Umwerthung aller Werthe*, with the title *The Immoralist*.

38–44: These deal with modernity, society and politics.

All of these sections were added in the first half of October 1888, after he had finished *Der Antichrist* and just before he began *Ecce homo* (see Table 5.2 and Table A.1 in the appendix).

The first six of these sections, 32–7, are closely associated with chapters 5–7, which deal with ethics and religion. It can be well argued that these six sections really belong to the first half of the book, and they also seem to be based on notes written for the third volume of the *Umwerthung aller Werthe* with the title *The Immoralist*. Although not as closely thematically tied as the chapters of the first half of the book, these six sections could have been added as an extra chapter, perhaps with the title of the first section, 'The Immoralist Speaks' (or 'The Immoralist Speaks of the Real and Healthy Versus the Ideal and Sickly') as title of the whole chapter, and perhaps placed before the chapter 'What the Germans Lack'. However, by the time Nietzsche added these sections, between 4 and 13 October, the printing of the text had already begun (by 4 October Nietzsche had received and corrected three instalments of proofs), and this is likely to have been the main reason why these sections landed in the long 'Expeditions of an Untimely Man' chapter instead.

The first six sections, 32–7, are all built around one dichotomy, between, on the one side, the real, the natural and the healthy, and on the other side, the idealistic (or false), the unnatural and the sickly. By means of this dichotomy, Nietzsche revalues

Table 5.2 Summary of the Contents of the Late (4–13 October 1888) Added Sections, 32–44, to the Chapter 'Expeditions of an Untimely Man'.

Characteristics of the Dichotomy	32	33	34	35	36	37
Realistic, natural, healthy and good	The *real* human being.	Egoism. Two forms: Ascending types – good egoism; Descending types – bad egoism.	-	[Egoism, seeking one's own advantage.]	[Those that have a meaning of life.]	Antiquity. The Renaissance. Vitality. Pathos of distance.
Idealistic, unnatural, sickly and bad	The *ideal* human. The ideals are worthless, sickly, nihilistic.	[Altruism]	Anarchists and Christians. Both governed by *ressentiment*.	Décadence morality, altruistic morality. 'I am worthless' = 'Life is worthless'	Those that lack meaning of life. Critique of pessimists and decadents. Praise of suicide.	We have not become more moral, only weaker, older, more delicate and more cowardly. Critique of equality.

	38	39	41	42	43	44
Antimodern	Freedom *for*. Striving. Will to power. Self-discipline.	Aristocratic society. Fighting for liberal institutions. Old marriage had meaning.	Self-discipline. *Bildung*.	Integrity	-	Great men not great because useful, but because long prepared. Squandering. Dangerous.
Modern	Freedom *from*. Seeking comfort. Undermining the will to power.	Democracy. Liberal institutions. Against authority. Modern marriage has no meaning.	The modern = physiological contradiction. 'Freedom'.	Integrity lacking among moralists, saints and philosophers – who only admit publicly sanctioned truths.	Going backwards, reaction – as priests and moralists wants – is not possible.	Modern interpretations of great men false: *not* useful, 'holy' or due to environment.

Brackets are used to signal where the other side of the dichotomy is more implied than explicitly discussed. © Thomas H. Brobjer.

a number of themes relating to ethics and society: the *real* human is more valuable than any *ideal* human (and thereby criticizes conventional morality), egoism more than altruism, he revalues suicide as an honourable way to die, criticizes that present morality (decadence morality) as made by and for those who deny themselves, life and lack any meaning of life, and ends by stating that we have not become more moral (than people in earlier epochs), only weaker, older, more delicate and more cowardly, and contrasts modernity with the vitality of antiquity and the Renaissance – as well as contrasting equality (a theme he will return to in the following sections) with his own emphasis on 'pathos of distance' (and by implication, the associated 'order of rank', although that expression is not explicitly mentioned here).

In the first, section 32, in line with his critique of metaphysics and the 'beyond' in chapters 3 and 4, he claims that actual humans and human actions are of much greater value than human ideals (which are mostly absurd, sick and nihilistic). This can be seen as a revaluation of the conventional view that ideals (especially moral ideals) are of greater value than life actually lived.[151]

In sections 33 and 35 he revalues the conventional view that egoism is something bad and ought to be replaced by altruism. Nietzsche claims that egoism is an essential ingredient of a healthy life – 'the best is lacking when egoism begins to be lacking' – and thus it is on the whole a valuable rather than disreputable character trait. However, its actual value depends on *who* is egoistic – when it is someone who is life-affirming (part of ascending life) it is of great value, but if it is someone who is life-denying its value is negative.

In section 34, Nietzsche argues that what is often regarded as two opposing attitudes towards life and the world, and on the opposite side of the religious and the political scale, the Christian (traditionalist) and the anarchist (revolutionary) are, in fact, in the eyes of an immoralist, all but identical. They are both life-denying and governed by *ressentiment*. They need to blame someone or something, and to vent their suffering by revenge (or by the expression of *feelings* of revenge), and can be characterized as denying and befouling the world and society, respectively.

Section 36 is a direct continuation of sections 33, 34 and 35 (about egoism and ascending and descending forms of life). Originally, the section primarily dealt with a revaluation of suicide (also called 'free' or 'voluntary' death in German), and had as title 'The Rehabilitation of Suicide, of "Voluntary Death"'.[152] It follows fairly naturally from Nietzsche's naturalistic and 'heroic' morality and love of antiquity that he would – unlike the Church – affirm suicide: 'To die proudly when it is no longer possible to live proudly'.[153] It also follows naturally from Nietzsche's emphasis on the quality of life rather than on its quantity.

However, in the final version of this section – possibly the most provocative in the book and perhaps in all of his published writings[154] – he goes two steps further. In the last third of the section, he speaks to those who are life-denying, Christians, pessimists and other decadents (those on the 'negative' side of the dichotomy, which he discusses throughout those sections), and claims that they ought to follow their own prescriptions and to commit suicide – not only is that the logical conclusion of their views, but it would also mean that they do not live as parasites on the more life-affirming (by arguing and exemplifying that life is not worth living). Instead of suicide (which they condemn), they recommend 'the slow suicide' – life, small, poor, without vitality, but as long as possible. This step is made explicit in a note from the spring of 1888.[155]

However, Nietzsche adds at the very beginning of the text ten lines (and a new title) which are highly provocative and ambiguous in its meaning but which nonetheless follow directly from the previous sections 33, 34 and 35 (with their themes of the life-denying being 'parasites' and the 'contagious' nature of such life-denials). However, in these sections it is clear that Nietzsche speaks of Christians and pessimists, while at the beginning of section 36 it seems as if he is referring to 'the invalid' or the 'sick person'.[156]

> The invalid is a parasite on society. In a certain state it is indecent to go on living. To vegetate on in a cowardly dependence on physicians and medicaments after the meaning of life, the *right* to life, has been lost ought to entail the profound contempt of society. [. . .] To create a new responsibility, that of the physician, in all cases in which the highest interest of life, of *ascending* life, demands the most ruthless suppression and sequestration of degenerating life – for example in determining the right to reproduce, the right to be born, the right to live.

It is true that as a negative consequence of Darwinism, apart from increased racism, is that many at the end of the nineteenth century did use illness as an argument for not being worthy to live and to procreate. However, this is unlikely to be Nietzsche's position. Not only was he a severe critic of Darwinism as applied to humans, but when we see this section as a continuation from the earlier (sections 33, 34 and 35) and the purpose of the whole book, as well as when we examine earlier versions of the text, it is clear that what he is referring to are Christians, nihilists and pessimists – those who are philosophically 'sickly' (or who hold 'sickly' values) – rather than those who are clinically ill. When read straightforward, the text may seem to indicate that Nietzsche here is referring to the sick or the invalid (those afflicted by cancer, diabetes etc.), but when read in that manner the text of the whole section makes no sense (first speaking of the ill, then suicide and finally of pessimists). However, Nietzsche must here, as so often is the case, be speaking in similes and parables (just as when he in two sections further down claims that: 'The free man is a *warrior* [*Krieger*]' he does not actually mean a soldier or a warrior with deadly weapons, but someone who strives). With the 'sick' person he must refer to those decadents who are infused by sickly values, and by 'physicians', philosophers concerned with human values (Nietzsche often referred to physicians who can heal philosophically illnesses, see e.g. FW, Preface, 2 (1887): 'I am still waiting for a philosophical *physician*'). The whole argument then hangs together. He begins by discussing and criticizing pessimists and Christians who hold 'sickly' and life-denying values, then discusses and argues for suicide in general (it is a good and honourable way to die, rather than the opposite), and it is furthermore the logical conclusion of pessimists' and Christian's views (pessimism was defined as the view that it is better not to live than to live,[157] and Christians emphasize the afterlife more than life – it was there that they found their meaning of life), and ends by discussing and criticizing pessimists generally.

Furthermore, that Nietzsche is not referring to the physically ill becomes apparent when we realize not only that he himself was very sickly and had ten years earlier been forced to resign from his professorship due to illness (and since then had been living on a small pension from the University of Basel – essentially a sick-pension) but also that he often spoke well of physical illness, and emphasized the importance of illness and recovery. He, for example, claims at the very beginning of *Ecce homo* (written just days after this section) that he would not have developed his philosophy and become life-affirming were it not for his illness.[158] Furthermore, the illness he speaks of in the section is the loss of 'the meaning of life' – which surely relates to a philosophical, not a clinical illness.[159] Thus, in truth, this section, like the ones before it, is aimed at Christians and pessimists,[160] who claim that life is not worth living, but who also deny or fear death, and thus proclaim and spread life-denying ideologies.

What Nietzsche does is thus to claim that what is valuable is not life at any cost (life without meaning or life that is life-denying) but a worthy life. Death is part of life, and it is not wrong to choose a voluntary death at the right time (which the church claims). Christians and pessimists ought to draw the practical conclusion of their own views. He ends the section by claiming that the contagiousness of pessimism is not really so dangerous as it might appear for it does not make an era or people in general more sickly or life-denying – he argues just as he had in the Socrates chapter – only those who anyway are morbid or life-denying succumb to it.

In section 37, the longest of these first added six sections, Nietzsche claims against general belief – that we have not become more moral, but only weaker and more delicate – we have in fact declined. Our 'progress' is merely the effect of 'our general decay of *vitality*'. He especially criticizes the morality of pity, closely related to Christian morality as well as to Schopenhauerian pessimism. He therefore criticizes equality (which continues in the next two sections, and especially in section 48) and against it places his own concept of pathos of distance (*Pathos der Distanz*): 'the will to be oneself, to stand out' – an important concept for Nietzsche's revaluation project which recurs in the following section (as 'that one preserves the distance which divides us'). This is a concept which Nietzsche (and many others) strongly associates with the ancient Greeks.

In the beginning of this section Nietzsche makes his only reference to *Übermensch* in the book – but it is stated in response to reviews of his *Jenseits von Gut und Böse* (Nietzsche seems to be paraphrasing his reviewers), and it is doubtful if it can be used to better understand his concept of *Übermensch*: 'compared to *us*, a Cesare Borgia was certainly not to be set up as a "higher man", as a kind of *Übermensch*, in the way I set him up'.[161]

The last seven of these added sections, 38–44, are not as closely tied together as the previous group was, but most of them revolve around the dichotomy of modernity contra anti-modernity. Possibly these seven sections could have been placed (as a chapter in the first half of the book) maybe under a title like 'The Immoralist Speaks of Aristocratic Versus Modern Ideals and Values'.

In section 38, the first of the second and more socially oriented part of these added sections, Nietzsche defines his conception of freedom – against the liberal and 'negative' freedom (free *from* something) – as 'positive' freedom (free *for* something) – as that one has the will to self-responsibility. He uses a rather bombastic and military language – 'the free man is a *warrior*' – but what he argues is fully in line with what he had argued in chapter 5 ('Morality as Anti-Nature' as well as what is referred to in the short epilogue 'The Hammer Speaks'), for self-determination, self-discipline, strength, pride and vitality against the desire for 'peace of soul'.

This critique of modernity and liberalism – as lacking the instincts and the discipline necessary to give direction to the future, continuous in section 39, there applied to political institutions (including democracy) and the institution of marriage.

In the first of the following five sections, 40, he briefly discusses the workers' question (a much-debated problem at this time)[162] from what can appear to be a reactionary position, but actually seems to be from a mostly hypothetical position (Nietzsche does not offer a solution, but questions if the current view and position is a consistent one) – in line with that he in *Ecce homo* calls himself 'the last anti-political German' and what he had written earlier in the chapter 'What the Germans Lack'. A few sections later, he also distances himself from the conservative or reactionary view by claiming that it is not possible to go back (43). He claims that modern instincts are turned against one another (decadence) leading to individual and social anarchy and nihilism (41) and that intellectual integrity is lacking among moralists and philosophers – who instead conform to the 'truths' of their time (42).

In the last of these late added sections, 44, Nietzsche describes his view of great men – as spontaneous overflowing of great energy which has long been accumulated (more à la Lamarck than according to Darwin, compare section 47) – as against theories which emphasize the importance of the environment (à la H. Taine), and against great men interpreted as democratically useful (à la Buckle) or religiously (à la Carlyle).

There is no great breach with the following sections, written for the book earlier. In fact, sections 45–8, suit well as a continuation of similar and related reflections – on the criminal, as often a strong human being in unfavourable conditions – with allusions to the kinship with those who revalue or reconstitute values (45). Sections 46 and 47 continue the theme of great men, and 48 is a critique of equality and progress, ending with references to Goethe as a concrete and real (rather than ideal, but nonetheless, somewhat idealized) example of a great man, and thereby pointing to the final theme of the chapter. In fact, it is possible to argue that all of sections 44–51 concern great men.

Great men and Goethe as *exemplum*

Götzen-Dämmerung is a primarily critical book, where many of the values, views, ideologies, assumptions and world views which have characterized the past two thousand years have been severely criticized. However, like the case with most chapters, the end of this chapter (which when he wrote it was meant to end the whole book) is overtly affirmative, with Goethe as the specific *exemplum*. 'Goethe' is also the title for the last three sections of the chapter, 49–51.

Goethe is throughout Nietzsche's writings the human being who he praises more than any other.[163] Nietzsche gives a number of reasons for this – and they are important if we want to understand Nietzsche's values, and his critique of values. However, even more important is his ethics of character approach that what determines and characterizes the 'good' or valuable human being is *not* some set of abstract virtues, properties, principles and so on as almost all of us assume. On the contrary, for Nietzsche it is the supreme human being that determines what properties and virtues are worthy. We do not, or at least we should not begin with abstract principles or goals and from these determine who best fulfil these but instead naturally begin with concrete examples and from them come to give high regard to many of their characteristics, such as honesty, courage, high-spiritedness and so on. That in different situations (or contexts) and to different persons, different supreme humans seem especially worthy is natural and not a complication.[164] For Nietzsche, with much kinship to Greek thought, it is thus not principles which determine who are great but great people who determine what characteristics are worthy. Character or personality is primary, prior also to action. He, for example, points out that 'it is obvious that moral designations were everywhere first applied to *human beings* and only later, derivatively, to actions.'[165] In a note from the same time, he writes:

> 'It seems to me as if you have bad intentions for the future, one can believe that you would want to condemn mankind to go under?' – I once said to the god Dionysos. 'Perhaps, answered the god, but so that something thereby for him comes out of it.' – What then? I asked curiously. – *Who* then? You should ask'. Thus spoke Dionysos.[166]

Shortly after *Götzen-Dämmerung*, Nietzsche specifies his problem thus:

> The problem I raise is not what ought to succeed mankind in the sequence of species (– the human being is an *end* –): but what type of human being one ought to *breed*, ought to *will*, as more valuable, more worthy of life, more certain of the future.[167]

However, if we return to more conventional ways of thought, we can note that it is possible to delete the references to Goethe, and hence here find a description of Nietzsche's human ideal (and perhaps even the characteristics which can be associated with the *Übermensch*). However, before we do that, we can briefly look at two other instances where Nietzsche speaks of human greatness:

> Yesterday I noted [. . .] a quantity of traits by which I detect 'distinction' or 'nobility' in people – and, vice versa, what pertains to the 'rabble' in us. [. . .] It is distinguished to give a steadfast impression of frivolity, which masks a stoic hardness and self-control. It is distinguished to go slowly, in every respect, also to have the slow-paced eye. It is difficult for us to wonder at things. There are not many valuable things; and these come to us of their own accord, and *want* to come to us. It is distinguished to avoid small honours and to distrust anyone who is quick to praise. It is distinguished to doubt the communicability of the heart; solitude is distinguished – not chosen but given. To be convinced that one has duties only to one's equals, and to act toward others as one thinks fit; to feel always that one is a person who has honours to give, and seldom concedes that another

has honours to give that are meant for us; to live almost always in disguise, to travel *incognito*, as it were – so as to spare oneself much shame; to be capable of *otium* [idleness], and not only be busy as a chicken – clucking, laying an egg, clucking again, and so on. And so on. (Letter to Peter Gast, 23 July, 1885)

In *Ecce homo* Nietzsche gives an *ideal* portrait of himself, which also illuminates many of the characteristics he finds worthy:

> And in what does one really recognize that someone has *turned out well*! In that a human being who has turned out well does our senses good: that he is carved out of wood at once hard, delicate and sweet-smelling. He has a taste only for what is beneficial to him; his pleasure, his joy ceases where the measure of what is beneficial is overstepped. He divines cures for injuries, he employs ill chances to his own advantage; what does not kill him makes him stronger. Out of everything he sees, hears, experiences he instinctively collects together *his* sum: he is a principle of selection, he rejects much. He is always in *his* company, whether he traffics with books, people or landscapes: he does honour when he *chooses*, when he *admits*, when he *trusts*. He reacts slowly to every kind of stimulus, with that slowness which a protracted caution and a willed pride have bred in him – he tests an approaching stimulus, he is far from going out to meet it. He believes in neither 'misfortune' nor in 'guilt': he knows how to *forget* – he is strong enough for everything to *have* to turn out for the best for him. Very well, I am the *opposite* of a *décadent*: for I have just described *myself*. (EH, 'Why I Am so Wise', 2)

When we return to Goethe, we can observe that the primary reason for Nietzsche's admiration and praise of Goethe is his high respect for, not his works, but his character and personality – a character that Nietzsche found to be artistic and yet a convinced realist, noble and life-affirming. We can note that Nietzsche was fairly sceptical of Goethe's *magnum opus*, *Faust,* and very rarely speaks of his scientific work – although having read Goethe very extensively. The one work which he places before all else is Goethe's *Conversations with Eckermann* (a more biographical type of work which brings forth Goethe's character and personality). Nietzsche furthermore agrees with and praises a number of Goethe's opinions: Goethe's rejection of nationalism, Goethe's low opinion of the French Revolution, Goethe's high regard to Napoleon, his paganism, his sensuality, his apolitical or anti-political stance, his 'realism' and, perhaps most importantly, his scepticism in regard to Christianity:

> *Goethe* – not a German event but a European one: [. . .] What he aspired to was *totality*; he strove against the separation of reason, sensuality, feeling, will (– preached in the most horrible scholasticism by Kant, the antipodes of Goethe); he disciplined himself to a whole, he *created* himself. . . . Goethe was, in an epoch disposed to the unreal, a convinced realist: he affirmed everything which was related to him in this respect – he had no greater experience than that *ens realissimum* called Napoleon. Goethe conceived of a strong, highly cultured human being, skilled in all physical accomplishments, who, keeping himself in check and

having reverence for himself, dares to allow himself the whole compass and wealth of naturalness, who is strong enough for this freedom; a man of tolerance, not out of weakness, but out of strength, because he knows how to employ to his advantage what would destroy an average nature; a man to whom nothing is forbidden, except it be *weakness*, whether that weakness be called vice or virtue. [. . .] what Goethe as a person strove for: universality in understanding and affirmation, amenability to experience of whatever kind, reckless realism, reverence for everything factual. [...] But one misunderstands great human beings if one views them from the paltry perspective of public utility. That one does not know how to make any use of it *perhaps even pertains* to greatness . . . (GD, 'Expeditions of an Untimely Man', 49–50)

We can also note that Nietzsche describes Goethe (and thus the supreme human being) as someone who affirms the idea of eternal recurrence and *amor fati* (although these expressions are not explicitly used) and he is therefore associated with Dionysos:

He did not sever himself from life, he placed himself within it; nothing could discourage him and he took as much as possible upon himself, above himself, within himself. What he aspired to was *totality* [. . .] a convinced realist: he affirmed everything which was related to him in this respect [. . .] stands in the midst of the universe with a joyful and trusting fatalism, in the *faith* that only what is separate and individual may be rejected, that in the totality everything is redeemed and affirmed – *he no longer denies*. . . . But such a faith is the highest of all possible faiths: I have baptized it with the name *Dionysos*. (GD, 'Expeditions of an Untimely Man', 49)

After the discussion of Goethe, at what was to be the end of the book, Nietzsche added a one-sentence new paragraph: 'I have given mankind the most profound book it possesses, my *Zarathustra*: I shall shortly give it the most independent.' He is obviously referring to the forthcoming *Hauptwerk*, the *Umwerthung aller Werthe* (also mentioned several times in the foreword). In fact, the whole idea of a *Hauptwerk* began after he had discovered the idea of eternal recurrence in August 1881, before Zarathustra – and *Also sprach Zarathustra* is closely related to that *Hauptwerk* – in both *Also sprach Zarathustra* and the *Umwerthung aller Werthe* the idea of eternal recurrence is a, or the, pivotal concept. *Also sprach Zarathustra* constituted the poetical expression of the *Hauptwerk* (and that is the reason why Nietzsche emphasizes it so strongly in the late books), while the *Umwerthung aller Werthe* was to be the philosophical and more argumentative version – therefore these two works are here at the end of *Götzen-Dämmerung* associated together (as they also are in *Ecce homo* and in the foreword to *Der Antichrist*).

Pointers and references in this chapter to the *Umwerthung aller Werthe*

As we observed at the beginning of this chapter, it is more 'timely' than the other parts of *Götzen-Dämmerung*, and we should therefore probably not expect many explicit pointers to the *Umwerthung aller Werthe*, which he regarded as immensely important, serious and untimely, in it. It is therefore not surprising that there is only one very explicit and prominent pointer to the *Umwerthung aller Werthe* in this chapter. That is its last sentence, which also was to be the last sentence of the whole book when he wrote it: 'I have given mankind the most profound book it possesses, my *Zarathustra*: I shall shortly give it the most independent' (section 51). It can thus not be doubted that Nietzsche planned to complete the four-volume *Umwerthung aller Werthe* in the near future – as is also confirmed by letters from this time as well as by the foreword. It seems most likely that those plans also affected the purpose and contents of *Götzen-Dämmerung*. However, there are a number of further pointers and references to that *Hauptwerk* – sometimes obvious ones but others are more hidden (see Table A.4 in the appendix).

Many of the sections of this chapter contain severe critique of Christianity. Considering that Nietzsche at the time when he wrote this was working on *Der Antichrist* as the first volume of the *Umwerthung aller Werthe* there is an obvious overlap and thus indirect pointing to that coming work. The critique of Christianity in *Götzen-Dämmerung* was probably meant to prepare the reader for the more systematic and still hasher critique of it there. This is especially noticeable in section 5 with its severe critique of agnostics and free-thinkers (whom Nietzsche sees, perhaps correctly, as especially common in England). George Eliot had, among others, translated David Strauss' important agnostic study *Das Leben Jesu* into English, but both of them, according to Nietzsche, had failed to draw even the necessary and most obvious consequences from their non-belief.

> When one gives up Christian belief one thereby deprives oneself of the *right* to Christian morality. For the latter is absolutely *not* self-evident [. . .] Christianity is a system, a consistently thought out and *complete* view of things. If one breaks out of it a fundamental idea, the belief in God, one thereby breaks the whole thing to pieces. (Expeditions, 5)

The pointing to *Der Antichrist* becomes more specific in sections 45 and 47. In both of them Nietzsche promises or claims that Christianity is coming to an end. This is the main purpose of *Der Antichrist*, and the most explicit theme at the very end of *Der Antichrist*, section 62, and in the 'Law against Christianity' with even the suggestion that we enter a new era and a new chronology from the 30 September 1888 – the day when Nietzsche finished *Der Antichrist* – ('according to the old false chronology') as the first day of year one.

When Nietzsche in section 47 writes that 'Christianity, which despised the body, has *up till now* been mankind's greatest misfortune' (my italics), with its suggestion that that will in the near future no longer be the case, this is a pointer to *Der Antichrist* and the revaluation project. This is perhaps even more apparent in section 45 where Nietzsche writes: 'A time is coming – I promise it – when he [the priest] will be considered the *lowest*, as our Chandala, as the most mendacious, as the most indecent kind of human being . . .'. Nietzsche's promise – 'I promise it' – is surely a pointer to *Der Antichrist*. A severe critique of the priest is indeed a major theme in *Der Antichrist* (it occurs in sections 8, 12, 26, 38, 49 and 65) and these claims also correspond closely to the fourth and fifth propositions of the 'Law against Christianity':

> *Fourth proposition.* – The preacher of chastity is a public incitement to anti-nature. Contempt for sexuality, making it unclean with the concept of 'uncleanliness', these are the real sins against the holy spirit of life.
>
> *Fifth proposition.* – Eating at the same table as a priest ostracizes: you are excommunicated from honest society. The priest is *our* Chandala, – he should be ostracized, starved, driven into every type of desert.

It may thus far seem possible that the 'most independent' book which Nietzsche promises in section 51 refers to, and only to, *Der Antichrist* (and not to the complete *Umwerthung aller Werthe* in four volumes). However, that this was not the case is shown by a number of other pointers, as well as by the fact that *Der Antichrist* is referred to as 'the first book of the *Revaluation of All Values*' at the end of the foreword.

Nietzsche interrupts the theme of 'Among Artists and Authors' of sections 1–18, by the five more wide-ranging and theoretical sections 7–11. These five sections built up to, before 'Among Artists and Authors' again continues, a brief presentation of grand style at the end of section 11:

> The highest feeling of power and security finds expression in that which possesses *grand style*. Power which no longer requires proving; which distains to please; which is slow to answer; which is conscious of no witnesses around it; which lives oblivious of the existence of any opposition; which reposes in *itself*, fatalistic, a law among laws: *that* is what speaks of itself in the form of grand style.

Nietzsche had referred to 'grand style' earlier, especially a few times in *Jenseits von Gut und Böse*, but it becomes very much more prevalent and focused in his notes from 1887 and 1888. The expression also occurs once importantly near the end of *Der Antichrist*, section 59 (but it obviously does not primarily concern a critique of Christianity), and once in *Ecce homo*, but it is from its occurrence in the late notes that suggests that this was probably a theme Nietzsche planned to discuss in the *Umwerthung aller Werthe*, probably in the third or fourth volume.

In section 19 Nietzsche discusses how our concepts of the beautiful and the ugly are anthropomorphic and a reflection of ourselves: 'Man has *humanized* the world', and he ends the section with the open question of how would a higher being respond to our sense of beauty (suggesting, perhaps, both the *Übermensch* and Dionysos). However, rather abruptly, three further lines are added, not obviously or only weakly related to the earlier discussion:

> 'O Dionysos, divine one, why do you pull my ears?' Ariadne once asked her philosophical lover during one of those celebrated dialogues on Naxos. 'I find a kind of humour in your ears, Ariadne: why are they not longer?'

It is not clear what this section means, or what those supposedly 'celebrated dialogues on Naxos' refer to although it seems likely that Dionysos here represents a non-human, over-human, 'higher arbiter of taste' – and thus to Nietzsche's probably planned discussions of aesthetics in volume 4 of the *Umwerthung aller Werthe*: 'Dionysos philosophos'. Nietzsche had already once earlier, in the penultimate section of *Jenseits von Gut und Böse* (which points forward to Dionysos and the coming *Umwerthung aller Werthe*, and which Nietzsche quoted extensively in *Ecce homo*) referred to these dialogues in a forward-pointing manner. In a three-page long note from October 1887, he discusses the whole *Hauptwerk* project; primarily stylistically, he ends the discussion by writing: '*Satyr-Play* at the end. *Insert*: short talks between Theseus, Dionysos and Ariadne.' Thereafter he writes notes for some of them on half a page.[168] Almost certainly, it was Nietzsche's intention, already from 1886 onwards, to let this be part of the *Hauptwerk*, and, that the fourth volume was going to end with these Dionysian dialogues.

Sections 32–7 were part of the addition Nietzsche made in October (after *Der Antichrist* was finished), and these all deal with ethics. The first section, 32, has the title 'The Immoralist Speaks' – and seems to be a reference to – or a pointing forward to – the third volume of the *Umwerthung aller Werthe*, with the planned title: 'The Immoralist'. In this section Nietzsche discusses human ideals and argues that one 'finds nothingness behind all the ideals of men'. He continues: 'The history of his desiderata has hitherto been the *partie honteuse* [shameful part] of man – one should take care not to read too long in it.' We here again come across the little word 'hitherto' (*bisher*), possibly suggesting that he meant that this was something that would soon change (with his revaluation). It is not obvious, but Nietzsche's critique of human ideals and talk of a 'history' of them is probably a reference to the planned content of volume 3 of the *Umwerthung aller Werthe*. This view is strengthened when we realize that he in section 6 of *Der Antichrist* again speaks of this theme: 'A history of the 'higher feelings', of the 'ideals of mankind' – and it is possible that I shall have to narrate it – would almost also constitute an explanation of *why* man is so depraved'. We can furthermore note that two chapters which Nietzsche planned for the *Hauptwerk* were entitled: 'The Origin of Ideals' and 'Critique of Christian Ideals'.[169]

In section 33, Nietzsche speaks more explicit than earlier of two alternatives, two relations towards life: 'Every individual may be regarded as representing the ascending or descending line of life' – or expressed differently, representing affirmation or denial of life. This is one of the fundamental themes in *Götzen-Dämmerung*. The book begins by arguing that Socrates represents the descending line (and several other metaphysical or Christian thinkers are later added), and ends by arguing that Goethe and the early Greeks represent the ascending line. In Nietzsche's last draft of a complete outline of the *Hauptwerk*, including with specific chapter titles, written at the time of writing *Götzen-Dämmerung*, the fourth volume consists of three chapters: the first one on 'Order of Rank', and the third one on 'Eternal Recurrence', and between is a chapter with the title 'The Two Ways' (or 'The Two Roads').[170] At first it may seem far from obvious what this refers to, but it almost certainly indicates that Nietzsche planned to perform a more detailed discussion of the ascending and descending ways of life.

Section 34, with the title 'Christian and Anarchist' – added to the text after *Der Antichrist* was finished – is again a severe critique of Christians (and anarchists and socialists) as representing the descending line and being motivated by resentment and desire for revenge.

Section 35, with the title 'A Critique of *Décadence* Morality', on the theme of altruism and other moralities which lack 'egoism', is almost certainly a pointer to the third volume of the *Umwerthung aller Werthe*, where Nietzsche, among others, planned to discuss and criticize the morality of unselfing oneself (*Entselbstungsmoral*) and depersonalization (*Entpersönlichung*) (also briefly mentioned in *Ecce homo*).[171]

In section 24, Nietzsche argues that art is not without purpose, it constitutes instead 'the great stimulus to life'. But art also accounts for the ugly, the difficult, the questionable in life – does it thereby suffer from life? To answer that we need to ask the artists themselves:

> *What does the tragic artist communicate of himself?* Does he not display precisely the condition of *fearlessness* in the face of the fearsome and questionable? [. . .] In the face of tragedy the warlike in our soul celebrates its Saturnalias; whoever is accustomed to suffering, whoever seeks out suffering, the *heroic* man, extols his existence by means of tragedy – for him alone does the tragic poet pour this draught of sweetest cruelty.

Nietzsche thus here brings up tragedy and the tragic artist – a theme he will discuss more in the next chapter (but that was added long after section 24 was written) – and this was also a theme planned to be discussed further in the fourth volume of the *Umwerthung aller Werthe*.[172] Furthermore, one of the chapters planned for his *Hauptwerk* had the title 'The Opposite Movement: Art' (the opposite here refers to the opposing movement to that which Nietzsche objects to, Christianity, metaphysics and morality). In one of these notes, the content of this chapter is further characterized by the words: 'The problem of the tragic'.[173]

Closely related to the tragic and the tragic *Weltanschauung* is, according to Nietzsche, the Dionysian, the idea of eternal recurrence and the affirmation of reality (*amor fati*). These themes come together at the end of section 49 (but Nietzsche will also discuss them further in the next and last chapter, which he added later):

> A spirit thus *emancipated* stands in the midst of the universe with a joyful and trusting fatalism, in the *faith* that only what is separate and individual may be rejected, that in the totality everything is redeemed and affirmed – *he no longer denies* . . . But such a faith is the highest of all possible faiths: I have baptized it with the name *Dionysos*.

This too is a pointer to the *Umwerthung aller Werthe*, especially to its fourth volume with the planned title 'Dionysos' or 'Dionysos Philosophos'. Likewise, Dionysos, as a pointer to the *Umwerthung aller Werthe*, is also referred to at the very end of *Jenseits von Gut und Böse*, the last sentence of *Ecce homo*, as well as at the very end of the next and last chapter in *Götzen-Dämmerung*.

That there is a close relation between *Götzen-Dämmerung* and the *Umwerthung aller Werthe*, and that Nietzsche in *Götzen-Dämmerung* on many occasions points at the future work, cannot be doubted.

5.7 The last chapter on antiquity and the Dionysian (10)

Unlike the previous chapter, except its very end, the last and tenth chapter – 'What I Owe to the Ancients', added to the book somewhat unexpectedly after it really was finished, during the proofreading period (and after he had finished the first volume of *Umwerthung aller Werthe*, *Der Antichrist*) – is more closely and explicitly related to the *Umwerthung aller Werthe*, and especially to its fourth volume, *Dionysos* or *Dionysos philosophos*, than the rest of the book. This chapter arguably constitutes the late Nietzsche's most important text and gives a sort of key to understanding his philosophy. After having added it, Nietzsche wrote to Peter Gast, on 30 October 1888:

> Are you satisfied with that I ended it with the *Dionysos-morality*? It struck me that this set of concepts at no price should be missing from this *vade mecum* to my philosophy. With these few sentences about the Greeks, I challenge everything that has been said about them.

He begins the chapter with the words: 'In conclusion, a word on that world into which I have sought to find a way, into which I have perhaps found a new way – the ancient world'. However, the first section and the beginning of the second section are somewhat misleading, in that he there seems to imply that Roman antiquity is, and has been for him, more important than Greek antiquity. This is far from true (except in regard to style); that which Nietzsche has sought, and perhaps found, a new road to Greek antiquity, and to the closely related concepts of tragedy and the Dionysian, not Rome! This somewhat misleading impression that Nietzsche gives can easily be resolved by noticing that he, in the first and the early part of the second section, is exclusively dealing with literary style, the rest and the more important part of the chapter actually deals with the Greeks (which is also stated in the last sentence of the chapter, with its reference to Nietzsche's *Die Geburt der Tragödie*, which deals exclusively with Greek culture and thought).

After in the first section having praised the style of Sallust and Horace,[174] and claimed to have learnt from them, he in the rest of the second section, expresses his critique of Plato and Platonism ('higher swindle') and contrasts him with Thucydides and sophistic culture ('realist culture'):

> *Courage* in face of reality ultimately distinguishes such natures as Thucydides and Plato: Plato is a coward in face of reality – consequently he flees into the ideal; Thucydides has *himself* under control – consequently he retains control over things.

He summarizes much of the content of the first six chapters – affirmation of reality and critique of metaphysics and morality (which are based on a denial of reality) – when he praises Thucydides (and Machiavelli) as closely related to him in 'their unconditional will not to deceive themselves and to see reason in *reality* – not in "reason", still less in "morality"'. This emphasis of an affirmation of reality is likely to have been meant as a major theme in *Umwerthung aller Werthe* (see the discussion in Chapter 6). We can note that Nietzsche here places history (the treatment of reality) above traditional philosophy (life-denying speculation), although good or Dionysian philosophy ('the philosophers of the future') are meant to combine the best of them – accepting reality but thinking beyond it in the sense of giving direction, value and meaning to our *relation* to reality.[175]

In the third section, he contrasts his own more complex and darker understanding of the Greeks (as agonal, tyrannical and childish, but also as good at sublimation and development) against the traditional 'classic and sublime' view à la Winckelmann and Goethe. Nietzsche here also makes one of his, in this book, very rare references to his concept of will to power: 'I saw their strongest instinct, the will to power, I saw them trembling at the intractable force of this drive.'[176] Some commentators have concluded that he gave up on this concept of will to power since it is almost absent in this 'summary' of his philosophy. Earlier Nietzsche had much emphasized this concept or philosopheme and claimed that everything is really will to power.[177] He is certainly emphasizing it less in *Götzen-Dämmerung* than earlier, but he cannot have rejected it. The fact remains that he refers to it here, and continues to refer to it in the following two books, *Der Antichrist* and *Ecce homo*, where it again is given supreme importance.[178] Will to power remains a central tenet of Nietzsche's view of human nature and psychology (and related to such concepts as creativity, *agon*, striving, *Bildung* and becoming), which he continually contrasts to the more passive and idealistic emphasis typical of the nineteenth-century psychology. My argument is that its relative absence in *Götzen-Dämmerung* (as well as that of several other Nietzschean concepts such as eternal recurrence and *amor fati*) is due to the purpose of *Götzen-Dämmerung*, which was to give an extract of his critical philosophy and to be preparatory for his coming *Hauptwerk* (but not to present his own constructive alternatives – that was to have been done in the *Umwerthung aller Werthe*, mainly in the fourth volume). However, in this last chapter, added late, Nietzsche allowed himself to more explicitly hint at his own affirmative philosophy, just as the epilogue to his previous book, *Der Fall Wagner*, served the same purpose.[179] This is especially noticeable in the last two sections (4 and 5), where he introduces the for Nietzsche closely intertwined and related concepts of the Dionysian, the tragic and eternal recurrence, an account of which were to constitute the kernel of the fourth book of *Umwerthung aller Werthe*. *Götzen-Dämmerung* thus ends with a direct pointer to the coming *Umwerthung aller Werthe* (just as, but perhaps even more so, than in the previous chapter, which originally was to constitute the end).

> For it is only in the Dionysian mysteries, in the psychology of the Dionysian condition, that the *fundamental fact* of the Hellenic instinct expresses itself – its 'will to life'. *What* did the Hellene guarantee to himself with these mysteries? *Eternal* life, the eternal recurrence of life; the future promised and consecrated in the past; the triumphant Yes to life beyond death and change; *true* life as collective

continuation of life through procreation, through the mysteries of sexuality. [. . .] All this is contained in the word Dionysos: I know of no more exalted symbolism than this *Greek* symbolism, the symbolism of the Dionysian. The profoundest instinct of life, the instinct for the future of life, for the eternity of life, is in this word experienced religiously [. . .] The psychology of the orgy as an overflowing feeling of life and energy, within which even pain acts as a stimulus provided me with the key to the concept of the *tragic* feeling, which was misunderstood as much by Aristotle as it especially was by our pessimists. [. . .] Affirmation of life even in its strangest and sternest problems, the will to life rejoicing in its own inexhaustibility through the *sacrifice* of its highest types – *that* is what I called Dionysian, *that* is what I recognized as the bridge to the psychology of the *tragic* poet. [. . .] *to realize in oneself* the eternal joy of becoming – that joy which also encompasses *joy in destruction*.[180]

The keys we are here given to enable us to understand the late Nietzsche's affirmative and life-affirmative philosophy are centred on the concepts Dionysian (surplus of power), the tragic and eternal recurrence. We also in this final chapter encounter brief allusions to the more minor affirmative concepts of 'will to power', immorality, realism, *agon* (Greek term for competition and striving), creativity and 'the eternal joy of becoming'.[181]

The values held by the early Greeks represent to Nietzsche, more clearly than those of any other era or people, healthy, natural and life-affirming values. This emphasis of the high value of the Greeks is visible already in the second chapter on Socrates (where he is set up against the older Greek way of thought and living) and is a prominent theme in all of Nietzsche's books from 1888. In all of these he sets up a contrast between decadent modernity and healthy early antiquity. He argues that metaphysical philosophy, Platonism, abstract thought, pessimism and Christianity have falsified and corrupted our view of the world and our values. This is one of the fundamental assumptions behind his whole attempt of a revaluation of all values – that which separates the ascending (affirmation of) life from the descending (rejection of) life. However, Nietzsche, educated as a classical scholar and historian, does not believe that it is either possible or desirable to merely copy early Greek cultures and values, or that we could possibly return to them.[182] He often emphasizes how different they were compared to our culture and values. However, we can learn from them, we can be inspired by them and they can constitute an alternative point of reference. That this was to a large extent true for Nietzsche himself, he states in the last sentence of the book: 'the *Birth of Tragedy* was my first revaluation of all values: with that I again plant myself in the soil out of which I draw all that I will and *can*'. We can furthermore note that he during the spring of 1888 wrote a very large number of notes based on and relating to *Die Geburt der Tragödie* into his notebooks.

This emphasis of early Greek culture as a contrast to modernity is present in all the books from 1888. In *Der Fall Wagner*, about modern aesthetics, and in *Nietzsche contra Wagner*, he claims that 'there is an aesthetics of *décadence*, and there is a classical aesthetics'.[183] Furthermore, *Nietzsche contra Wagner* ends with high praise of the Greeks; *Götzen-Dämmerung*, as we have just seen, likewise ends with a chapter on what he owes to the Greeks. At the end of *Der Antichrist*, Christianity is negatively contrasted with antiquity and the Renaissance (the revival of antiquity), *Ecce homo* ends with the words '*Dionysos against the crucified one*' and his late collection of poems, *Dionysos-Dithyramben*, constitutes a praise of the dithyramb, Dionysos and the tragic.

Already in the summer of 1883 (while reading Leopold Schmidt's *Die Ethik der alten Griechen*, two volumes (Berlin, 1882), Nietzsche felt that the Greeks may even have discovered the idea of eternal recurrence. In a long note from this time he writes: '*I have discovered the Greek world: they believed in eternal recurrence! That is the [secret of the] mysteries!* (Place in Cratylus) *Plato believes that the dead in Hades are true philosophers, liberated from their bodies*'.[184]

This whole chapter, and *Götzen-Dämmerung*, then ends with the claim: 'the *Birth of Tragedy* was my first revaluation of all values: with that I again plant myself in the soil out of which I draw all that I will and *can* – I, the last disciple of the philosopher Dionysus – I, the teacher of the eternal recurrence . . .'.

The reference to Dionysos is probably also a pointer to his coming *Umwerthung aller Werthe*. This is also how *Ecce homo* ends: '*Dionysos against the crucified one* . . .' as well as *Jenseits von Gut und Böse*, where, in the penultimate section, 295, Nietzsche calls himself 'the last disciple and initiate of the god Dionysos'[185] and he claims, since *Die Geburt der Tragödie*, to have 'learned much, all too much more about the philosophy of this god' and states that 'perhaps I might at last one day begin to give you, my friends, a little taste of this philosophy' – referring to the project *Umwerthung aller Werthe*, and specifically its fourth volume.[186]

Most of the drafts for the fourth book of the *Umwerthung aller Werthe* and all the drafts from October (when this chapter was written and added) give it the title *Dionysos* or *Dionysos philosophos*.[187] The central thought of the whole *Hauptwerk* project, already from the very beginning (one of its first planned titles was *The Philosophy of Eternal Recurrence: An Attempt at a Revaluation of All Values*),[188] was eternal recurrence, and that was to be the main theme of the fourth book. That is what he is pointing at here at the very end of *Götzen-Dämmerung*.

5.8 The epilogue: The hammer speaks

The epilogue 'The Hammer Speaks' was added late by Nietzsche, at the same time as the last chapter, and meant much to him. The text is a direct quotation (with only insignificant changes, apart from the title which is new) from *Also sprach Zarathustra*, III, 'Of Old and New Law-Tables', 29. This is the penultimate section of this chapter, at the end of the third book of *Also sprach Zarathustra*, which to a large extent summarizes much of the whole of *Also sprach Zarathustra*. Originally, he seems to have meant this section 29 to end the first volume of *Umwerthung aller Werthe*, *Der Antichrist*, but during the middle of October decided to place it at the end of *Götzen-Dämmerung* instead.[189] For a long time, after he had written *Götzen-Dämmerung*, he seems to have intended to end *Ecce homo* with the following, the last section, 30, of this chapter (for a discussion of the contents of this section, see the following).

He wrote to Gast, in reference to the epilogue to *Götzen-Dämmerung*: 'At the end, that hammer-speech from Zarathustra – perhaps, *after* this book, *audible* . . . I myself do not hear it without an ice-cold shudder through my whole body.'[190] Why did he decide to add it, why was it so important to him, and what does it mean?

1. What or who is the hammer that speaks in the title 'The Hammer Speaks'? As we discussed earlier in this chapter, the hammer can mean many different sorts of hammers; in particular a diagnostic hammer, a sculptor's hammer and a sort of sledgehammer. However, these (and others) do not suit well here. But we also there saw that Nietzsche often used the term 'hammer' for his idea of eternal recurrence (since it both can force us to affirm reality and ourselves and crush those who are unable to do so). This interpretation of the hammer as both destructive and creative makes sense of the hammer in the subtitle of *Götzen-Dämmerung*, in the foreword and in the epilogue. It is thus the idea of eternal recurrence that speaks here. We can note that in the original text in *Also sprach Zarathustra*, it is Zarathustra – 'the teacher of eternal recurrence'[191] – who speaks. This interpretation is also consistent with that it was so important to Nietzsche, that he felt 'an ice-cold shudder' – it is probably only the idea of eternal recurrence that could have this affect on him. We should also remember that the last sentence before the epilogue was: 'I, the teacher of the eternal recurrence', and we are with the epilogue given one consequence or aspect of the idea of eternal recurrence – it requires that you are or become hard.
2. When we attempt to understand the meaning of the epilogue, we can note that the dichotomy of soft and hard (coal versus diamond) are poised against one another. The soft represents that or those that has 'denial and abnegation' in their hearts, that is those who share or accept conventional philosophy (metaphysics), morality and religion. However, a revaluation of all values and the idea of eternal recurrence require us to be different, hard against ourselves and against our environment.
3. The hammer lets the diamond state that one should instead of being unresisting and yielding want to be fates or destinies – and those that are fates must be hard and inexorable. The words 'fate' and 'destiny' are throughout the late Nietzsche's writings closely associated with the idea of eternal recurrence.[192]
4. Being a creator means being both a creator and a destroyer. Nietzsche gives a sort of explication of this epilogue in the last chapter of *Ecce homo*, 'Why I Am a Destiny', 2:[193]

    Do you want a formula for a destiny like that, *which becomes man*? – You will find it in my *Zarathustra*.
     – *And whatever wants to be a creator in good and evil: verily, he must first be an annihilator and shatter values.*
    Thus does the highest evil belong to the highest good: but this latter is the creative.
    I am by far the most terrifying human being there has ever been; this does not prevent me from being the most benevolent in future. [. . .] my Dionysian nature, which is incapable of separating no-saying from yes-saying.

To be able to create new values, both for oneself and for other, one needs to destroy old values – and for that one needs to be hard.

5. It may seem as if this emphasis on both creating and destroying, as well as the great amount of critique that Nietzsche expresses in *Götzen-Dämmerung*, is in contradiction to his other many claims in *Götzen-Dämmerung* (and in *Ecce homo*) that his nature is affirmative: 'To be true to my nature, which is *affirmative* and has dealings with contradictions and criticism only indirectly and when compelled' ('What the Germans Lack', 6).[194] However, that is not necessarily the case. Apart from the view that creating and destroying inevitably belong together, one can also argue that it is possible to criticize and destroy in an affirmative spirit, as a child plays, because one loves the game, the challenge, the resistance, the fight – not for 'rational reasons', not just as the means justifies the end (not just as necessary for the constructive or affirmative aspect which one hopes will replace it) but in itself, for the love of battle, out of overflowing.[195] That is why Nietzsche refers to it as Dionysian.

6. Some of the themes touched upon in this short epilogue are relevant for Nietzsche's whole revaluation project, though not discussed explicitly in *Götzen-Dämmerung*. This is probably due to the fact that *Götzen-Dämmerung* summarizes Nietzsche's critical philosophy, while the epilogue is taken from *Also sprach Zarathustra*, an earlier text which emphasizes the yes-saying much more than the no-saying (this is also how Nietzsche describes these works in *Ecce homo*).

   (i) The theme of not being so yielding, can easily be associated with Nietzsche's harsh critique of ideologies and moralities of unselfing oneself (*Entselbstungs-Moral*), a theme which Nietzsche briefly mentions in all his books after *Also sprach Zarathustra*, except *Götzen-Dämmerung*, and which, judging from his notes, was going to be a theme in the third volume of the *Umwerthung aller Werthe*.

   (ii) The theme of being a fate or a destiny is closely related to the idea of eternal recurrence and to a total acceptance of reality. This is a strong implicit theme in *Götzen-Dämmerung*, as I have argued earlier, although *Schicksal*, *Fatum* and related words occur only rarely in the book.[196] In *Ecce homo* these words become prevalent (even in the title of the last chapter – 'Why I Am a Destiny' – which can be read as a direct introduction and foreword to the *Umwerthung aller Werthe*) and they occur frequently in many of Nietzsche's late notes.

   (iii) The theme of creation and being a creator is an immensely important and prevalent theme in much of Nietzsche's writings, especially in *Also sprach Zarathustra*, but is not especially prevalent in *Götzen-Dämmerung* (except a little in the long ninth chapter and in the last chapter where he points at his constructive and affirmative views).

   (iv) The noble ('only the noblest is perfectly hard') is another affirmative theme throughout Nietzsche's writings, but which is not especially prevalent in *Götzen-Dämmerung*.

The relative absence of all these constructive or affirmative themes shows again that *Götzen-Dämmerung* is not a summary or extract of Nietzsche's affirmative philosophy, but mostly of his more critical philosophy, his *'philosophical heterodoxy'*.

7. What does 'become hard!' mean? And why should we desire it? To become hard means to have power over oneself so that one can remain authentic and not become 'soft, yielding and submitting' to the wills of others, and hard to others means to be able to criticize all that denies life and reality, especially 'the good and the just' (which had been the theme of the last few sections before this one in *Also sprach Zarathustra*).[197] Hard enough to be able to create ('all creators are hard') – but create what? It is not obvious, but much (including the last aphorisms in the first chapter 'Formula of my happiness: a Yes, a No, a straight line, a *goal* . . . ') suggests that it is a goal, a purpose – it is such creating which makes one a destiny.

Nietzsche once returns to this imperative: 'Become hard!' after *Götzen-Dämmerung*, in the last sentences of his review of *Also sprach Zarathustra* in *Ecce homo*, where he writes in line with this interpretation:

> I will emphasize one final point, prompted by the highlighted verse. For a *Dionysian* task the hardness of the hammer, the *pleasure even in destroying* are crucial preconditions. The imperative 'Become hard!', the deepest conviction *that all creators are hard*, is the true badge of a Dionysian nature.

The problem Nietzsche responds to is that the one who is soft and yielding (friendly and willing to compromise) will never be able to create new values since that task inevitably requires denial and destruction of old values.

Dionysos, or the Dionysian, mentioned in the quotation, is often by Nietzsche associated with his own affirmative philosophy, and related to the idea of eternal recurrence (as in the last chapter of *Götzen-Dämmerung*) and with a total acceptance of reality.[198]

8. Nietzsche's philosophy can in part be described as ecstatic and Dionysian, but it is also true that it apart from that emphasizes, what might appear as the opposite; self-discipline, self-control and hardness. This was also very much part of Nietzsche's personality, which had a strong stoic tendency, and it goes well with his strong emphasis on *Bildung*, striving, excelsior and attempting to affirm and realize the highest form of life. To take a personal example; in a letter to Malwida von Meysenbug, 12 May 1887, he writes about the '*ruthless* honesty' in regard to himself he had used while writing his prefaces in 1886–7, 'that way I kept "the many", once and for all, off me, for nothing aggravates people so much as to let them notice something of the severity and hardness of discipline with which one treats and have treated *oneself* in regard to one's own ideals'. He also refers to this hardness towards himself in several places in *Ecce homo*: 'One must never have spared oneself, one must have become accustomed to *harshness* to feel high-spirited and cheerful among nothing but harsh truths',[199] and when he describes how we can know that a person 'has turned out well': 'By the fact that someone who has turned out well is good for our senses: the wood he is made of is at once hard, delicate and fragrant.'[200] He also describes what he wanted to do in his *Unzeitgemäße Betrachtungen* as 'an unparalleled problem of education, a

new concept of *self-discipline*, of *self-defence* to the point of harshness, a path to greatness and to world-historic tasks was clamouring for its first expression'.[201]
9. Although the text of the epilogue comes from *Also sprach Zarathustra*, being and becoming hard is in fact also a major theme in *Götzen-Dämmerung* and his other late books. In *Götzen-Dämmerung* he describes Thucydides and the older Hellenes as possessing 'strong, stern, hard matter-of-factness'.[202] Already in the foreword to *Der Antichrist* he writes: 'One must be honest in intellectual matters to the point of harshness to so much as endure my seriousness, my passion', and in section 57 of the same book he emphasizes that the most spiritual persons, as the strongest, also must be the hardest towards themselves and others. In the foreword to *Ecce homo* he writes: 'Every achievement, every step forwards in knowledge is the *consequence* of courage, of toughness towards oneself, of sincerity towards oneself'.
10. In the last section of the chapter 'Of Old and New Law-Tables', 30, of the original text in *Also sprach Zarathustra* (which was meant to constitute an epilogue to *Ecce homo* until 29 December 1888)[203] we are given a few further hints as to the meaning of the epilogue. However, this last section is even more poetical and metaphorical – with the corresponding difficulty of finding a definitive interpretation.

> O my Will! My essential, *my* necessity, dispeller of need! [. . .] Preserve and spare me for a great destiny! [. . .] That I may one day be ready and ripe in the great noontide [. . .] ready for myself and my most secret Will: a bow eager for its arrow, an arrow eager for its star [. . .] O my Will! My essential, *my* necessity, dispeller of need! Spare me for one great victory!'[204]

Where 'becoming hard' and 'creating' was emphasized in 29, 'will' and 'victory' are emphasized more in 30, both being related to having (or creating) a goal,[205] – 'Formula of my happiness: a Yes, a No, a straight line, a *goal* . . .'[206] – and attempting to realize that goal (great victory). The theme of being a fate (and its close relation to eternal recurrence) continues and is made even more explicit in that 'the great noontide' (*grossen Mittage*) is mentioned twice, which Nietzsche elsewhere uses as a synonym for eternal recurrence (including in the chapter following this one in Za, III, 'The Convalescent', 2).[207] Thus, what seems clear is that the becoming hard and possessing will, creating purpose and striving to realize it (victory) is related to the idea of eternal recurrence.[208] This interpretation is further supported by the fact in that the following chapter Zarathustra is described as 'the teacher of eternal recurrence' and the following three last chapters are centred on this idea, with the final poem 'O Man! Attend!' with its final lines: 'But all joy wants eternity / – wants deep, deep, deep eternity!' and the very last chapter 'The Song of Yes and Amen' with its refrain: 'For I love you, O Eternity!' – thus *Also sprach Zarathustra* (as Nietzsche published it in three books) ends with references to eternal recurrence and to a total affirmation of reality in eternity. The epilogue of *Götzen-Dämmerung* points at a necessary step to achieve such total affirmation – becoming hard and creative. Hard because it is difficult to liberate oneself of that which limits one and from all that which teaches us to negate the world (conventional philosophy, morality and religion). This has also been the main focus of *Götzen-Dämmerung*.

In conclusion, knowing that it is the hammer (the idea of eternal recurrence) that speaks – '*Become hard!*' means *become hard so that you can become a creator of your own will and purpose so that you can affirm yourself and reality* – and perhaps also *a creator of a purpose and meaning beyond yourself* – is also an accurate summary and conclusion of the affirmative content of *Götzen-Dämmerung*. Furthermore, it seems likely that it also means that becoming hard in this manner also prevents you from being crushed by the idea of eternal recurrence (the idea that there is no external goal or purpose which Nietzsche believed would crush many persons) – and instead allows you to be able to affirm it.

5.9 References to the *Revaluation of All Values* in *Götzen-Dämmerung*

In this section we will examine the presence of references to the four-volume book project *Umwerthung aller Werthe* in *Götzen-Dämmerung* – first the explicit references and thereafter discuss the more hidden or uncertain references. This is summarized in Table A.4 in the appendix.

The several explicit references to the *Umwerthung aller Werthe* are at the very beginning of the book, in the foreword, and in what was originally to have been the book's last sentence – the last sentence of the chapter 'Expeditions of an Untimely Man', 51.

The foreword begins with a reference to his work on the *Umwerthung aller Werthe*:

To stay cheerful when involved in a gloomy and exceedingly responsible business is no inconsiderable art: yet what could be more necessary than cheerfulness? Nothing succeeds in which high spirits play no part. Only excess of strength is proof of strength. – A *revaluation of all values* [A *Revaluation of All Values*], this question-mark so black, so huge it casts a shadow over him who sets it up – such a destiny of a task compels one every instant to run out into the sunshine so as to shake off a seriousness grown all too oppressive. Every expedient for doing so is justified, every 'occasion' a joyful occasion.[209]

He seems to say that the work on the *Umwerthung aller Werthe* is 'exceedingly responsible' and so difficult that he needed to write *Götzen-Dämmerung* as a sort of relaxation from that work. That he is referring to the *Umwerthung aller Werthe* is confirmed at the end of the foreword where he writes: 'Turin, 30 September 1888, on the day the first book of the *Revaluation of all Values* was completed'.[210]

In the last sentence of the chapter 'Expeditions', which was to have been the last sentence of the book when he wrote it, he writes: 'I have given mankind the most profound book it possesses, my *Zarathustra*: I shall shortly give it the most independent one – '. This refers, of course, to the *Hauptwerk*, in line with that he writes in letters that *Götzen-Dämmerung* was meant to be preparatory for the *Umwerthung aller Werthe*.

In no other book by Nietzsche does he so explicitly refer to and point to a future coming work, with the possible exception of *Ecce homo*, where he points at the same forthcoming *Umwerthung aller Werthe*.

Most of the implicit references to the *Umwerthung aller Werthe* in *Götzen-Dämmerung* are vague, hidden and difficult to discover, especially without detailed knowledge of what Nietzsche intended to discuss in that work. Among the more obvious ones are references to immoralism and immoralists – the third volume was planned to be called *The Immoralist*. Furthermore, he begins the discussion of the morality of 'improving' in *Götzen-Dämmerung* (a theme he seems to have intended to enlarge upon in the *Umwerthung aller Werthe*) with the words: 'A first example, merely as an introduction'.[211] Other examples were surely meant to follow in the *Umwerthung aller Werthe*. Also the critical reference to and brief discussion of all human ideals 'But the philosopher despises [...] all the *ideals* of man' ('Expeditions of an Untimely Man', 32) – which together with his statement in *Der Antichrist*, 6 – 'A history of the 'higher feelings', of the 'ideals of mankind' – and it is possible I shall have to narrate it – would almost also constitute an explanation of *why* man is so depraved' – probably refers to intended contents of volume 3 of the *Hauptwerk* (we can see in Table 3.2 that Nietzsche planned two chapters entitled 'Critique of the Christian Ideals' and 'The Origin of Ideals' for the *Hauptwerk*). Another fairly obvious reference to both Nietzsche's revaluation and the *Umwerthung aller Werthe* is his claim: 'As long as the *priest* was considered the highest type *every* valuable kind of human being was disvalued. . . . The time is coming – I promise it – when he will be considered the *lowest*' ('Expeditions of an Untimely Man', 45). This is something which Nietzsche both argued and claimed in the first book of the *Umwerthung aller Werthe*, *Der Antichrist*.

Another reference – but which may be difficult for a reader to realize – is the reference to 'the famous dialogues on Naxos', in the chapter 'Expeditions of an Untimely Man', 19. He makes a similar reference to these dialogues also in *The Antichrist*, 39: 'a *spectacle for the gods* – for those divinities which are at the same time philosophers and which I encountered, for example, during those celebrated dialogues on Naxos'. These 'Dialogues on Naxos', between Theseus, Dionysos and Ariadne, had not yet been written, but which, according to his notes, he intended to include in the *Umwerthung aller Werthe*.[212]

Other likely references to the *Umwerthung aller Werthe* are where he in *Götzen-Dämmerung* mentions the themes which (from his plans and notes) are likely to have been intended to be discussed there, such as 'great style', 'pathos of distance', 'the great human being', 'the innocence of becoming' – as well as concepts like nihilism, will to power, revaluation, Dionysos, the distinction between ascending and descending life, and eternal recurrence.

5.10 Some conclusions

Having examined *Götzen-Dämmerung* with special reference to its purpose and its relation to Nietzsche's work on a *magnum opus* in four volumes, the first volume which he had already finished before he made the last more major revisions of *Götzen-Dämmerung* (he added the last chapter, the epilogue and sections 32–44 in the chapter 'Expeditions of an Untimely Man', made changes in the foreword and changed the title *after Der Antichrist* was finished). We can now draw some general conclusions as to the nature and purpose of this work. Several of them will be presented and elaborated on in the succeeding chapters, but we can summarize them here.

Götzen-Dämmerung is primarily a *critical* work – its purpose is primarily to present critique of accepted views of philosophy, religion, aesthetics and morality. Occasionally throughout the book he presents or suggests affirmative alternatives to this, but the *emphasis* is on critique. Only in the last chapter on antiquity, added late, does the affirmative predominate – with such 'affirmative' themes as the tragic, the Dionysian and eternal recurrence. That it primarily is a critical book is confirmed – apart from being obvious when one examines its contents, as we have done in this chapter – also by his review of it in *Ecce homo*: 'Anyone who wants to get a quick idea of how topsy-turvy everything was before I came along should make a start with this work',[213] and in his claim there that after he had finished *Also sprach Zarathustra*: 'Now that the yes-saying part of my task was solved, it was the turn of the no-saying, *no-doing* half: the revaluation of previous values itself, the great war – the conjuring up of a day of decision'.[214] It is also consistent – in the sense that it is easier to present critique than to construct a completely new philosophy – with Nietzsche's claims in the foreword (and in letters) that the book is a resting place as compared to the much more difficult task of writing the *Umwerthung aller Werthe* – which was not meant to be merely critical but also to present his own constructive philosophy. In this sense *Götzen-Dämmerung* can be regarded as a partial summary of Nietzsche's 'heterodoxy', of his heresy (deviation from orthodox or accepted views). It can be regarded as giving a partial summary, *not* of his philosophy, but of his critique of philosophy.

The book is divided into three parts, two main parts, with the last chapter and the epilogue as a more affirmative *addendum* (also actually added last to the text). The six early chapters, after the first one with aphorisms, contain focused miniature essays or treatises with severe critique of an overemphasis of reason, pessimism, metaphysics, morality and Christianity. These can be regarded as excerpts from his work on the *Hauptwerk*. The second main part, consisting of the chapter on the Germans and the long penultimate one, is more 'timely' and less focused, containing many miscellaneous themes, but primarily reflections on aesthetics. Parts of this material are also drawn from the work on the *Hauptwerk*, but mostly from less finished material, and some of it seems not to have any direct relation to that work, but can rather be seen as miscellaneous notes and thoughts which would not suit that future work, and therefore it was presented here instead. In the foreword Nietzsche had claimed that the book deals only with 'eternal' idols (probably reflecting that he regarded the first part of the book as much more important than the second), but in *Ecce homo*, written later, he says more correctly that the book touches on 'not just the *eternal* idols, but also the most recent of all'.[215] The last chapter and the epilogue constitute a more affirmative third part.

When we examined the secondary literature about *Götzen-Dämmerung* in Chapter 2, we made two main observations:

A. Almost nothing was said about the relation between *Götzen-Dämmerung* and the *Hauptwerk* project.
B. Almost all the more serious studies of *Götzen-Dämmerung* accepted it as a summary of Nietzsche's philosophy. This was not questioned or qualified, and oddly enough, one can think, also not used to discuss and actually summarize his philosophy.

In the present chapter we have made a number of observations that go counter to these views and we are thus forced to draw other conclusions.

A. About the relation between *Götzen-Dämmerung* and the *Umwerthung aller Werthe*:
   1. We have seen that there is a very close relation between *Götzen-Dämmerung* and the *Umwerthung aller Werthe*.
   2. The relation of *Götzen-Dämmerung* to the *Umwerthung aller Werthe* can be summarized by a few observations:
      (i) *Götzen-Dämmerung* was written (from Nietzsche's own perspective) in part as a relaxation from the difficult task of writing *Umwerthung aller Werthe* (as he says in the foreword and in several letters). The writing of *Götzen-Dämmerung* was in part much easier because he used or excerpted already finished material for that work.
      (ii) *Götzen-Dämmerung* frequently points at and alludes to the planned volumes of *Umwerthung aller Werthe*, as we have seen in this chapter (and which is summarized in Table A.4 in the appendix).
      (iii) Much of the material for *Götzen-Dämmerung* was drawn from Nietzsche's notes originally written for his work on the *Hauptwerk*, as Montinari correctly has emphasized. Nietzsche had collected notes into three large bound notebooks, W II 1–3, for this specific purpose (but there are also other notes meant primarily for his *Hauptwerk*), and he often returned to them and revised them, including striking out some of them which he either has used or changed his view about.[216]
      (iv) The purpose of *Götzen-Dämmerung* can be described as to tempt, to prepare and to initiate readers for the coming *Umwerthung aller Werthe* – this is how Nietzsche describes the purpose in letters – thus to ignore *Götzen-Dämmerung*'s relation to the planned *Hauptwerk* is to completely fail to realize the purpose of the book.
      (v) This tempting and preparing by Nietzsche is done by very briefly summarizing, or better, exemplifying or giving excerpts from, some of the planned contents of the first three critical volumes of the *Umwerthung aller Werthe* – by briefly saying what no one else says about the misconceptions about life and reality, and especially about how we value and evaluate life and reality, that has reigned for thousands of years.
      (vi) The planned *Umwerthung aller Werthe* also influenced what Nietzsche decided *not* to include in the book. A fairly large number of themes and

philosophemes Nietzsche seems to have avoided in *Götzen-Dämmerung* because he planned to deal with them in the *Umwerthung aller Werthe*.
  (vii) To better illuminate Nietzsche's constructive philosophy requires very focused reading of *Götzen-Dämmerung* and his other late books, in combination with careful study of his late notes.
B. To regard *Götzen-Dämmerung* as a summary of Nietzsche's late philosophy is problematic (and would lead to a severe misrepresentation of his philosophy), and fails to take into account several important qualifications.
  1. *Götzen-Dämmerung* is not a straightforward summary of Nietzsche's philosophy (in spite of Nietzsche's own words that may lead one to assume that it is). Most importantly, it can in no way be regarded as a summary of Nietzsche's late books, *Also sprach Zarathustra*, *Jenseits von Gut und Böse*, *Zur Genealogie der Moral* and *Der Fall Wagner* (as shown in the next chapter).
  2. Nietzsche is with and in this book not backward-looking, but forward-looking. What *Götzen-Dämmerung* perhaps can be said to summarize or to give extracts from – a selection of themes from – is *not* his late books, but his work on the planned *Hauptwerk*, especially of the first three more critical volumes. Compare the examination in the next chapter.
  3. *Götzen-Dämmerung* does not summarize or give much of an extract of Nietzsche's affirmative philosophy (his alternative philosophy or his own answers and solutions to the problems he addresses in this book and elsewhere). Those who accept it as a summary of his philosophy, which seems to be the case with almost all commentators, will inevitably strongly overemphasize Nietzsche's critical philosophy and underemphasize his constructive philosophy.
  4. However, that affirmative philosophy is not completely absent in the book. Occasionally it shines through in his critique, and most noticeably, almost every chapter ends by pointing at or alluding to it (see the discussion in Chapters 6 and 7). It is also quite strongly present in the last chapter, 'What I Owe to the Ancients', added long after the rest of the text was finished.
  5. *Götzen-Dämmerung* is not well described as a summary of Nietzsche's critique of philosophy and culture, but, can, if a better description is lacking, perhaps be called at most a *partial* 'summary'. However, it is much better and more accurately described as consisting of a selection of themes from his work on his *Hauptwerk* (which is also consistent with his original subtitle of *Götzen-Dämmerung* as an 'Auszug', as consisting of extracts or excerpts or selections of themes).
  6. It is far from a complete account (or summary) of that *Hauptwerk*. Many important planned critical themes, such as, for example, discussions of nihilism, of the will to truth and of the morality of unselfing oneself are missing. Compare the discussions in Chapter 6 as follows.
  7. Nietzsche did not extract and use notes from his work on the planned *Hauptwerk* because he had given up on the project (because he had nothing better to do with the notes for it), but for the purpose of producing a text which would tempt and help prepare the reader for that coming work.

That this is the case follows from the fact that the whole spirit of the book is forward-looking, not backward-looking. This is especially apparent in the foreword and in the last section of 'Expeditions of an Untimely Man' where he says that he will soon publish 'the most independent' book, but also at many other places in the book. It is perhaps even more apparent in his letters where he refers to *Götzen-Dämmerung* as preparatory for that which was to come. Shortly before he wrote *Götzen-Dämmerung*, at the end of June 1888, he wrote that 'it is my innermost conviction that these my problems, this whole position as an "immoralist" is yet far too early, yet far too unprepared'.[217] In a draft to a letter to H. Taine, 8 December 1888, he writes that *Götzen-Dämmerung* 'is perhaps the most radical book that has so far been written – and in regard to that which it *prepares*, almost a piece of fate' (Nietzsche's emphasis). When he a couple of weeks later, in a letter to his publisher, discusses his plans to have *Götzen-Dämmerung* translated into French, he refers to *Götzen-Dämmerung* as: 'it is short and in the highest degree preparatory'.[218] What it prepares the readers for is the planned *Umwerthung aller Werthe*, which first volume he had then completed.

8. The themes, arguments and questions which Nietzsche brings up in *Götzen-Dämmerung* did not pre-empt or exhaust these themes and questions (and much less the whole of that *Hauptwerk*) – we are here only given examples or excerpts in a 'nut-shell' version[219] to tempt and prepare us for a future more thorough discussion. That this was the case can be 'confirmed' by examining the critique of Christianity in *Götzen-Dämmerung* and comparing it with that of the first volume of the *Umwerthung aller Werthe*, *Der Antichrist*, as is done in Chapter 9. Expressed differently, the fact that Nietzsche had criticized Christianity and religion severely in *Götzen-Dämmerung* did not prevent him from writing the more extensive, focused, systematic and elaborate critique of it in *Der Antichrist*.

9. It follows that *Götzen-Dämmerung* can be used to say something about the planned contents of the *Umwerthung aller Werthe* – as we have done throughout this study. However, a detailed discussion of the planned contents of the *Hauptwerk* requires a much more thorough examination of Nietzsche's late notes than is possible in this study. Such work would also inherently be significantly more speculative than our discussion here based on the contents of the published *Götzen-Dämmerung*. We have to limit ourselves in this study to preliminary results and to pointing at the more obvious conclusions as to the planned contents of the three further volumes of the *Umwerthung aller Werthe*.

In short, *Götzen-Dämmerung* can be regarded as a partial 'summary' not of Nietzsche's late books but forward-looking, of his work on the critical volumes of his *Hauptwerk*. However, it is better described as consisting of excerpts or extracts or a selection of topics from his work on the *Umwerthung aller Werthe* (which only in part coincides with what he had written in his later books). As such, it gives us an immensely important partial overview of Nietzsche's last philosophical position – but, as can be seen from his notes and from brief allusions in the text, he also left much out of it – including much of that which was most important to him (including most of his affirmative philosophy) since he expected to present that in the near future.

6

What is not included in *Twilight of the Idols*

Or what is it a 'summary' of?

6.1	Introduction	125
6.2	Can *Götzen-Dämmerung* be regarded as a summary of Nietzsche's late books?	125
6.3	Does *Götzen-Dämmerung* contain anything new?	128
6.4	Can *Götzen-Dämmerung* be regarded as containing extracts of or excerpts from the planned *Hauptwerk*?	129
6.5	Do the contents of *Götzen-Dämmerung* pre-empt or exhaust the contents of the *Hauptwerk*?	130
6.6	What is not included in *Götzen-Dämmerung*? – Nietzsche's own philosophemes	133
6.7	The affirmative contents of *Götzen-Dämmerung*	140

6.1 Introduction

In this chapter we will examine and discuss five important questions about the nature of *Götzen-Dämmerung*, each constituting a section of this chapter, questions that mostly cannot easily be answered by a simple yes or no. Often we will have to be satisfied by tendencies or vague answers rather than definite ones, but for several of the questions, the answers are fairly definite. At the end of the chapter we will examine the somewhat hidden affirmative contents of *Götzen-Dämmerung*.

6.2 Can *Götzen-Dämmerung* be regarded as a summary of Nietzsche's late books?

The standard view of *Götzen-Dämmerung*, as we saw in Chapter 2, is that it constitutes a sort of summary (or failed summary) of Nietzsche's philosophy. That it constitutes a summary is supported in part by Nietzsche himself who seems to say or suggest so in a number of letters. However, this description is rather vague and problematic. Most commentators here take 'Nietzsche's philosophy' to mean 'the late Nietzsche's philosophy', but I have found no one who has specified it further. 'The late Nietzsche's philosophy' remains vague, but by implication it, for most commentators and readers, means what he published in his late books. We will in this section examine whether *Götzen-Dämmerung* can be regarded as a summary of the post-*Zarathustra* books, the last three books Nietzsche published before *Götzen-Dämmerung* – *Jenseits von Gut und Böse* (1886), *Zur Genealogie der Moral* (1887) and *Der Fall Wagner* (1888) – and which conventionally coincide with those attributed to his 'late' period.[1]

We will see that *Götzen-Dämmerung* cannot be regarded as a summary or extract of his late books. Let us examine them in reverse chronological order, thus starting with the books closest to *Götzen-Dämmerung*, beginning with *Der Fall Wagner*. We can almost immediately realize that *Götzen-Dämmerung* is very far from being a summary of *Der Fall Wagner*. Not only is Richard Wagner hardly present at all in *Götzen-Dämmerung*,[2] and discussions of music are also kept very much in the background. Nietzsche summarizes *Der Fall Wagner* at the very end of that book:

> But who would still doubt what I want – what are the *three demands* for which my wrath, my concern, my love of art has this time opened my mouth?
> *That the theater should not lord it over the arts.*
> *That the actor should not seduce those who are authentic.*
> *That music should not become an art of lying.*

None of these themes are discussed in *Götzen-Dämmerung*.

Götzen-Dämmerung can also not be regarded as a summary of *Zur Genealogie der Moral*. The overlap between the two books is minor. The themes of *Götzen-Dämmerung* are not present in *Zur Genealogie der Moral*, and more importantly, the major themes of *Zur Genealogie der Moral* are not present in *Götzen-Dämmerung*. *Zur Genealogie der Moral* consists of three essays, and according to Nietzsche's own review of *Zur Genealogie der Moral* in *Ecce homo*, 'the truth of the *first* essay is the psychology of Christianity: the birth of Christianity out of the spirit of resentment [...] essentially a counter-movement'. The title of this first essay is '"Good and Evil" and "Good and Bad"', and it explains how two value systems, original noble morality and reactive slave (or Christian) morality arose, and the dichotomy of active-reactive is pivotal in it. None of these themes are discussed in *Götzen-Dämmerung*, and the dichotomy between master and slave morality is not even mentioned once in it. The second essay is called '"Guilt", "Bad Conscience" and Related Matters', and is described by Nietzsche as giving 'the psychology of *conscience*' as the result of an instinct of cruelty turned back on itself. Guilt and conscience are mentioned a few times in *Götzen-Dämmerung*, but their roles are very minor, and he seems not to refer back to his dissection of them in *Zur Genealogie der Moral*. Instead he in *Götzen-Dämmerung* is forward-looking and hopes for a future without guilt,[3] and bad conscience is mentioned but not discussed. Cruelty is also mentioned (twice) in *Götzen-Dämmerung*, but in an altogether different context. The third essay deals with 'ascetic ideals', which is a term and concept which does not even once occur in *Götzen-Dämmerung*. We can thus conclude that *Götzen-Dämmerung* does not contain a summary of *Zur Genealogie der Moral*. This is obviously *not* because Nietzsche had changed his mind and no longer held to what he wrote the previous year (as can, for example, be seen in *Ecce homo* where he describes the three essays as 'three *preliminary* works of a psychologist towards a revaluation of all values').

The case with *Jenseits von Gut und Böse* is slightly more complicated, for it is significantly longer, more wide-ranging in content and deals with many more themes.

Jenseits von Gut und Böse consists of nine major sections or chapters. With most of them there is very little or no overlap with *Götzen-Dämmerung*, but for a few of them there is some overlap. This is true for the first chapter on the prejudices of philosophers, the third on religious nature and the fifth on the natural history of morals. However, the overlap is small, and even if it was much greater, *Götzen-Dämmerung* could certainly not be regarded as a summary of three chapters of *Jenseits von Gut und Böse* – the summary would be longer than the text summarized. More importantly, the overlap, even with these three chapters is small.

In fact, if *Götzen-Dämmerung* was to be regarded as a summary of any of Nietzsche's earlier books, *Die Geburt der Tragödie* is probably the best candidate, at least for two of the chapters. The chapters 'The Problem of Socrates' and 'What I Owe to the Ancients' can to a fairly large degree be described as summaries of some of the contents of Nietzsche's first book. However, they also contain much that was not included in *Die Geburt der Tragödie* (and some of that which originally was part of the contents in *Die Geburt der Tragödie* has been significantly changed in these chapters: Socrates is now less of an isolated individual and seen more as an expression of a general decline in Greece, and the Dionysian has gone from being one important ingredient in tragedy to be almost synonymous with it). Not included in *Die Geburt der Tragödie*, but present in *Götzen-Dämmerung* is, for example, a much stronger naturalistic tendency, the use of medical language, including such concepts as decadence and degeneranz, as well as a much stronger emphasis on physiology. *Die Geburt der Tragödie* was not only almost metaphysical in character, and in it Nietzsche also emphasized the importance of music and regarded art as the essence of reality – while in *Götzen-Dämmerung* metaphysics is rejected with severe hostility and discussions of music is essentially lacking. In *Götzen-Dämmerung* it is 'reality' and daring to see and accept reality as it *is* rather than art that is most fundamental. Therefore his praise of the sophists.

The *Die Geburt der Tragödie* is perhaps not a pessimistic book, but it contains aspects of Schopenhauerian pessimism, while pessimism is one of the things Nietzsche most strongly opposes and criticizes in *Götzen-Dämmerung*.

The theme of the last half of the last chapter in *Götzen-Dämmerung* is eternal recurrence – a philosopheme that he only discovered in 1881 and which certainly was not present in *Die Geburt der Tragödie* (although he now, in 1888, retrospectively, associates it to Greek tragedy and to their mysteries). Thus, *Götzen-Dämmerung* is no summary of *Die Geburt der Tragödie*. However, the late Nietzsche was much concerned with *Die Geburt der Tragödie*, Dionysos and the ancient Greeks generally, and the presence of these two chapters represents more his present and forward-looking attitude than any will to summarize an older book.

We can thus conclude that *Götzen-Dämmerung* is *not* a summary of Nietzsche's published books (although that seems to be the view of almost all commentators).

6.3 Does *Götzen-Dämmerung* contain anything new?

Several commentators, as we saw in Chapter 2, claim that *Götzen-Dämmerung* does not contain anything new. The question whether a book contains anything new in relation to earlier works is often much more difficult to answer (i.e. to verify or falsify) than at first may appear to be the case. Does *Jenseits von Gut und Böse* contain anything new? Does *Zur Genealogie der Moral*? Does *Der Fall Wagner*? Does *Götzen-Dämmerung*? Does *Der Antichrist*? Often the difference between books is rather a question of degrees, of perspectives, of emphases and of nuances.

The question whether a book contains anything fundamentally new or not is almost impossible to answer per se. It can almost only be answered comparatively, but even then it is very difficult. Possibly it is correct to argue that *Die Geburt der Tragödie*, where everything is new since it was his first book, and *Die fröhliche Wissenschaft* and *Also sprach Zarathustra*, in which he introduces a number of philosophemes such as the death of God, eternal recurrence, *Übermensch, amor fati* and so on contain unusually many new ideas. But almost as obvious is that *Human, All Too Human* also contains much that is new (and many of the themes that are new in *Die fröhliche Wissenschaft* and *Also sprach Zarathustra* have their origin earlier).

However, being aware that the answer is much more difficult and vague than the question seems to imply, I believe that the question of this section must be answered in the affirmative. The most obvious first step to realize this is what we have seen earlier – that it is very far from being a summary of his last books, *Jenseits von Gut und Böse*, *Zur Genealogie der Moral* and *Der Fall Wagner* – that it is far from presenting the same contents as can be found in them. Nor is it a summary of his earlier books.

A second step may be to realize that there is a new tone of and emphasis on being concise, on naturalism, on medical language and on a sense of urgency in *Götzen-Dämmerung*. Many commentators may not like some of these new tones and the resulting new emphases, but that does not change the fact that they are present. From this follows an increased intensity in his critique of Christianity, morality, the Germans, traditional philosophy, modernity and many other themes which Nietzsche dismisses as signs of decadence.

Perhaps the most obvious theme which is new in *Götzen-Dämmerung* is the strong emphasis on realism and accepting reality as it is. In fact, the most obvious common denominator of what Nietzsche affirms in all chapters is an affirmation of reality, and that what he criticizes is different versions of a denial of reality, including metaphysics, idealism, religion and morality. This emphasis of reality is not completely absent in his earlier books, but it is there a more minor theme, often shadowed by a stronger emphasis on the importance of art and creating, even as creating our view of reality. This is also confirmed when we study the occurrence of the word 'real' and different variants of it in *Götzen-Dämmerung* and earlier books. It is rarely used before *Götzen-Dämmerung* (and then often in a different sense) but is common in it and the use of it increases still further in the works after it.

Götzen-Dämmerung also contains a large number of more specific themes which are new or partially new: the appraisal of the sophists,[4] viewing morality as a symptom, the explicit claim of the possibility of 'natural' or healthy morality, several of the 'four great errors' (the first three) are new (the fourth, of free will, he had discussed extensively before), the emphasis on 'improvers' of mankind (and the related discussion of, and comparison with the Laws of Manu), the strong emphasis of sense-perceptions, and therefore also his emphasis on the nose, that the value of life cannot be estimated, the emphasis of sublimation and *Vergeistigung* ('spiritualization', especially in relation to morality), the praise of Roman style, his philosopheme of the innocence of becoming, and the tying his concept of eternal recurrence to Greek thought. One could go on for quite some time. To me, it seems obviously false to claim, as many commentators have done, that *Götzen-Dämmerung* does not contain anything new.

6.4 Can *Götzen-Dämmerung* be regarded as containing extracts of or excerpts from the planned *Hauptwerk*?

This too is not an altogether uncomplicated question to answer – but the simple answer is undoubtedly yes – as we have already seen in Chapters 3 and 5 earlier, and as can be seen when one studies the origin of the texts of *Götzen-Dämmerung*. Much of the material for the book is taken from notes obviously intended for the *Hauptwerk*,[5] and this is especially noticeable in that some of the early chapters in *Götzen-Dämmerung* almost completely coincide with the intended contents of chapters of that work (as can be seen in the preliminary lists of chapters for the four volumes, see Table 3.2 where some of these drafts of chapter titles are summarized).

However, there are several complications.

1. This is not equally true for all parts of *Götzen-Dämmerung*, but is most true for the first half.
2. The *Hauptwerk* was a continually evolving project, and thus the most reasonable approach is not to select only one draft of it and compare the contents of *Götzen-Dämmerung* to this, but to realize the great similarity of the many versions of this project, and thus to refer to it over an extended period of time.[6] If this is done, one is left with a fairly large number of notes – and sometimes it is difficult to know whether specific notes should be regarded as working material for this project or not. Nonetheless, it is clear that a large proportion of the contents in *Götzen-Dämmerung* is taken from this material.

However, *Götzen-Dämmerung* cannot be regarded as a summary of the planned *Umwerthung aller Werthe*. The planned contents of book 4 seem not dealt with in *Götzen-Dämmerung* at all, and also much of the planned contents of books 2 and 3 are not mentioned in *Götzen-Dämmerung*. Although there is a fair amount of overlap between Nietzsche's critique of Christianity in *Götzen-Dämmerung* and *Der Antichrist* (as we will discuss in Chapter 9), *Götzen-Dämmerung* cannot be regarded as a summary of that work. As we concluded in the previous chapter, it is better regarded as consisting of extracts of work on the *Umwerthung aller Werthe*.

6.5 Do the contents of *Götzen-Dämmerung* pre-empt or exhaust the contents of the *Hauptwerk*?

Most commentators – following Mazzini Montinari (as discussed in Section 2.2) – assume that Nietzsche gave up on writing a *Hauptwerk* in November 1888. Although rarely explicitly stated they seem to assume that Nietzsche with *Götzen-Dämmerung* (and perhaps also with *Der Antichrist*) had said all he wanted or could.[7] They thus assume that *Götzen-Dämmerung* (possibly together with other works) pre-empts and exhausts the contents planned for several years of the four volumes of the *Umwerthung aller Werthe*.

The main argument for this is that he used notes written for it while writing *Götzen-Dämmerung* and that no *Hauptwerk* (in four volumes) was ever written.

As I have argued earlier, I do not agree with the view that Nietzsche gave up on writing the *Hauptwerk*. If he did give up on writing the *Hauptwerk*, not only was it *after* the writing of *Götzen-Dämmerung*, as well as *after* having finished *Der Antichrist* and also after the writing of his last book, *Ecce homo*. For this study, which examines the relation between *Götzen-Dämmerung* and the planned *Hauptwerk*, *it hardly matters since it could not affect his intentions while writing and revising Götzen-Dämmerung* if he changed his mind about the *Hauptwerk* in late November, in December or not at all. Anyway, as late as 18 December 1888 (just two weeks before his mental collapse) he still referred to *Der Antichrist* as 'the first volume of *Revaluation of All Values*'.[8] Only the last days before his collapse, when under the influence of the immanent mental breakdown, did he strike out 'the first book of' on the title page of *Der Antichrist* and in a reference to the work in *Ecce homo*. But even this does not necessarily mean that he had changed his mind about the *Hauptwerk*. The new title simply avoids stating how many volumes or books, or in which order they will come. It would be perfectly consistent with this title if Nietzsche later produced further works entitled, for example, *Der freie Geist: Umwerthung aller Werthe* and *Der Immoralist: Umwerthung aller Werthe*.

There are three possible ways to answer the question if Nietzsche with *Götzen-Dämmerung* had exhausted or pre-empted the contents of the planned *Hauptwerk*.

1. To examine Nietzsche's late notes thoroughly and compare them with the contents of *Götzen-Dämmerung*. This is a 'possible' but very difficult task that goes beyond the scope of this book, even if we have and will discuss many aspects of it.
2. A more direct way is to examine the relation between *Götzen-Dämmerung* and the first volume of the *Hauptwerk*, which Nietzsche actually wrote, *Der Antichrist*. This will be done in detail in Chapter 9, but we can already here note that although *Götzen-Dämmerung* contains fairly much and very severe critique of Christianity, this did not prevent him from writing *Der Antichrist* – with the obvious conclusion that at least Nietzsche did not regard *Götzen-Dämmerung* as pre-empting or exhausting the critique of Christianity he wanted to present as *Der Antichrist*, the first volume of his *Hauptwerk*.

3. An even more direct way to examine if Nietzsche regarded *Götzen-Dämmerung* as exhausting the material for the *Umwerthung aller Werthe* is to examine his late plans for this work in his notebooks. There are almost no extant notes from Nietzsche's last two months before the collapse, November and December 1888, but in late September and October – that is, including after he sent the cleanly written manuscript of *Der Antichrist* to his publisher – Nietzsche makes several drafts of the planned continued contents (of volumes 2–4) of the *Umwerthung aller Werthe*, which thus clearly indicates that he did not see the project as pre-empted by either *Götzen-Dämmerung* or *Der Antichrist*.

Other indications – apart from the explicit statements in the foreword and at the very end of the long chapter – that Nietzsche had not regarded, and did not regard, himself as having pre-empted the planned work on the *Umwerthung aller Werthe* are expressions in *Götzen-Dämmerung* such as '*first* example of my "revaluation of all values"' and 'A first example, merely as an introduction' ('The "Improvers" of Mankind', 2), and that which was meant to follow up on this does not come in *Götzen-Dämmerung*, but surely refers to what he planned was coming in the *Der Immoralist* (the third book of *Umwerthung aller Werthe*). Furthermore, all the chapters in *Götzen-Dämmerung* are very short, not much more than five to six pages each, while Nietzsche, when planning his *Hauptwerk*, seems to have intended the chapters to be thirty-five to thirty-seven pages each.[9] Several of the planned chapters (à thirty-five to thirty-seven pages) listed in this note deal not with the contents of whole chapters in *Götzen-Dämmerung*, but only with parts of them: '1) Verwechslung von Ursache und Wirkung' (confusing cause and effect) which corresponds only to the first one or two sections of the chapter 'The Four Great Errors' in *Götzen-Dämmerung*, and '3) Verwechslung des Bewusstseins mit der Ursächlichkeit' (confusing conscious thought with causality), which corresponds to only section 3 of the same chapter in *Götzen-Dämmerung*.

That Nietzsche had nothing against first writing a very condensed text (which he often called aphorism) and thereafter expounding on it, we can see in the third essay of *Zur Genealogie der Moral* (1887), for in the preface, section 8, he states: 'In the third essay of this book I have offered a model for what I mean by 'interpretation' in such a case – the essay opens with an aphorism [i.e. section 1, about one page] and is itself a commentary upon it [in sections 2–28].' It is not altogether unlikely that this was also the approach he intended to use for, at least, parts of *Götzen-Dämmerung*. First he presents themes briefly in *Götzen-Dämmerung*, then expounds and interprets them further in the *Umwerthung aller Werthe*. Basically, that is what we see about the relation between *Götzen-Dämmerung* and the first book of the *Umwerthung aller Werthe*, that is, *Der Antichrist*.

What we are left to examine here is what of Nietzsche's late notes and especially his plans for the *Hauptwerk* did he not include in *Götzen-Dämmerung*. One way to see this is as an examination of whether *Götzen-Dämmerung* can be regarded as having pre-empted or used up most of the relevant content of that *Hauptwerk*, and therefore perhaps explain the fact that it was never finished. That this was not the case is easily seen by comparing *Götzen-Dämmerung* to a detailed table of contents for his *Hauptwerk* from the time when he was in the middle of working on *Götzen-*

Dämmerung and a list of the four books constituting it, from *after* he had finished *Götzen-Dämmerung*.

<table>
<tr><td>

KSA 13, 18[17] Last reference to the *Hauptwerk* as *Will to Power*. Dated to 26 Augusti 1888.
[The chapter titles below have been translated in table 3.2 above.]

Entwurf des
Plans zu:
der Wille zur Macht.
Versuch
einer Umwerthung aller Werthe.
— Sils Maria
am letzten Sonntag des
Monat August 1888

Wir Hyperboreer. — *Grundsteinlegung des Problems*.

Erstes Buch: *„was ist Wahrheit?"*
Erstes Capitel. Psychologie des Irrthums.
Zweites Capitel. Werth von Wahrheit und Irrthum.
Drittes Capitel. Der Wille zur Wahrheit (erst gerechtfertigt im Ja-Werth des Lebens

Zweites Buch: *Herkunft der Werthe*.
Erstes Capitel. Die Metaphysiker.
Zweites Capitel. Die homines religiosi.
Drittes Capitel. Die Guten und die Verbesserer.

Drittes Buch: *Kampf der Werthe*
Erstes Capitel. Gedanken über das Christenthum.
Zweites Capitel. Zur Physiologie der Kunst.
Drittes Capitel. Zur Geschichte des europäischen Nihilismus.

Psychologen-Kurzweil.

Viertes Buch: *Der grosse Mittag*.
Erstes Capitel. Das Princip des Lebens „Rangordnung".
Zweites Capitel. Die zwei Wege.
Drittes Capitel. Die ewige Wiederkunft.

</td><td>

KSA 13, 19[8], September 1888
Written after Nietzsche had finished both *Götzen-Dämmerung* and *Der Antichrist*

Umwerthung aller Werthe.

Erstes Buch.
Der Antichrist.   Versuch einer Kritik des Christenthums.

Zweites Buch.
Der freie Geist.   Kritik der Philosophie als einer nihilistischen Bewegung.

Drittes Buch.
Der Immoralist.   Kritik der verhängnissvollsten Art von Unwissenheit, der Moral.

Viertes Buch.
Dionysos.   Philosophie der ewigen Wiederkunft.

</td></tr>
</table>

One can almost immediately see that what is important here is not so much *Götzen-Dämmerung* as the fact that Nietzsche sometime after 26 August decided to put all of his critique of Christianity (which previously had been distributed throughout the whole work) into the first book, *Der Antichrist*, and therefore he had to rearrange the contents of the rest of the work (except for the fourth book which probably could remain relatively unchanged). The second plan of the *Hauptwerk*, listed earlier, KSA 13, 19[8], shows, before all else, that Nietzsche intended and planned to work on his *Hauptwerk* also after he had written *Götzen-Dämmerung*, as well as *Der Antichrist*, and this is further confirmed by a few other later notes. Nietzsche worked on *Götzen-Dämmerung* from mid-August until 7 September 1888, when he sent a clean-written copy to his publisher, so the more detailed table of contents, listed earlier, was written down almost exactly in the middle of the time he worked on *Götzen-Dämmerung*, and there are good reasons to estimate that he at that time had written most or all of the first half of the book. If we ignore the fourth book, which seems, at least explicitly, almost completely absent in *Götzen-Dämmerung* and *Der Antichrist* (again showing that Nietzsche obviously intended to write further works after these two books), the first plan listed earlier consists of three books and nine chapters, three chapters per book. These chapters are thus much longer than the short *Götzen-Dämmerung*-chapters. Of these, two chapters, 'The homines religiosi', II.2, and 'Thoughts about Christianity', III.1 (and probably part of the planned contents of some of the others), were shortly thereafter redirected to constitute *Der Antichrist*.

We can further see that the value of 'truth and error', and 'the will to truth' were meant to be perhaps the most prominent theme of the first book in the first listing, but then, after *Der Antichrist* was written as the first book, moved to the second book, *The Free Spirit*, of the *Umwerthung aller Werthe*. However, these themes are almost completely absent in *Götzen-Dämmerung*.

Judging from the chapter titles, two, three or four chapters seem to overlap with, or be planned expansions of themes dealt with in *Götzen-Dämmerung*: 'The Psychology of Error', I.1, 'The Metaphysicians', II.1, 'The Good and the Improvers', II.3, and maybe 'Towards a Physiology of Art', III.2. (Although Nietzsche mentions 'physiology of art' in *Götzen-Dämmerung*, and it plays a part in six sections in 'Expeditions' it is not systematically treated and not given a treatise-like chapter, so I suspect that Nietzsche felt he had much more to say about it – for he had publically promised to address this field in his coming *Hauptwerk* in both *Zur Genealogie der Moral* and *Der Fall Wagner* – the unsystematic comments about it in *Götzen-Dämmerung* are probably not a treatment of it, but merely pointers to a future treatment.) The other chapters in the table of contents earlier seem to have no or little overlap with the contents of *Götzen-Dämmerung*.

Another theme one could expect a summary of Nietzsche's late philosophy and the planned *Umwerthung aller Werthe* would discuss and treat is that of the importance of the herd and the herd-instinct in Nietzsche's analysis of ethics. Nietzsche had mentioned it in *Zur Genealogie der Moral* and clearly intended to discuss it in his *Hauptwerk*,[10] but it is not treated at all in *Götzen-Dämmerung* (only briefly mentioned once, in 'Expeditions', 38), and thus the book in no way exhausts the plans for the *Hauptwerk* in this respect. In a letter to Franz Overbeck, 4 January 1888, Nietzsche discusses his *Zur Genealogie der Moral*, where each of the three treatises isolates one single genealogical theme, as he says, but

> a fourth, a fifth and even the most important ('the herd instinct') are missing – these had to be set aside for a time, as too broad, as well as the final putting together all different elements and thus a sort of *settlement of accounts with morality*. Therefore we are [with *Zur Genealogie der Moral*] still in the 'prelude' to my philosophy.[11]

This is clearly things he intended to do in the third book of the *Umwerthung aller Werthe* dealing with ethics, *The Immoralist*.

6.6 What is not included in *Götzen-Dämmerung*? – Nietzsche's own philosophemes

If it is difficult to answer whether a book contains anything new, it is near impossible to answer what is *not* included in it in any relevant manner. Thus the question must be seen in a somewhat more limited sense – what is not included of what we could expect it to contain if it was to be a summary of his (late) philosophy? This can be divided into three partly overlapping questions: we could expect it to contain themes discussed in his late books (but we have already seen that all in all that is not the case), parts of the planned contents of the *Hauptwerk* (and we have seen earlier that that seems to be the case) and finally Nietzsche's own affirmative philosophy (which we will examine in Section 6.7).

The perhaps most surprising aspect of *Götzen-Dämmerung* – assuming that it in any sense is true that it contains a summary of Nietzsche's philosophy – is the absence of a number of philosophemes that most readers of Nietzsche would expect to be present in any summary – such as the idea of eternal recurrence, will to power, the *Übermensch*, nihilism, the revaluation of all values and so on.

Nietzsche had discussed most of these themes previously, especially in *Also sprach Zarathustra*, and from his late notes it is obvious that he intended further discussions and elaborations of them (with the possible exception of the *Übermensch*). Let us summarize what he says about these five major Nietzschean themes (all of them usually emphasized in every general account of Nietzsche's philosophy).

Will to power

The concept of the will to power is an explanatory one – everything wants to expand and to 'control' its surroundings. Nietzsche used it mainly for human psychology but sometimes applied it to all life and perhaps even to inorganic matter. An important aspect of Nietzsche's view of psychology is thus his belief that the will to power is the most fundamental of all drives, motives or desires in all living beings.

> All psychology has hitherto remained anchored to moral prejudices and timidities: it has not ventured into the depths. To conceive it as morphology and the *development-theory of the will to power*, as I conceive it – has never yet so much as entered the mind of anyone else.[12]

Nietzsche proposes the will to power in opposition to 'the will to life' or the Platonic eros or to more partial wills like the will to truth.[13] The desired state is the feeling of increased power.[14] This power includes power over others as well as over oneself, but also more sublimated forms, such as the power to interpret one's surroundings: 'it will have to be the will to power incarnate, it will want to grow, expand, draw to itself, gain ascendancy – not out of any morality or immorality, but because it *lives*, and because life *is* will to power.'[15] Will to power is for Nietzsche a motive force, not a criterion of the value of an action or feeling. Will to power lies behind all actions and feelings, good ones (e.g. exuberance) as well as bad ones (e.g. resentment).

Nietzsche first publicly presented the will to power in the chapter 'Of Self-Overcoming' in the second book of *Thus Spoke Zarathustra* (1883), (but he had 'discovered' it long before then), and he treats it fairly frequently in *Jenseits von Gut und Böse* (1886).

In *Götzen-Dämmerung* Nietzsche only refers to will to power on four occasions – and at no time does he strongly emphasize this concept or idea.[16] In fact, in none of these does he refer to will to power as philosopheme, as an important philosophical concept, the way he had done in earlier books, and seems to do again in *Der Antichrist*.[17] Some commentators have even argued that Nietzsche gave up on will to power, but that is clearly not the case. The expression is after all present in *Götzen-Dämmerung*, although not emphasized. Furthermore, it is more strongly present and emphasized in *Der Antichrist* and *Ecce homo*, written after *Götzen-Dämmerung*, as well as being very present in many notes from 1888. It seems very likely that Nietzsche had intended to discuss it further in his *Hauptwerk*, which for a long time even was named after this philosopheme, as *The Will to Power: Attempt at a Revaluation of All Values*. Its limited presence in *Götzen-Dämmerung* is likely to be due to that the book is not a summary of Nietzsche's philosophy but consists of extracts of his philosophy, and the selected excerpts happen not to contain discussions of this theme.

Revaluation of values

The word 'revaluation' which is related both to the title of his *Hauptwerk* and to a philosophical project concerning values occurs four times in *Götzen-Dämmerung* (in three separate paragraphs or sections), twice in the foreword with reference to the planned *Hauptwerk* with the title *Umwerthung aller Werthe* (as well as to the philosophical project of actually revaluating values). Nietzsche is here strongly emphasizing the importance of the *Umwerthung aller Werthe* as his major philosophical project. In the foreword to *Götzen-Dämmerung* he actually states that he is working on a much more important project, *Götzen-Dämmerung* is really only the result of a relaxation from that work, and, at the end of the foreword, he states that he has just finished the first volume of that work!

In the actual text of *Götzen-Dämmerung* he does not explicitly say much about either the *Umwerthung aller Werthe* or about revaluating values. However, the word occurs twice, when he gives two different examples of his own revaluations – one specific but fundamental one and the other a broad general one.

'In my mouth this formula ["The most general formula at the basis of every religion and morality is: 'Do this and this, refrain from this and this – and you will be happy! Otherwise . . ."] is converted into its reverse – *first* example of my "revaluation of all values": a well-constituted human being, a "happy one", *must* perform certain actions and instinctively shrinks from other actions' (GD, 'The Four Great Errors', 2).

In the last sentence of the book, in the chapter 'What I Owe to the Ancients', 5, he states: 'the *The Birth of Tragedy* was my first revaluation of all values'.

The second statement is not very clear, but I take it to mean that, at least in some sense, Nietzsche says that already in his first book, *Die Geburt der Tragödie* (1872), he had proclaimed that pre-Classical, Dionysian or 'tragic' values are of higher value than classical (Platonic), Christian and modern values. The first of these statements in *Götzen-Dämmerung*, where he says: '*first* example of my "revaluation of all values"' surely means that he intends to give further examples, which even the title of his planned *Hauptwerk* promises: *Umwerthung aller Werthe*.

The *Übermensch*

For many readers of Nietzsche the *Übermensch* is probably Nietzsche's most famous philosopheme, and it is surprisingly absent in *Götzen-Dämmerung*. The word occurs once, but then not directly Nietzsche's own view of it but with reference to what one or several reviewers had said about it:

> *Whether we have grown more moral.* [. . .] Above all, I was invited to reflect on the 'undeniable superiority' of our age in moral judgement, our real *advance* in this respect: compared with *us*, a Cesare Borgia was certainly not to be set up as a 'higher man', as a kind of *superman*, in the way I set him up. ('Expeditions', 37)

Nietzsche scholars know that Nietzsche almost only used the term *Übermensch* in *Also sprach Zarathustra* (and in notes from that time) and then as a metaphor. Quite what the poetic concept of *Übermensch* is a metaphor of there is no full consensus, but most, including myself, argue that it is for the higher human being, the 'lucky exceptions' (as he says in *Der Antichrist*), the one who can affirm reality and life even to the extent of affirming eternal recurrence. Even in this expanded meaning of *Übermensch*, the higher human being seems not particularly present in *Götzen-Dämmerung* (at least not as a philosopheme). However, the idea is not completely absent but present not as a philosopheme but in the form of *exempla*, references to human beings to emulate, but also others used as negative examples.

Nietzsche's description of Goethe at the end of the long chapter (which originally was to have ended the book) is surely a description of what Nietzsche regarded as an ideal character and attitude to life – and it seems close to how he describes the *Übermensch* much more poetically in *Also sprach Zarathustra* (see Section 5.6, where much of this is quoted). Likewise, *Götzen-Dämmerung* is filled with negative examples, such as Kant, Socrates and Plato.

Nietzsche hardly ever refers to the concept of *Übermensch* in his late notes, including in the working notes for the *Umwerthung aller Werthe*. My conclusion from this is that Nietzsche had given up, or rather stopped using, the metaphor *Übermensch*, but *not* the underlying view or concept of higher forms of human life – relating to a person's ability to affirm reality and life. In Table 3.2 we can see that Nietzsche during 1888 planned chapters discussing higher human beings, such as 'The Type of the Law-Giver', 'The principle of life: "Order of rank"' and 'The Two Ways'.

Nihilism

The late Nietzsche was profoundly involved with the problem of nihilism. Although he sometimes discussed the concept in his published writings, from *Beyond Good and Evil* onwards,[18] there is much more on this theme in his notebooks than in his published works, and he clearly intended to publish more on it.[19]

Nietzsche's first reference to nihilism dates from the summer of 1880 and was a direct response to his reading of Turgenev's *Fathers and Sons*, in a French translation with a preface by Mérimée, which – like the text of the book itself – discusses the concept of nihilism.[20] Nietzsche later made only a few rare references to nihilism until 1884, when he began to use the term more frequently, and then even more so from 1886 onwards.

Surprisingly, the word 'nihilism' is not mentioned at all in *Götzen-Dämmerung*, but the word 'nihilist' is used four times: in aphorism 34 (about Flaubert) in the first chapter, and in sections 21, 32 and 50 in the long 'Expedition' chapter.

The first and fourth of these, at least on a first reading, say relatively little about Nietzsche's concept and use of nihilism. In the first of these he accuses Flaubert of being a nihilist, since he thinks ideas can be won by sitting (i.e. by pure abstract thought) rather than by walking (activity, actual lived life). In the fourth one, he claims that the nineteenth century is resulting in a nihilistic sigh, in a not knowing which way to turn. In the second one, he states what he often claims also at other times, that the Christian approach is a nihilistic one (21). The whole of section 32 is a critique of all human ideals, and as such can be interpreted as dealing with nihilism, but the explicit statement there is somewhat less general.

We can conclude that the problem of nihilism is central to Nietzsche, but that he does not directly address it in *Götzen-Dämmerung*. He planned to do that in the coming *Hauptwerk*.

Of special interest concerning nihilism and its place in *Götzen-Dämmerung* and the *Hauptwerk* is the essay: '*European Nihilism*',[21] now found in Nietzsche's notebooks, but planned to constitute part of the third chapter of the third book (in the last extensive table of contents of his *Hauptwerk*) and later probably as part of the second book (which he sometimes changed into being the third book).

Assuming that *Götzen-Dämmerung* (at least the first half of it) consists of excerpts from Nietzsche's notes for his *Hauptwerk* – there is one such text one perhaps would have expected Nietzsche to include before all else – and that is the text he wrote in June 1887 at Lenzer Heide entitled '*European Nihilism*' in sixteen short sections, and which summarizes much of his thought about nihilism.

It is impossible to be certain as to why Nietzsche did not include a particular text in *Götzen-Dämmerung* – in this case the '*European Nihilism*' text – but it is possible to present a reasonable explanation for it. Had '*European Nihilism*' been included in *Götzen-Dämmerung* – perhaps before or after the 'Socrates' or before the 'Fable' chapter, or just before 'What the Germans Lack', for it suits very well as such a chapter, both in structure and in length – it would surely have attracted much attention. It has received much attention even as it is – 'hidden' in his notebooks and not even fully reproduced in Elisabeth's and Peter Gast's *Der Wille zur Macht* (there it was split up in parts and published at three different places).[22] The text is since the late 1970s found in KSA 12, 5[71] – but that 'standard version' contains not only an important misreading (and sixteen other more minor ones)[23] but its place in the KSA is also highly misleading. Today, the best text is that published in KGW IX.3, where the whole notebook is reproduced in facsimile and diplomatic form, and this text is on pages 13–24 of the notebook. In KSA 12 it is placed as the 71st note of notebook N VII 3, and followed by further notes until the last, 110th, one – implying that it is somewhere in the middle of the notebook.[24] In reality, the text seems to have been *cleanly* written on separate pages at the end of the notebook (actually at the beginning, since Nietzsche almost always wrote in his notebooks, as in this case, from back to front).[25] As is shown in a draft for his *Hauptwerk* from this time, the summer of 1887, KSA 12, 5[75], this essay was clearly meant to constitute part of that work or at least be closely associated with it:

> *Der Wille zur Macht.*
> Versuch einer Umwerthung aller Werthe.
>
> 1.
> Vom Werth der Wahrheit.
> 2.
> Was daraus folgt.
> 3.
> Zur Geschichte des europäischen Nihilismus.
> 4.
> Die ewige Wiederkunft.[26]

That Nietzsche intended to include the essay 'European Nihilism' in his *Hauptwerk* is explicitly and publicly promised at the very end of *Zur Genealogie der Moral* where he explicitly points forward and refers to his future intention: 'I shall probe these things [the ascetic ideal] more thoroughly and severely in another connection (under the title "On the History of European Nihilism"; it will be contained in a work in progress: *The Will to Power: Attempt at a Revaluation of All Values*)'.[27]

However, the third planned book or volume (in the table of contents quoted earlier) entitled 'On a History of European Nihilism'[28] is almost certainly not equivalent to 'European Nihilism' as one at first can believe, but a planned expansion of it. The first third of the essay, sections 1–5, seems to correspond to or constitute a summary draft for a history of European nihilism. This is setting up the problem. Thereafter, the essay changes nature – begins to address a possible solution – by introducing the idea of eternal recurrence, 'the most extreme form of nihilism'. There are, Nietzsche claims, two possible attitudes towards such extreme nihilism (the idea of eternal recurrence) – either with dejection or with affirmation (sections 6–8). There are correspondingly two sorts of people: active and reactive, masters and slaves, commanders and obeyers. The latter will be dejected and seek self-destruction (9–14). But what about those 'richest in health', he asks, and the text ends with the rhetorical question: 'what would such a man think of eternal recurrence?' (15–16).[29]

Thus, most of the essay, especially the latter part, concerns the idea of eternal recurrence – and thus belongs more to volume 4 of the *Umwerthung aller Werthe* than to the earlier volumes. It seems to me that Nietzsche could not include this essay in *Götzen-Dämmerung* without saying more about eternal recurrence – and from the actual text of the *Götzen-Dämmerung*, this seems not to have been Nietzsche's intention. In *Götzen-Dämmerung*, eternal recurrence is only explicitly mentioned twice, at the end of the last chapter, including in the very last sentence, obviously pointing forward to the *Umwerthung aller Werthe*, especially to its fourth and final volume. And even these references, as pointers of what was to come, were added more than a month after the rest of the book was completed. We can also note that both in the note of a table of contents, 5[75], quoted earlier, and 18[17], also quoted earlier, this book or chapter, respectively, is placed just before the fourth book, which was meant to deal with eternal recurrence, so that it becomes a pointer to, or leads on to the fourth book.

That was thus not a suitable use for *Götzen-Dämmerung* (which does not discuss eternal recurrence) and thus it is my hypothesis that he could not use this text, 'European Nihilism', there, but saved it for the *Hauptwerk*.

The idea of eternal recurrence

Nietzsche 'discovered' the idea of eternal recurrence – a central theme of the mature Nietzsche's philosophy – in August 1881, and publicly first expressed it in 1882:

> *The greatest weight.* – What, if some day or night a demon were to steal after you into your loneliest loneliness and say to you: 'This life as you now live it and have lived it, you will have to live once more and innumerable times more; and there will be nothing new in it, but every pain and every joy and every thought and sigh and everything unutterably small or great in your life will have to return to you, all in the same succession and sequence – even this spider and this moonlight between the trees, and even this moment and I myself. The eternal hourglass of existence is turned upside down again and again, and you with it, speck of dust!'
>
> Would you not throw yourself down and gnash your teeth and curse the demon who spoke thus? Or have you once experienced a tremendous moment when you would have answered him: 'You are a god and never have I heard anything more divine.' If this thought gained possession of you, it would change you as you are or perhaps crush you. The question in each and every thing, 'Do you desire this once more and innumerable times more?' would lie upon your actions as the greatest weight. Or how well disposed would you have to become to yourself and to life *to crave nothing more fervently* than this ultimate eternal confirmation and seal?[30]

The meaning of Nietzsche's idea of eternal recurrence can be summarized as the hypothesis that the world process is cyclical and that we therefore will re-live our lives an infinite number of times in identically the same way. We would not be aware of this (and certainly not remember it), but philosophically and theologically it would mean the complete rejection of every external sense of purpose, of *telos*, of the universe and of human life having a final goal. The idea of eternal recurrence is thus a form of extreme nihilism, which only can be overcome by affirming the present life, not its *telos*. Nietzsche's primary use of this idea seems to be as an existential question – do you affirm reality and life sufficiently to be willing, even desiring to live life again and again in exactly the same way.

I have argued in Section 5.2 that Nietzsche in fact uses eternal recurrence throughout *Götzen-Dämmerung*, that he in it philosophizes from the perspective of eternal recurrence – philosophizes with the hammer (eternal recurrence) – i.e. from the perspective of testing whether the different things he discusses make us reject or affirm reality and life. However, explicitly, there was no reference to eternal recurrence at all in the book until he at a late stage of the proofreading, in the second half of October, added the last chapter 'What I Owe to the Ancients', which contains two important references to it. First: '*Eternal* life, the eternal recurrence of life; the future promised and consecrated in the past; the triumphant Yes to life beyond death and change; *true* life as collective continuation of life through procreation, through the mysteries of sexuality' (section 4), and the second of them exclusively as a pointer: 'I, the last disciple of the philosopher Dionysus – I, the teacher of the eternal recurrence ...' (section 5) – but these references say almost nothing about what eternal recurrence means or has for consequences. That was to be explained and elaborated on in his soon-to-be-published *Hauptwerk*. We know this for this is the most consistent theme (although almost never elaborated upon) in his notes for a *Hauptwerk*, ever since 1884 (see the discussion in the next chapter).

We have thus seen that these five major philosophemes of the late Nietzsche's thought, although present, are not discussed explicitly or elaborated on at all in the book. However, judging from his notes, all of these (except perhaps the *Übermensch*) have prominent roles in his plans for the *Hauptwerk*.

6.7 The affirmative contents of *Götzen-Dämmerung*

Götzen-Dämmerung is primarily a critical book, and that is how Nietzsche describes it. In fact, since it has been generally understood as a summary of Nietzsche's thought and it contains much more critique than giving answers and alternatives, this has contributed to that most commentators generally have overemphasized the critical and underemphasized the affirmative aspects of Nietzsche's thought, underemphasized his solutions, alternatives and philosophemes. However, this does not mean that there is no affirmative content in the book and that Nietzsche does not sometimes hint at or allude to his own solutions.

We will in this section briefly summarize two of the fundamental affirmative contents of *Götzen-Dämmerung*, and thereafter point at five different ways to recognize much of the book's affirmative content, some of which is fairly well hidden.

Nietzsche's affirmation of reality and life

Most obvious is Nietzsche's affirmation of reality (and realism) in *Götzen-Dämmerung*, never previously so strongly emphasized. It echoes in almost every chapter (this will be further discussed and elaborated on in Chapter 8). In short, the common denominator of what Nietzsche affirms in all chapters is an affirmation of reality and what he criticizes is different versions of a denial of, or a denigration of, reality. One of the many examples of this is his comparison of Plato and Thucydides: 'Thucydides as the grand summation, the last manifestation of that strong, stern, hard matter-of-factness instinctive to the older Hellenes. *Courage* in face of reality ultimately distinguishes such natures as Thucydides and Plato: Plato is a coward in face of reality – consequently he flees into the ideal; Thucydides has *himself* under control – consequently he retains control over things ...' (GD, Ancients, 2). One way to describe the affirmative contents of *Götzen-Dämmerung* is to observe how closely related to this affirmation of reality certain assumptions (or knowledge) about the nature of reality are – such as that it is ever-changing, evolving, that everything is interconnected (fate) and so on. Nietzsche does not seem to doubt that we acquire knowledge about the world through our senses ('they never lie'). He in this regard belongs to the Epicurean and empiricist tradition, and the importance of the senses is strongly emphasized in the text. This also leads to a thoroughgoing empiricism, naturalism and positivism in regard to methods.

The other major fundamental affirmative topos in *Götzen-Dämmerung* concern healthy life, and that which belongs to it, such as instincts, the unconscious and so on, and exemplified by Goethe.

These naturalist and empiricist assumptions led to the conclusion that Nietzsche does not hesitate to claim that man is an animal, and driven by instincts, drives and the subconscious. We can (and should), and in fact almost inevitably do, sublimate these into more complex and more permanent character traits. Too little sublimation leads to that we do not fulfil our potentiality, but wrong or too much sublimation leads to rationalism, idealism and decadence (and a denial of our bodies, instincts, reality etc.). Healthy instincts and good sublimation can lead to natural morality, *Bildung* and noble culture.

Five ways to recognize other affirmative aspects of *Götzen-Dämmerung*

One way to discover the affirmative contents of *Götzen-Dämmerung* is simply to observe it as the counter-positions to that which he criticizes. This is summarized in Table A.3 in the appendix.

A second way is to discover what philosophical and cultural traditions and epochs Nietzsche affirms. The two most obvious epochs he affirms are the ancient world and the Renaissance (the revival of antiquity after the religious Middle Ages). Most important is undoubtedly the Greek ancient world (except for in questions of style and writing where the Latin Roman world has priority), but his relation to it is ambiguous. He affirms the early Greek world, but is highly critical of Socrates, Plato and Euripides. The importance of antiquity can be seen in his claim that: 'the *Birth of Tragedy* was my first revaluation of all values: with that I again plant myself in the soil out of which I draw all that I will and *can*' (GD, Ancients, 5). Even more fundamental is that many of the 'revalued' values which Nietzsche seems to approve of have close kinship with ancient values: 'I sought in history the beginning of the construction of reverse ideals (the concepts "pagan", "classical", "noble" newly discovered and expounded –)'.[31]

There are few explicit cultural and philosophical schools or traditions which Nietzsche seems to affirm in *Götzen-Dämmerung*. The three most obvious ones seem to be the closely related early Greek culture (which Nietzsche tends to refer to as tragic culture or the tragic *Weltanschauung*) and the Presocratics, as well as the somewhat later tradition of the Greek sophists.

A third way is to study the thinkers and persons whom he affirms in *Götzen-Dämmerung*. When we examine Nietzsche's evaluations and relations to the circa sixty persons he refers to by name in *Götzen-Dämmerung*, we can again confirm that the book is primarily critical, for he is critical to two-thirds of them (and many of these he returns to and mentions several times unlike almost all of the ones he affirms),[32] but he is not only critical, for almost a third of the persons he refers to he affirms. Of the circa eighteen names that he seems to affirm,[33] one stands out from all the others in the strength of affirmation and the number of times referred to – Goethe. He is by far the most obvious example of the sort of man and life Nietzsche affirms in *Götzen-Dämmerung*, but also throughout all of his writings (compare the discussion of Goethe in Section 5.6 earlier).

Among these eighteen affirmed names, the by far the largest category to which they can be classified are those nine that are primarily authors. However, all of them, with the exception of Goethe, are only referred to a single time. Several of them seem to be mentioned by Nietzsche because he regarded them as good psychologists; this is true for Dostoevsky and Stendhal, and perhaps also for Baudelaire, Emerson and Goethe.

The perhaps most surprising, and yet a prominent group, is that of 'men of action', to which Cesare Borgia, Caesar and Napoleon belong. Borgia, who is only mentioned once, and then in response to a review of one of Nietzsche's own earlier books, is probably of less importance (but he is also referred to in Nietzsche's next two books, *Der Antichrist* and *Ecce homo*), but Caesar and Napoleon are repeatedly referred to, also in other late books. However, when we examine what he says about them, we see that it is not as military men they are mentioned, but as men of genius who have affirmed and formed themselves by being active and by becoming hard, the importance of which he emphasizes in the epilogue of *Götzen-Dämmerung*.

Nietzsche mentions and discusses a fairly large number of philosophers in *Götzen-Dämmerung*, but only four of them are mentioned in a positive or affirmative vein,[34] which is the theme of this section: Hegel, Machiavelli, Emerson and Heraclitus. The result, however, of analysing statements regarding these thinkers in *Götzen-Dämmerung* is sparse. All but one of them he refers to only once, the exception being Hegel – a philosopher whom Nietzsche showed little interest in, and both of the two references to him in *Götzen-Dämmerung* are not actually Nietzsche's own but merely to the fact that Hegel traditionally is regarded as a great (i.e. influential) German philosopher. Nietzsche's references to the three remaining thinkers, Machiavelli, Emerson and Heraclitus, are brief but very positive and affirmative: Machiavelli as a realist (and perhaps as an early 'immoralist'), Heraclitus as a philosopher of struggle and change and Emerson as a healthy thinker and writer.[35] These are all important topics and themes affirmed by the late Nietzsche.

The last group among those whom Nietzsche affirm, we can briefly note, are historians (who accept the world rather than attempt to falsify it), Thucydides, Burckhardt, Sallust and Machiavelli. Nietzsche was educated as a historian, and history was immensely important to him. A historical approach and historical knowledge colours much of Nietzsche's methods, approach, manner of argument and, most importantly, what he regarded as possible alternatives to what he saw as the decadent present.[36]

It is thus primarily a few Greeks (Heraclitus, Thucydides and the sophists) and Goethe, Machiavelli and Burckhardt, and perhaps Caesar, Borgia and Napoleon, whom Nietzsche uses in *Götzen-Dämmerung* to signal or symbolize that which he affirms.

A fourth way to discover and describe the affirmative contents of *Götzen-Dämmerung* is to discuss Nietzsche's own affirmative philosophemes (philosophical topics or metaphors) in the book. However, as we have seen earlier, Nietzsche seems to avoid discussions of most of them. He, for most of them, only briefly mentions them in *Götzen-Dämmerung*, but does not elaborate on them. The most likely reason for this is that he saves such discussions of them for his *Hauptwerk*.

However, there is one philosopheme or expression which he uses for the first time in *Götzen-Dämmerung*, and that is 'the innocence of becoming', which he refers to twice.[37] It refers both to 'reality' and 'life', and he proclaims that man is a natural part of reality, that we are 'innocent' in contrast to the claims of morality and religion that we are guilty and sinners, and we are part of the flow and development of reality (in contrast to those who, like Plato, claim that everything true and valuable is static, which was still a common view in the nineteenth century). It seems likely that he was going to discuss it in book 4 of the *Umwerthung aller Werthe*, but the expression itself hardly occurs in the late notes.[38]

A fifth and last way is to carefully read *Götzen-Dämmerung* and examine all instances of affirmation. One will then discover that he especially ends almost every chapter by presenting or more often only vaguely alluding to his own solutions – which mostly were to be discussed in the fourth volume of *Umwerthung aller Werthe*.

The first chapter of aphorisms ends with the important aphorism: 'Formula of my happiness: a Yes, a No, a straight line, a *goal* . . . ', which seems to connect the book both to *Der Antichrist* (where it is further discussed) and to the *Hauptwerk* where this theme of creating one's own goal and meaning, although there exists no external and universal goal, was meant to be further discussed.

In the second chapter, 'The Problem of Socrates', it is not the short last twelfth section (which says that Socrates himself realized that he was sick), but at the end of the previous, penultimate, section, in which he summarizes his alternative to Socrates' 'Reason = virtue = happiness' (section 10) with his statement that 'as long as life is ascending, happiness and instinct are one. –'.

The third chapter ends with the claim (which connects with the fourth book of the *Umwerthung aller Werthe* which was called *Dionysos* or *Dionysos philosophos*): 'The tragic artist is *not* a pessimist – it is precisely he who *affirms* all that is questionable and terrible in existence, he is *Dionysian* . . . ' (6).

The short fourth, 'Myth', chapter about 'the history of an error' ends with the last (Nietzschean) stage: 'Midday; moment of the shortest shadow; end of the longest error; zenith of mankind; INCIPIT ZARATHUSTRA'. Almost every statement here seems to point at especially the fourth book of *Umwerthung aller Werthe*.

The fifth chapter ends, after having criticized religious and moralizing views, by giving a contrast to that: 'But we ourselves, we immoralists, are the answer to that . . . ' (and the title of the third book of the *Umwerthung aller Werthe* was precisely *The Immoralist*).

In the next chapter, 'The Four Great Errors', the whole last section (8) gives Nietzsche's alternative, and begins 'What alone can *our* teaching be?' and continues to argue along the line of the innocence of becoming and that each of us is part of an ever-changing totality.

In the following, seventh, chapter, it is more the first section and not the last which proclaims Nietzsche's philosophy: that philosophers should 'place themselves *beyond good and evil* – that they have the illusion of moral judgement *beneath* them' and that '*there are no moral facts whatever*'.

The eighth chapter, where his affirmative view of culture, *Bildung* and university education is present, does not really contain any special section which summarizes it.

The long ninth chapter, which originally was meant to end the book, is not and probably cannot be summarized in the manner we have brought forth in this section – but it nonetheless ends with a very clear pointer to the coming *Hauptwerk*: 'I have given mankind the most profound book it possesses, my *Zarathustra*: I shall shortly give it the most independent one –', obviously referring to the *Umwerthung aller Werthe*, which he also had strongly introduced in the foreword.

The same is true for the last chapter which ends with references to the 'philosopher Dionysos' (the title of the fourth book of *Umwerthung aller Werthe* was either *Dionysos* or *Dionysos philosophos*) and to eternal recurrence (the planned main theme of the book): 'I, the last disciple of the philosopher Dionysus – I, the teacher of the eternal recurrence . . .'.

7

The role and place of the idea of eternal recurrence in *Twilight of the Idols*

7.1 Introduction   145
7.2 The discovery of eternal recurrence in 1881   147
7.3 The place and role of eternal recurrence in Nietzsche's published books   148
7.4 The presence of eternal recurrence in *Götzen-Dämmerung*   151
7.5 The role and place of eternal recurrence in Nietzsche's plans for a *Hauptwerk*   157
7.6 What ought we to learn from the place of eternal recurrence in
     Götzen-Dämmerung?   162

7.1 Introduction

What does it mean that Nietzsche ends *Götzen-Dämmerung* by saying 'I, the teacher of eternal recurrence . . .'? It is the last sentence of the book (except for the short epilogue in the form of a quotation) and with it he seems to summarize or describe the essence of his affirmative philosophy, but what does it then mean, considering that he did not discuss or elaborate on the idea in the book (nor in any other post-Zarathustra books)? If he is the teacher of eternal recurrence, why is this theme not more present in this account of his philosophy? If *Götzen-Dämmerung* was to be regarded as a summary of Nietzsche's philosophy, this makes no sense at all. However, if *Götzen-Dämmerung* is regarded as consisting of excerpts from his work on the *Hauptwerk* – and thus as pointing forward – it makes sense assuming that eternal recurrence was an important philosopheme for him (as that last sentence in *Götzen-Dämmerung* certainly seems to suggest) and that he planned to discuss it in the *Umwerthung aller Werthe*. These are questions and topics which we will discuss and answer in this chapter.

In the introduction to this book, I mentioned the problem of the apparent absence of several of Nietzsche's most well-known ideas, concepts and views, and what this means. In this chapter, we will concentrate on Nietzsche's most important affirmative philosopheme, eternal recurrence, and discover that it is in fact present (although kept in the background), and thus that it is wrong to believe that Nietzsche had given up on the idea, or even that it had become less important to him.

However, we need to begin by answering the question of what does the idea of eternal recurrence actually mean? Let us here start with a preliminary description of it that will be refined in the following.

In *Ecce homo* Nietzsche briefly describes 'the doctrine of the "eternal recurrence", in other words of the unconditional and infinitely repeated circulation of all things – ultimately this doctrine of Zarathustra's *could* also have been taught already by Heraclitus'.[1] The idea is closely related to fate and to accepting reality and that which is necessary, and to the complete connectedness of everything. This is visible in several of his notes, for example, when he writes:

My drawing fatalism to its conclusion:
1) through the eternal recurrence and pre-existence
2) through the elimination of the concept of 'will'.[2]

The meaning of Nietzsche's idea of eternal recurrence can thus be summarized as the hypothesis that the world process is cyclical and that we therefore will relive our lives an infinite number of times in identically the same way. We would not be aware of this (and certainly not remember it), but philosophically and theologically it would mean the complete rejection of every external sense of purpose, of *telos*, of the universe and of human life. The idea of eternal recurrence is thus a form of extreme nihilism, which only can be overcome by affirming the present life, not its *telos*.

The fundamental point of the idea of eternal recurrence is thus, in a sense, destructive (and that is why Nietzsche often refers to it as 'the hammer'). It is meant – in a simplified form – to show how meaningless your life and everything is – whatever you do, whatever you think, you are not part of any grand purpose and do not contribute to any fundamental progress. The idea says that you will have to relive your life in identically the same way again and again, and this is meaningless since then there can be no great purpose (*telos*) outside of you, no progress, no god, no universal goal, to which you can contribute or be a part of. In his notebooks Nietzsche even calls his idea of eternal recurrence 'the most extreme form of nihilism'.[3] However, Nietzsche believed that out of this idea another contrary process could also grow – liberated from every grand *telos* (related, of course, to the death of God – announced in the same book as was eternal recurrence, *Die fröhliche Wissenschaft*), we can instead create our own, here and now, goal and purpose, and strive to realize that. If that goal and purpose are truly separate and independent of every false idea of a grand *telos*, then one is also immune to the destructive (nihilistic) aspect of the hammer – of the eternal recurrence. If your purpose lies in your life,[4] in your here and now – then you will rather affirm the ideal of eternal recurrence than reject it. And that affirmation, that *Weltanschauung*, leads (or can lead) to a general and total affirmation of life and reality.

The idea of eternal recurrence can thus be seen as primarily a psychological test of life-affirming and healthy instincts consisting of one's response (joy or dejection) to an emphasis, or awareness, of the total lack of external value and meaning of human life, in combination with the idea of having to relive one's life in identically the same manner, not just once or twice but an infinite number of times. It can be regarded as a test of man's, or an individual's, character and of his self-sufficiency in regard to fundamental values, and it is closely associated with tragedy (which according to Nietzsche also denies any comprehensive teleology).

There is also another aspect of the idea of eternal recurrence, hardly present in the published books at all, but discussed by Nietzsche in his notes: eternal recurrence as a physical theory of the universe – not then merely as a psychological or existential test but as a description of the nature and evolution of the universe (which, if true, would make the test not just hypothetical but actual).[5] I will not be much concerned with these discussions in this study. I will also not here be concerned with defending or criticizing the idea of eternal recurrence, but accept that Nietzsche regarded it as important.

There is still much debate over whether Nietzsche meant it to be a natural scientific hypothesis (or truth) or an existential one. I find the evidence much more convincing that the centre of gravity for Nietzsche was on the existential sense, even if in his notebooks he also contemplated it as a scientific theory. However, it is true that Nietzsche's reading of natural scientific books is likely to have contributed importantly to, and been a stimulus for, his 'discovery' of the idea.

Before we examine the idea of eternal recurrence itself in more detail, and its place in *Götzen-Dämmerung* and in the plans and notes for the *Hauptwerk*, let us summarize Nietzsche's discussions of it and its 'history' in Nietzsche's thought and its place in his earlier books.

Already the number of synonyms used by Nietzsche to describe or refer to this idea shows how important it was to him. I have identified about twenty-five expressions he used to signify the idea, some of them more descriptive, such as eternal recurrence, return, circular movement and circular process, to much more poetic ones such as the ring of rings, ring of eternity, the most abysmal thought, da capo and so on.

7.2 The discovery of eternal recurrence in 1881

Nietzsche claimed that the idea of the eternal recurrence came to him suddenly in early August 1881 while walking near Sils-Maria in Switzerland, and this is confirmed by Nietzsche's notes from this time,[6] and by his account of it in *Ecce homo*:

> Now I shall relate the story of Zarathustra. The basic conception of the work – the *thought of eternal recurrence*, this highest attainable formula of affirmation – belongs to the August of 1881: it was dashed off on a sheet of paper with the caption '6000 feet beyond man and time'. On that day I was walking through the woods by Lake Silvaplana; not far from Surlei I stopped next to a massive block of stone that towered up in the shape of a pyramid. Then this thought came to me. – [. . .]. This interval includes the '*gaya scienza*', which gives a hundred indications that something incomparable is near; latterly it gives the opening of *Zarathustra* itself, and in the penultimate section of the fourth book it gives Zarathustra's fundamental thought.[7]

We know that Nietzsche both had read about and knew of the idea of eternal recurrence before that, but for his own version of the idea his statement is likely to be correct.

What happened in August 1881 was probably not so much that Nietzsche discovered the idea, but that he suddenly discovered its consequences and made it into *his* idea.

The idea of eternal recurrence is far from unique to Nietzsche. It is present in much of ancient thought, for example, among the Pythagoreans and the Stoics – the idea (at least in a vague form) is natural in societies with a more or less cyclical view of time; versions of it is present in Buddhism and Christianity,[8] and it was discussed in many contemporary scientific and literary texts in Nietzsche's day, several of which Nietzsche had read. Nietzsche's version of the idea, however, differs from all, or almost all, of these by the fact that he gives the idea a much stronger existential orientation and connects it with the question of nihilism and with the value of life. For him, it is no mere idea or hypothesis about the nature of the universe, but an existential test and touchstone: 'My teaching says: the task is to live so that you must wish to live again.'[9]

A large number of possible sources or influences on Nietzsche's view of 'eternal recurrence' have been suggested, including Heine, Schopenhauer, Hölderlin, Hume, Spinoza, the pre-Socratics (Pythagoras, Heraclitus and the Stoics, all of these ancient Greeks Nietzsche himself associated with the idea),[10] and several others, including among contemporary thinkers, A. Blanqui, E. Dühring, J. G. Vogt and especially O. Caspari, but no definite source has been identified with certainty.[11]

We will, however, concentrate on Nietzsche's version of the idea. To do this, we need to be aware that closely related to the idea of eternal recurrence is the concept of *amor fati* (love of fate), which to Nietzsche meant an affirmation of life and the world (fate) in its totality. This idea constitutes a central aspect of Nietzsche's view of tragedy, philosophy and of himself. Nietzsche discovered and used the expression *amor fati* more or less simultaneously with his discovery of the eternal recurrence, in the autumn of 1881.[12]

The discovery of the idea of eternal recurrence in August 1881 had a profound affect on Nietzsche's thought and outlook, and it seems that it was this discovery which more than anything else made Nietzsche move into a new phase of his thought (into that which is conventionally called his late phase). Furthermore, just weeks after the discovery, Nietzsche discovered Zarathustra – who not only was going to become the symbol of his spokesman for much of this period but whom he describes as 'the teacher of the eternal recurrence'.[13] The idea is given a prominent place and role at the end of *Die fröhliche Wissenschaft*, and very much so in *Also sprach Zarathustra*, but thereafter it is hardly visible in Nietzsche's published books.

7.3 The place and role of eternal recurrence in Nietzsche's published books

Nietzsche first presented the idea of eternal recurrence, after much hesitation,[14] in the penultimate section, 341,[15] of the first edition of *Die fröhliche Wissenschaft* (1882). Here it is presented as an existential question and test:

> *The greatest weight.* – What, if some day or night a demon were to steal after you into your loneliest lonelines and say to you: 'This life as you now live it and have

lived it, you will have to live once more and innumerable times more; and there will be nothing new in it, but every pain and every joy and every thought and sigh and everything unutterably small or great in your life will have to return to you, all in the same succession and sequence – even this spider and this moonlight between the trees, and even this moment and I myself. The eternal hourglass of existence is turned upside down again and again, and you withit, speck of dust!'

Would you not throw yourself down and gnash your teeth and curse the demon who spoke thus? Or have you once experienced a tremendous moment when you would have answered him: 'You are a god and never have I heard anything more divine.' If this thought gained possession of you, it would change you as you are or perhaps crush you. The question in each and every thing, 'Do you desire this once more and innumerable times more?' would lie upon your actions as the greatest weight. Or how well disposed would you have to become to yourself and to life *to crave nothing more fervently* than this ultimate eternal confirmation and seal?[16]

This is not only the penultimate section of the book, followed by the section which introduces Zarathustra (and is almost identical to the beginning of *Also sprach Zarathustra*), who eventually will proclaim this idea. Nietzsche is here – as so often at the end of his books – looking forward, promising further discussions of this idea – as we also can see from his letters – and which was also fulfilled in the next book.

The idea of eternal recurrence then also becomes the major theme in *Also sprach Zarathustra* – although Zarathustra at first avoids speaking of it – and Nietzsche thus builds up expectations and emphasizes its importance – because it is so difficult a topic. However, it is eventually presented poetically and metaphorically in the third book of that work.

I, Zarathustra, the advocate of life, the advocate of suffering, the advocate of the circle – I call you, my most abysmal thought! [. . .]

'For your animals well know, O Zarathustra, who you are and must become: behold, *you are the teacher of the eternal recurrence*, that is now *your* destiny!

'That you have to be the first to teach this doctrine – how should this great destiny not also be your greatest danger and sickness!

'Behold, we know what you teach: that all things recur eternally and we ourselves with them, and that we have already existed an infinite number of times before and all things with us.[17]

And in the very last chapter of the third (and last) book, called 'The Seven Seals (or: The Song of Yes and Amen)', seven times the refrain is sounded:

Oh how could I not lust for eternity and for the wedding ring of rings – the Ring of Recurrence!

Never yet did I find the woman by whom I wanted children, unless it be this woman, whom I love: for I love you, O Eternity!

For I love you, O Eternity!

It is not just a theme of that book but its central theme. The expression eternal recurrence only occurs about fifteen times (but about half of them are as a refrain in a poem), but many synonyms are used and the whole latter third of the book alludes to and gives different descriptions of it.

However, after *Also sprach Zarathustra* the idea of eternal recurrence is hardly present in the published books at all. Considering that Nietzsche obviously regarded it as so important, this is surprising. An explanation for this is that it is due to Nietzsche's plans for his *Hauptwerk* (and thus also closely connected to the theme of this study). From at least 1884, Nietzsche intended eternal recurrence to constitute the kernel of the *Hauptwerk* (as we will see later) – while the books actually published after *Also sprach Zarathustra* were merely side-productions – not suitable for the presentation, discussion and elaboration of the idea of eternal recurrence but suitable for hinting at and alluding to it – and that is what is done in *Jenseits von Gut und Böse*, *Zur Genealogie der Moral* and *Götzen-Dämmerung*.

In *Jenseits von Gut und Böse* (1886) – 'Prelude to a Philosophy of the Future' – this idea is very much held in the background. The only almost explicit mentioning of it is in section 56:

> Whoever, like myself, prompted by some enigmatical desire, has long endeavoured to go to the bottom of the question of pessimism and free it from the half-Christian, half-German narrowness and stupidity in which it has finally presented itself to this century [. . .]; whoever [. . .] has actually looked inside, and into the most world-renouncing of all possible modes of thought – beyond good and evil [. . .] – whoever has done this, has perhaps just thereby, without really desiring it, opened his eyes to behold the opposite ideal: the ideal of the most world-approving, exuberant, and vivacious man, who has not only learnt to compromise and arrange with that which was and is, but wishes to have it again *as it was and is*, for all eternity, insatiably calling out *da capo*, not only to himself, but to the whole piece and play; and not only the play, but actually to him who requires the play – and makes it necessary; because he always requires himself anew – and makes himself necessary. – What? And this would not be – *circulus vitiosus deus*?

There are also references to the hammer in three or four sections, of which at least two are probably hidden references to the idea of eternal recurrence.[18] This is not much, but the idea is nonetheless obviously present and not rejected. *Jenseits von Gut und Böse* was not based on his notes for the *Hauptwerk*, which he obviously worked on at this time. He, for example, announced it on the cover of *Jenseits von Gut und Böse* as a work in preparation, and *Jenseits von Gut und Böse* points at it on several occasions, including in its subtitle: 'Prelude to a Philosophy of the Future'. We can note that in several drafts of the title of *Jenseits von Gut und Böse*, he describes the book as preliminary to the idea of eternal recurrence. For example, *Beyond Good and Evil: Foreword to a Philosophy of Eternal Recurrence*.[19]

However, in the two following books, *Zur Genealogie der Moral* and *Der Fall Wagner*, it does not surface at all. After *Götzen-Dämmerung* (discussed in the next section), it also is not present in *Der Antichrist* – importantly, for this is the only volume of his

Hauptwerk which he wrote before his collapse – but in *Ecce homo* – written as a preface and introduction to the *Umwerthung aller Werthe* – the idea of eternal recurrence is very present again.

We ought also to be aware of the fact, that although the idea of eternal recurrence is hardly mentioned in the published books between *Also sprach Zarathustra* and *Ecce homo*, it is nonetheless very present in his notes (see Section 7.5).

7.4 The presence of eternal recurrence in *Götzen-Dämmerung*

There can be no doubt, as I will show in this and the next section, that Nietzsche also after 1885 continued to regard eternal recurrence as the kernel of his philosophy – why then is it so absent in *Götzen-Dämmerung* (as well as in his other published books after *Also sprach Zarathustra*)?

It has been argued that Nietzsche gave up on the idea of eternal recurrence. That could be the explanation for its absence in *Götzen-Dämmerung* and other late books. However, that is not a persuasive and defensible position. After all, the idea of eternal recurrence is not absent in *Götzen-Dämmerung* (and several other late books), only much less present than one could expect. He, after all, ends the book with the statement: 'I, the last disciple of the philosopher Dionysos – I, the teacher of eternal recurrence . . .'. Furthermore, he highly praises *Also sprach Zarathustra* in *Götzen-Dämmerung* (and in other late books), which at least in part also implies an emphasis of the idea of eternal recurrence, which he describes as 'the basic conception' of that work. And, as mentioned earlier, in Nietzsche's last book, *Ecce homo*, the idea is much more present, and it is definitely present in his late notes.

I will attempt to show that the idea of eternal recurrence is more present in *Götzen-Dämmerung* than what at first appears to be the case (summarized in Table 5A in the appendix), and secondly, argue that the reason why it is not expounded upon more explicitly in this work is due to that it was planned for the *Hauptwerk*.

At first it may appear that the only place in *Götzen-Dämmerung* where the idea of eternal recurrence is present is in its last sentence (before the epilogue), or more accurately, only in the last two sections (for it is present throughout in both of them). However, I will show that, even if kept very much in the background, the idea of eternal recurrence is present in most chapters, often it becomes more apparent at the very end of them. We can do this analysis by considering the presence of the idea of eternal recurrence on three levels. At the first level, it is expressly presented and explicitly mentioned – which is only the case in the last two sections of *Götzen-Dämmerung* (more strictly perhaps only in the last sentence). At the second level, it is present but not explicitly mentioned (although more 'hidden' synonyms may be used). This is the case with its only clear presence in *Jenseits von Gut und Böse* (section 56), and in several instances in *Götzen-Dämmerung*, including the subtitle (discussed in Chapter 5 and in the following). At the third level, the idea of eternal recurrence seems to be present, but its presence is vague and uncertain, and one can thus not be certain of its presence – although repeated such instances make it probable (at least in a context which also includes first- or second-level instances).

As I have argued earlier, the first occurrence of the idea of eternal recurrence is present already in the subtitle of the book: 'or How to Philosophize with the Hammer' (as well as in the foreword – 'for once to pose questions here with the *hammer*' – and the epilogue), for the hammer is a synonym to the idea of eternal recurrence as is explicit in many notes.[20] Although the idea of eternal recurrence is not explicitly discussed or elaborated on in *Götzen-Dämmerung*, the book nonetheless can be said to exemplify how one can philosophize from the perspective of the idea of eternal recurrence, not in any cosmological sense, but in emphasizing, with affirmation, the here and the now – and it thus follows that the book contains severe critique of that which centres life elsewhere – metaphysics, religion and morality. Another way to put it is to state that eternal recurrence is used diagnostically when we examine whether ideals and values (idols) aid us in affirming ourselves and reality or inhibit and prevent such affirmation.

Several of the aphorisms in the first chapter can, on the third level, be related to the idea of eternal recurrence. This is true for aphorisms 2: 'Even the bravest of us rarely has the courage for what he really *knows* . . .', which has a general meaning, but it is also an accurate description of Zarathustra's relation to the idea of eternal recurrence, as well as Nietzsche's own.

Aphorisms 10–12 are also related to this philosopheme:

10. Let us not be cowardly in face of our actions! Let us not afterwards leave them in the lurch! – Remorse of conscience is indecent.

11. Can an *ass* be tragic? – To be crushed by a burden one can neither bear nor throw off? . . . The case of the philosopher.

12. If we possess our *why* of life we can put up with almost any *how*. [. . .]

One aspect of the eternal recurrence is that it emphasizes fatalism – that everything is connected and necessary – it follows that 'remorse of conscience is indecent'. In Nietzsche's first presentation of eternal recurrence in *Die fröhliche Wissenschaft*, quoted earlier, it was referred to as 'the heaviest weight' and he continually discusses or refers to how it can crush the individual (that is also why he uses the hammer as a synonym). There may be other burdens, but the idea of eternal recurrence is almost certainly one of those Nietzsche had in mind when he wrote aphorism 11. The probably most important and most obvious point of the idea of eternal recurrence is that there is no external *telos* or purpose – and the necessity of possessing or creating one (otherwise one will become crushed or a nihilist). This is also the main point of aphorism 12. This point becomes even more explicit in the last of the aphorisms, aphorism 44 (also present in the same sense in the first section of *Der Antichrist*):[21]

44. Formula of my happiness: a Yes, a No, a straight line, a *goal* . . .

The idea of eternal recurrence, in the form of *amor fati*, seems to lie behind the whole main theme of the second chapter, 'The Problem of Socrates'. Although almost everything in the chapter is aimed at the critique of pessimism, of those who deny themselves and life, of those whom Nietzsche calls decadents – it is actually based on a dichotomy between these and those who affirm themselves and reality, those who possess *amor fati*. Those whom Nietzsche criticizes in this chapter lack the insight of eternal recurrence, and thus are not wise. The late Nietzsche frequently differentiates between ascending and descending life – and this is the theme also of this chapter. The ascending life is associated with *amor fati* (and eternal recurrence), while the descending life is associated with morality, moralism (and Christianity). The affirmative alternative is almost only visible in the last sentence of section 11: 'as long as life is *ascending*, happiness and instinct are one. –'. The failure, physiological as well as intellectual, of Socrates et al, becomes even more evident when this chapter is compared to the last one, where Nietzsche speaks of:

> the Dionysian condition, that the *fundamental fact* of the Hellenic instinct expresses itself – its 'will to life'. *What* did the Hellene guarantee to himself with these mysteries? *Eternal* life, the eternal recurrence of life; the future promised and consecrated in the past; the triumphant Yes to life beyond death and change; *true* life as collective continuation of life through procreation, through the mysteries of sexuality. [. . .] All this is contained in the word Dionysos. (GD, 'Ancients', 4)

Here, in this last chapter, the affirmative alternative to Socrates and pessimism becomes visible, and it is closely associated with eternal recurrence.

In the third chapter, '"Reason " in Philosophy', the idea of eternal recurrence is present in three ways, but the first two – more general aspects – only vaguely and on the third level. First, the idea of eternal recurrence forces us to accept and live in the here and now – and that which Nietzsche criticizes in this whole chapter (and the next) is just the opposite of this. Secondly, and somewhat more specific, what the philosophers want, according to Nietzsche, is 'being', duration and unity – 'Death, change, age, as well as procreation and growth, are for them objections' (section 1). Nietzsche instead emphasizes change and 'becoming' – and one of the things which characterizes the idea of eternal recurrence is that it is Heraclitean and ever-dynamic. The third aspect is perhaps more explicit and is expressed in the last sentence of the chapter: 'The tragic artist is *not* a pessimist – it is precisely he who *affirms* all that is questionable and terrible in existence, he is *Dionysian* . . . ' (6). As we will see at the end of this section, Dionysos is very closely related to the idea of eternal recurrence, but perhaps still more important is that the best response to the idea of eternal recurrence – or, in fact, the very essence of the idea – is to 'affirm all', which is done by the tragic artist, according to Nietzsche.

The next brief 'Fable' or 'Myth' chapter is really a direct continuation of the previous one. The sixth and last section here is a fairly obvious, second level, reference to the idea of eternal recurrence – and to Nietzsche's planned further elaboration in the *Hauptwerk* of this idea and its consequences. The result of the fable – and thus that which we are left with in section 6 – is the here and the now (that which previously has been called the apparent world) – that is, that which also is emphasized by the idea of eternal recurrence. And the description in parenthesis '(Midday; [. . .] zenith of mankind; INCIPIT ZARATHUSTRA)' points at the idea of eternal recurrence – both 'Midday' and 'zenith of mankind' are symbols for the time when mankind has come to realize this teaching, and Zarathustra *is* the teacher of eternal recurrence. 'Incipit Zarathustra' means 'here begins *Also sprach Zarathustra*' – and thus also the philosophy of eternal recurrence. That eternal recurrence is the most fundamental idea of *Also sprach Zarathustra* is stated explicitly in Nietzsche's description of the book in *Ecce homo*: 'The basic conception of the work – the *thought of eternal recurrence*, this highest attainable formula of affirmation.'[22]

In chapter 5 (and 7) Nietzsche presents a severe critique of morality as anti-natural, which is against accepting reality as it is, against *amor fati*. Morality (anti-natural) is just another name for 'denial of the will to life' (section 5), while a natural and healthy morality would be an affirmation of the will to life. This *amor fati* assumption and alternative is present as a background for the arguments in the whole chapter – but in the last, sixth section, it and the idea of eternal recurrence become explicit:

> the individual is, in his future and in his past, a piece of fate, one law more, one necessity more for everything that is and everything that will be. To say to him 'change yourself' means to demand that everything should change, even in the past. . . . [. . .] We others, we immoralists, have on the contrary opened wide our hearts to every kind of understanding, comprehension, *approval*. We do not readily deny, we seek our honour in *affirming*.

The five most obvious references or allusions to the idea of eternal recurrence in *Götzen-Dämmerung* – apart from the explicit one at the end of the book – are the use of the word 'hammer' in the subtitle, which is a synonym to eternal recurrence, the last section of the 'fable' chapter (with reference to Midday and to Zarathustra), the last section of the fifth chapter (just quoted), the last section of the sixth chapter, 'The Four Great Errors' (discussed here), and in section 49 of the penultimate chapter. The first two of these are primarily pointers to the idea of eternal recurrence (and thus also to the *Umwerthung aller Werthe*), and the three other ones give descriptions of the idea of eternal recurrence, important but not complete descriptions.

After having shown and discussed four fundamental misconceptions about the world and about human psychology and thought in chapter 6, Nietzsche at the end of section 7 and in the whole of section 8 presents his own view with the words: 'What alone can *our* teaching be?' His answer, although not mentioned by name, is actually a fairly detailed description of the idea of eternal recurrence in terms of fate, necessity, the absence of general purpose, that each person is part of the whole, that no one is accountable and with the concept of the 'innocence of becoming':

> *No one* is accountable for existing at all, or for being constituted as he is [. . .] The fatality of his nature cannot be disentangled from the fatality of all that which has been and will be. [. . .] in reality purpose is *lacking* . . . One is necessary, one is a piece of fate, one belongs to the whole, one *is* in the whole [. . .] thus alone is the *innocence* of becoming restored. (8)

It may seem surprising that Nietzsche denies that one should attempt to improve man – '*the entire morality of improvement, the Christian included, has been a misunderstanding*

. . .' (GD, 'Socrates', 11) – as he argues in the whole of chapter 7, 'The "Improvers" of Mankind'. Is that not one of the fundamental thoughts of *Also sprach Zarathustra*, and present in almost all of Nietzsche's writings, for example, in *Der Antichrist* 3: 'The problem I raise here is not what ought to succeed mankind in the sequence of species [...] but what type of human being one ought to *breed*, ought to *will*, as more valuable, more worthy of life, more certain of the future'? The answer, I believe, is that there are two ways of attempting to 'improve' man – one which Nietzsche rejects, another which he affirms – the former, done by means of morality and religion, is motivated by a *desire to change reality* because one denies or objects to it (and that is what he is discussing in this whole chapter). The second way – in parallel to how the tragic artist works and what Nietzsche called '*healthy* morality' in chapter 5 – does not wish to change reality as such, but to affirm it (and affirm it still more). It is thus not motivated by any denial of reality, but by *amor fati* – and thus of an aspect of the idea of eternal recurrence. Even sublimation – Nietzsche's alternative to moralizing (together with the importance of examples) can be motivated by fear or denial of reality (moralism) and is then not a good solution – only when it also is an expression of affirmation of reality is it Nietzsche's approved solution. Thus, in this, the seventh chapter, the idea of eternal recurrence is not visible or directly present, since Nietzsche here is only concerned with the 'negative' manner of 'improving' man. However, an awareness of eternal recurrence and Nietzsche's affirmative philosophy nonetheless affects the reading of this chapter for it allows us to realize that what he rejected in the chapter is just one alternative. There is another more affirmative and Dionysian alternative to improve man which Nietzsche recommends, but that is not discussed here.

In chapter 8, containing a 'timely' critique of the Germans and of higher education, there is no discussion of eternal recurrence. The only very hidden and vague possible reference to the idea is in section 6 where Nietzsche claims to be affirmative: 'To be true to my nature, which is *affirmative* and has dealings with contradictions and criticism only indirectly and when compelled'.

The long penultimate 'Expedition' chapter is like the previous chapter more 'timely', and in it Nietzsche comments on more specific phenomena (often on art and aesthetics) and thus the idea of eternal recurrence is not especially present until at the end. One can find some vague third-level probable reflections of, or references to it, such as in Nietzsche's account of 'grand style' in section 11, which suits to that 'which no longer requires proving; which distains to please; which is slow to answer; which is conscious of no witnesses around it; which lives oblivious in *itself*, fatalistic, a law among laws'. It is perhaps also hinted at in sections 17 (honouring life even when most difficult), 22–23 (beauty incites to procreation), 24 (the tragic artist), 32 (real persons are more valuable than 'any sort of *ideal* man'), but all of these are very vague. It is also possible to argue that the idea of eternal recurrence and *amor fati* constitute a necessary backdrop to that which Nietzsche criticizes in this chapter, the more specific examples of Christianity and decadence which we encounter in his critique of, for example, Renan, Eliot and Carlyle – while Emerson is described as someone in tune with life. Some of Nietzsche's reflections on art and aesthetics also suggest a parallel between art and life; both are healthy only when they are based on an acceptance and affirmation of life. However, there are only two more explicit and important references to the idea of eternal recurrence in this long chapter. The first is in section 49, as part of the affirmative finale of the chapter. Here Nietzsche describes Goethe as *exempla* of human life, and when he describes his attitude and relation to life, what he describes is one who has accepted the idea of eternal recurrence, although that expression is not used.

> He [Goethe] placed himself within it [life] [. . .] What he aspired to was *totality*; [. . .] a convinced realist [. . .] a man of tolerance, not out of weakness, but out of strength [. . .] a man to whom nothing is forbidden, except it be *weakness*, whether that weakness be called vice or virtue. . . . A spirit thus *emancipated* stands in the midst of the universe with a joyful and trusting fatalism, in the *faith* that only what is separate and individual may be rejected, that in the totality everything is redeemed and affirmed – *he no longer denies*. . . . But such a faith is the highest of all possible faiths: I have baptized it with the name *Dionysos*. –

At the end of this quotation Nietzsche also pronounces the close connection, or even identity, of Dionysos with the idea of eternal recurrence. Not in *Die Geburt der Tragödie*, but in the later 1880s, Dionysos has become another synonym of the idea of eternal recurrence. This becomes even more explicit in the last chapter – and is consistent with that in Nietzsche's last drafts for the *Umwerthung aller Werthe*, the fourth volume planned to discuss eternal recurrence, is called either *Dionysos* or *Dionysos philosophos* (see the end of the next Section 7.5). The second fairly explicit reference to eternal recurrence in this chapter is in its last sentence where he calls *Also sprach Zarathustra* – the book in which he expounds on the idea of eternal recurrence – the most profound book, and thereafter promises to soon publish the *Umwerthung aller Werthe*.

It is in the last chapter of *Götzen-Dämmerung* that Nietzsche allows himself to be more specific about his affirmative philosophy, including the idea of eternal recurrence. Here, in the last two sections, the close association between the idea of eternal recurrence, Dionysos and the tragic is made very apparent:

> For it is only in the Dionysian mysteries, in the psychology of the Dionysian condition, that the *fundamental fact* of the Hellenic instinct expresses itself – its 'will to life'. What did the Hellene guarantee to himself with these mysteries? *Eternal* life, the eternal recurrence of life; the future promised and consecrated in the past; the triumphant Yes to life beyond death and change; *true* life as collective continuation of life through procreation, through the mysteries of sexuality. [. . .] All this is contained in the word Dionysos: I know of no more exalted symbolism than this *Greek* symbolism, the symbolism of the Dionysian. The profoundest instinct of life, the instinct for the future of life, for the eternity of life, is in this word experienced religiously [. . .] The psychology of the orgy as an overflowing feeling of life and energy, within which even pain acts as a stimulus provided me with the key to the concept of the *tragic* feeling, which was misunderstood as much by Aristotle as it especially was by our pessimists. [. . .] Affirmation of life even in its strangest and sternest problems, the will to life rejoicing in its own inexhaustibility through the *sacrifice* of its highest types – *that* is what I called

Dionysian, *that* is what I recognized as the bridge to the psychology of the *tragic poet*. [. . .] *to realize in oneself* the eternal joy of becoming – that joy which also encompasses *joy in destruction*. . . . [. . .] – I, the last disciple of the philosopher Dionysos – I, the teacher of eternal recurrence . . .

We have thus seen that *Götzen-Dämmerung* not only ends by explicitly announcing eternal recurrence (and also pointing forward to a future presentation of this idea) but also that it contains many other references to this idea – sufficiently for it to be reasonable for him to regard it as an example of philosophizing with a hammer – as philosophizing from the perspective of the idea of eternal recurrence.

7.5 The role and place of eternal recurrence in Nietzsche's plans for a *Hauptwerk*

From the very beginning, the idea of eternal recurrence constituted the most fundamental thought and topic of the *Hauptwerk*. In fact, the *Hauptwerk* seems to have started as a work on the eternal recurrence, and with that expression in its title. This also makes sense, if we look at the first references to the *Hauptwerk* a few years later – where *Also sprach Zarathustra* (with its poetic description of eternal recurrence) is described as the entrance hall and the *Hauptwerk* as the main building (in which the idea of eternal recurrence was going to be elaborated on in the last volume).

The very first occasion of the idea of (and of the expression) eternal recurrence in Nietzsche's writings is in the form of a draft of what presumably was to be a book, with five numbered sections, entitled, '*The Recurrence of the Same*: Outline [or Draft]', from early August 1881.[23] The next outline for a book among Nietzsche's notes consists of three notes which are written on 26 August 1881, now entitled, 'Midday and Eternity', with the subtitle 'Outline for a New Way to Live', divided into four books. Zarathustra is mentioned, but this is clearly *not* an outline for *Also sprach Zarathustra*, but, in fact, has more similarity to that which will eventually become his notes for the *Hauptwerk*. However, it is probably best seen as an early stage of a work, before it eventually became two works; *Also sprach Zarathustra* and the *Hauptwerk*. These three notes show that the first book was intended to discuss the 'de-anthropomorphizing nature',[24] the second, knowledge, the third, 'the *last happiness of the one who is alone*' and the fourth, eternal recurrence: 'Dithyramic-comprehensive "*Annulus aeternitatis*". Desire to experience everything once again and an infinite number of times again'.[25]

Nietzsche seems from now on to make notes and plans both for what eventually would become *Also sprach Zarathustra* and the *Hauptwerk*, as well as a continuation of *Morgonröthe*, which eventually became *Die fröhliche Wissenschaft* (which ends by foreshadowing *Also sprach Zarathustra*). For us here, the relevant path to follow is the second one, the one leading towards the plan of a *Hauptwerk* (eventually entitled *Der Wille zur Macht* and thereafter *Umwerthung aller Werthe*). However, we need to be aware that at this early stage this path crosses and sometimes temporarily merges with that leading to *Also sprach Zarathustra* – frequently it is not possible to keep them apart. This is an important lesson for us. Not only did *Also sprach Zarathustra* and the *Hauptwerk* arise out of the same thoughts, notes and drafts of books – and for both of them the kernel is the idea of eternal recurrence. This close kinship of the two works remains an important fact also in the later 1880s and explains why he mentions both *Also sprach Zarathustra* and the *Umwerthung aller Werthe* at the end of *Götzen-Dämmerung*, why *Also sprach Zarathustra* is so prominent in *Ecce homo*, written as a preface to the *Umwerthung aller Werthe*, as well as why he can claim that perhaps the only readers who can understand the first volume of the *Umwerthung aller Werthe*, i.e. *Der Antichrist*, are 'the readers who understand my *Also sprach Zarathustra*'.[26]

In the summer of 1882 Nietzsche writes down a note, with the title 'Towards a Philosophy of Recurrence',[27] and shortly thereafter the title 'Midday and Eternity' ['*Mittag und Ewigkeit*'] returns for a second time.[28] It will thereafter be used another twenty times as a title (either as a title or subtitle), sometimes for a book project, sometimes for a book or a chapter (or part of a book), sometimes related to *Also sprach Zarathustra*, for example, it is on several occasions used as the title of the fourth book of *Also sprach Zarathustra*, or, alternatively, it was also used for a collection of poems. The same is also true for the title 'The Great Midday' [*Der grosse Mittag*]. We can draw the same conclusion as above – the same title 'Midday and Eternity' (as well as 'The Great Midday') – was used both for *Also sprach Zarathustra* (and parts of it)[29] and for the *Hauptwerk* (or parts of it).

During the period of writing *Also sprach Zarathustra*, I–IV, January 1883 to early in 1885, most of the very many notes mentioning or discussing eternal recurrence are more metaphorical and related to that work, but not all of them. In some notes he also plans a non-metaphorical and more systematic account (with discussions of the 'theoretical prerequisites and consequences', proofs, consequences of if it was to be believed to be true, how to live with the idea, its place in history and its social consequences).[30] From 1884 onwards there exists a number of drafts for titles and subtitles, several of which have similarities to *Jenseits von Gut und Böse*,[31] and one can see that the subtitle, 'Prelude to a Philosophy of the Future', at least in its original form meant prelude to 'a Philosophy of Eternal Recurrence'.[32] There are good reasons to accept this conclusion, and to regard *Jenseits von Gut und Böse* as being a prelude to the planned *Hauptwerk*, to the *Umwerthung aller Werthe*, in which the idea of eternal recurrence was going to be the kernel. I will give some further arguments for this later.

It is also interesting to see that the expression 'An Attempt at the Revaluation of All Values', which for a long time was the subtitle to *Der Wille zur Macht*, and then, slightly altered, became the main title of the *Hauptwerk*, actually began as a subtitle to a work called 'Philosophy of the Eternal Recurrence'.[33]

It is in 1884 that the plan for a four-volume *Hauptwerk* begins to crystallize,[34] and at the early stage it continues to be clearly centred on the idea of eternal recurrence (which most frequently is meant to be dealt with in the last part or volume).[35] Some of these drafts are already now similar to the structure the *Hauptwerk* will have in 1886–8, with one part for truth and knowledge, one for morality, one for art, one for the highest forms of humans and the last for the idea of eternal recurrence.[36]

The intention to write a *Hauptwerk* becomes visible and explicit in his letters for the first time in four letters from the spring of 1884 where Nietzsche speaks of *Also sprach*

Zarathustra as merely an entrance hall to his philosophy, and that he was working on the main building. In a letter to Meysenbug at the end of March 1884, he writes that he has finished his *Also sprach Zarathustra* (in three books) and immediately thereafter he calls that work 'an entrance hall to my philosophy – built for me, to give me courage'. He hints that he is working on the main building. In three further letters from this time he refers to *Also sprach Zarathustra* as merely the 'Vorhalle' to his philosophy, and to his strong sense of purpose and mission. It seems clear that he had in mind a more philosophical (and less metaphorical) work than *Also sprach Zarathustra*, but which, in all likelihood, would elaborate on the same fundamental ideas.

> If I get to Sils Maria in the summer, I mean to set about revising my metaphysical and epistemological views. I must now proceed step by step through a series of disciplines, for I have decided to spend the next five years on an elaboration of my 'philosophy', the entrance hall of which I have built with my *Zarathustra*. (Letter to Overbeck, 7 April 1884)

A month later, he repeats the intention to work on a *Hauptwerk*, then referred to as 'Haupt-Bau'.

> Now, after that that I have built for me this entrance hall to my philosophy, I will have to start again and not grow tired until the main building stands finished before me. (Letter to Meysenbug, early May 1884)

In fact, this was not only an intention, for during much of 1884 Nietzsche actually planned and worked on this *Hauptwerk* or 'main building' of his philosophy. At this early stage it seems most frequently to have been called 'Philosophy of Eternal Recurrence' as title or subtitle, or occasionally 'The Innocence of Becoming' ['*Unschuld des Werdens*'].[37] His notes, as well as numerous letters, show this:

> In the coming days I will leave from here, and since I for the next 3 months have determined to perform a revision of the most subtle things (the problems of epistemology), I ask forgiveness if I during this time remain completely silent and also do not want any letters from anyone. (Letter to Franziska, 14 June 1884)

In the early autumn of 1884 Nietzsche seems to confirm that he had fulfilled his plans.

> I have practically finished the main task which I set myself for this summer; the next six years will be for working out a scheme which I have sketched for my 'philosophy'. It has gone well and looks hopeful. (Letter to Gast, 2 Sept. 1884)

During 1885 Nietzsche continued to plan and prepare for producing a *Hauptwerk*.

> I notice everywhere that it is over with what has so far been the case, and that I now must create, without every form of too great haste, *definitive* circumstances, which

must last at least for 10 years, for the purpose of being able, with complete calm, to begin to tackle the work of my life. A surrounding which *suits* me, I mean my *work*! (Letter to Franziska, 29 January 1885)

After the *Also sprach Zarathustra* books were finished by the spring of 1885 – although Nietzsche occasionally continued also thereafter to write a few notes on possible continuations – he wrote down a number of more theoretical reflections concerning the idea of eternal recurrence, as well as other notes for his *Hauptwerk*. For a time these notes possibly overlapped with the notes for *Jenseits von Gut und Böse*,[38] but mostly they were kept separate, and these notes and ideas were not included in *Jenseits von Gut und Böse*.[39] Montinari, in the commentary to *Jenseits von Gut und Böse*, expresses it still stronger:

> That *Beyond Good and Evil* was *not* developed out of the so-called *Will to Power* material is clear from this history of its origin and development. It was, in fact, prepatory for, a 'Prelude' to, something that still was to come but – at least as *Will to Power* – did not come.[40]

In fact, in a draft to a preface to a second volume of *Jenseits von Gut und Böse*, which was never written, Nietzsche seems to describe *Jenseits von Gut und Böse* as written for the purpose of aiding to make comprehensible the origin of his thoughts from the *Also sprach Zarathustra* period. That is, as a sort of commentary ahead of time – thus seemingly saying that it does not deal with the actual ideas of that period – which was planned to be discussed in the *Hauptwerk* – but merely with their origin.[41]

After *Jenseits von Gut und Böse* Nietzsche would not refer explicitly to the idea of eternal recurrence for two years in his published books, then at the end of *Götzen-Dämmerung* and thereafter in *Ecce homo*. However, in his notes the idea, expression and synonyms are very present – in many drafts for titles, in general discussions, in more poetical writings and also in more natural scientific speculation (such as 'The principle of conservation of energy demands the eternal recurrence').[42] Of special interest is the long essay 'The European Nihilism', dated, Lenzer Heide, the 10 June 1887 (exactly one month before he began *Zur Genealogie der Moral*, written in July), which contains several examinations of the relation between nihilism and the idea of eternal recurrence.[43]

All in all, the expression eternal recurrence (with synonyms) occurs about sixty times in the notes, approximately equally distributed in time, during these last two and a half years. By far the most frequently, it occurs in drafts for titles – mostly for the last volume of the *Hauptwerk*. To exemplify with just a few of the very last instances. The last draft for the *Hauptwerk* when it still had the title *Der Wille zur Macht*, from 28 August 1888:[44]

> Fourth Book: *The Great Midday*
> First Chapter. *The Principle of Life: Order of Rank*
> Second Chapter. *The Two Ways*
> Third Chapter. *The Eternal Recurrence*

The same is true – the fourth volume is dedicated to the idea of eternal recurrence – also for the continued project under the title *Umwerthung aller Werthe*:[45]

> *Fourth Book*
> *Dionysos.* Philosophy of Eternal Recurrence

Dionysos is closely related to the idea of eternal recurrence in the late Nietzsche's thought. This is a natural association from Greek religion and mythology, for he was not only the god of *exstasis* (ecstasy), the mask and the theatre but also of seasonal change and of life, death and rebirth. In *Götzen-Dämmerung*, although the idea of eternal recurrence is hardly explicitly mentioned, this association is nonetheless made explicit both at the end of section 49 of the penultimate chapter and in the last two sections of the last chapter, including in the last sentence, where Nietzsche suggests that he is the teacher of eternal recurrence because he is a disciple of Dionysos. In many notes from 1888, Nietzsche also extensively discusses Dionysos and the Dionysian, and relates it to the idea of eternal recurrence:

> The word '*Dionysian*' means: an urge to unity, a reaching out beyond personality, the everyday, society, reality, across the abyss of transitoriness: a passionate-painful overflowing into darker, fuller, more floating states; an ecstatic affirmation of the total character of life as that which remains the same, just as powerful, just as blissful, through all change; the great pantheistic sharing of joy and sorrow that sanctifies and calls good even the most terrible and questionable qualities of life; the eternal will to procreation, to fruitfulness, to recurrence; the feeling of the necessary unity of creation and destruction.[46]

This affirmative – and Dionysian – and tragic – view of the world is referred to in a number of late notes: 'A highest form of state of affirmation of existence will be created, in which even pain, every sort of pain, is ever included as means to ascending: the *tragic-Dionysian* state.'[47] In another important two-page note from May 1888, Nietzsche combines and relates the idea of eternal recurrence, Dionysos and the Dionysian, *amor fati* and the revaluation of all values:

> Dionysian affirmation of the world as it is, without subtraction, exception, or selection – it wants the eternal circulation: – the same things, the same logic and illogic of entanglements. The highest state a philosopher can attain: to stand in a Dionysian relationship to existence – my formula for this is *amor fati*. [. . .] It is also part of this state to depreciate that side of existence which alone has been affirmed hitherto; to perceive the origin of this valuation and how little a Dionysian value standard for existence is obliged to it.[48]

This strong emphasis of Dionysos with affirmation (and by implication also the idea of eternal recurrence) is present at several places in *Ecce homo*, for example, in the third section of the review of *Die Geburt der Tragödie*. The section begins by referring to a total affirmation of life as Dionysian, and that before Nietzsche 'this transformation of the Dionysian into a philosophical pathos: *tragic wisdom*' was lacking. He refers to the idea of eternal recurrence, and claims that it was central to Zarathustra: 'the doctrine of the "eternal recurrence", in other words of the unconditional and infinitely repeated circulation of all things – ultimately this doctrine of Zarathustra's'. He continues in the next section:

> *But that is the concept of Dionysos himself.* [. . .] Zarathustra [. . .] the opposite of a no-saying spirit [. . .] Zarathustra is a dancer [. . .] who has the harshest, most terrible insight into reality, who has thought the 'most abyssal thought', nevertheless finds in it no objection to existence, or even to the eternal recurrence of existence – but rather yet another reason *to be himself* the eternal 'yes' to all things, 'the enormous and unbounded Yes- and Amen-saying' . . . 'Into all abysses I carry my blessing Yes-saying' . . . *But that is the concept of Dionysos once again.*

Although Nietzsche in the end was unable to elaborate on his Dionysian philosophy and the idea of eternal recurrence due to his mental collapse, it clearly was his intention to do so in the *Umwerthung aller Werthe*. Eternal recurrence, the Dionysian and the tragic were key elements of *Also sprach Zarathustra*, which he now planned to elaborate on – and which he regarded as closely associated to his attempt of a revaluation of all values. According to Nietzsche, our present values, Christian and modern values, are fundamentally life-denying. To enable one to promote a contrasting set of life-affirmative values, these concepts and especially eternal recurrence, which can function as a touching-stone for values, seemed pivotal to him.[49]

7.6 What ought we to learn from the place of eternal recurrence in *Götzen-Dämmerung*?

We started this chapter with an awareness of only a single reference to the idea of eternal recurrence in *Götzen-Dämmerung*, and that at the very end of the work, but we have now come to realize that it is in fact possible to see almost the whole book as a response to and following from this idea (although the idea itself is almost throughout hidden in the background) – *Götzen-Dämmerung* as constituting a philosophizing from the perspective of eternal recurrence (as the subtitle indicated when we realize that the hammer symbolizes eternal recurrence). Or expressed differently, *Götzen-Dämmerung* constitutes a philosophizing from the perspective of life- and reality-affirmation – although still concentrating on the critical aspects, on what has been wrong with philosophizing the past two and a half thousand years, rather than on how such an affirmative philosophy (including morality) could actually function and appear.

The term 'life-affirming' can be misleading, for what Nietzsche refers to is certainly not life as such, much less life at any cost, but rather the highest possible forms of life.

> The problem I raise is not what ought to succeed mankind in the sequence of species (– the human being is an *end* –): but what type of human being one ought

to *breed*, ought to *will*, as more valuable, more worthy of life, more certain of the future. (*Der Antichrist*, 3)

It seems as if both *Also sprach Zarathustra* and the *Hauptwerk* originated as different ways to work out the idea of eternal recurrence in 1883–5 – the former poetically and metaphorically, the latter more philosophically. Both works arose from the same fundamental thought and from the same set of notes. The idea of eternal recurrence constituted the central idea of *Also sprach Zarathustra*, as well as in the plans for the *Hauptwerk*.

It follows from this that *Götzen-Dämmerung* cannot be a summary of Nietzsche's thought – the most important, the idea of eternal recurrence, is explicitly almost completely missing. It is even less a summary of his late books – *Jenseits von Gut und Böse*, *Zur Genealogie der Moral* and *Der Fall Wagner* – in which he specifically avoided the idea of eternal recurrence and related concepts of his affirmative philosophy. In *Götzen-Dämmerung* he does not explicitly deal with eternal recurrence, but he nonetheless to a large extent philosophizes from that perspective. As we already concluded at the end of the fifth chapter, *Götzen-Dämmerung* can be described as consisting of excerpts or extracts or a selection of topics from his work on the *Umwerthung aller Werthe*. As such, it gives us an immensely important *partial* overview of Nietzsche's last philosophical position – but, as can be seen from his notes, he also left much out of it – including more explicit elaboration of the idea of eternal recurrence, since he expected to present that in the near future.

This present chapter also confirms that *Götzen-Dämmerung* points forward – otherwise it is very difficult to understand the meaning of that last sentence's reference to the idea of eternal recurrence (which we have been able to realize only because we have all of Nietzsche's notes available and because we here read *Götzen-Dämmerung* as related to his *Umwerthung aller Werthe* project). However, having realized this, it is easy to see that last sentence 'I, the last disciple of the philosopher Dionysos – I, the teacher of eternal recurrence . . .' as referring to and pointing at the content of the book he in the last sentence of the penultimate chapter promises to soon publish: 'I shall shortly give it [mankind] the most independent [book]'.

The fact that eternal recurrence is so relatively absent from his late books has led many commentators to undervalue the importance for Nietzsche of this idea (especially since mostly the more poetical *Also sprach Zarathustra* is less used in academic studies of Nietzsche's thought). To acquire a better understanding of eternal recurrence requires us, apart from reading *Also sprach Zarathustra*, to closely study especially *Götzen-Dämmerung* and *Ecce homo* carefully with this question in mind (as has been done in this chapter for *Götzen-Dämmerung*), as well as carefully examine Nietzsche's late notes.

It has also become clear that *Der Antichrist* (or *Der Antichrist* together with *Götzen-Dämmerung*) cannot constitute the whole *Hauptwerk* – since the idea of eternal recurrence is missing in *Der Antichrist* (as well as Dionysos, the proclaimer of the idea of eternal recurrence) and they are explicitly only hinted at in *Götzen-Dämmerung*. In *Der Antichrist* Nietzsche is even more concerned with a critique of our present tradition (Christianity) than in *Götzen-Dämmerung*.

We have in this chapter also found a plausible explanation as to why the idea of eternal recurrence is not more explicitly present in *Götzen-Dämmerung* (and other late books). From our examination of the idea of eternal recurrence in the late notes we could see that in almost all of the drafts for the *Hauptwerk* – planned to be published shortly after *Götzen-Dämmerung* – the fourth volume was meant to deal with eternal recurrence, and as it seems, in a more affirmative sense, that is, not only using it as a contrast to that being criticized (metaphysics, morality etc.) but actually working out some of its constructive consequences. It seems from the notes that Nietzsche had not yet performed or finished such a philosophical analysis and drawn conclusions from this (even though he had done it more poetically in *Also sprach Zarathustra*). Undoubtedly, he, like Zarathustra, found that very difficult. It seems as a reasonable conclusion that Nietzsche did not emphasize the idea of eternal recurrence more in *Götzen-Dämmerung*, both because he had not yet concluded his examination of the idea and because he anyway wanted to save that kernel of his philosophy for his *Hauptwerk*, that he expected to publish in the near future.

8

The role of psychology, reason and instinct in *Twilight of the Idols*

8.1	Introduction	165
8.2	Nietzsche's new psychology and his critique of old psychology	166
8.3	Nietzsche's view of sublimation	170
8.4	The status and role of reason and instinct in *Götzen-Dämmerung*	173

8.1 Introduction

I will begin this chapter by briefly commenting on Nietzsche as a psychologist – a theme especially relevant for *Götzen-Dämmerung* which originally was entitled 'A Psychologist's Leisure' and where he emphasizes his role as psychologist in the foreword as well as throughout the text. I will thereafter discuss the presence of the closely related dichotomies between reason and instinct, between mind and body, and between conscious and subconscious in two different ways.

Nietzsche is a complex thinker, and his texts often contain apparent or real contradictions. One such major possible contradiction in *Götzen-Dämmerung* (and in most of his other late books) is, on the one hand, his strong emphasis of the body, instincts, the senses, physiology and naturalism. He can even appear as a radical 'materialist', or at least sharing much with empirists, naturalists and positivists. On the other hand, he strongly emphasizes the mind and its products (culture and *Bildung*). A strong case can be made that Nietzsche's main concerns are cultural ones: philosophy, music (and other forms of art), morals and values, and negatively religion. He claims that the goal of life and of the state is *Bildung* and culture, he emphasizes the importance of seeing and interpreting the world from a human, an anthropomorphic perspective,[1] and his best *exemplum* on how to live is not some healthy 'blond beast' or sportsman, but Goethe, the German Shakespeare, who was both a scientist and a poet.

Is this a contradiction? How does he view the relation between mind and body, between intellect and instinct? What was his relation to the classical mind–body problem? How far does his physiological reductionism go? How high does his spiritual and cultural ambition go? Is it possible to make a synthesis of these two aspects of his thought?

I will after the discussion of Nietzsche's psychology begin by setting up the earlier suggested dichotomy between a strong emphasis of the body contra Nietzsche's concern with values and culture, and thereafter discuss their relation.

8.2 Nietzsche's new psychology and his critique of old psychology

To describe the importance of psychology in Nietzsche's thought, and his insights and contributions to psychology, is almost as vast and complicated a task as it would be to do the same in regard to philosophy. I can here therefore only point at some of the more obvious aspects and especially at those relevant for *Götzen-Dämmerung* and the late Nietzsche's thought. That Nietzsche regarded psychology and a psychological approach as supremely important can be seen, for example, by his claim that 'psychology shall again be recognized as the queen of the sciences, to serve and prepare for which the other sciences exist. For psychology is now once again the road to the fundamental problems'.[2]

Nietzsche regarded himself as a psychologist, and were it not for Peter Gast *Twilight of the Idols* would have been called *The Leisure of a Psychologist* (the 'leisure' may not be obvious, but he explains it in the foreword as a relaxation from the difficult task of thinking through and writing the *Umwerthung aller Werthe*).

In a letter from June 1888, where Nietzsche describes his philosophy, he writes: 'My pretension is that my books are of the first rank by virtue of their wealth of psychological experience, their fearlessness in face of the greatest dangers, and their sublime candour.'[3] When he a few months later writes *Ecce homo* he again emphasizes the psychological side of his thought: ' That out of my writings there speaks a *psychologist* who has not his equal, that is perhaps the first thing a good reader will notice.'[4] He goes on to claim that one of his contributions to philosophy is psychology: 'Who before me at all among philosophers has been a *psychologist* and not rather its opposite "higher swindler", "idealist"? Before me there was no psychology.'[5] He explains that a major reason for this was because 'Christian morality' has led to a 'false-coinage *in psychologicis* to the point of crime'.[6]

The most striking of all of Nietzsche's psychological insights, and the one having the most far-reaching consequences, is his emphasis on the importance of the sub- or unconscious and hence on the surface and epiphenomenal nature of consciousness. This is a major theme in all of his books, from *Die Geburt der Tragödie* to *Ecce homo* and one of the foundation-stones of his thought.[7] Some of the innumerable consequences of this belief are Nietzsche's rejection of systems (since they are by necessity built merely on surface considerations), his claim that all merely rational explanations are insufficient, his rejection of reason and rationality as causes, and his acceptance that self-observation and self-knowledge are almost always misleading and extremely difficult. This last insight explains, at least partially, why we have accepted so many errors and false suppositions concerning human psychology which has had ramifications into the heart of philosophy, religion and culture.

Another fundamental psychological assumption of Nietzsche's thought is that man is an animal,[8] that we are biological beings governed by the same natural laws as all other organic, and even inorganic, matter. Nietzsche denies all 'spiritual causes' and accepts that all causes must be physical[9] leading him on towards a physiological view of man.[10] 'Indeed, every table of values, every 'thou shalt' known to history or ethnology, requires first a *physiological* investigation and interpretation, rather than a psychological one; and every one of them needs a critique on the part of medical science.'[11]

There is an interesting potential tension between the two fundamental assumptions of psychology versus physiology in Nietzsche's thought. The former points towards depth psychology and the latter towards behaviourism and sociobiology. There is, however, nothing inevitable about this tension. Nietzsche fully appreciated the speculative and introspective psychology of a Heraclitus, a Montaigne, a Rochefoucauld, a Stendhal, a Shakespeare and a Dostoevsky, while at the same time reading books about physiology and claiming: 'our knowledge of man today is real knowledge precisely to the extent that it is knowledge of him as a machine'.[12] Instead of assuming that they give conflicting and opposing results one can view them as yielding complementary results where the speculative depth-psychology approach goes downwards from the psychological level and the biological approach goes upwards from the physiological level.

A third important assumption for Nietzsche's psychology is his belief in the will to power as the most fundamental of all drives, motives or desires in all living beings. 'All psychology has hitherto remained anchored to moral prejudices and timidities: it has not ventured into the depths. To conceive it as morphology and the *development-theory of the will to power*, as I conceive it – has never yet so much as entered the mind of anyone else.'[13] Nietzsche proposes the will to power in opposition to 'the will to life',[14] or the Platonic eros or to more partial wills like the will to truth.[15] The desired state is the feeling of increased power.[16] This power includes power over others as well as over oneself, but also more sublimated forms as the power to interpret one's surroundings: 'it will have to be the will to power incarnate, it will want to grow, expand, draw to itself, gain ascendancy – not out of any morality or immorality, but because it *lives*, and because life *is* will to power.'[17] Will to power is for Nietzsche a motive force, not a criterion of the value of an action or feeling. Will to power lies behind all actions and feelings, good ones (e.g. exuberance) as well as bad ones (e.g. resentment). That Nietzsche did not necessarily approve of power and especially physical, actual and political power is, for example, visible in sections 4–5 of the chapter 'What the Germans Lack' in Götzen-Dämmerung where he claims:

> After all, no one can spend more than he has – that is true of individuals, it is also true of nations. If one spends oneself on power, grand politics, economic affairs, world commerce, parliamentary institutions, military interests – if one expends in *this* direction the quantum of reason, seriousness, will, selfovercoming that one is, then there will be a shortage in the other direction [i.e. in regard to culture]. Culture and the state – one should not deceive oneself over this – are antagonists: the 'cultural state' is merely a modern idea. The one lives off the other, the one thrives at the expense of the other. All great cultural epochs are epochs

of political decline: that which is great in the cultural sense has been unpolitical, even *anti-political*. [...] the main thing – and that is still culture [...] The essential thing has gone out of the entire system of higher education in Germany: the *end*, as well as the *means* to the end. That education, *culture*, itself is the end – and *not* 'the Reich' – [...] has been forgotten.

The perhaps most important consequence of the belief that the will to power underlies all life is that life and human life thus become *active*, not merely reactive agents as suggested by Darwinism and much of modern views of man.

The concept and importance of will to power was introduced in *Also sprach Zarathustra*,[18] and strongly emphasized in *Jenseits von Gut und Böse* and *Zur Genealogie der Moral*,[19] but plays a much more modest role in *Götzen-Dämmerung*, where it is mentioned a few times, but not at all emphasized.[20]

The concept of the will to power is an explanatory one – everything wants to expand and to 'control' its surroundings. Nietzsche used it mainly for human psychology but sometimes applied it to all life and perhaps even to inorganic matter. An important aspect of Nietzsche's view of psychology is thus his belief that the will to power is the most fundamental of all drives, motives or desires in all living beings.

Will to power is frequently interpreted as a metaphysical principle, but there is nothing that supports that Nietzsche regarded it as such in *Götzen-Dämmerung* (or in the books written after that). All of his references to it (and to power) concern *human* psychology, with one exception (and then to biology in his discussion of Darwin and Malthus). Considering that Nietzsche regards man as an animal, it follows naturally that he also regards the will to power as the striving after power also as a motive force in biology and for all animals and plants.[21]

This relative absence of the concept of will to power in *Götzen-Dämmerung* is surprising, especially if the book was to constitute a summary of his philosophy. Since it is present, and continues to be present in the two books after *Götzen-Dämmerung*, *Der Antichrist* and *Ecce homo*, he cannot have rejected it as some have argued.[22] However, a reasonable first assumption for those who regard *Götzen-Dämmerung* as a summary of his philosophy would be that he believes much less in it and therefore emphasizes it less. However, against this stands that it is quite strongly present in *Der Antichrist* and *Ecce homo*. Furthermore, Nietzsche mentions it frequently in his notes from 1888.

Until the end of August 1888 even the projected name of the *Hauptwerk* was '*Der Wille zur Macht*', and many drafted chapters contained the concept of will to power in their titles.[23] From September onwards Nietzsche used the former subtitle, *Umwerthung aller Werthe*, instead of *Der Wille zur Macht* as the main title, but that need not suggest that he had given up on or rejected the concept of will to power.

All three of these tendencies of Nietzsche's psychological thought, the subconscious, the physiological approach and the emphasis on power, have had important repercussions. The emphasis of the subconscious foreshadowed (and possibly influenced) Freud; the second physiological approach has much similarity with the underlying view of modern experimental psychology, cognitive psychology, sociobiology and behaviourism, and the emphasis on power profoundly influenced A.

Adler, L. Klages and M. Foucauld, and much of modern analysis of social and political phenomena.

Nietzsche argues that will and willing not only is something complicated[24] but that conscious will is not a cause; it is merely an epiphenomenon. What we commonly believe to be willing is only a resultant of a large number of drives, where the ruling class of drives, instincts or 'under-souls' identify with the successes of the commonwealth.[25] From this follows Nietzsche's often repeated rejection of 'free will', as well as of 'unfree will'. The precondition of the 'old-style psychology, the psychology of will' was that every action had its origin in consciousness 'whereby the most *fundamental* falsification *in psychologicis* was made into the very principle of psychology'.[26] Nietzsche's views of consciousness as surface and epiphenomenon has been discussed earlier. Nietzsche rejects the ego as illusionary and as a higher swindle. For example, he writes:

> that a thought comes when 'it' wants, not when 'I' want; so it is a *falsification* of the facts to say: the subject 'I' is the condition of the predicate 'think'. *It* thinks [. . .] For even with this 'it thinks' one has already gone too far: this 'it' already contains an *interpretation* of the event and does not belong to the event itself. The inference here is in accordance with the habits of grammar: 'thinking is an activity, to every activity pertains one who acts, consequently – ' [. . .] and perhaps we [. . .] will one day accustom ourselves to getting along without that little 'it' (which is what the honest old 'I' has evaporated into).[27]

What is left if we accept Nietzsche's critique of consciousness, willing and the ego? Remarkably much. What Nietzsche is essentially rejecting is the Christian soul, and related concepts, and since these concepts are so deeply ingrained in us we at first feel as if little or nothing is left. Anyway, common sense tells us that Nietzsche is wrong, consciousness, willingness and the ego remain. The Christian picture of the individual (which is also applicable to Socrates, Plato and most everyday psychology) can be likened to an automobile with a driver or a horse with a rider. The driver is the soul, or the consciousness who 'drives' the body, including a number of instincts, emotions and so on. Nietzsche argues that the driver or rider is illusion, and in his picture the individual is only the automobile or the horse – that we are animal, that we are 'body entirely, and nothing beside; and soul is only a word for something in the body'.[28] It is this view that makes Nietzsche reject the old psychology of imaginary causes and of going in the direction of a new physio-psychology, as we can clearly see in *Götzen-Dämmerung*. But Nietzsche is always not only a destructive but also a constructive philosopher. He reconstructs the self, but now in a more biological and less idealistic manner. 'Behind your thoughts and feelings, my brother, stands a mighty commander, an unknown sage – he is called Self. He lives in your body, he is your body. There is more reason in your body than in your best wisdom.'[29] The self has become, not an '*individuum*' but a '*dividuum*',[30] an 'oligarchy', 'a multiplicity' where the drives or affects are continually competing with and against one another leading to a dynamic state of continual change.[31] But there is also unity, and the body is a unit,[32] 'a multiplicity with one sense',[33] some of the leading drives identify with the totality and Nietzsche assumes a certain stability in regard to the drives; he claims that who a man is depends on 'the order of rank the innermost drives of his nature stand in relation to one another'.[34]

8.3 Nietzsche's view of sublimation

A major theme throughout *Götzen-Dämmerung* which lies behind and to some extent explains Nietzsche's *ad hominem* approach and his physiological 'attempt' – that is, his tendency to reduce aesthetical, ethical and even political and social questions to psychological and 'physiological' ones – is his view of mind and body. Fundamentally, we are only body – or expressed differently – fundamentally we are animals – we are filled with instincts and other physiological needs and drives. But some of these are more complex, eventually leading to 'higher order bodies', consciousness and higher emotions and 'rational' thought: '*intelligere* is actually nothing but a certain behavior of the instincts toward one another' (FW, 333). An important aspect of this view of mind as being the resultant of something fundamentally corporal and physiological is his view of the possibility and occurrence of movements from the instinctual – towards the conscious (sublimation, spiritualization, metamorphosis) and also in the reverse direction, from the conscious and even the social to the bodily and physiological, that which is reflected in, for example, psychosomatic illness (incorporation and internalization).

Hence, the self remains, not as something independent which governs the body but as a name for the body. Willing remains, not as a conscious, independent and governing principle but as a resultant of a number of drives, instincts and experiences, in the manner of how we already in 'the old psychology' accepted that animals 'will'. Indeed, the concept of will, especially the distinction between strong and weak will, is important for Nietzsche, but the concept of free will becomes as superfluous as it already earlier was in discussions of insects. Nietzsche explicitly rejects and discusses some of the consequences of this rejection of free will in section 7 of the chapter 'Errors' of *Götzen-Dämmerung* (as well as in three sections each in *Der Antichrist* and *Ecce homo*).[35]

The feeling of 'free will' may remain in man, but the denial of it as a fact is not only necessary for the man with intellectual and scientific conscience, according to Nietzsche, but also for the purpose of destroying and preventing the enormous false structures and consequences of this belief. We still 'feel' the earth to be motionless and that the sun revolves around us, but today we *know* better. We still today feel consciousness, willing and the ego as independent and causal, but we *ought* to know better. When man took the step from the geocentric to the heliocentric world view he thereby began to reject the explanations of cosmic phenomena as anthropocentric, teleological, theological, as being of a fundamentally different nature from those on the earth (e.g. the Aristotelian dichotomy of the sub- and superlunar worlds) or simply as divine or mysterious omens (as was often the case with, for example, solar eclipses and comets). The cosmic phenomena remained, but they were reinterpreted. Nietzsche believes we now must take a similar step (shift of paradigm) in psychology *and* philosophy. Nietzsche draws a parallel to Copernicus, who 'persuaded us to believe, contrary to all the senses, that the earth does *not* stand firm'.[36] However, Nietzsche's new psychology does not only reject old beliefs and the apparent evidence of the senses but, more importantly, common sense and 'rationality'. In this sense it may be better to compare the changes brought about by Nietzsche's new psychology with that of modern physics which also led to a situation beyond common sense. What astronomy was to the seventeenth century, physiology or physio-psychology should be to the nineteenth, twentieth and twenty-first centuries. We can no longer accept the spiritual causes and interpretations of psychic phenomena, nor uphold the twofold distinction between body and soul even in its more modern version of body and spirit or as body and consciousness, where spirit and consciousness have their conceptual origin in the old concept of soul. Spirit or consciousness remains for Nietzsche, but their origin is now the body.

Having reinterpreted these fundamental assumptions Nietzsche goes on to reinterpret a large number of 'comets' in human psychology: for example, love, altruism, faith, 'peace of soul', pessimism and truth.[37]

It does not follow necessarily from what is most fundamental, for example, that man is an animal, that this also is the most interesting and relevant consideration. When phenomena are fundamentally similar it is often the small part that makes them different which is of most interest. Nietzsche believes that we should study man biologically and physiologically, and he does so himself in some of his reading and analysis (as well as in his 'experimenting' with diet and climate for the sake of his health), and that we should certainly never forget or deny that man is an animal, but it is man's spirituality and consciousness that makes man into the most interesting of animals, and it is as a cultural animal that Nietzsche is primarily interested in him – wanting him at the same time to become more spiritual and more natural (instinctive).

To approach it from a different angle, the newborn offspring is a purely physiological being, determined, according to Nietzsche, by biological drives and inherited capacities and potentialities depending on individual ancestors, and on which race and species one belongs to. One is not born as a 'tabula rasa' (that assumption too is based on the separation between the spiritual and the physical, of body and soul) but under 'the spell of *physiological* value judgements and racial conditions'.[38] Nietzsche, however, shows little interest in babies and young people. With time, however, consciousness and spirituality are developed, and what was from the beginning merely physiological responses becomes more and more determined not only by these responses but also by what we put into them, how we experience and interpret them, which is done both consciously and unconsciously.[39] Nietzsche believes that language and especially grammar is in the last resort physiologically grounded[40] but it is also a social and spiritual activity that profoundly affects how we interpret the world.[41] The same applies to religion, morality, philosophy and so on – they are ultimately physiologically founded but as conscious and semiconscious beliefs they also affect both our interpretation of the world and our physiology. Nietzsche is no stranger to how 'spiritual' beliefs can influence physiology, for example, in the form of illness and mental illness, and he claims that views 'through habit become instinct'.[42] However, most of his examples are to indicate the influence from the physiological to consciousness (since this was something that had been almost completely ignored by the old psychology, and even more by the old philosophy).[43]

Nietzsche writes in *Jenseits von Gut und Böse*: 'It has gradually become clear to me what every great philosophy has hitherto been: a confession on the part of its author and a kind of involuntary and unconscious memoir; moreover, that the moral (or immoral) intentions in every philosophy have every time constituted the real germ of life out of which the entire plant has grown.'[44] In still more general language Nietzsche states that he attempts 'to understand moral judgements as symptoms and sign language which betray the processes of physiological prosperity or failure'[45] and

> often I have asked myself whether taking a large view, philosophy has not been merely an interpretation of the body and a *misunderstanding of the body*. Behind the highest value judgements that have hitherto guided the history of thought, there are concealed misunderstandings of the physical constitution – of individuals or classes or even whole races. All those bold insanities of metaphysics, especially answers to the question about the *value* of existence, may always be considered first of all as the symptoms of certain bodies. And if such world affirmation or world negations *tout court* lack any grain of significance when measured scientifically, they are the more valuable for the historian and psychologist as hints or symptoms of the body, of its success or failure, its plenitude, power, and autocracy in history, or of its frustrations, weariness, impoverishment, its premonitions of the end, its will to the end. I am still waiting for a philosophical *physician* [. . .] what was at stake in all philosophizing hitherto was not at all 'truth' but something else – let us say, health, future, growth, power, life.[46]

Nietzsche uses such words as 'body', 'physiological' and so on because these represent the ultimate source of character and personality – 'a mere disciplining of thoughts and feelings is virtually nothing [. . .]: one first has to convince the *body*. [. . .] It is decisive for the fortune of nations and mankind that one should inaugurate culture in the *right place* – *not* in the 'soul' (as has been the fateful superstition of priests and quasi-priests): the right place is the body, demeanour, diet, physiology: the *rest* follows . . .'[47] It is, however, often reasonable to read these physiological words as instead referring to the broader concepts of character and personality. Such a reading is justified for two reasons. First, although Nietzsche theoretically wants to reduce philosophical systems and beliefs to physiological causes, in practice and in detail he is mostly only able to do so to the psychological level, or to a more general character level.[48] Second, because Nietzsche does not only assume that there is an influence from the physiological level and upwards but also in fact accepts a rather large degree of downward influence from the social and still more from the psychological level to the physiological level. This can be regarded as a Lamarckian and behaviouristic aspect of Nietzsche's thought which limits its reductive character.

8.4 The status and role of reason and instinct in *Götzen-Dämmerung*

Most readers of *Götzen-Dämmerung*, as well as of most of Nietzsche's other books, come away from it with a view that Nietzsche was highly critical of reason ('The harshest daylight, rationality at any cost, life bright, cold, circumspect, conscious, without instinct, in opposition to the instincts, has itself been no more than a form of sickness')[49] and largely favourable of instincts ('everything *good* is instinct').[50] On one level this is clearly true, but it is also misleading.

Reason and instinct (including related concepts) are two of the most prominent and central themes of *Götzen-Dämmerung*.[51] In this section we will examine them and their relation to one another. His view of the relation between them is of great importance for a general understanding of Nietzsche's philosophy, and more specifically for, for example, seeing how he anticipated Freud, for understanding how he reversed the conventional view in the history of philosophy that reason, mind and consciousness are more valuable than body, instinct and the subconscious, and for correctly understanding *Götzen-Dämmerung*.

I will here present three levels of interpretations of his view and analysis of reason and instinct and of the relation between them. The first one – that Nietzsche simply reverses the conventional view of placing reason above instinct – which I believe is the most common view among readers and commentators – is overly simplistic and, although containing much truth, leads to a severe misunderstanding of Nietzsche and his philosophy. The second-level interpretation removes much of this misconception by emphasizing that for Nietzsche reason and instinct do not necessarily represent opposing positions and showing how they for him belong together and how they, in fact, are closely related by emphasizing sublimation and incorporation. This interpretation, however, seems to leave some contradictions. The third-level interpretation, I believe, removes the contradictions and leaves us with a better understanding of Nietzsche's view of these questions, as well as of his philosophy generally.

First-level interpretation: Nietzsche reverses the conventional view of mind and body

There seem to be many reasons for accepting that Nietzsche places instincts (and body) high above reason (and intellect), and thus goes against Plato, Descartes and much of the history of philosophy, which has regarded man as the rational animal and philosophy as the study of reason (and in this shows kinship with David Hume). He, for example, claims that 'There is more reason in your body than in your best wisdom.'[52] Some commentators have argued that he even uses 'instinct' as a criterion for good and bad, and others see him as an irrationalist thinker, and thus as an opponent of reason.

At first Nietzsche's position can seem to simply be the reverse of the conventional one – instinct above reason ('of all forms of intelligence discovered hitherto, "instinct" is the most intelligent'),[53] and that which comes from instinct as good, while that which comes from reason and dialectics is bad ('with dialectics the rabble gets on top [. . .] One chooses dialectics only when one has no other expedient').[54]

Nietzsche certainly favours instinct, but it cannot be and is not his criterion for what is good. It is just like the case with the will to power, which, also cannot constitute a criterion, for it lies behind everything, good and bad – but where instinct or will to power is missing (or is misdirected, is decadent), that is certainly, according to Nietzsche, not of highest quality. We can, for example, see this in that Nietzsche frequently refers to 'negative' instincts, such as herd-instinct, decadence-instinct and sickly instinct. He also occasionally speaks ill of instincts or the effect of them, as when he refers to the 'dissolutioness and anarchy of his [Socrates'] instincts'.[55]

Nonetheless, even without using instinct as criteria, this is indeed a radical view which seems to invert the whole concept of philosophy. But is it Nietzsche's view? We are in that case left with a very contradictory Nietzsche, which is also the view of, for example, G. Funke, who wrote the article 'Instinkt' for *Historisches Wörterbuch der Philosophie*. This picture fits many of Nietzsche's provocative statements about instincts and reason, and much of what he says about mind and body, as well as for his praise of Dionysos and the importance of *extasis*.[56]

But equally much goes against this interpretation – not only Nietzsche's whole concern for high culture and *Bildung* ('the main thing [. . .] is still culture'),[57] but also his interest in more advanced philosophy, psychology and science (which presupposes higher faculties than mere drives and instincts), as well as that he often emphasizes the importance of cool thinking and to be sceptical, and of the importance of reading well, rather than to react immediately to every impulse and stimuli.[58] Furthermore, this 'reversal' view is inconsistent with the results when we examine what sort of individuals Nietzsche approves of and admires. They are not primitive men of actions, but highly sophisticated cultural persons, such as Goethe, Homer, Shakespeare, Beethoven, Napoleon, Voltaire, Sophocles, Aeschylus, Heraclitus, Byron, Horace, Raphael and Montaigne. These are the most often referred to and praised persons in Nietzsche's published books, in this order.[59] To take one pertinent example, *Götzen-Dämmerung* was originally to end with the chapter 'Expeditions of an Untimely Man', which ends with the last four sections in a crescendo of praise of Goethe – presumably this is not just a portrait of Goethe but also at the same time an exemplar of what man can become. According to Nietzsche:

> Goethe was, in an epoch disposed to the unreal, a convinced realist: he affirmed everything which was related to him in this respect [. . .] Goethe conceived of a strong, highly cultured human being, skilled in all physical accomplishments, who, keeping himself in check and having reverence for himself, dares to allow himself the whole compass and wealth of naturalness, who is strong enough for this freedom; a man of tolerance, not out of weakness, but out of strength, because he knows how to employ to his advantage what would destroy an average nature; a man to whom nothing is forbidden, except it be *weakness*, whether that weakness be called vice or virtue.

This lack of consistency leads us on to another, deeper, second-level interpretation.

Second-level interpretation: Reason and instinct are not opposites but related

A less radical, but related, interpretation than the first level one would be to emphasize:

1. Nietzsche upgrades instincts and the body, contra Plato, Descartes, et al.
2. Nietzsche emphasizes that thinking and valuing must be related to the body or instincts – otherwise it is useless or dangerous (leads to alienation, abstraction, 'idealism' etc.).
3. This can be understood by realizing the importance of the concept of sublimation (*Sublimirung* and *Vergeistigung*) as well as the opposing concepts of incorporation and assimilation (*Einverleibung* and *Aneignung*) for Nietzsche.

This leads to a much more accurate picture, but it still contains several important lacunas and problems. In particular, it is then perhaps not so very different from that of Plato's view and that of most members of the philosophical tradition.

Third-level interpretation: Dynamic affirmation of not a static average but of both poles, of both mind and body

This interpretation adds an extra dimension to the previous, second, level. We need to realize that Nietzsche affirms both instinct and reason, and still admitting that they can often be contradictory, and therefore we need to affirm them dynamically, moving from one to another ('It is by being "natural" that one best recovers from one's unnaturalness, from one's spirituality . . .')[60] and affirming *both*. In so doing, Nietzsche also emphasizes that reason (and the conscious) and instinct (and the unconscious) are not really distinct and separate spheres but overlapping and interdependent. He also builds in an inherent conflict and dynamism in his view of human psychology and thought.[61] Unlike earlier views, it is according to him not possible to find a perfect synthesis or compromise between reason and instinct (or mind and body) – and thus no static or equilibrium ideal – instead one must accept a dynamic swing between reason and instinct – sometimes emphasizing the one, sometimes the other. This interpretation fits and illuminates his many statements in regard to mind and body in *Götzen-Dämmerung*.

9

The critique of Christianity in *Twilight of the Idols* and its relation to *The Antichrist*

9.1 Introduction 177
9.2 The critique of Christianity in *Götzen-Dämmerung* 177
9.3 The critique of Christianity in *Der Antichrist* 183
9.4 Conclusions: The relation between *Götzen-Dämmerung*, *Der Antichrist*
and the further volumes of the *Revaluation of All Values* 185

9.1 Introduction

Nietzsche wrote *Götzen-Dämmerung* and *Der Antichrist* essentially at the same time in August and September 1888. What is the relation between them? The probably best answer is that Nietzsche regarded the former as a sort of summary or extract of his revaluation project and the latter as the first volume of the *Umwerthung aller Werthe*. More specifically, what is the relation between his critique of Christianity in *Götzen-Dämmerung* and in *Der Antichrist*? Does the critique of Christianity in *Götzen-Dämmerung* pre-empt that of *Der Antichrist*? Or summarize it? Or is it meant as a complement to it? Can *Götzen-Dämmerung* in this respect be regarded as preparatory for *Der Antichrist*? How? Or is the relation best described in another manner?

The main question we are examining in this chapter is more far-reaching than it first appears. If we can determine something tangible about the relation between *Götzen-Dämmerung* and *Der Antichrist* (the first and only of the books of the *Umwerthung aller Werthe* to be written), then we ought to be able to say something, in parallel, also about its relation to the other planned volumes, and thus also something about these planned but never written books.

9.2 The critique of Christianity in *Götzen-Dämmerung*

One could perhaps at first expect that *Götzen-Dämmerung* should contain only little critique of Christianity, since that was to be the theme of the first volume of the *Umwerthung aller Werthe*, *Der Antichrist*, which he wrote at the same time. On the other hand, one could also expect it to contain a 'summary' or extract of the severe critique of Christianity which he was writing for *Der Antichrist* in line with his general statements and what seems to be the case for the other three planned but not written books. Furthermore, Nietzsche, for personal reasons, seems to have been unable to refrain from critique of it (as well as to refrain from criticizing contemporary Germany) during his last one or two years. However, more importantly, for anyone who wants to perform a revaluation of all values, the influence of Christianity is so all-pervasive that it simply was impossible for him not to discuss it and refer to it on numerous occasions. Furthermore, it is likely that Nietzsche felt that it was necessary for him to prepare his readers for the coming critique.

Critique of Christianity is present in every chapter of *Götzen-Dämmerung*, but in none is it the main and exclusive theme.[1] It is most prominent in chapters 6 and 7 ('The Four Great Errors' and 'The "Improvers" of Mankind'), and, somewhat less in chapter 5 ('Morality as Anti-Nature'). It seems fair to say that the critique of Christianity, of theoretical philosophy and metaphysics, and of morality constitute approximately equally important parts of *Götzen-Dämmerung*. This is especially true for the first half of the book, chapters 1–7. The treatment of these three themes differ in that the critique of theoretical philosophy and ethics constitute the primary theme of several chapters, chapters 2–4 (and possibly also 6) and 5–7 respectively, while Christianity is mentioned throughout, but is not made the primary target of any one chapter (with the possible exception of chapter 6). In the foreword, where Nietzsche describes the purpose of the book as sounding-out idols – '*eternal* idols' – he is probably referring to these aspects: religion, metaphysics and morality – but in the last sentence he seems especially to emphasize Christianity (God): 'That does not prevent their being the *most believed in*; and they are not, especially in the most eminent case, called idols [*Götzen*]'.[2]

Let us examine the critique of Christianity in *Götzen-Dämmerung*, which is also summarized in Tables 9.1 and 9.2. The first chapter of aphorisms contains about an equal number of maxims which vaguely refers to Christianity, philosophy and ethics respectively. The second chapter, 'Socrates', contains a single explicit reference to Christianity (actually to Christian morality) – which points to chapters 6 and 7, where the theme is discussed further: '*the entire morality of improvement, the Christian included, has been a misunderstanding*' (section 11). In the two following chapters, the critique of Christianity is tied to the critique of philosophy and metaphysics, including the nature of language: '"Reason" in language: oh what a deceitful old woman! I fear we are not getting rid of God because we still believe in grammar' (5). The Christian division between a life here and a 'beyond' is closely associated to the philosophical separation of a 'true' and an 'apparent' world, and, Nietzsche claims that this dichotomy is created out of a desire to denigrate life here and now.

The following three morality-critical chapters contain many more explicit references to Christianity. In chapter 6 ('The Four Great Errors') the emphasis is on epistemology and view of reality. Christianity is tied to each of the four fundamental errors Nietzsche discusses. The first error is the one of mistaking cause for consequence: 'every proposition formulated by religion and morality' is based on this first error. The second error – the error of false causality – concerns primarily the psychology of 'inner facts', based on will, conscience (spirit) and the ego – also

Table 9.1 Summary of the Critique of Religion and Christianity in *Götzen-Dämmerung*

Twilight of the Idols Chapters	Where (Section in Chapter) and What Sort of Critique	Summary of Critique
Foreword	God as an idol	Christianity included in the critique of idols
1. Maxims and Arrows	7, 9, 18, (29), (31), 32	Is man God's mistake, or God man's mistake?
2. The Problem of Socrates	11. 'The entire morality of improvement, the Christian included, has been a misunderstanding.'	Christian morality a misunderstanding
3. 'Reason' in Philosophy	The death of God and metaphysics. Many minor arguments. Language: 'I fear we are not getting rid of God because we still believe in grammar'	Rejection of Christian metaphysics
4. How the 'Real World' at last Became a Myth	The death of Platonic and Christian metaphysics.	Rejection of Christian metaphysics
5. Morality as Anti-Nature	Much critique. (1) 'the practice of the Church is *hostile to life*'. (4) 'Life is at the end where the "Kingdom of God" begins'.	Severe rejection of Christian morality. As anti-natural, as life-denying, as wanting to exterminate all passions.
6. The Four Great Errors	(5) Christian 'criterion of truth' as pleasure or potency is wrong. (6) 'Morality and religion fall entirely under the *psychology of error*'. (7) 'Free will' created by theologians and priests for the purpose of making man responsible and guilty. (8) 'We deny God; in denying God, we deny accountability: only by doing *that* do we redeem the world'.	Christianity and morality are based on all four of these errors.
7. The 'Improvers' of Mankind	(2) Christian morality = taming man. (4) Christianity, the revolt of the failed, motivated by hatred and revenge, but claims to be motivated by love. (4) 'Christianity, growing from Jewish roots and comprehensible only as a product of this soil'. (5) Christian morality is 'thoroughly *immoral*'.	Severe rejection of Christian morality. Close association of Christianity with Judaism – a major theme in AC.
8. What the Germans Lack	(2) Christianity as narcotics.	Christianity as narcotics.
9. Expeditions of an Untimely Man	The critique of Christianity is present in many of these mini-essays, especially in: 2, 4, 5, 9, 34, 35 and 47.	(2) Renan, a freethinker, but a priest in his bowels. (5) Many free themselves of Christianity, but feel obliged to cling more firmly to Christian morality. 'Christianity is a system'. 'When one gives up Christian belief one thereby deprives oneself of the *right* to Christian morality'.

(*Continued*)

Table 9.1 (Continued)

Twilight of the Idols Chapters	Where (Section in Chapter) and What Sort of Critique	Summary of Critique
		(9) A Christian cannot be an artist (for artists are life-affirming)
		(34) Christians and anarchists are declining types and motivated by feelings of revenge.
		(35) The decadent and Christian says '*life* is not worth anything' – when they should say '*I* am no longer worth anything'. This nihilism is contagious and therefore dangerous.
		(47) 'Christianity, which despised the body, has up till now been mankind's greatest misfortune'.
10. What I Owe to the Ancients	(2) Plato 'an antecedent Christian'. (4) 'Christianity, with *ressentiment against* life [...] made sexuality something impure'.	Nietzsche finds/creates ideals and values among and from the Greeks – not in or from Christianity.
The Hammer Speaks	Become hard! And self-confident, a creator and a destiny.	The opposite of the Christian teaching of humility.

© Thomas H. Brobjer
Column 1 lists the chapters of *Götzen-Dämmerung*. Column 2 the main sections where critique of Christianity is expressed, and often briefly summarizing it. Column 3, briefly summarizes the essence of Nietzsche's critique in the whole chapter.

Table 9.2 The Relation between *Götzen-Dämmerung* and *Der Antichrist* (as the First Volume of the *Umwerthung aller Werthe*)

Götzen-Dämmerung contains brief presentations of the following themes also present in *Der Antichrist*:

Critique of Christianity, the Church and God generally.
Critique of Christian metaphysics
Critique of Christian morality, as a misunderstanding, anti-natural, life-denying, decadent
Critique of Christian disregard for reality, science and truth
Comparison of Christian morality with that of the Laws of Manu
Severe critique of priests (and philosophers are regarded as closely allied to them)
Critique of Kant as essentially a Christian thinker

Götzen-Dämmerung does not contain discussions of the following major themes in *Der Antichrist*:

Analysis of Jesus and his psychology (AC 27–40)
Discussion of the relation between St. Paul and Jesus – Paul as the originator of the Church (AC 41–7)
Götzen-Dämmerung contains very limited comparisons of Christianity with Buddhism (AC 20–3), Judaism (AC 24–7), antiquity, Islam and the Renaissance (AC 58–61).

There is nothing important in relation to a critique of Christianity in *Götzen-Dämmerung* which is not also present in *Der Antichrist*.

© Thomas H. Brobjer

has consequences for religion, which is based on the assumption of effective 'spiritual causes', which we no longer can believe in: 'The error of spirit as cause mistaken for reality! And made the measure of reality! And called God!' (3). The entire realm of religion (and morality) also falls under the third similar error, the concept of imaginary causes, that is, giving (false) spiritual causes for physiological affects (often understood religiously or morally, such as feelings of 'sin' or something being due to 'good conscience'). The fourth error, the error of free will, is, according to him, constructed by theologians and priests to make mankind 'accountable' and thus guilty and dependent on them. While discussing these four errors, Nietzsche also briefly criticizes the Christian criterion and proof of truth – 'Proof by *pleasure* ("by potency") as criterion of truth', in other words, conviction as a criterion of truth (5). This anti-scientific attitude receives Nietzsche's scorn and is returned to in *Der Antichrist*.[3]

In chapter 5 ('Morality as Anti-Nature') one main argument in regard to religion is put forward: Christianity is hostile to life (by being hostile to the fundament of life, instincts, passions and the body) and therefore the morality associated with Christianity is anti-natural and life-denying.

In the seventh chapter, 'The "Improvers" of Mankind', morality is severely criticized in the first and last section (as simply fictitious, but also including that Christians and other moralists have never doubted their right to use immoral means to make people moral). In the middle part of the chapter, two forms of morality ('improvements') are discussed and rejected – 'taming' and 'breeding', represented by Christianity and the Laws of Manu, respectively. To 'tame' is not to improve, but to make weak and sick – to make 'in short, a "Christian"' (2). Nietzsche here also briefly, in a subclause, mentions the thesis that Christianity is a direct continuation of Jewish religion, a major theme in *Der Antichrist* (sections 24–7): 'Christianity, growing from Jewish roots and comprehensible only as a product of this soil' (4).

While presenting these more major points in these three chapters, Nietzsche also briefly mentions a fairly large number of other more minor points.

In the eighth chapter, 'What the Germans Lack', there is no explicit discussion of Christianity, except the claim that it, together with alcohol, is one of the two great European narcotics, and thus possibly regarded by Nietzsche as the cause for German (and European) decline.

The long ninth chapter, 'Expeditions of a Untimely Man', contains a fairly large number of scattered remarks (some of them highly condemning) in regard to Christianity, several of them repetitions of things stated earlier in the book, such as 'Christianity, which despised the body, has up till now been mankind's greatest misfortune' (47).

Two new larger themes are also briefly discussed. One of these concerns modern agnosticism and free-thinking – those who claim that they do not believe in God or are not Christians but nonetheless are profoundly indebted to it and who base much of their values on the Christian paradigm. This is elaborated on especially in section 5, and mentioned in regard to Renan, Comte, Eliot, Carlyle and Schopenhauer.

The other major theme concerns the contrast between higher and lower persons and forms of life: 'As long as the *priest* was considered the highest type *every* valuable kind of human being was disvalued' (45). He exemplifies with Renan, on his knees before 'the *évangile des humbles*' (2), who is contrasted to Goethe's healthy atheism (51). This theme is, of course, closely related to a revaluation of all values.

Many other points are also briefly touched on in this long chapter.

In the last chapter, 'What I Owe to the Ancients', Nietzsche briefly refers to Christianity as 'the great fatality' (2) and repeats his view of it as life-denying: 'It was only Christianity, with *ressentiment against* life in its foundations, which made sexuality something impure: it threw *filth* on the beginning, on the prerequisite of our life' (4). He also refers to Plato as 'so much an antecedent Christian' (2) and elaborates on this theme, which he also has mentioned in several of his earlier books.[4] He also suggests that early Greek society and thought constitutes a life-affirming alternative to Christianity.

The epilogue contains no discussion of Christianity but can be regarded as setting up the ideal 'become hard' in opposition to the Christian ideal of humility and self-sacrifice.

One important underlying claim in much of Nietzsche's critique of Christianity is that our conception of God and religion is merely a reflection and expression of human psychology and values. His critique of Christianity is in fact largely a critique of man and man's view of himself.[5]

Perhaps it is not unreasonable to summarize the explicit and unsystematic critique of Christianity in *Götzen-Dämmerung* under five headings, of which the first is the most important and the last least important (and given least space in the book), and the three middle ones of approximately equal importance and prominence.

1. Much general critique, some of which is very fundamental (and hostile): This includes arguing that Christianity is against life, our instincts and the body. Christianity is decadent, nihilistic and pessimistic. Christianity is based on resentment (this is also one of the important similarities between Christians, socialists and anarchists). He also refers to two fundamental value systems: early Greek contra Christian (and modern), with, however, Plato as an antecedent Christian.
2. Critique of Christian metaphysics and a two-world system: His account of how the 'real world' became a myth has great similarity to and is written in parallel to his claim that God is dead, but we have still not drawn the consequences of this. To do so constitutes a large part of Nietzsche's philosophical task. Associated with this is also a critique of language as containing conceptions of spiritual causality and metaphysics in its very foundation, and thus reinforcing our belief in God.
3. Epistemological critique of Christianity: Nietzsche constructs four fundamental errors (discussed earlier in this book), all related to Christianity. He also briefly criticizes the Christian criterion of truth, based merely on the degree of conviction.
4. Much and fundamental critique of Christian morality.[6]
5. Critique of agnostics, atheists and free-thinkers, who claim to have left Christianity but who nonetheless continue to hold fast to Christian values: Nietzsche here argues that 'Christianity is a system' which one either must accept or reject.

9.3 The critique of Christianity in *Der Antichrist*

Der Antichrist, slightly shorter than *Götzen-Dämmerung*, written during September 1888, is a much more focused and worked-out study than the multifarious *Götzen-Dämmerung* in which no theme is treated in depth. With the exception of the first short seven sections which are more general and introductory, the rest of the book is completely focused on a critique of Christianity. Nietzsche had produced subtitles or divisions for the first half of the book, although not included in the final version (and I have constructed further ones, given in parenthesis), which help us summarize and get an overview of what it contains:

1–7: We Hyperboreans
8–14: For us – against us
15–19: The concept of a décadence-religion
20–3: Buddhism and Christianity
(24–7): The roots of Christianity [the Jewish religion]
(27–33): Jesus and Jesus' psychology
(33–40): Jesus contra Christianity
(41–7): Paul and his reinterpretation of the Evangelium
(48–55): Christianity contra science and truth
(56–8): Christianity contra Manu
(58–61): Christianity contra antiquity, Islam and the Renaissance
(62): Conclusion and condemnation of Christianity
(Law against Christianity): Seven antichristian theses

Der Antichrist is furthermore a much more worked-out and almost 'academic' treatise as compared to *Götzen-Dämmerung* (if we ignore the polemics). This is especially visible in that *Der Antichrist* was in part constructed by studying, using and going into critical dialogue with a row of specific religious studies, including the Bible (although many of these books and studies are not explicitly mentioned by Nietzsche). Nietzsche's reading of religious books was extensive from early childhood, and already when he began school he was called 'the little pastor' because he knew selections from the Bible by heart. He left the Christian faith before the age of twenty, but he nonetheless continued reading relevant Christian literature. Especially around 1879 and 1880 he read religious literature extensively, in a critical vein (which influenced, among others, his views of Christianity generally, Luther, Paul and the relation between religion and morality, which is visible in *Morgonröthe*). Intensive reading of Christian literature continued in 1887 and 1888.

Among the relevant reading during the mid-1880s was his detailed and critical reading of Augustine's *Confessions* in 1885 (discussed in *Der Antichrist*)[7] and the following year of Julius Lipperts *Christentum, Volksglaube und Volksbrauch: Geschichtliche Entwicklung ihres Vorstellungsinhaltes* (Berlin, 1882), of which he says, 'it contains much of *my* way of thinking about religion, and a large number of suggestive facts',[8] together with several other works. Let us summarize his fairly extensive and most explicit reading concerning religion in 1887 and 1888, that is, shortly before he wrote *Der Antichrist*.⁹ For the year 1887, this includes the Bible, Julius Wellhausen (a well-known historian of religion, by whom Nietzsche read three books, important for the account of early Christianity, Jewish religion and Islam), Ernst Renan (perhaps six massive volumes of his *Les origines du christianisme*, of which one was called *L'antichrist*), probably a re-reading of Thomas à Kempis *Imitatio Christi*, probably Pascal, Simplicius' commentary to Epiktetus (Nietzsche's copy is heavily annotated, and he claims to see the contrast between Epiktetus' ancient *Weltanschauung* and Simplicius' Christian attitudes and values – in spite of the fact that Simplicius, sixth century AD, was not a believing Christian), perhaps the church father Tertullian and the book into which Nietzsche made more annotations than into any other during that year, Guyaus *L'irréligion de l'avenir* (Paris, 1887). In 1888 he continued to intensively read books on religion, including: Louis Jacolliot, *Les legislateurs religieux: Manou*, Tolstoj, *Ma religion*, Dostoevsky, *Les possédés*, Wellhausen, the Bible and a re-reading of Renan's *Vie de Jésus*, the first volume of seven of *Les origines du christianisme*.

We can thus see that Nietzsche worked on, studied and carefully prepared his more focused critique of Christianity and the writing of *Der Antichrist*.

In summary, one can say that Nietzsche does three things in *Der Antichrist*:

1. In the first seven or fourteen sections, he sets up a dichotomy between his own ideal (here referred to as 'Hyperborean') and contrasts that with that of Christianity and modernity. The first seven sections were originally written as a foreword to the whole *Umwerthung aller Werthe* volumes, and thus they are broader than the rest of the book. In the following seven sections, 8–14, the critique of Christianity (and everyone with 'the blood of theologians') become much more apparent, but the emphasis on a dichotomy remains, and these sections too can be regarded as introductory, or as constituting a transition from the introduction to the actual main arguments of the book.¹⁰
2. The greater middle part of the book contains a severe, in large part detailed and unrelenting critique of Christianity, some of which is summarized in section 47. We can here see that it was not only directed against the Church, not only directed against the existence of God or on our ability to know and prove this but emphasizing the *values* inherent in Christianity:

   > What sets *us* apart is not that we recognize no God, either in history or in nature or behind nature – but that we find that which has been reverenced as God not 'godlike' but pitiable, absurd, harmful, not merely an error but a *crime against life*. . . . We deny God as God. . . . If this God of the Christians were *proved* to us to exist, we should know even less how to believe in him. – In a formula: *Deus, qualem Paulus creavit, dei negatio*.¹¹

As a special aspect of his strategy – in contrast to the general contemporary view (which was often anti-Semitic), but in line with, among others, the still-today respected scholar of the history of Christianity Julius Wellhausen's research (but without naming him) – he ties Christianity closely to Jewish religion – and regards it as a continuation of Jewish values, that Nietzsche describes as a slave-morality. Second – also in contrast to the general contemporary view – he

separates and treats as distinctly different Jesus' and St. Paul's Christianity. Third, he expends much space on discussing the psychology of Jesus, arguing that it differs fundamentally from how it has been interpreted by later Christianity. Fourth, *Der Antichrist* contains a large number of quotations from, and critical discussions of, the Bible.
3. In the latter part of the book, sections 48–61 (and sections 20–3), he compares Christianity to, and contrasts it with, other phenomena: Buddhism, (Judaism), truth and science, Manu, antiquity, Islam and the Renaissance.

9.4 Conclusions: The relation between *Götzen-Dämmerung*, *Der Antichrist* and the further volumes of the *Revaluation of All Values*

One of the most obvious differences in regard to Christianity between *Götzen-Dämmerung* and *Der Antichrist* is that in *Götzen-Dämmerung*, although prevalent, there is no consistent critique of Christianity, while in *Der Antichrist* this is obviously the main and exclusive theme. Another difference is that the critique in *Götzen-Dämmerung* is throughout general, while it becomes much more detailed, worked out and consistent in *Der Antichrist*. In *Götzen-Dämmerung* most of his critique is stated rather than argued (or, at least, the line of arguments is very short) and he makes very limited use of history, while much of his critique in *Der Antichrist* is historical in nature and his lines of arguments are longer.

Using the three-part division of *Der Antichrist* discussed earlier, as consisting of an introduction (1–14), the focused and thematic middle part (15–47) and the comparative final part (48–61), we can draw some general conclusions about the critique of Christianity in *Götzen-Dämmerung* and *Der Antichrist*.

The first sections of *Der Antichrist* are in fact equally general and introductory to the whole *Umwerthung aller Werthe*-project as *Götzen-Dämmerung* (which Nietzsche explicitly referred to as preparatory for that project, and, alternatively, as consisting of excerpts from work on that project). This is not altogether surprising when we realize that *Der Antichrist* is not only the first of four planned volumes but that half of this beginning (sections 1–7) was originally written as a foreword to that whole project.

In fact, if one compares the critique of Christianity in these first fourteen sections with that in *Götzen-Dämmerung*, it turns out that it is similar – general in nature, Christianity as supporting everything 'weak, base, ill-constituted' against that which is valuable, Christianity and priests as denying truth and reality, much of it is highly condemning and hostile, and Christianity is described as decadent and nihilistic, and much of the critique is based upon an assumption of the existence of two fundamental and opposing sets of values, life-affirming (Hyperborean, Dionysian and non-Christian) and life-denying (Christian and decadent). Both texts also contain severe critique of priests (which, however, is made more extensive and explicitly includes theologians in *Der Antichrist*), and both stress a close relationship between philosophy (especially German philosophy) and Christianity, exemplified in both books by Kant.

The probably greatest difference is that in these first fourteen sections of *Der Antichrist* there is a strong critique of pity or compassion and the morality of pity (in sections 2 and elaborated on in section 7), while this theme is only briefly mentioned in *Götzen-Dämmerung* (section 37 in the 'Expedition' chapter). We can thus conclude that there is much similarity between the critique of Christianity in *Götzen-Dämmerung* and in the first part of *Der Antichrist*. Both of them are furthermore introductory not only to the critique of Christianity, but to the whole *Umwerthung aller Werthe*-project.

In contrast, there is only limited overlap between the critique of Christianity in *Götzen-Dämmerung* and in the *thematic* larger middle part of *Der Antichrist* (sections 15–47). In the former there is, for example, no mention at all of Jesus, Paul and Luther, while they are main characters in *Der Antichrist*. Furthermore, Nietzsche in the latter also extensively quotes and discusses the Bible, something which is almost completely absent in *Götzen-Dämmerung*. *Götzen-Dämmerung* can thus in no way be regarded as a summary of this central part of *Der Antichrist*. That central part can be regarded as an elaboration and much more detailed analysis and critique of Christianity than is done in *Götzen-Dämmerung*.

Also in regard to the third *comparative* part of *Der Antichrist*, *Götzen-Dämmerung* can *not* be regarded as a summary, since several of the phenomena discussed in *Der Antichrist* are completely missing in *Götzen-Dämmerung* (such as Buddhism and Islam, and Judaism is only briefly mentioned in a subclause), but there is nonetheless a very significant overlap with several other themes (truth, Manu, antiquity and the Renaissance). *Götzen-Dämmerung* seems concerning these four latter themes or phenomena to contain more than an extract or summary. In general, in regard to these four themes there is much similarity between what is said in *Götzen-Dämmerung* and in *Der Antichrist*.[12]

We have thus concluded that *Der Antichrist* contains significantly more and further information and arguments than those present in *Götzen-Dämmerung*, but little or nothing that goes against what can be found there. Compare Tables 9.1 and 9.2, where the similarities and differences between *Götzen-Dämmerung* and *Der Antichrist* are summarized.

How is the reverse situation? Is almost all of the discussion and critique of Christianity in *Götzen-Dämmerung* also present in *Der Antichrist*, or does *Der Antichrist* only contain a smaller proportion of that? All important critique of Christianity in *Götzen-Dämmerung* seems also to be included in, and often expanded on, *Der Antichrist*, with one exception. Christian morality is discussed more in *Götzen-Dämmerung* than in *Der Antichrist* – Nietzsche seems to avoid discussing it in *Der Antichrist* since it was intended to be discussed together with other critique of morality in volume 3 of the *Umwerthung aller Werthe*.

There seems to exist no difference or contradiction between in how Christianity is treated in *Götzen-Dämmerung* and in *Der Antichrist*.[13]

Primarily due to the almost complete lack of overlap between the critique of Christianity in *Götzen-Dämmerung* and the central part of *Der Antichrist*, *Götzen-Dämmerung* cannot be regarded as a summary of *Der Antichrist*. What we have in *Götzen-Dämmerung* is instead a broad, general critique of Christianity, suitable as a general introduction to *Der Antichrist* and for introducing an awareness of the existence of two opposing sets of fundamental values – the foundation of Nietzsche's project of a revaluation of values.

It follows from this that the contents of *Der Antichrist* cannot be constructed from only an extrapolation of the contents of *Götzen-Dämmerung*. If one were, as a test case, to attempt to construct the contents of *Der Antichrist* out of *Götzen-Dämmerung* (the way one could attempt it in a more relevant sense for the three further volumes of the *Umwerthung aller Werthe*), one would, for example, have failed to realize the extent of, and the detailed discussion of, Jesus, Paul and Luther, the fairly detailed discussion of the Bible and the comparison of Christianity with Buddhism, Islam and Judaism. However, except these (and a few other) major themes, *Götzen-Dämmerung* actually contains – although often without elaboration – many of the most important aspects of Nietzsche's critique of Christianity. Furthermore, there is little in *Götzen-Dämmerung* that is not included in *Der Antichrist*, and almost nothing in it that goes against the argument in *Der Antichrist*. Such a reconstruction would thus be interesting and relevant, and give a reasonable account of the general contents of *Der Antichrist*, although also contain major lacunas, as well as much less argued and elaborated views and interpretations. Knowing this about the relation between *Götzen-Dämmerung* and *Der Antichrist*, one could, in parallel, attempt to construct the contents of the further volumes of the *Umwerthung aller Werthe*, at least of the more critical volumes two and three, with the realization that they would, if they actually had been written by Nietzsche, almost certainly also contain significant material not mentioned in *Götzen-Dämmerung* (which thus would be missed in such an extrapolation).

However, the situation for an extrapolation to reach an approximation of the possible contents of the *Umwerthung aller Werthe* is significantly better than this suggests if we also utilize the available information in Nietzsche's late notes. When one combines the relevant contents of *Götzen-Dämmerung* with Nietzsche's critique of Christianity in his late notes (from before September 1888, when he began *Der Antichrist*), the result would improve significantly, and become much more similar to what *Der Antichrist* actually contains. Most of what he says of Jesus and Jesus' psychology is present in the notes from the winter of 1887–8, just as most of his discussion of Paul, Luther and his quotations and critique of the Bible are present in the notes from the autumn of 1887 and the spring of 1888.

A reasonable starting point for such an attempt to provisionally reconstruct the contents of the four volumes of the *Umwerthung aller Werthe* (of which the construction of the contents of the first volume is only a test case) can be aided by using not only his notes in general, but his extensive collection of notes, which he calls 'the first written version of my "Umwerthung aller Werthe" is finished',[14] and the attribution of them into the different four volumes of the *Umwerthung aller Werthe*.[15] However, it must be kept in mind that at that stage the plans for the four volumes were somewhat different (especially in regard to the critique of Christianity), but this can at least in part be adjusted for. Of these 374 numbered notes, about 63 relate to Christianity (almost all of them at this stage attributed to book II of the *Umwerthung aller Werthe*). When one examines them, one finds that they, in a skeleton version, express most of Nietzsche's general critique of Christianity and that Jesus, Paulus, Luther and Buddhism are discussed, and much of the central parts of *Der Antichrist* are at least sketchily present. The situation further improves when we include the notes written down immediately after these numbered notes, in the same notebook.[16] These notes include, apart from further notes for the *Umwerthung aller Werthe*-project, also fairly extensive excerpts from a number of books, including Tolstoy, *Ma religion*, Julius Wellhausen *Prolegomena zur Geschichte Isreals* (1883) and *Skizzen und Vorarbeiten* (1887), Dostoevsky *Les Possides (Bési)* (1886) and Renan *Vie de Jésus*, all of which were important for Nietzsche's argument in *Der Antichrist*. It is thus during the winter of 1887–8 and the early spring that Nietzsche works out much of the central contents of *Der Antichrist*. From these notes alone, or in combination with *Götzen-Dämmerung*, one is able to extrapolate a critique of Christianity which largely coincides with that of *Der Antichrist*.

It seems likely that a parallel scenario would also be the case for the three further volumes of the *Umwerthung aller Werthe*.

We can thus conclude that *Götzen-Dämmerung* cannot really be regarded as a summary of *Der Antichrist*, but in its many brief critical statements and claims about Christianity it suits well as an introduction to *Der Antichrist*.

We have also seen that it is not possible to construct the contents of *Der Antichrist* from an extrapolation of the contents of *Götzen-Dämmerung* – although it is true that much of the *general* critique is similar. Much of the specific nature of *Der Antichrist* could not be extrapolated. However, if we, apart from *Götzen-Dämmerung*, also use Nietzsche's late notes, it is in fact possible to extrapolate much of the contents of *Der Antichrist*. It would seem reasonable that that would also be possible for the other volumes of the *Umwerthung aller Werthe*, at least the two critical ones, volumes 2 and 3, containing critique of philosophy, metaphysics and nihilism in the former and of morality in the latter.

10

Conclusion and summary

Twilight of the Idols is a late, short, rich and stimulating work to read, and it contains and summarizes much of the late Nietzsche's philosophy. He himself describes it as 'my philosophy in a nutshell', 'this *vade mecum* to my philosophy' and it had as a subtitle for a while 'My Philosophy in Extract'. In this study we have examined *Twilight of the Idols*, its contents and its purpose, and especially its relation to Nietzsche's planned four-volume *magnum opus* or *Hauptwerk*, from September 1888 and onwards called *Revaluation of All Values*. He had been working on this project, which he on several occasions refers to as his *Hauptwerk*, ever since 1884, but with especial intensity since the autumn of 1887. We have seen that *Twilight of the Idols* is indeed greatly influenced by the presence of the plans and work on that *Hauptwerk* – both in what *Twilight of the Idols* contains and in what Nietzsche decided to leave out of it. Nietzsche refers to *Twilight of the Idols* as 'preparatory' to and its purpose as 'initiating and whetting the appetite for' that *Hauptwerk* in letters. It is preparatory in the sense that *Twilight of the Idols* often points to that coming *Hauptwerk* and to its planned contents – it gives extracts of some of the critique of religion, philosophy and morality (planned to be dealt with in the first three volumes of the *Revaluation of All Values* respectively). This perspective has been missed by previous commentators who have ignored its relation to the planned *Hauptwerk*. While reviewing all of his books in *Ecce homo*, Nietzsche writes that after *Also sprach Zarathustra* 'it was the turn of the no-saying, *no-doing* half: the revaluation of previous values itself, the great war [the work relating to the first three volumes of the *Umwerthung aller Werthe*] – the conjuring up of a day of decision' Much of that no-saying Nietzsche briefly summarizes in *Twilight of the Idols*.

He also refers to *Twilight of the Idols* as an 'extract', 'a handbook' and a 'summary' of his philosophy, a claim generally accepted by commentators. However, it is far from a complete summary, for many of the critical themes of his late philosophy (which he planned to discuss in the *Revaluation of All Values*) are absent in it, such as nihilism, questions relating to truth and the will to truth, the morality of unselfing oneself, and slave and noble morality. This absence is even more pronounced in that he avoided speaking of or elaborating on much of his own affirmative philosophy, and such Nietzschean themes as eternal recurrence, *amor fati*, will to power, perspectivism, order of rank and the *Übermensch* (or higher humans), which he planned to deal with in the fourth volume of the *Revaluation of All Values*, entitled *Dionysos* or *Dionysos philosophos*. When Nietzsche wrote the books after *Also sprach Zarathustra*, *Jenseits von Gut und Böse* and *Zur Genealogie der Moral*, but also *Der Fall Wagner*, he emphasized that they were *not* part of his work on the *Hauptwerk* – that they were not part of that fundamental work, but were more like resting places from that work (*Der Fall Wagner* and *Jenseits von Gut und Böse*) or pointers to that work (*Jenseits von Gut und Böse* and *Zur Genealogie der Moral*) – and he seems, on the whole, not to have utilized the notes he had written for work on the *Hauptwerk* for the writing of them. This is not the case for *Götzen-Dämmerung*. It too contains pointers to the *Umwerthung aller Werthe*, but in writing it Nietzsche extensively used (excerpted from) the notes for the *Hauptwerk*. I thus argue that *Twilight of the Idols* is not a good or accurate 'summary' and 'handbook' of his late philosophy, that is, it does not summarize the contents of his later books, in particular *Jenseits von Gut und Böse, Zur Genealogie der Moral* and *Der Fall Wagner* (which we examined in Chapter 6). Instead it can be regarded as containing a summary, or, more accurately, several 'extracts' or 'excerpts', *not* of his late books, but forward-looking, of his work on his *Hauptwerk*, especially of the first three more critical volumes, which he intended to publish in the near future.

This explains why he was able to write the book so quickly, it is consistent with his first draft of the subtitle to the work: 'Extracts of My Philosophy', it can explain much of the structure of the book and it makes comprehensible how Nietzsche can call it a 'summary' while yet so many of his most well-known philosophemes are missing in it. That it is forward-looking rather than backward-looking is furthermore more or less 'confirmed' by the fact that the text has been constructed largely from notes for his *Hauptwerk*.

Twilight of the Idols is a rich, profound and provocative book, but its contents are also extremely condensed and much of it and its meaning are easily misunderstood if one fails to realize the close connection between it and the four-volume *Revaluation of All Values* which he worked on at the same time. In fact, the best account of the purpose of *Twilight of the Idols* is that it was written to tempt, prepare and initiate readers for the planned *Revaluation of All Values*. He states: 'the book can serve the purpose of *initiating* and *whetting the appetite* for my *Revaluation of Values* (which first book is almost completed)'.[1] He also wrote it to give him a break from the difficult work of writing this *magnum opus*, as he describes in the preface. Thus to ignore its relation to that planned but only partially executed *Hauptwerk* is to completely fail to realize the purpose of the book. It follows from this that *Twilight of the Idols* also contains information and a sort of overview of the planned contents of the unfinished volumes of the *Hauptwerk*, which, in part, can be uncovered when it is correctly read.

Is it possible that we have a completely false conception of the world? Nietzsche thinks that we do. It is as if we still believed that the earth was placed immobile at the centre of the universe. It required a major revolution of our thinking for us to realize that that is not the case. Nietzsche makes a parallel claim concerning the view of the physical world in the nineteenth century. The world is not constituted as one thought then (or now). Reality is much less anthropocentric, less static and more complex than we believe – and many of the great discoveries of twentieth-century science – relativity, quantum mechanics, big bang and dark energy – are, broadly speaking, in line with his thought. We will inevitably and continually discover that the world is much more complex than we expect since we are ever limited by our human horizon, while we, perhaps necessarily, tend to assume that we are close to the 'true' world.

However, more central to Nietzsche's concern in *Götzen-Dämmerung* and elsewhere than the physical world is our conception of life and values, and that which is related to them, such as morality, religion and truth. There are many views of the value and meaning of life – but Nietzsche finds that there are among thinkers two related ones which are more common and fundamental than others – that life is not worth living (pessimism) and that life is meaningless (nihilism, basically a consequence of the death of God and the belief in a mechanistic universe). The former is primarily related to how we attribute value, the latter also to our conception of truth and nature. In *Götzen-Dämmerung* Nietzsche diagnoses this situation, and suggests that it is possible to have another attitude towards life, one which is healthier and more life-affirming. He argues that many of our present ideals were in fact constructed for the purpose of negating and denigrating life. Two of the fundamental themes of *Götzen-Dämmerung* are to point out the errors of our present views of values and of the nature and value of the world and to prepare for constructing better and more life-affirming alternatives.

Nietzsche's philosophy has received enormous amount of attention and influence since the early 1890s. There are those who claim that he is the most influential philosopher ever or at least the one most written about. Be that as it may, he is at least one of the most influential ones since *c.* 1900. My claim in this study is that his thinking is even more interesting and relevant than has generally been realized. Nietzsche's late books, especially *Götzen-Dämmerung*, *Ecce homo* and *Der Antichrist* have almost always been interpreted as backward-looking (*Götzen-Dämmerung* as a summary of his philosophy, *Ecce homo* as a summary of his life and *Der Antichrist* as the complete *Revaluation* project, consisting merely of a critique of Christianity, which he had already presented in his earlier books), and as such been shown to be unsatisfactory and as containing many problems. Commentators and scholars generally say that they accept Nietzsche's statement that *Götzen-Dämmerung* constitutes a summary of his philosophy, but rarely, if ever, use it as such – since, in truth, it is a bad summary of the philosophy presented in his earlier books. Likewise with *Ecce homo*, most commentators accept it as an autobiography but rarely use it as such since it is strange and unreliable. If one accepts *Der Antichrist* as the complete *Hauptwerk*, the complete *Umwerthung aller Werthe*, this means that Nietzsche regarded his philosophy as almost exclusively a critique of Christianity, and many other aspects of his philosophy inexplicably fall away. I have instead argued and showed that it is more correct and more constructive to regard these three books as forward-looking (*Götzen-Dämmerung* as being preparatory for his *Revaluation of All Values* by given extracts from that work for the sake of initiating and tempting readers, *Ecce homo* as being preparatory for that work by explaining why specifically he is able to revalue values when no one else seems even to see the problem, and that *Der Antichrist* was only the first of four planned volumes of that major revaluation project). Furthermore, these three books contain more information than has been realized. Among other things, they contain hints and pointers to the planned contents of his *Hauptwerk*, *philosophy of the future*, *Revaluation of All Values* – and project of a revaluation of all values.

It is probably true that Nietzsche has been more influential as a critical philosopher (the death of God, critique of Christianity, morality, metaphysics, nihilism and truth) than as someone who builds new structures (perspectivism, accepting our senses and bodies, existentialism and axiology), not to speak of some of his own affirmative claims and ideas (such as eternal recurrence, *amor fati*, *Übermensch*, will to power, etc) or as one who points forward towards the future (but for which philosopher is this not true?). However, both the critical and the constructive aspects of Nietzsche's thought have on the whole been regarded as a set of determined positions, which can be extracted from his published texts. Most would agree that his thought is generally dynamic and even hyperdynamic – and yet treat his work as a determinate set of claims. My thesis is that also his whole philosophy was evolving and that it contains and implies more than what can be found in his published texts. When Nietzsche collapsed at the age of forty-four, he had been working for several years on developing his thinking in a direction which it is in part possible to disentangle from his late books and notes, which implies several further views and positions to those generally determined from his published texts. Not fundamentally different ones perhaps but further ones pointing forward – especially concerning the nature of values and the revaluation of values. We have in this study examined this in regard to *Götzen-Dämmerung*.

Appendix

Tables summarizing aspects of *Twilight of the Idols*

1. Chapters, Thematic Listing and the Chronology of the Chapters of *Götzen-Dämmerung*.
2. Summary of Themes in *Götzen-Dämmerung*.
3. Summary of Nietzsche's Critique and Affirmation in *Götzen-Dämmerung*.
4. Pointers in *Götzen-Dämmerung* to the *Umwerthung aller Werthe*.
5. The Presence of (or Pointers to) the Idea of Eternal Recurrence in *Götzen-Dämmerung*.

Table A.1 Chapters, Thematic Listing and the Chronology of the Chapters of *Götzen-Dämmerung*

The broken lines in the middle column signify thematic breaks, and the double lines major breaks, as discussed in Chapter 5, especially in 5.1.

Table of Contents	Thematic Listing	Chronological Listing
Foreword	Foreword	[**The following constituted the original ms sent to publisher 7 September 1888**]
1. Maxims and Arrows	1. Maxims and Arrows	Part of 'What the Germans Lack' as foreword
	-------------------------------	1. Maxims and Arrows
2. The Problem of Socrates	2. The Problem of Socrates	2. The Problem of Socrates
		3. 'Reason' in Philosophy
3. 'Reason' in Philosophy	3. 'Reason' in Philosophy	4. How the 'Real World' at last Became a Myth
		5. Morality as Anti-Nature
4. How the 'Real World' at last Became a Myth	4. How the 'Real World' at last Became a Myth	6. The Four Great Errors (except § 1–2)
	-------------------------------	7. The 'Improvers' of Mankind
5. Morality as Anti-Nature	6. The Four Great Errors [on which religion and morality are based]	9. Expeditions of an Untimely Man, sections 1–31 and 45–51
		-------------------------------
6. The Four Great Errors	5. Morality as Anti-Nature	[**Later additions:**]
7. The 'Improvers' of Mankind	7. The 'Improvers' of Mankind	(6). §1–2 of 'The Four Great Errors'
	===========================	Foreword (18 and 30 September)
8. What the Germans Lack	8. What the Germans Lack	8. What the Germans Lack (18 September)
	-------------------------------	Title changed from 'The Idle Hours of a Psychologist' to GD (c. 27 September)
9. Expeditions of an Untimely Man	9. Expeditions of an Untimely Man [About half the chapter deals with aesthetics.]	(9). Expeditions of an Untimely Man, sections 32–44 (4–13 October)
	===========================	
10. What I Owe to the Ancients	10. What I Owe to the Ancients	10. What I Owe to the Ancients (c. 16 October)
The Hammer Speaks	The Hammer Speaks	Epilogue: The Hammer Speaks (c. 16 October)

© Thomas H. Brobjer

Appendix

Table A.2 Summary of Themes in *Götzen-Dämmerung*

Götzen-Dämmerung is more critical than affirming – its purpose is primarily to present the critique of accepted views (of an overemphasis of reason and its consequences, of pessimism, of metaphysics, of morality, of Christianity and of our view of aesthetics).

One principle common denominator of what Nietzsche affirms in all chapters is an affirmation of reality and what he criticizes is different versions of a denial of reality.

Twilight of the Idols	The Main Themes of Each Chapter
Foreword	The book's relation to the *Revaluation of All Values*, as a relaxation, and the purpose of the text (as a declaration of war) – testing and questioning truths, values and systems.
1. Maxims and Arrows	Many themes, including autobiographical ones, and questions and existential questions to the reader.
2. The Problem of Socrates	Critique of Socrates and pessimists who claim that life is worthless. The value of life cannot be estimated – such judgements are only symptoms. Those who negate life are decadents. Socrates used dialectics and 'rationality at any costs' to deal with reality.
3. 'Reason' in Philosophy	Critique of the overemphasis of reason in philosophy. Three errors which arise from this; denial of change (lack of historical sense), denial of the senses and mistaking the last (most developed) for the first.
4. How the 'Real World' at last Became a Myth	A summary of how the belief in the two-world metaphysics has gradually weakened. The consequences of this have still not been drawn, except in *Also sprach Zarathustra* and with Nietzsche's new philosophy.
5. Morality as Anti-Nature	Morality as life-denying and anti-natural. But a natural and healthy morality is possible. We should not exterminate the passions, but sublimate them.
6. The Four Great Errors	Four errors which lie behind morality, religion and the falsification of the world are discussed; mistaking cause for consequence, false causality, imaginary causality and free will.
7. The 'Improvers' of Mankind	Philosophers must stand *beyond* good and evil. Morality is a misrepresentation and useful only as a symptom. Morality wants to 'improve' men. By taming (Christianity) or by breeding (Manu). Both are mistaken and both are immoral.
8. What the Germans Lack	Critique of contemporary Germany and its emphasis on politics and nationalism. Culture and the state 'are antagonists'. German education and culture are declining. Instead Nietzsche affirms 'noble culture'. What is needed is to learn to see, think, speak and write – as forms of dancing.
9. Expeditions of an Untimely Man	Mostly discussions of aesthetics and literary critique. [Too many themes to be adequately summarized – see Chapter 5.6.]
10. What I Owe to the Ancients	Praise of Roman literary style – which Nietzsche learnt from Sallust and Horace. 'Plato is a coward in face of reality' and represents idealism and 'higher swindle' – while Thucydides and the sophists were realists. The Greeks instead affirmed life – as we can see in their concept of tragedy and the Dionysian. Nietzsche connects with this his idea of eternal recurrence.
The Hammer Speaks	'Become hard!' Become hard so that you can become a creator of your own will and purpose so that you can affirm yourself and reality.

© Thomas H. Brobjer

Table A.3 Summary of Nietzsche's Critique and Affirmation in *Götzen-Dämmerung*

Twilight of the Idols	The Main Critical and Affirmative Themes of Each Chapter
Foreword	**Against**: Idols (false ideals and truths). **For**: Cheerfulness. Struggle, fight, war. Sounding-out idols.
1. Maxims and Arrows	Many themes, including autobiographical ones, and questions and existential questions to the reader.
2. The Problem of Socrates	**Against**: Pessimism (and by implication nihilism), dialectics, conscious reason. **For**: Instincts, the subconscious, the aristocratic.
3. 'Reason' in Philosophy	**Against**: Philosophy which overemphasizes reason, idealistic views of origins, the static. **For**: Change and evolution (like Heraclitus' claimed), the senses.
4. How the 'Real World' at last Became a Myth	**Against**: Two-world metaphysics, reason, rejection of the present (or 'apparent') world. **For**: The apparent world as the only one. Here begins philosophy, here begins Zarathustra.
5. Morality as Anti-Nature	**Against**: Morality, denial of passions, denial of life. **For**: Natural morality, sublimation of the passions.
6. The Four Great Errors	**Against**: Falsification of the world. Moralizing. Religion. **For**: Accept oneself and the world. You are necessary, a piece of fate.
7. The 'Improvers' of Mankind	**Against**: Morality, religion, 'taming morality', 'breeding morality', every means hitherto to 'improve' man. **For**: Morality can be used as semeiotics. [Sublimation instead of taming or breeding]
8. What the Germans Lack	**Against**: German politics and nationalism. The decline of education and culture. **For**: *Bildung* and culture. Examples and educators of educators. Learn to see, think and write – as forms of dancing – for the purpose of noble culture.
9. Expeditions of an Untimely Man	[Too many critical and affirmative themes to summarize]
10. What I Owe to the Ancients	**Against**: Cowards in face of reality (Plato and idealists). **For**: Roman style. Realism. Tragedy. Dionysos. Eternal recurrence.
The Hammer Speaks	**Against**: Weakness, softness, lacking creativity and destiny. **For**: Become hard!

© Thomas H. Brobjer

Table A.4 Pointers in *Götzen-Dämmerung* to the *Umwerthung aller Werthe*

The first column simply lists the chapters of *Götzen-Dämmerung* (GD). The second column lists and summarizes what in each chapter points toward the *Umwerthung aller Werthe* (UAW). The third column briefly lists what the text in GD seems to be pointing at; the work as a totality (UAW), the first three more critical books (UAW:1-3), the first volume (AC), or any of the three planned but not written volumes (UAW:2 or 3 or 4), each dealing with a critique truth and epistemology, a critique of morality and giving Nietzsche's alternatives to this, especially eternal recurrence, respectively.

Twilight of the Idols (Chapters)	Pointers in *Götzen-Dämmerung*	To *Umwerthung aller Werthe* (UAW)
Title and subtitle	*Twilight of the Idols* Subtitle: Philosophize with the Hammer (where hammer is a symbol for the thought of eternal recurrence)	To UAW: 1–3. The end of old ideals and truths. The subtitle (Hammer) especially to volume 4, on eternal recurrence.
Foreword	GD as resting place from work on UAW. Announces the completion of the first volume (AC).	Complete UAW. Announces the completion of the first volume (AC).
1. Maxims and Arrows	Last aphorism 44 (the importance of having a goal).	AC, 1 (the aphorism 44 in GD is repeated at the end of section 1 of AC)
2. The Problem of Socrates	Critique of pessimism. (11) '*the entire morality of improvement, the Christian included, has been a misunderstanding* . . .'	AC and UAW: 3 'The Immoralist', was to contain a chapter 'The Good and the Improvers'.
3. 'Reason' in Philosophy	'The tragic artist [. . .] *affirms* all [. . .] he is *Dionysian*'.	UAW: 4: 'Dionysos philosophos'.
4. How the 'Real World' at last Became a Myth	(6) Last part, 'Incipit Zarathustra'. To the consequences of a liberation from metaphysics.	Points to Za and the UAW-project.
5. Morality as Anti-Nature	(3) GD as resting place from his revaluation of values. (6) 'we immoralists' are the advantage of priests.	Complete UAW. UAW:3: 'The Immoralist'.
6. The Four Great Errors	(2) '*first* example of my revaluation of all values'. (7) 'we immoralists'. 'remove the concept of guilt and [. . .] punishment'. (8) 'we are necessary, we are fates'. (8) 'the *innocence* of becoming'.	Revaluation of all values. UAW:3. UAW:3: 'The Immoralist'. Removing the concept of guilt and punishment. UAW:4: 'Dionysos'. Nietzsche's concept of eternal recurrence. UAW: 3 or 4.
7. The 'Improvers' of Mankind	(2) 'A first example, merely as an introduction'. (4) 'Christianity, growing from Jewish roots and comprehensible only as a product of this soil'. (3–5) Manu. (5) 'the psychology of the "improvers" of mankind'.	An introduction to UAW. This is a major theme in AC. AC, 55–8 (Manu) UAW:3: 'The Immoralist', planned to deal with 'The Good and the Improvers'.

(*Continued*)

Table A.4 (Continued)

Twilight of the Idols (Chapters)	Pointers in *Götzen-Dämmerung*	To *Umwerthung aller Werthe* (UAW)
8. What the Germans Lack	(3) GD as resting place from a 'profound seriousness' that is UAW. (6) Nietzsche's nature is affirmative.	Complete UAW. UAW:4: 'Dionysos'.
9. Expeditions of an Untimely Man	(5) Critique of agnostics and free-thinkers. (11) 'Grand style'. (19) Dionysos and Ariadne, and their 'celebrated dialogues on Naxos'. (24) Tragedy and 'tragic artist'. (32) 'The immoralist'. Critique of human ideals. (33) 'the ascending or descending line of life'. (45) The priest has been regarded as the highest type. 'A time is coming – I promise it' when the priest will be regarded as the lowest. (47) 'Christianity, which despised the body, has *up till now* been mankind's greatest misfortune' [my italics]. (49) Dionysos = 'that in the totality everything is redeemed and affirmed' [i.e. eternal recurrence]. (51) Promise to soon publish 'the most independent' book.	AC Present in many late notes. UAW: 4: 'Dionysos philosophos'. Cf KSA 12, 9[115]. Also to DD, 'Ariadne'. UAW: 4. Cf. KSA 13, 12[1](271) + 14[168]. AC and UAW: 3: 'The Immoralist'. Chapter: 'The Origin of Ideals'. Cf the planned chapter: 'The Two Ways' for UAW. AC Cf. AC, 51 and 62. Christianity should come to an end. UAW: 4: 'Dionysos philosophos'. Cf also the end of EH (pointing forwards): '*Dionysos against the crucified one . . .*'. Complete UAW in four volumes.
10. What I Owe to the Ancients	(2) Affirmation of reality. (4-5) Affirmation of tragedy and the Dionysian. (5) 'Affirmation of life'. 'revaluation of all values'. 'I, the last disciple of the philosopher Dionysos – I, the teacher of eternal recurrence . . .'.	UAW: 2 and 4. UAW: 4. UAW: 4: 'Dionysos philosophos'. The main theme in this volume was planned to be eternal recurrence.
The Hammer Speaks	Become hard, but also noble, a destiny and creative.	UAW: 4.

© Thomas H. Brobjer

Table A.5 The Presence of (and Pointers to) the Idea of Eternal Recurrence in *Götzen-Dämmerung*

Twilight of the Idols	**The Presence of 'Eternal Recurrence'**
Title and subtitle	The subtitle [The Hammer is a symbol of eternal recurrence].
Foreword	'For once to pose questions here with the *hammer*' (i.e. from the perspective of eternal recurrence, i.e. does this make us affirm life and reality or condemn it?).
1. Maxims and Arrows	(2, 10–12, 41–43), especially the last aphorism 44 (the importance of having a goal, one's own goal, since there is no *telos*, no universal goal).
2. The Problem of Socrates	Background. Two ways: ascending (*amor fati*) and descending (condemning) life. The chapter almost exclusively consists of a critique of pessimism, of the descending way.
3. 'Reason' in Philosophy	Background. The opposite of abstraction. Dynamic. (6) 'The tragic artist [...] *affirms* all [...] he is *Dionysian*' [Dionysos is another symbol of, and teacher of, eternal recurrence].
4. How the 'Real World' at last Became a Myth	(6) 'Midday' and '*Incipit Zarathustra*'. These are pointers to the idea of eternal recurrence. Eternal recurrence is 'Zarathustra's fundamental thought', *Ecce homo*, 'Za', 1.
5. Morality as Anti-Nature	Background – the opposite of that criticized. (6) 'the individual is, in his future and in his past, a piece of fate, one law more, one necessity more for everything that is and everything that will be. To say to him 'change yourself' means to demand that everything should change, even in the past.... [...] We others, we immoralists, have on the contrary opened wide our hearts to every kind of understanding, comprehension, *approval*. We do not readily deny, we seek our honour in *affirming*'.
6. The Four Great Errors	(7) 'to remove the concept of guilt and the concept of punishment from the world [...] the innocence of becoming'. (8) '*No one* is accountable for existing at all, or for being constituted as he is [...] The fatality of his nature cannot be disentangled from the fatality of all that which has been and will be. [...] in reality purpose is *lacking*... One is necessary, one is a piece of fate, one belongs to the whole, one *is* in the whole [...] thus alone is the *innocence* of becoming restored....'
7. The 'Improvers' of Mankind	-
8. What the Germans Lack	(Possibly, very vaguely in section 6, where Nietzsche claims that his nature is affirmative.)

(*Continued*)

Table A.5 (Continued)

Twilight of the Idols	**The Presence of 'Eternal Recurrence'**
9. Expeditions of an Untimely Man	(11) 'Grand style'. (24) Tragedy and 'tragic artist'. (33) 'the ascending or descending line of life'. (49) 'He [Goethe] placed himself within it [life] [...] What he aspired to was *totality*; [...] a convinced realist [...] a man of tolerance, not out of weakness, but out of strength [...] a man to whom nothing is forbidden, except it be *weakness*, whether that weakness be called vice or virtue.... A spirit thus *emancipated* stands in the midst of the universe with a joyful and trusting fatalism, in the *faith* that only what is separate and individual may be rejected, that in the totality everything is redeemed and affirmed – he no longer denies.... But such a faith is the highest of all possible faiths: I have baptized it with the name *Dionysos*. –'
10. What I Owe to the Ancients	(2) Affirmation of reality. (4-5) 'For it is only in the Dionysian mysteries, in the psychology of the Dionysian condition, that the *fundamental fact* of the Hellenic instinct expresses itself – its 'will to life'. What did the Hellene guarantee to himself with these mysteries? *Eternal* life, the eternal recurrence of life; the future promised and consecrated in the past; the triumphant Yes to life beyond death and change; *true* life as collective continuation of life through procreation, through the mysteries of sexuality. [...] All this is contained in the word Dionysos: I know of no more exalted symbolism than this *Greek* symbolism, the symbolism of the Dionysian. The profoundest instinct of life, the instinct for the future of life, for the eternity of life, is in this word experienced religiously [...] Affirmation of life even in its strangest and sternest problems, the will to life rejoicing in its own inexhaustibility through the *sacrifice* of its highest types — *that* is what I called Dionysian, *that* is what I recognized as the bridge to the psychology of the *tragic* poet. [...] *to realize in oneself* the eternal joy of becoming – that joy which also encompasses *joy in destruction* ... [...] – I, the last disciple of the philosopher Dionysos – I, the teacher of eternal recurrence ....'.
The Hammer Speaks	Hammer: Become hard so that you will not be crushed by the idea of eternal recurrence.

© Thomas H. Brobjer

Notes

Chapter 1

1 His other 1888 books are even less relevant here; *Nietzsche contra Wagner* contains a selection of his older statements regarding Wagner, and his book of poems, *Dionysos-Dithyramben*.
2 Letter to Peter Gast, 30 October 1888 and letter to Georg Brandes, 20 October 1888.
3 Note that for the present work, only Nietzsche's intention during August and September (and perhaps October) is relevant – and nobody denies that he then planned to continue the *Hauptwerk* in four volumes or parts. For my arguments that he continued to do so also after mid-November, see my 'The Origin and Early Context of Nietzsche's Revaluation of All Values', *Journal Nietzsche Studies* (2010): 12–29; 'The Place and Role of *Der Antichrist* in Nietzsche's Four Volume Project *Umwerthung aller Werthe*', *Nietzsche-Studien* 40 (2011): 244–55 and *Nietzsche's Ecce Homo and the Revaluation of All Values* (Bloomsbury, 2021), where the proofs of the first page of *Ecce homo*, where Nietzsche refers to *Der Antichrist* as the first volume of the *Revaluation of All Values*, and thus stating that more volumes were to follow, is reproduced in facsimile, including Nietzsche's words in his handwriting 'ready to be printed' and dated by him as 'Turin, 18 Dec. 1888', on page 93.
4 *Ecce homo*, 'Twilight of the Idols', sections 1 and 2.
5 Nietzsche uses the expression 'How to Philosophize with *the* Hammer' (italics added by me), but all English translations falsely use the indefinite article, 'a Hammer', which makes it more difficult to realize what Nietzsche meant with the expression.
6 'The eternal recurrence as hammer', KSA 12, 5[70]. See the discussion in Section 5.2. Compare also my article 'Götzen-Hammer: The Meaning of the Expression "To Philosophize with a Hammer"', *Nietzsche-Studien* 28 (1999): 38–41.
7 Nietzsche here plays with the title of his 'Hauptwerk', and immediately after the quoted text he will in a similar manner play with the title of his *Der Fall Wagner*. The German 'Eine *Umwerthung aller Werthe*' can be translated both as 'A *revaluation of all values*' and 'A *Revaluation of All Values*', the latter referring to the title of his work and the former to a philosophical theme. I argue that Nietzsche meant both of these meanings, both the book and the theme. In fact, the publication of the facsimile of Nietzsche's draft of the foreword, KGW IX,10, 79, shows that Nietzsche first wrote 'Die *Umwerthung aller Werthe*', obviously referring to the title of his work in progress, but then changed the definite article to 'Eine', leaving it more open and being a reference to both the title of his work and a philosopheme. Nietzsche writes it identically the same way here and at the end of the foreword, where he obviously refers to the literary work. The word 'war' in the last two sentences obviously means polemics.
8 See Nietzsche's claim in the letter to Georg Brandes, 20 October 1888: 'This book is my philosophy *in nuce* [in a nutshell] – so radical that it can be regarded as criminal

... ' ('Diese Schrift ist mein Philosophie *in nuce* – radikal bis zum Verbrechen ... '). With this letter Nietzsche included two copies of the book, one for Brandes and one for Strindberg. He makes a similar claim also in a letter to Gast, written the same day.

9   Nietzsche at a very late stage added the final chapter 'What I Owe to the Ancients' (which actually was part of the earliest version of the *Ecce homo* manuscript) and the short half-page epilogue to the manuscript.
10 Letter to Gast, 12 September 1888: 'so daß die Schrift [*Götzen-Dämmerung*] als *einweihend* und *appetitmachend* für meine *Umwerthung der Werthe* (deren erstes Buch beinahe in der Ausarbeitung fertig ist) dienen kann'.
11 Letter to Deussen, 14 September 1888. The quotation ends with '*Umwerthung aller Werthe*', which equally well can be translated as a title: '*Revaluation of All Values*' (italics in original).
12 Letter to Taine, 8 December 1888: 'und in Hinsicht auf das, was es vorbereitet, beinahe ein Stück Schicksal'.
13 'kurz und im höchsten Grade vorbereitend'.
14 See the discussion in Chapter 2.
15 *Nietzsche-Lexikon*, edited by Christian Niemeyer (Darmstadt, 2009), 114, 'GD ist sorgfältig komponiert und gibt einen gütigen Überblick über N.s philosophische Lebensthemen'.
16 *Ecce homo*, 'JGB', 1. This first section was added afterwards and stood originally without being numbered, as a sort of introductory paragraph, not only to *Jenseits von Gut und Böse*, but to the rest of this whole chapter (and the second section was numbered as '1'). This information is not given in KSA 14, but is visible in the *Ecce homo* manuscript. The numbering of the sections as '1' and '2' was done later, and with lead pencil. It is not clear to me if this was done by Nietzsche, Gast (who made his revisions on the manuscript with pencil) or some one else. Probably it is not known, since two single digits are too little to identify handwriting. In fact, this first section thus refers to his main interest and preoccupation during the years following *Also sprach Zarathustra* (1885/86–8). The quoted words earlier, in the main text, correspond well with what he says in *Ecce homo* about *Götzen-Dämmerung*, quoted earlier at the end of section 1.2.
17 *Ecce homo*, 'JGB', 1.
18 The 'review' of *Der Fall Wagner* is much longer, but after the first half page it turns into a general critique of the Germans and is no longer a discussion of the book.
19 I am here referring to his comparison of them to his planned *Umwerthung aller Werthe*, but he also compares them to 'ordinary' books, and then makes much more positive and affirmative statements about them.
20 *Ecce homo*, 'WA', 1.
21 *Ecce homo*, 'WA', 4. A few lines earlier, he writes: 'And so, roughly two years before the shattering lightning-bolt of the *Revaluation* [. . .] I sent *The Wagner Case* out into the world'.
22 Although I only very rarely and with much hesitation go beyond Nietzsche in this study, I hope that it will be a stimulus not only to further studies of *Götzen-Dämmerung*, of Nietzsche's late philosophy, of his project of *Umwerthung aller Werthe* and of other aspects of his thought, but also to thinking *with* Nietzsche and to thinking *beyond* Nietzsche. The nature and content of values remain, together with mind or consciousness, one of the great mysteries that need to be unravelled.

Chapter 2

1. Letter to Fuchs, 9 September 1888.
2. This is claimed, in spite of, as we have seen earlier, that Nietzsche repeatedly emphasizes the similarity of the two books *Götzen-Dämmerung* and *Der Fall Wagner*, and even calls them 'twin works'.
3. Janz, II, 625f.
4. Janz continues the quotation cited earlier with the words: 'But he fails already from the beginning'. This sentence is the last one of that section dealing with *Götzen-Dämmerung*. The next section deals with *Der Antichrist*. The meaning of that last sentence seems to refer to the *Umwerthung aller Werthe*, which, according to Janz, ought to have dealt with epistemological questions rather than with only 'einen Teilaspekt', with a partial aspect, that is the critique of Christianity – for Janz assumes that Nietzsche gave up on the idea of writing a four-volume *Umwerthung aller Werthe* and decided to write only *Der Antichrist*.
5. Ross, 752.
6. Ross, 753. Already at the very beginning of his discussion of *Götzen-Dämmerung*, at the bottom of page 751, he refers to the work as 'ein Ablenkung, ein Vorklang', 'a diversion, an overture', to what was to come, i.e. the *Umwerthung aller Werthe*, which for Ross means *Der Antichrist*.
7. Safranski, 324. The 'Dies' in the quotation from Nietzsche does not refer to the previous sentence, as Safranski suggests, but to what comes after, which Safranski does not include in the quotation.
8. Pages 163–7.
9. Rattner once, near the very end, refers to 'revaluation of all values', but it is then to the philosophical project, not to the *Hauptwerk*.
10. Mazzino Montinari, 'Nietzsche Lesen: Die Götzen-Dämmerung', *Nietzsche-Studien* 13 (1984): 69–79.
11. Mazzino Montinari, 'Nietzsches Nachlaß von 1885 bis 1888 oder Textkritik und Wille zur Macht', in *Nietzsche lesen* (Berlin, New York; Walter de Gruyter, 1982), 92–119, 114f.
12. KSA 14, 410. 'Daß die *Götzen-Dämmerung* als eine Art "Zwillingswerk" des *Antichrist* zu betrachten ist, wurde schon oben hervorgehoben'. Compare also the earlier statements on 383 and 400.
13. 'Aus den Aufzeichnungen zum "Willen zur Macht" sind die *Götzen-Dämmerung* und *Der Antichrist* entstanden; der Rest ist – Nachlaß'. Mazzino Montinari, *Nietzsche lesen* (Berlin, New York; Walter de Gruyter, 1982), 118.
14. Ibid., 118. '*Die Turiner Katastrophe kam, als Nietzsche wortwörtlich mit allem fertig war*'. See also Reto Winteler, 'Nietzsches *Antichrist* als (ganze) *Umwerthung aller Werthe*. Bemerkungen zum "scheitern" eines "Hauptwerks"', *Nietzsche-Studien* 38 (2009): 229–45, and my response to his text, 'The Place and Role of *Der Antichrist* in Nietzsche's Four Volume Project *Umwerthung aller Werthe*', *Nietzsche-Studien* 40 (2011): 244–55.
15. See letter to Elisabeth, 14 September 1888: 'Da ich mitten in der entscheidenden Arbeit meines Lebens bin, so ist mir eine vollkommne Regel für eine Anzahl Jahre die erste Bedingung. Winter Nizza, Frühling Turin, Sommer Sils, zwei Herbstmonate Turin – dies ist der Plan'. Compare also the letter to Overbeck, written on the same day.

16 See my discussion in 'Nietzsche's *magnum opus*', History of European Ideas 32 (2006): 278–94.
17 See letter to Meta von Salis, 7 September 1888: 'Inzwischen war ich sehr fleißig [...] Es ist mir sogar etwas *mehr* gelungen, Etwas, das ich mir nicht zugetraut hatte ... Die Folge war allerdings, daß mein Leben in den letzten Wochen in einige Unordnung gerieth. Ich stand mehrere Male nachts um 2 auf, "vom Geist getrieben" und schrieb nieder, was mir vorher durch den Kopf gegangen war. Dann hörte ich wohl, wie mein Hauswirth, Herr Durisch, vorsichtig die Hausthür öffnete und zur Gemsen-Jagd davon schlich. Wer weiß! vielleicht war ich auch auf der Gemsenjagd. ... Der *dritte* September war ein sehr merkwürdiger Tag. Früh schrieb ich die Vorrede zu meiner *Umwerthung aller Werthe*, die stolzeste Vorrede, die vielleicht bisher geschrieben worden ist. Nachher gieng ich hinaus – und siehe da! der schönste Tag, den ich im Engadin gesehn habe'.
18 Letter to Overbeck, 14 September 1888. In a later letter to Gast, he says that it only took him ten days, but even that is more than allowed for by Montinari's scheme.
19 See Nietzsche's letter to his publisher, 7 September 1888. Compare also his letter to Gast, 12 September 1888.
20 See my *Nietzsche's Ecce Homo and the Revaluation of All Values* (Bloomsbury, 2021), as well as my earlier articles 'The Origin and Early Context of Nietzsche's Revaluation of All Values', *Journal Nietzsche Studies* (2010): 12–29 and 'The Place and Role of *Der Antichrist* in Nietzsche's Four Volume Project *Umwerthung aller Werthe*', *Nietzsche-Studien* 40 (2011): 244–55.
21 Brusotti has written a similar account for the *Kindlers Neues Literatur Lexikon* and for *Grosses Werklexikon der Philosophie*, edited by Franco Volpi (Stuttgart, 1999).
22 *Nietzsche-Lexikon*, ed. Christian Niemeyer (Darmstadt, 2009), 112 and 114. 'N. betrachtete GD als "vollkommene Gesammt-Einführung" in sein Denken [...] GD ist sorgfältig komponiert und gibt einen gütigen Überblick über N.s philosophische Lebensthemen'.
23 Another outstanding Nietzsche-scholar, H. G. Hödl, in his immensely rich Habilitationsschrift *Der letzte Jünger des Philosophen Dionysos: Studien zur systematischen Bedeutung von Nietzsches Selbstthematisierungen im Kontext seiner Religionskritik* (Berlin, New York, 2009) does not examine *Götzen-Dämmerung*, but nonetheless makes a number of valuable comments about its last chapter 'What I Owe to the Ancient'.
24 Some of it may also be found in *Also sprach Zarathustra*, and in the notes from the period, 1881–5. Nietzsche, at least sometimes, saw the contents of the planned *Haupwerk* as the working out philosophically what he poetically had said or alluded to in his *Also sprach Zarathustra*. This is also the main reason for his excessive praise of and continual reference to *Zarathustra* in *Ecce homo*. I examine the relation between *Also sprach Zarathustra* and the planned *Hauptwerk* in my study *The Close Relationship Between Nietzsche's Two Most Important Books* (2023).
25 Hollingdale, 200.
26 However, Nietzsche's severe critique of metaphysics began in *Menschliches, Allzumenschliches* and the naturalistic and positivistic tendency of *Götzen-Dämmerung* is similar to that of *Menschliches, Allzumenschliches*.
27 Pages 520 and 523–5.
28 Young assumes, similar to me, that *Götzen-Dämmerung* was written between 18 August and 7 September, based on Nietzsche's claim in a letter that he wrote it in 20 days. Oddly enough, Young later adds on the same page (497) the erroneous

29 There is, of course, much that one could discuss or notice. This is also true for what is absent in Young's often profound and interesting interpretations. We can, for example, note that in the answer to the last question on Nietzsche's relation to art, there is no mention of the theme of the physiology of art, a theme which Nietzsche touches on in the book, and which he already both in *Zur Genealogie der Moral* ('I shall return to this point on another occasion, in connection with the still more delicate problems of the *physiology of aesthetics*, which is practically untouched and unexplored so far', GM, III, 8) and in *Der Fall Wagner*, 7, had promised to discuss later (in his *Hauptwerk*).
30 Duncan Large, ix, xi and xii.
31 It is also claimed that *Götzen-Dämmerung* was written between 26 August and 3 September, the shortest interval of all proposals (while Nietzsche's own claim was 20 days). Part of the text is based on Duncan Large's introduction to his translation of *Götzen-Dämmerung*.
32 Thatcher very briefly once alludes to the hammer as the idea of eternal recurrence (which frequently occurs in Nietzsche's notes, see my following discussion), but it is subsumed under the category 'The Lawgiver's Hammer', which is rejected by him.
33 This comment is hidden at the end of footnote 35, and certainly, would at least, require a discussion.
34 See especially 201.
35 On the penultimate page, she seems to deviate from this view (and come close to mine and the one I will present in this study), when she states that 'in several of his plans for the *Revaluation of All Values*, eternal recurrence is directly linked to Dionysus, and Nietzsche no doubt intended to pursue that theme thoroughly', and implying that he had more to say, but that he did not say that 'given the looming catastrophe of his collapse' (334).
36 On the penultimate page of the text she seems to retreat from that statement: 'as though the whole of *Twilight of the Idols* really has been a summary of his philosophy, instead of an expedition to revisit old ideas and introduce some new ones' (334).
37 In Chapter 5, I will argue for that there is a sort of overall pattern, in that it can be divided into three parts with different contents and purposes.

Chapter 3

1 Including also the philological commentary to them, KGW III.7/3.1 and 7/3.2, and KSA 14, as well as to his letters, KSB and the letters to him in KGB III.6 and KGB III.7/3.2.
2 On 9 August Nietzsche sends back the corrected proofs of most of *Der Fall Wagner*, except the end. He received that second (smaller) part of the proofs on or shortly before 12 August, which he then seems to have sent back to his publisher later the same day.
3 In the letter to Meta von Salis, 7 September 1888, and to Fuchs, 9 September, he speaks about having been extra inspired and producing more than expected in the last weeks ['in den letzten Wochen']. Nietzsche does not explicitly mention *Götzen-Dämmerung*, but hints at *Der Antichrist* (or rather the *Umwerthung aller Werthe*), but it seems clear that these statements must refer to the work on *both* books.

4 Such information may not be particularly philosophical, but is often very useful for dating Nietzsche's notes.
5 The complete texts contained in these folders will presumably eventually be published in facsimile in KGW IX. This work has progressed far, but is yet not completed. However, this work will not include the different *Druckmanuskripten* (printer's copies) etc.
6 Montinari refers to it in KSA 14, p. 422 (comments to *Götzen-Dämmerung*): 'Im ersten Dm . . .'. Also on page 397, and in his article on *Götzen-Dämmerung*, discussed in Chapter 2, pages 72 and 74.
7 Finding no information about the manuscript, a possible interpretation could be that Montinari refers to a stage of the manuscript (for an early version of *Götzen-Dämmerung*) which no longer exists. Perhaps what he does is to reconstruct this 'erste Dm' consisting of a number of thematic essays, which (he assumes?) later was separated into the manuscripts for *Götzen-Dämmerung* and *Der Antichrist*. His comment (KSA 14, 398) that the titles of essays 1, 7–9 (in the note KSA 13, 19[4]) 'the titles, which one – crossed out – still can read in the *Druckmanuskript* of *Der Antichrist*', suggests this. Little or no information on how reliable (and on what it is based) such a reconstruction would be is given.
8 KSA 14, 398. Compare also his similar statement twice in his article on reading *Götzen-Dämmerung*, 'Nietzsche lesen: Die Götzen-Dämmerung', *Nietzsche-Studien* 13 (1984), pages 72 and 74.
9 Nietzsche numbered and summarized 374 of these notes, and attributed them (except the last ones) into the four planned volumes of the *Hauptwerk*, see KSA 13, 12[1–2], from early 1888. The contents of these four large notebooks have been published in facsimile and diplomatic text in KGW IX.6 and IX.7.
10 Letter to Peter Gast, 30 October 1888. With 'the Dionysos-morality' Nietzsche includes the idea of eternal recurrence.
11 See his letter to Overbeck, 14 September 1888, quoted at the beginning of the fifth chapter, 5.1.
12 However, it can be argued that the earlier titles of parts of this chapter – 'Among Artists and Authors' and 'From My Aesthetics' – overlap with some of the earlier chapter listings.
13 KSA 13, 19[8], 11[416] (this note is placed at the end of an earlier notebook, but was written at the end of the summer according to Montinari), 22[3, 14, 24], 23[8 and 13].
14 Except that books 2 and 3 have exchanged places in two of them.
15 These three more detailed tables of contents are KSA 13, 12[2], 16[51] and 18[17]. It is true that it is unclear whereto two distinct themes, 'critique of modernity' and 'aesthetics', mentioned in them belong, or, possibly that he decided not to include these themes (which seems less likely to me, but possible). It is easy to imagine that aesthetics where then meant to be discussed in the third volume (mostly dealing with morality), and that the theme of critique of modernity probably now fell apart and was meant to be discussed in all three of the first volumes (in relation to Christianity, nihilism and morality).
16 KSA 11, 39[1].
17 KSA 12, 2[100]. This note is dated by Nietzsche as having been written in the summer of 1886.
18 See KGW VI.2, 257 (unfortunately this page is not included in KSA, and therefore usually not reproduced or mentioned in English translations of *Beyond Good and Evil*).

19 KSA 13, 18[17]. Dated by Nietzsche as 26 August 1888. The chapter titles are given in Table 3.2.
20 KSA 13, 19[8], 11[416] (this note is placed at the end of an earlier notebook, but was written at the end of the summer according to Montinari, 22[3, 14, 24], 23[8 and 13]. Four of these seven drafts contain the title *Umwerthung aller Werthe*, the other three simply lists the titles and or planned contents of two, four and three of the volumes of this work, respectively.
21 I have argued for this view in more detail in my article 'Nietzsche's *magnum opus*', *History of European Ideas* 32 (September 2006): 278–94.
22 It is true that he in letters to Meta von Salis, 22 August 1888 and to his mother, 30 August (note that this is before and after he wrote the detailed table of contents for *Der Wille zur Macht* on 26 August), seems disappointed that he has done less work this summer than he had hoped for (he probably had hoped to write, or at least begin, the first volume of the *Hauptwerk*), but in a letter to Meta von Salis, 7 September, he then withdraws that statement and states that he feels that his work is going well.
23 KSA 12, 7[64].
24 Montinari writes in the commentary volume: '*Die Lücke ist mit Sicherheit zu ergänzen*: <Der Wille zur Macht Versuch einer Umwerthung> aller Werthe. *nach 2[100]*'. KSA 14, 740. This is indeed possible, perhaps probable, but *not* certain. That other note, 2[100], is after all written about eight months earlier.
25 I have been unable to examine what this page and note looks like in the original, KSA 12, 7[64], from end of 1886 to early 1887 (Mp XVII 3b). It has not been published in KGW IX.
26 Letter to Overbeck, 13 February 1888: 'Als factum brutum ausgedrückt: die erste Niederschrift meiner 'Umwerthung aller Werthe' ist fertig. Die Gesammt-Conception dafür war bei weitem die längste Tortur, die ich erlebt habe, eine wirkliche Krankheit'.
    Letter to Gast, 13 February 1888. 'Ich habe die erste Niederschrift meines "Versuchs einer Umwerthung" fertig: es war, Alles in Allem, eine Tortur, auch habe ich durchaus noch nicht den Muth dazu. Zehn Jahre später will ichs besser machen'.
27 The notebook is dated as beginning on 24 November 1887, and he seems to have used it until February or March 1888.
28 This is given as note KSA 13, 11[416]. This note is *not* written at the end of the notebook (as this number signifies), but on an empty page opposite the notes 11[96, 97 and 98], KGW IX.7, W II 3, 157, in this notebook in which Nietzsche collected notes to be used for the *Hauptwerk*. Montinari claims that this note was written later, when Nietzsche returned to and worked through the notebook, and that seems very plausible also to me. Montinari, in the commentary KSA 14, claims that several notes in this notebook were re-written or edited during the summer of 1888 ('Überarbeitet im Sommer 1888'), but dates the last two notes as having been added 'in late summer'. Montinari does not explain the reason for the dating of the last two notes, KSA 13, 11[416 and 417] as having been added during the late summer, 'Spätsommer', but one can perhaps suspect that the dating is based on that he regarded *Der Wille zur Macht* as the title until 26 August, the new title can only have been written after that, but also by the fact that the first volume is given as *Der Antichrist*, which never occurred elsewhere as such before early September 1888. These notes are published in facsimile in KGW IX.7.
29 In particular to KSA 13, 11[416], 19[8], 22[14 and 24].
30 With the exception of a little in the note KSA 13, 23[2], there is no discussion of art or aesthetic questions after early September. The last note in which he claims that he

is going to discuss it is his listing of chapter titles for that combined stage of *Götzen-Dämmerung* and *Der Antichrist*, KSA 13, 19[4].
31 KSA 13, 16[70].
32 See for example the two notes: KSA 13, 11[416]:

Umwerthung der Werthe.
Buch 1: *der Antichrist.*
Buch 2: *der Misosoph.*
Buch 3: *der Immoralist*
Buch 4: *Dionysos*
Umwerthung aller Werthe

and KSA 13, 22[24]
I. Die Erlösung   vom *Christenthum*: der Antichrist
II.   von der *Moral*: der Immoralist
III.   von der *Wahrheit*: der freie Geist.
IV.   vom *Nihilismus*:

Chapter 4

1 Although there is much to say about Nietzsche's reading related to the chapter 'Expeditions of an Untimely Man', it has little bearing on the main theme of this study, the relation of and dependence between *Götzen-Dämmerung* and the *Umwerthung aller Werthe*, and therefore I have decided to largely ignore that chapter in this discussion of sources.
2 Much of such specific reading is given in Andreas Urs Sommer's useful German commentary to *Götzen-Dämmerung, Nietzsche-Kommentar: Band 6/1*.
3 I discuss the philosophical influences on Nietzsche in my study *Nietzsche's Philosophical Context: An Intellectual Biography*, Urbana and Chicago, 2008.
4 It may be that the increased discussion of Hartmann in his notes from this period instead is due to his reading of Sully, who discusses Hartmann (whom Nietzsche had intensively read several works by earlier) extensively.
5 The table of contents of Fouillée's *La science sociale contemporaine* lists the following content:
   1. Le contrat social et l'ecole idéaliste, 1.
   2. L'organisme social et l'ecole naturaliste, 74.
   3. La conscience sociale, 192.
   4. La justice pénale et les collisions de droits dans le société, 259.
   5. La fraternité et la justice réparative, 323.
   Conclusion, 379–421.

   Nietzsche's copy of the book is heavily annotated with many '!', 'NB', 'gut', 'ja' and other comments in the margins of the pages.
6 KSA 12, 10[17] and KSA 13, 11[137 and 147].
7 However, Nietzsche also read a fair number of other books about sociology and society, most of them in the 1880s; H. Spencer's *Einleitung in das Studium der Sociologie* (Leipzig, 1875), A. Espinas's *Die tierischen Gesellschaften. Eine vergleichend-psychologische Untersuchung* (Braunschweig, 1879), A Bordier's *La vie des sociétés*

(Paris, 1887), J. Michelet's *Das Volk* (Mannheim, 1846), W. Bagehot's *Der Ursprung der Nationen Betrachtungen über den Einfluss der natürlichen Zuchtwahl und der Vererbung auf die Bildung politischer Gemeinwesen* (Leipzig, 1874) and E. Hermann's *Kultur und Natur: Studien im Gebiete der Wirtschaft* (Berlin, 1887). More information about all the books in Nietzsche's private library can be found in the valuable *Nietzsches persönliche Bibliothek*, ed. G. Campioni. P. D'Iorio, M. C. Fornari, F. Fronterotta and A. Orsucci (Berlin, New York, 2003).

8 Letter to Overbeck, 9 January 1887.
9 A copy of *Le prince de Nicolaus Machiavel* (1873), 190 pages, is in Nietzsche's private library. Several of the pages of the preface have not been cut open, but those of the main text were 'cut' with a pencil, which led to small pencilled lines across some of the pages. The book contains no real annotations. It is not known when Nietzsche read this work.
10 'Thucydides, and perhaps the *Principe* of Machiavelli, are related to me closely by their unconditional will not to deceive themselves and to see reason in *reality* – not in "reason", still less in "morality"', *Twilight of the Idols*, 'What I Owe to the Ancients', 2.
11 KSA 12, 7[4], 259–70. See 'Beiträge zur Quellenforschung mitgeteilt von Thomas H. Brobjer', *Nietzsche-Studien* 30 (2001): 421.
12 There is also a brief reference to Spinoza in 'Expeditions', 49, but there only that Goethe was inspired by him.
13 For Nietzsche's relation to and reading about the sophists, see my 'Nietzsche's Relation to the Greek Sophists', *Nietzsche-Studien* 34 (2005): 255–76 and 'Nietzsche's Disinterest and Ambivalence toward the Greek Sophists', *International Studies in Philosophy* 33 (Fall 2001): 5–23. For his reading of Brochard, see also my 'Beiträge zur Quellenforschung', *Nietzsche-Studien* 26 (1997): 574–9. I have also discussed Nietzsche's relation to the sophists Trasymachos and Callicles in my article 'Nietzsche's Wrestling with Plato', in *Nietzsche and Antiquity: His Reaction and Response to the Classical Tradition*, ed. Paul Bishop (Rochester, 2004), 241–59.
14 See Andreas Urs Sommer's *Friedrich Nietzsches 'Der Antichrist': Ein philosophisch-historischer Kommentar* (Basel, 2000), 783 pages, for a detailed account of Nietzsche's reading of Renan, and its relevance for *Der Antichrist*. This work contains much further useful information about Nietzsche's reading relevant for *Der Antichrist*.
15 Actually, the Roux volume in Nietzsche's library contains no annotations, but according to a note by Rudolf Steiner who worked in the Nietzsche Archive under the guidance of Elisabeth Förster-Nietzsche, Nietzsche's copy then contained annotations in the form of marginal lines. Most probably Nietzsche's copy has been lost and replaced by a new one.
16 The 'Anhang', 'Die Schranken der naturwissenschaflichen Erkenntniss', 555–682, contains the following chapters:

Vorwort, 555
Einleitung, 560
Beschaffung und Befähigung des erkennenden Ich, 565
Beschaffung und Zugänglichkeit der Natur, 570
Wesen des Erkennens, 578
Keine principielle Verschiedenheit zwischen unorganischer und organischer Natur, 585
Keine principielle Verschiedenheit zwischen unbeseelter und beseelter Natur, 590–602.

This is followed by nine added essays, for example, '1. Physische und metaphysische Atomistik', '3. Naturphilosophische Weltanschauungen: Entropie' and '4. Bedingungen für empirisches Wissen und Erkennen: Morphologische Wissenschaften'.

Apart from the preface and introduction, Nietzsche has annotated all of these chapters and essays, many of them heavily, including with comments.

17 See e.g. *KSA* 12, 7[9 and 25]. On Dumont, see Maria Christina Berti, 'Beiträge zur Quellenforschung', *Nietzsche-Studien* 26 (1997): 580–1. On Rolph, see Greg Moore, *Nietzsche, Biology and Metaphor* (Cambridge: Cambridge University Press, 2002), 46–54. On Nägeli, see Andrea Orsucci, 'Beiträge zur Quellenforschung', *Nietzsche-Studien* 22 (1992): 371–88.

18 Nietzsche discovered Dostoyevsky in early 1887 and read him intensively that year and in 1888. A possible stimulus for his discovery of Dostoyevsky is Joseph Viktor Widmann's review of *Jenseits von Gut und Böse* (Nietzsche knew Widmann and repeatedly refers to this review, also in *Götzen-Dämmerung*), which was published in September 1886 in *Der Bund*, and which begins with a long quotation from Dostoyevsky's *Junger Nachwuchs* as motto, and relates Nietzsche's books to it.

19 Nietzsche had earlier read about Tolstoy in his reading of French literary critics, and now read Tolstoy's *Ma religion* (Paris, 1885), 266 pages, in 1888.

20 Nietzsche corresponded with Strindberg in 1888 and during that year he also read three of his works in French translations; *Les mariés*, *Père* (which Nietzsche read twice) and a short story *Remords*. Both Nietzsche and Strindberg (as well as Georg Brandes) observes that their views of the psychology of women were very similar.

21 The table of contents of Höffding's *Psychologie in Umrissen auf Grundlage der Erfahrung* (Leipzig, 1887) lists the following main chapters:

1. Gegenstand und Methode der Psychologie, 1
2. Seele und Körper, 36
3. Das Bewusste und das Unbewusste, 88
4. Einteilung der psychologische Elemente, 107
5. Die Psychologie der Erkenntnis, 124
   A. Empfindung, 124
   B. Vorstellung, 150
   C. Auffassung des Zeit und des Raums, 231
   D. Die Auffassung des Wirklichen, 258
6. Die Psychologie des Gefühls, 278
   A. Gefühl und Sinnesempfindung, 278
   B. Gefühl und Vorstellung, 293
   C. Egoistisches und sympathisches Gefühl, 305
   D. Die Physiologie und Biologie des Gefühls, 338
   E. Die Gültigkeit des Gesetzes der Beziehung für die Gefühle, 348
   F. Einfluss des Gefühls auf die Erkenntnis, 377
7. Die Psychologie des Willens, 391
   A. Die Ursprünglichkeit des Willens, 391
   B. Der Wille und die andern Bewusstseinselemente, 408
   C. Der individuelle Charakter, 443–463.

22 For three such example, see 'Beiträge zur Quellenforschung mitgeteilt von Marco Brusotti', *Nietzsche-Studien* 21 (1992): 390f., and for another six see 'Beiträge zur Quellenforschung mitgeteilt von Thomas H. Brobjer', *Nietzsche-Studien* 30 (2001): 418–21. All of these are in *Zur Genealogie der Moral*, except one in the chapter '"Reason" in Philosophy', in *Götzen-Dämmerung*.

23 The table of contents of Joly's *Psychologie des grands hommes* (Paris, 1883) lists the following main chapters:

1. La préparation par la race.
2. La préparation par l'hérédité dans la famille.
3. Le grand homme et le milieu contemporain.
4. Le génie et l'inspiration.

24 On Richet, see Greg Moore, 'Beiträge zur Quellenforschung', *Nietzsche-Studien* 27 (1998): 535–51 (546).
25 For a discussion of Nietzsche's reading of these three works, see B. Wahrig-Schmidt's article '"Irgendwie – jedenfalls physiologisch". Friedrich Nietzsche, Alexandre Herzen (fils) und Charles Féré 1888', *Nietzsche-Studien* 17 (1988): 434–64. Another work which emphasizes the biological influences on Nietzsche's view of decadence is Anette Horn's *Nietzsches Begriff der Décadence: Kritik and Analyse der Moderne* (Frankfurt, 2000).
26 The book contains extensive discussion about pleasure and pain (compare Dumont's study which he read earlier), including a short appendix on the physiology of them: 'Physiologie du plaisir et de la peine', 442–4.

   Several of Nietzsche's comments in the margins of the book are written in French, which implies a late reading, at least after 1884, probably later.

   This probably late reading makes it somewhat less relevant, but it is possible that the work nonetheless was important for Nietzsche's continued view of will to power, for the will is extensively discussed in the book, and Nietzsche has annotated many of these discussions.
27 This work is a mixture of philosophical, psychological and physiological speculation and theories. The main headings in the table of contents are:

1.	L'étude de l'illusion	The Study of Illusions
2.	Classification des illusions	The Classifications of Illusions
3–6.	Illusions de la perception	Illusions of Perceptions
7.	Les rêves	Dreams
8.	Les illusions de l'introspection	Illusions of Introspection
9.	Autres illusions quasi présentatives	Other Quasi-Presentative Illusions : Errors of Insight
10.	Les illusions de la mémoire	Illusions of Memory
11.	Les illusions de la croyance	Illusions of Belief
12.	Les résultats	Results

Nietzsche's annotations are in chapters 10 and 11, 205–34 (10 pages annotated) (with some dog-ears in other chapters). It is likely that the reading of this work influenced Nietzsche's *On the Genealogy of Morals*, and possibly as background för *Götzen-Dämmerung*.
28 In the Introduction Stricker writes: 'Die Rechtsidee, so behaupte ich, entwickelt sich im Menschen aus zweierlei Erfahrungsreihen. Die eine Erfahrungsreihe resultirt aus den willkürlichen Bewegungen [i.e. conscious muscular movements]. Die Beziehungen des Willens zu den Muskeln bilden aber gleichzeitig die erste Quelle des Machtbewusstseins. Ich sage daher in Kürze, dass sich die Rechtidee aus der Machtidee entwickle. [. . .] Die Idee von der eigenen Macht und der Macht der anderen Menschenbilden also gleichsam die Keime der Rechtsidee. [. . .] Und die Macht, oder richtiger gesagt, *die durch den Vertrag bestimmte Machtquote ist es, welche von der Gerechtigkeit gewogen wird*'. (iiif.) Compare also the discussion of power as the motive of men, on page 75, annotated by Nietzsche.

29　KSA 11, 29[67].
30　Other titles relating to psychology and/or physiology in Nietzsche's library are:

> L. Hermann's *Grundriss der Physiologie des Menschen* (Berlin, 1874), 526 pages, which according to R. Steiner had not been completely cut open (but this, nonetheless, suggests reading of parts of it).
> F. A. v. Hartsen, *Grundzüge der Psychologie* (Halle, 1877).
> Bernstein, J., *Die fünf Sinne des Menschen* (Leipzig, 1875).
> Dumont, Léon, *Vergnügen und Schmerz. Zur Lehre von den Gefühlen* (Leipzig, Brockhaus, 1876).
> Foster, M., *Lehrbuch der Physiologie*. Übers. v. N. Kleinenberg (Heidelberg, 1881).
> Hartmann, Eduard v., *Das Unbewusste vom Standpunkt der Physiologie und Descendenztheorie. Eine kritische Beleuchtung des naturphilosophischen Teils der Philosophie des Unbewussten aus naturwissenschaftlichen Gesichtspunkten* (Berlin, 1872).
> His, Wilhelm, *Unsere Körperform und das physiologische Problem ihrer Entstehung. Briefe an einen befreundeten Naturforscher* (Leipzig, 1874).
> Löwenfeld, L., *Die moderne Behandlung der Nervenschwäche (Neurasthenie), der Hysterie und verwandter Leiden* (Wiesbaden, 1887).
> Mantegazza, Paul, *Die Physiologie der Liebe*. Übers. v. Eduard Engel (Jena, 1877).
> Mantegazza, Paul, *Physiologie des Genusses*. Übers. aus dem Italienischen. (Oberhausen u. Leipzig, 1881).
> Oettingen, Alexander v., *Die Moralstatistik in ihrer Bedeutung für eine Sozialethik* 3. Aufl. (Erlangen 1882).
> Paulhan, Fr., *Les phénomènes affectifs et les lois de leur apparition. Essai de psychologie générale* (Paris, 1887).
> Roux, Wilhelm, *Der Kampf der Teile im Organismus. Ein Beitrag zur Vervollständigung der mechanichen Zweckmässigkeitslehre* (Leipzig, 1881).

31　See Gregory Moore's examination and discussion of this reading in 'Nietzsche, Medicine and Meteorology', in *Nietzsche and Science*, ed. Gregory Moore and Thomas H. Brobjer (2004).
32　Nietzsche only used the word *décadence* once at this time, in a note relating to his reading of the brothers Goncourt's novel *Manette Salomon* (1867), where he referred to Delacroix as related to Wagner and both of them as representing *décadence*. Shortly before, in a note with a page reference to the chapter on décadence in Bourget's book, he had discussed the 'style of decline by Wagner' ['Stil des Verfalls bei Wagner'], KSA 11, 24[7], from the winter 1883–84.

In his *Essais de psychologie contemporaine* (Paris, 1883) Bourget discusses Baudelaire, Renan, Flaubert, Taine and Stendhal. Two of the chapters on Baudelaire are called 'Le Pessimisme de Baudelaire', 9–17, and 'Théorie de la décadence', 18–25. Two further chapters on Flaubert are also of special importance: 'Du Romantisime', 123–38, and 'Du Nihilisme de Gustave Flaubert', 139–50.

This book is not in Nietzsche's library. He seems to have borrowed it from the public library in Nice. However, he also possessed, read and annotated the second volume by Bourget, *Nouveaux essais de psychologie contemporaine* (Paris, 1885) in 1885. This work contained discussions of decadence and nihilism, and a related emphasis on Schopenhauer's influence on French literature.

33　In the 1880s Nietzsche read, among others, French literary critical works by Sainte-Beuve, Taine, Renan, Brunetière, Bourget, d'Autrevilly, Paul Albert, Lois

Desprez, Eugène Fromentin, Bérard Varagnac, Émile Gebhart, Jules Lemaître, Emil Montégut, Edmont Scherer and the brothers Goncourt. For example, in Desprez's *L'évolution naturaliste* (1884), which Nietzsche read, probably in 1888, he would have encountered discussions of *décadence* in the chapter 'Baudelaire et les Baudelairiens', 271–92. Nietzsche annotated the chapter sparingly.

34 Nietzsche's reading of Jacolliot is reflected in a large number of notes, for example: KSA 13, 14[106, 175–78, 189, 190, 191, 193, 195, 196, 198–204, 212–18, 220, 221, 223, 224 and 225], 15[21, 24, 42, 44, 45, 47, 62 and 109], 16[53 and 60], 18[3] and 22[10].

35 I discuss Nietzsche's reading of this work in some detail in 'The Absence of Political Ideals in Nietzsche's Writings: The Case of the Laws of Manu and the Associated Caste-Society', *Nietzsche-Studien* 27 (1998): 300–18.

36 A. Etter, 'Nietzsche und das Gesetzbuch des Manu', *Nietzsche-Studien* 16 (1987): 349–52. This interesting article contains much information about Jacolliot and Hinduism, but says little about Nietzsche. It would more apply be entitled 'Jacolliot und das Gesetzbuch des Manu'.

37 This issue of the *Atlantic Monthly* is still in Nietzsche's library, with annotations. For a discussion of Nietzsche's reading of it, see S. L. Gilman, 'Nietzsche's Reading on the Dionysian: From Nietzsche's Library', *Nietzsche-Studien* 6 (1977): 292–4, and S. L. Gilman, 'Nietzsches Emerson-Lektüre: Eine unbekannte Quelle', *Nietzsche-Studien* 9 (1980): 406–31.

38 Two brief exceptions are that utilitarianism is critically alluded to, but not mentioned, in aphorism 12 of the first chapter and there is an unimportant reference to the number of printed copies of Cornaro's book in England in the first section of the 'Error' chapter. In both *Jenseits von Gut und Böse* (1886) and *Zur Genealogie der Moral* (1887) Nietzsche had spent some time on expressing critique of 'English' philosophy and philosophers.

39 Carlyle, Spencer, J. S. Mill, G. Eliot, Darwin, Malthus and Buckle are mentioned.

40 Although Shakespeare and Byron (and even Bacon, but as the person behind Shakespeare) have positive roles in *Ecce homo*.

41 'But at the bottom of us, "right down deep", there is, to be sure, something unteachable, a granite stratum of spiritual fate, of predetermined decision and answer to predetermined selected questions'. *Jenseits von Gut und Böse*, 231.

42 I discuss Nietzsche's relation to, and reading of, British and American thinkers in greater detail in my study *Nietzsche and the 'English'* (2008).

43 Mill, John Stuart, *Gesammelte Werke*. Authorized translation under the direction of Theodor Gomperz. Volumes 1 (Leipzig, 1869/80), 9–12.

Vol. I. Die Freiheit – Das Nützlichkeitsprinzip – Rektoratsrede;
Vol. IX. August Comte und der Positivismus – Vermischte Schriften politischen, philosophischen und historischen Inhalts;
Volumes X. and XI. Vermischte Schriften politischen, philosophischen und historischen Inhalts;
Vol. XII. Über Frauenemanzipation – Plato – Arbeiterfrage – Sozialismus.

44 Nietzsche, in the summer of 1879, ordered Mill's *Autobiography* in German, but it had been sold out (letter from Louise Rothpletz to Nietzsche, probably middle of June 1879).

45 Letter to Schmeitzner, 22 November 1879. Nietzsche still refers to Spencer praisingly: 'hochberümt', 'höchst *lehrreich* für uns' and he further claims that a translation would be the best alternative against Hartmann's latest impudence, that is, latest book.

46 KSA 10, 20[3].
47 KSA 11, 35[34].
48 'I have read the life of *Thomas Carlyle*, that unwitting and involuntary farce, that heroical-moralistical interpretation of dyspepsia. [. . .] continually agitated by the desire for a strong faith *and* the feeling of incapacity for it (– in this a typical Romantic!) [. . .] Fundamentally, Carlyle is an English atheist who wants to be honoured for *not* being one'. *Twilight of the Idols*, 'Expeditions of an Untimely Man', 12.
49 Letter to Schmeitzner, 21 June 1881. Buckle was one of eleven books Nietzsche requested in this letter.
50 Letter to Peter Gast, 20 May 1887.
51 *On the Genealogy of Morals*, First essay, 4.
52 KSA 13, 11[409]. 'Autoren, an denen heute noch Wohlgefallen zu haben, ein für alle Mal compromittirt: Rousseau, Schiller, George Sand, Michelet, Buckle, Carlyle, die imitatio'.

This is an early version of *Twilight of the Idols*, 'Expeditions', 1, and only Buckle and Thomas à Kempis are not included in the published version – but they are dismissed elsewhere in the book.
53 See KSA 13, 16[39].
54 I discuss the extent to which Nietzsche's ethics can be regarded as a form of ethics of virtue in my study *Nietzsche's Ethics of Character: A Study of Nietzsche's Ethics and its Place in the History of Moral Thinking* (Uppsala, 1995) and in 'Nietzsche's Affirmative Morality: An Ethics of Virtue', *Journal of Nietzsche Studies* 26 (2003): 64–78.
55 KSA 13, 11[16].
56 KSA 12, 9[11].
57 KSA 13, 11[16]. Written between November 1887 and March 1888. The French quotation at the end ['I shall look at myself, I shall read myself, I shall delight myself and I shall say: Can I really have had so much wit?'] Nietzsche has been taken from F. Galiani, *Lettres à Madame d'Epinay, Voltaire, Diderot, Grimm, etc. Publiées avec notice biographique par Eugene Asse*. 2 vols. (Paris, 1882), Galiani an Madam d'Epinay, 18 September 1769, but there, of course, it is not associated with Eliot.

Chapter 5

1 See, however, the article by Reto Winteler, in which he argues that *Der Antichrist* does represent the whole of the planned *Hauptwerk*, 'Nietzsches *Antichrist* als (ganze) *Umwerthung aller Werthe*. Bemerkungen zum "scheitern" eines "Hauptwerks"', *Nietzsche-Studien* 38 (2009): 229–45 and my response to that article in 'The Place and Role of *Der Antichrist* in Nietzsche's Four Volume Project *Umwerthung aller Werthe*', *Nietzsche-Studien* 40 (2011): 244–55.
2 We can note that even if Nietzsche later, in November or December 1888, gave up on writing the rest of the *Umwerthung aller Werthe*, this does not actually affect the present study at all, which is concerned with Nietzsche's view of and work on it up until at the latest October 1888. However, I do not believe Nietzsche gave up on that project, and we can note that he continued to regard *Götzen-Dämmerung* as 'preparatory' for that *Hauptwerk* also in his letters from November and December 1888.

3 This is largely due to the important work of the editors of the modern critical edition of Nietzsche's work (KSA and KGW), G. Colli and M. Montinari, especially of the latter. Of additional aid and advantage is the ongoing project to make all of Nietzsche's notebooks, or late notebooks, available in full, in facsimile and diplomatic text, within the two projects; KGW, section IX and the *Nietzsche Source*, that together plan to make all notebooks available in facsimile in the future.
4 Bernd Magnus, 'The Deification of the Commonplace: Twilight of the Idol', in *Reading Nietzsche*, ed. R. Solomon and K. Higgins (1988), 152–81 and 'Nietzsche's Philosophy in 1888: *The Will to Power* and the *Übermensch*', *Journal of the History of Philosophy* 24 (1986): 79–98.
5 Jing Huang has recently well summarized much of the discussion of the value of Nietzsche's notes in her 'Did Nietzsche Want His Notes Burned? Some Reflections on the *Nachlass* Problem', *British Journal of the History of Philosophy* 27 (2019): 1194–214.
6 This is perhaps most obvious where he speaks of that work most explicitly, as in the foreword, at the end of 'Expeditions of an Untimely Man' and at the very end of the last chapter. But many others can also be found, for example, the reference to the future low status of the priests in 'Expeditions of an Untimely Man', 25, which is a theme continued in *Der Antichrist*.
7 That Nietzsche regarded the *Umwerthung aller Werthe* as much more important and comprehensive than *Götzen-Dämmerung* is apparent in the foreword to *Götzen-Dämmerung* and in many letters, and also in the prologue to *Ecce homo*.
8 See the two notes KSA 13, 19[3 and 5].

   Gedanken für Übermorgen.
   Auszug meiner Philosophie

   Weisheit für Übermorgen
   Meine Philosophie
   im Auszug.

   Magnum in parvo.
   Eine Philosophie
   im Auszug.

   Multum in parvo.
   Meine Philosophie
   im Auszug.

9 That Nietzsche found the process of revaluation highly difficult and strenuous is stated in the preface, and in several letters, for example letters to Overbeck, and to Gast, both from 13 February 1888, where he refers to it as torture and as an illness.
10 'Der Titel' *Müssiggang* eines Ps<ychologen> 'klingt mir, wenn ich mir vergegenwärtige, wie er auf Nebenmenschen wirken könne, zu anspruchslos. Sie haben Ihre Artillerie auf die höchsten Berge gefahren; haben Geschütze wie es noch keine gegeben, und brauchen nur blind zu schiessen, um die Umgegend in Schrecken zu versetzen. Eines Riesen Gang, bei dem die Berge in den Urgründen erzittern, ist schon kein Müssiggang mehr. In unsrer Zeit kommt ausserdem der Müssiggang gewöhnlich erst *nach* der Arbeit, und das Mü kommt auch in Müdigkeit vor. Ach

ich bitte, wenn ein unfähiger Mensch bitten darf: einen prangenderen glanzvolleren Titel!'. KGB III.6, 309f.

11 He then wrote to Gast: 'Was den *Titel* angeht, so kam Ihrem *sehr humanen* Einwande mein eignes Bedenken zuvor: schließlich fand ich aus den Worten der *Vorrede* die Formel, die vielleicht auch Ihrem Bedürfnisse genugthut. Was Sie mir von der "großen Artillerie"' schreiben, muss ich, mitten im Fertig-machen des *ersten* Buchs der '*Umwerthung*' einfach annehmen. [. . .] Der neue *Titel* (der an 3 bis 4 Stellen ganz bescheidne Veränderungen nach sich zieht) soll sein:

> *Götzen-Dämmerung.*
> Oder:
> wie man mit dem Hammer philosophirt.
> Von
> F. N.

Der Sinn der Worte, zuletzt auch an sich errathbar, ist, wie gesagt, das Thema der *kurzen* Vorrede. [. . .] Auch in diesem Sinne wird der neue Titel *Götzen-Dämmerung* gehört werden, – also *noch eine Bosheit* gegen Wagner . . . .'.

12 *Ecce homo*, 'GD', 2.
13 *Ecce homo*, 'GD', 1.
14 It is symptomatic that even this primary meaning of the title is not mentioned in the otherwise rich and valuable paper by David Thatcher, 'A Diagnosis of Idols: Percussions and Repercussions of a Distant Hammer', *Nietzsche-Studien* 14 (1985): 250–68, in which he hopes to 'dispel some persistent misconceptions surrounding Nietzsche's title'. In fact, nothing at all is said in the paper about the relation between *Götzen-Dämmerung* and the *Umwerthung aller Werthe* project. Furthermore, that whole paper ends with a strong emphasis, following Nietzsche's words, of *Götzen-Dämmerung* as a summary, an epitome, a *vade mecum* of his philosophy – without examining or questioning in which sense this is true and in which sense it is not.
15 *Twilight of the Idols or How to Philosophize with a Hammer*. All English translations seem to use 'a Hammer' although the German original clearly has 'the Hammer'. I discuss the consequences of this at the end of the discussion of the subtitle. The note where Nietzsche constructs or finds the new title is published as KSA 13, 22[6]:

> *Götzen-Hammer.* / oder / Heiterkeiten / eines Psychologen.
> *Götzen-Hammer.* / Oder: / wie ein Psycholog Fragen stellt.
> *Götzen-Hammer.* / Müssiggang / eines Psychologen.
> *Götzen-Hammer.* / Oder: / wie ein Psycholog Fragen stellt.
> *Götzen-Dämmerung.* / Oder: / wie man mit dem Hammer / philosophirt.

That Nietzsche was equally fond of the early version 'Götzen-Hammer' as the final version is shown by two letters written in December 1888, after the book was printed and just beginning to be distributed. In a letter to Helen Zimmern, 17 December 1888, Nietzsche wrote: 'Man könnte der Titel vereinfachen: *Götzen-Hammer*' and the same day he also wrote a letter to Jean Bourdeau in Paris, whom he hoped would translate the book into French, suggesting *Marteau des Idoles* (i.e. Götzen-Hammer) as the French title.

16 Both these sentences are taken from Nietzsche's review of *Twilight of the Idols* in *Ecce homo*, the first from the first section, the second from the second section.
17 One can note that a number of commentators strongly argue against this view, for example, Kaufmann, Magnus, Thatcher, et al, probably in order to 'protect' against 'vulgar' interpretations of Nietzsche.
18 Nietzsche's statements in the foreword has special importance not only because they are explanatory and come immediately after the title and subtitle, but this is also reinforced through Nietzsche's words in the letter to Peter Gast, 27 September 1888, after having given the new (i.e. the present) title, he continues: 'Der Sinn der Worte, zuletzt auch an sich errathbar, ist, wie gesagt, das Thema der kurzen Vorrede'.
19 *Götzen-Dämmerung*, Foreword (Hollingdale's translation). In *Ecce homo* Nietzsche explains the meaning of 'idols': 'That which is called idol on the title-page is quite simply that which has hitherto been called truth'.
20 See Walter Kaufmann's preface to his translation of *Götzen-Dämmerung* published in *The Portable Nietzsche* (New York, 1954), 463f. 'The spectacular title was an afterthrought. [...] It is usually assumed that he means a sledgehammer. The preface, however, from which the image is derived as an afterthought, explains: idols "are here touched with a hammer as with a tuning fork"'. Similar statements are made in Kaufmann's translation of *Ecce homo* (New York, 1967), 314, footnote 1 and *The Will to Power* (London, 1967), 46.
21 David S. Thatcher, 'A Diagnosis of Idols: Percussions and Repercussions of a Distant Hammer', *Nietzsche-Studien* 14 (1985): 250–68. In the article he claims: 'In fact, Nietzsche's hammer is neither a club nor a sledgehammer: strange as it may seem, it has more in common with the railwayman's hammer, used to check for cracks in the wheels of trains, than it has with any weapon of force or destruction. What makes the issue even more confusing is that it does not resemble any of the three types of hammer which can be classified in Nietzsche's previous work [...] It constitutes a metaphor novel to Nietzsche and, by virtue of its oddity, unique to him as well'. Thatcher discusses the three types of hammer – the sculptor's, the blacksmith's and the lawgiver's – which he claims can be found in Nietzsche's writings before his construction of the '*Götzen*-Hammer' and the title to *Götzen-Dämmerung* in 1888, but which he claims have nothing to do with its meaning in 1888.
22 Peter Georgsson has in an interesting article in *Nietzsche-Studien* 29 (2000): 342–50, 'Nietzsche's Hammer Again' defended and refined Thatcher's view that the hammer is primarily diagnostic (i.e. has the task of unmasking), and argues that 'the clang' produced by the hammer needs something to 'be judged against' for a diagnostic to be possible. He suggests for this purpose 'Nietzsche's view of the conditions for self-realization' (350), that is, 'giving style to one's character'. This brings forth an important aspect of Nietzsche's thought (self-realization), and yields an interesting interpretation of the epilogue, but it contains several weaknesses. It is far-fetched considering that 'giving style to one's character' is not a primary theme in *Götzen-Dämmerung* (as Georgsson himself admits, and he has instead found it in *Die fröhliche Wissenschaft*). He defends its relevance by pointing out that 'the main "idol" to be exposed' in *Götzen-Dämmerung* is morality, and points at the three chapters where this is true (chapters 5–7). However, this is a far too simplistic view of the book. Those three chapters constitute only 29 out of the 144 pages of the original edition, and it ignores other major themes of the book such as the critique of metaphysics and of Christianity generally, for which this explanation of the hammer makes little sense.

Furthermore, Nietzsche claims to have created the title out of the foreword, but there is no discussion of self-realization and giving style to one's character there.

23 It is true that there is a fundamental difference between a hammer and a tuning fork, but Thatcher seems not to notice both that Nietzsche says 'as a tuning fork' and the fact that a tuning fork can also work well 'diagnostically' – but not in the medical sense perhaps – for it gives off very different sounds depending on the object it touches while sounding, the sounding-board, for example, whether it is hollow or solid.

24 Letter to Gast, 27 September 1888. Quoted earlier.

25 *Präge-Hammer*, as has been emphasized by Andreas Urs Sommer.

26 The present text is an in part rewritten and expanded version of my short article 'Götzen-Hammer: The Meaning of the Expression 'To Philosophize with a Hammer'', *Nietzsche-Studien* 28 (1999): 38–41.

27 In *Ecce homo*, 'WA', 4, he says that that will occur in 1890 or 1891.

28 That Nietzsche would write something in one book, which would not be fully comprehensible until a later (and not yet written) book was published, may at first seem improbable. However, there are several instances of this in Nietzsche's production, most obvious in that the first edition of *Die fröhliche Wissenschaft* ends with an introduction of *Also sprach Zarathustra*, which made little sense until that work was actually published. Another example, is the last sentence of *Götzen-Dämmerung*, Nietzsche as 'the teacher of eternal recurrence', which makes fairly little sense unless he will later explain what he means by it.

29 This interpretation is also consistent with Nietzsche's claim that he constructed the title out of the foreword, letter to Gast, 27 September 1888, for half the foreword is dealing with the *Umwerthung aller Werthe*, and the idea of eternal recurrence was to be the pinnacle idea of that work and project.

30 KSA 10, 16[49]: 'Die schwerste Erkenntniß als Hammer'. However, already earlier, for example, in the note KSA 10, 15[48], where Nietzsche plans the text for *Also sprach Zarathustra*, III, he writes about the end of it (where eternal recurrence is present throughout): 'The end: I have the hammer!'.

31 KSA 11, 26[298]: 'Der schwerste Gedanke als Hammer'. However, the hammer is also used as such a symbol in several other notes before this, for example, KSA 10, 17[69], 21[3 and 6], and 25[249].

32 KSA 11, 27[80] written during the summer-autumn 1884: 'Die Lehre der ewigen Wiederkunft als *Hammer* in der Hand der *mächtigsten* Menschen, – – – '

33 KSA 11, 27[82].

34 For example, in KSA 11, 29[27], 31[2], 32[15] and 34[199]. See also the somewhat later notes 35[9 and 82].

35 KSA 11, 34[33, 78, 188 and 191]. Compare also 34[129] in which the hammer is not used, but the last part is there called (with the same sense) 'The Thought that Disciplines'. Compare also 34[201]. This is also repeated in 1885/86, KSA 12, 2[129].

36 KSA 12, 2[100, 118, 129 and 131].

37 KSA 12, 2[100].

38 KSA 12, 2[118].

39 KSA 12, 5[70]: 'Die ewige Wiederkunft als Hammer', written between the summer 1886 and the autumn 1887.

KSA 12, 7[45]: 'Die Umgekehrten / ihr Hammer, die Lehre von der Wiederkunft', written during the end of 1886 or the beginning of 1887.

KSA 13, 13[3]: 'IV Zur Lehre von der ewigen Wiederkunft. Als Hammer', written during early 1888.

KSA 13, 13[4]: 'Der Hammer: Lehre von der ewigen Wiederkunft', written during early 1888.

40 There is in Nietzsche's thought a direct parallel between the idea of the eternal recurrence and the idea of the death of God. They both deal with our need for an eternal telos, for an external purpose, with our relation to metaphysical conceptions. The ideas of the death of God is destructive in that it can lead to nihilism and a world devoid of values, it is diagnostic in that it tests the strength of our courage and intellectual conscience and it is constructive in the sense that it places us on a higher stage of history – 'must we ourselves not become gods simply to appear worthy of it?' (*Die fröhliche Wissenschaft*, 125).

41 See, for example, the interesting note KSA 13, 17[8].

42 KSA 9, 11[143].

43 KSA 9, 11[161].

44 Compare the last aphorism, 44, in the first chapter, which seems to have a meaning very similar to this. I discuss it later in the chapter.

45 That the *Umwerthung aller Werthe* is a more 'serious' work is confirmed when we examine *Der Antichrist* with *Götzen-Dämmerung*.

46 KSA 13, 18[17]. This is the last detailed draft for a table of contents of the *Hauptwerk*. There are several later ones, but they only list the titles of the books, not chapters.

47 KSA 12, 9[52]. This is one of the many notes Nietzsche numbered and designated for use in his work on the *Umwerthung aller Werthe*.

48 Note that already here, in *Jenseits von Gut und Böse*, 'hammer' is associated with the revaluation of all values (and by implication with the idea of eternal recurrence), and these, in turn with 'a heart transformed to brass' [*Erz*], which is the theme of the epilogue of *Götzen-Dämmerung*. The same German word, *Erz*, is used in both of them.

49 KSA 12, 9[154]. This is another of the many notes which Nietzsche numbered and designated for use in his work on the *Umwerthung aller Werthe*.

50 KSA 13, 18[4], from early 1888. Compare also the very similar texts, *Morgonröthe*, 318, KSA 12, 9[188], KSA 13, 11[410] and 15[118].

51 *Der Fall Wagner*, Epilogue.

52 Nietzsche re-read his *Zur Genealogie der Moral* during July–August 1888, and Montinari has suggested that these essays constituted a model and stimulus for how he was to write his *Revaluation of All Values*. I agree that this seems likely.

53 'Es handelt sich jetzt auch bei mir um eine conceptio [in the sense of a teaching, a programme, a totality]: Du wirst es aus dem Umschlage meines letzterschienenen Werks errathen [i.e. the cover of *Jenseits von Gut und Böse*, where the *Hauptwerk* was announced as a work in progress]' Letter to Seydlitz, 17 August 1886.

54 Letter to Overbeck, 24 March 1887, '*einen zusammenhängenden Bau von Gedanken*'.

55 Letter to Brandes, 4 May 1888, 'meine Gesammt-Conception'. Compare also letter to Overbeck, 13 February 1888, where the expression also occurs.

56 Letter to Overbeck, 7 April 1884, 'Ausarbeitung meiner "Philosophie"'.

57 Letter to Gast, 2 September 1884, 'Ausarbeitung eines Schema's an, mit welchem ich meine "Philosophie" umrissen habe'.

58 'Ich brauche jetzt, für lange lange Jahre, tiefe Ruhe: denn es steht die Ausarbeitung meines ganzen Gedankensystems vor mir'. (Letter to Fritzsch, end of December 1886).

59 Letter to Naumann, 7 September 1888, 'sehr strengen und ernsten Charakter'.
60 KSA 12, 1[168, 186, 187], 2[185] and 5[50].
61 It is likely that what he speaks of here is that which he planned to present in the fourth, more affirmative, volume of the *Hauptwerk*.
62 The metaphor of 'a straight line' also occurs in 'Expeditions of an Untimely Man', 18, where it seems to symbolize being consistent and being genuine. In the first section of *Der Antichrist* it seems to mean 'a road'.
63 'Lauter absolute Stellungen z.B. *Glück*!! z.B. Geschichte / ungeheurer Genuß und Triumph am Schluß, *lauter klare Ja's und Nein's zu haben* . . . Erlösung von der *Ungewißheit*!'. KSA 13, 14[156], written in May–June 1888. Compare also KSA 13, 15[13].
64 Before Nietzsche wrote *Der Antichrist*, nihilism was in almost all drafts planned to be discussed in the first volume.
65 These drafts of chapter titles were all made during 1888, but before he decided to name his *Hauptwerk* as *Umwerthung aller Werthe*. (There are several further drafts for the *Hauptwerk*, and further chapter titles could be added to these.) These are all taken from the three drafts of table of contents KSA 13, 12[2], 16[51] and 18[17], respectively. The first two comes from the first, the following four from the second and the last four from 18[17].
66 I have argued for this view in my paper 'Nietzsche's *magnum opus*', *History of European Ideas* 32 (September 2006): 278–94.
67 KSA 13, 18[17]. Its contents are reproduced in the last column of Table 3.2.
68 In section 5 and the concept of *agon* (competition) in section 8. In an early version of the end of section 4, Nietzsche wrote down as a contrast to the Socratic equation, reason=virtue=happiness a parenthesis, which he later struck out: '(the older equality was: Virtue=Instinct=Fundamental unconsciousness)'. See KSA 14, 413f.
69 This whole chapter can be seen as an answer or further elaboration of the third last section of the first edition of *Die fröhliche Wissenschaft*, section 340, with the title 'The Dying Socrates'.
70 As is visible in the last chapter, and in *Ecce homo*, Nietzsche now claims that he already then began his revaluation project. This is a dubious claim, and was certainly not true in the 1870s, but can, perhaps, with hindsight, be claimed to contain some truth. However, Nietzsche's concept of Dionysos, life-affirmation (*amor fati*) and even Socrates had in fact changed significantly since then.
71 A very large number of notes from KSA 13, 14[14] until 17[3].
72 Nietzsche is frequently interpreted as an anti-historical thinker, but this is far from true. He was educated as a historian, and his approach to philosophy was almost always historical. I have examined and argued for this in a number of articles, for example: 'Nietzsche's View of the Value of Historical Studies and Methods', *Journal of the History of Ideas* 65 (2004): 301–22, 'Nietzsche's Relation to Historical Methods and Nineteenth Century German Historiography', *History and Theory* 46 (May 2007): 155–79 and 'The Late Nietzsche's Fundamental Critique of Historical Scholarship', in *Nietzsche on Time and History*, ed. Manuel Dries (Berlin, New York, 2008), 51–60.
73 Nietzsche treats both these aspects (i) and (ii) as the first 'idiosyncracy'.
74 Julian Young, 498. I much agree with Young's view that Nietzsche himself had held many of the views he now criticizes. I think there is a strong case for arguing that Nietzsche also held the first position, Platonism (as a student). It is true that he first was a Christian, but here he is concerned with a general historical trend and start

with Platonism and continues to Christianity ('Platonism for the people', as he says in the foreword to *Jenseits von Gut und Böse*). I have argued that this is an important aspect of Nietzsche's thought (which he himself referred to as self-overcoming), and examined it in regard to his view of ethics, in my article 'The Development of Nietzsche's Ethical Thinking', in *Nietzsche and Ethics*, ed. Gudrun von Tevenar (Bern, 2007), 283–310.

75 The reference to Zarathustra here is probably to him as 'the teacher of the idea of eternal recurrence'.
76 See, for example, Bernd Magnus, 'The Deification of the Commonplace: Twilight of the Idol', in *Reading Nietzsche*, ed. R. Solomon and K. Higgins (1988), 152–81.
77 Young, 498.
78 See, for example, *Der Antichrist*, 47. Nietzsche often expresses critique of atheists and agnostics, such as for example David Strauss and George Eliot, who have not drawn *the consequences* of this denial of God (compare *Götzen-Dämmerung*, 'Expeditions of an Untimely Man', 5).
79 *Die fröhliche Wissenschaft*, 125.
80 See Nietzsche's note KSA 10, 15[58]: 'Law for Lawgivers: From *Praying*, We Must become *Praising* [or *Blessing*]!'.
81 The full text of the end is: 'Midday; moment of the shortest shadow; end of the longest error; zenith of mankind; INCIPIT ZARATHUSTRA'.
82 Nietzsche seems to be ambivalent about whether his affirmative philosophy was going to be represented by Zarathustra or Dionysos. For example, originally *Zur Genealogie der Moral* consisted of only two essays, and the latter (and thus the book) ends with a call for an 'Antichrist and Antinihilist [. . .] he must come one day . . . [. . .] Zarathustra the godless . . .'. See my discussion of this question in the fifth chapter 'The Roles of Zarathustra and Dionysos in *Ecce homo* and Other Late Texts' in my *Nietzsche's Ecce Homo and the Revaluation of All Values: Dionysian versus Christian Values* (2021), 97–120.
83 See, for example, KSA 9, 11[195 and 196].
84 For example in KSA 12, 6[26] and KSA 13, 14[77], 15[102] and 18[15 and 17].
85 KSA 13, 18[17].
86 KSA 13, 18[15].
87 These drafts of chapter titles were all made during 1888, but before he decided to name his *Hauptwerk* as *Umwerthung aller Werthe* (before he wrote *Der Antichrist*). They are all taken from the three drafts of table of contents KSA 13, 12[2], 16[51] and 18[17], respectively. The first five comes from the first, the following three from the second and the last two from 18[17].
88 KSA 14, 420. 'Die Hintergründe der Moral'.
89 For the second volume of *Zur Genealogie der Moral*, see KSA 12, 9[83], for later discussions and it being incorporated into his *magnum opus*, see, for example, KSA 12, 10[57 and 58], and many further notes. See also his important letter to Overbeck, 4 January 1888: 'Nur ein Wort hinsichtlich des Buchs [*Zur Genealogie der Moral*]: es war der Deutlichkeit wegen geboten, die verschiedenen Entstehungsheerde jenes complexen Gebildes, das Moral heißt, künstlich zu isoliren. Jede dieser 3 Abhandlungen bringt ein einzelnes primum mobile zum Ausdruck; es fehlt ein viertes, fünftes und sogar das wesentlichste ("der Heerdeninstinkt") – dasselbe mußte einstweilen, als zu umfänglich, bei Seite gelassen werden, wie auch die schließliche Zusammenrechnung aller verschiedenen Elemente und damit eine Art *Abrechnung mit der Moral*. Dafür sind wir eben noch im "Vorspiele" meiner Philosophie. (Zur

Genesis des Christenthums bringt jede Abhandlung einen Beitrag; nichts liegt mir ferner, als dasselbe mit Hülfe einer einzigen psychologischen Kategorie erklären zu wollen) Doch wozu schreibe ich das? Dergleichen versteht sich eigentlich zwischen Dir und mir von selbst. Treulich und dankbar Dein N'. (this letter is translated in Section 6.5), and compare also his letter to Deussen, 3 January 1888.

90 See, for example, *Zur Genealogie der Moral*, II, 24 and 25, and *Ecce homo*, 'Good Books', 1 and 4; *Ecce homo*, 'Götzen-Dämmerung', 2 and especially in the last chapter of *Ecce homo*, 'Destiny', 4, 5 and 8.

91 I treat chapter 6 before chapter 5, for it seems to me to be more fundamental and is more connected to the theme of the previous three chapters, but it would be no problem also to treat them in the order Nietzsche presented them.

92 Originally he presented three errors. The first error (sections 1–2) was added later.

93 KSA 12, 9[91].

94 See, for example, KSA 12, 1[40]: 'The *present* level of morality requires: a) no punishment! 2) no reward – no retribution! 3) no servility 4) no *pia fraus*!' Nietzsche writes many notes on these themes (punishment, guilt and retribution) during the winter 1887/88 and until the spring 1888.

95 The philosopheme of 'the innocence of becoming' (also 'the innocence of existence') Nietzsche discovered at the same time as the idea of eternal recurrence, and he discusses it frequently in notes from the autumn 1881 and also in 1883. Its close connection to eternal recurrence can, for example, be seen in the notes KSA 9, 11[141 and 144] and KSA 10, 16[49]. However, this philosopheme is not especially prevalent in the late Nietzsche's thought, though present in *Götzen-Dämmerung* as we have seen, and, for example, in the notes KSA 12, 9[91] and KSA 13, 15[30].

96 KSA 14, 416. Nietzsche had thus explicitly referred to 'Revaluation of All Values' in both chapters 5 and 6 (sections 3 and 2). In both of them, it is probably a reference to his project of a revaluation of values, but, for example, the quotation marks around the expression in chapter 6, means that we cannot exclude that it is meant (also) to refer to the *Hauptwerk*. The German expression *Umwerthung aller Werthe* (with or without italics, Nietzsche usually does not add italics to book titles) can, in English, both refer to the project and/or the title, i.e. can in written either as revaluation of all values or *Revaluation of All Values*.

97 According to Thatcher, footnote 48, one can see in the galley-proofs that Nietzsche first exchanged the old title with 'Götzen-Hammer', and only later changed it to *Götzen-Dämmerung*. See also KSA 14, 417.

98 I have discussed this question extensively in my book *Nietzsche's Ethics of Character: A Study of Nietzsche's Ethics and its Place in the History of Moral Thinking* (Uppsala, 1995).

99 At least on a first level, the claim that '*there are no moral facts whatever*' can perhaps be interpreted as aimed primarily at deontological ethics which assumes a transcendental objective moral world order, which Nietzsche denies. On a second level, one can claim that moral values and judgements are precisely values, which are separate from facts.

100 In German: 'Ein erstes Beispiel und ganz vorläufig'. This can perhaps better be translated as: 'A first example and very provisionally'.

101 For a more extensive discussion and interpretation of the meaning of the Laws of Manu, see my article 'The Absence of Political Ideals in Nietzsche's Writings: The Case of the Laws of Manu and the Associated Caste-Society', *Nietzsche-Studien* 27 (1998): 300–18.

102 See Nietzsche's letter to Theodor Fritsch, 23 and 29 March 1887, where Nietzsche is highly critical, and refers to the anti-Semitic 'falsification and justification by means of the vague concepts', including Aryan.
103 See Nietzsche's letter to mother and sister, 14 March 1885: 'Zum Enthousiasmus für "deutsches Wesen" habe ich's freilich noch wenig gebracht, noch weniger aber zum Wunsche, diese "herrliche" Rasse gar *rein* zu erhalten. Im Gegentheil, im Gegentheil – '. See also his response to reading an anti-Semitic journal, with a reference to *Also sprach Zarathustra* in it, sent to him by the publisher during the winter 1886-7, 'Disgust! Disgust! Disgust!' ['Ekel! Ekel! Ekel!'] as he wrote in his notebook, KSA 12, 7[67].
104 It should be noted that although the emphasis in the discussion appears to be on biological breeding, the German words *Zucht* and *Züchtung* can also have a substantial social and cultural component.
105 In *The Antichrist*, 3, written less than a month later, Nietzsche says that: 'The problem I raise here is not what ought to succeed mankind in the sequence of species (– the human being is an *end* –): but what type of human being one ought to *breed*, ought to *will*, as more valuable, more worthy of life, more certain of the future'. This implies that Nietzsche's emphasis in his own use of *Züchtung* is *not* the biological, at least not a strongly or exclusively biological one. This is made still more clear in an early version of this text, KSA 13, 15[120], and in KSA 13, 14[133].
106 Letter to Peter Gast, 31 May 1888. Compare also KSA 13, 11[228] and 14[25] where Nietzsche speaks of the Vedanta-philosophy and Brahmanism as nihilistic and as phenomena of decline.
107 Nietzsche's reading of Jacolliot is reflected in a large number of notes, for example: KSA 13, 14[106+175-178+189+190+191+193+195+196+198-204+212-218+220+2 21+223+224+225], 15[21+24+42+44+45+47+62+109], 16[53+60], 18[3] and 22[10].
108 KSA 13, 14[203], with the title 'Critique of Manu', KSA 13, 14[216], with the title 'Critique of the laws' and KSA 13, 15[45], with the title 'Toward a Critique of the Lawbook of Manu'.
109 KSA 13, 14[204].
110 For example, in KSA 13, 14[199+204+221].
111 KSA 13, 15[45].
112 In a note from the winter 1885-6 Nietzsche, as we have seen earlier, writes: 'The *present* level of morality requires: a) no punishment! 2) no reward – no retribution! 3) no servility 4) no *pia fraus*!'. KSA 12, 1[40].
113 KSA 12, 6[26], 8[4] and KSA 13, 18[17]. Also in a draft for a preface for the third volume of the *Umwerthung aller Werthe*: *The Immoralist*, written in October 1888, after he had finished both *Götzen-Dämmerung* and *Der Antichrist*, does he speak of 'improvers', KSA 13, 23[3] and 22[25].
114 See also Nietzsche's letter to Naumann, 12 August 1888, for his comments on the epilogue and its importance.
115 Also the contrary sort of morality, called slave morality in *Zur Genealogie der Moral*, is not mentioned in *Götzen-Dämmerung*.
116 Nietzsche sent the text to the epilogue to his publisher shortly before 12 August, but kept revising it until at least 18 August.
117 *Entselbstungmoral* is also briefly mentioned in *Jenseits von Gut und Böse* and *Zur Genealogie der Moral*, but more relevant is that he mentions it fairly frequently in his notes from 1887/88.

118 See, for example, his letter to Naumann, 18 September 1888: 'To be able to publish that extraordinary *serious* work, the *Umwerthung aller Werthe*, requires at least a years intervening space, *intervening period* in regard to *earlier* publications'.
119 Compare aphorism 23 in the first chapter.
120 It is remarkable how rarely the content of this chapter is discussed in the many studies of different aspects of Nietzsche as a political thinker. See two of my earlier articles in which this text is used and emphasized, 'Critical Aspects of Nietzsche's Relation to Politics and Democracy', in *Nietzsche, Power and Politics*, ed. Herman Siemens och Vasti Roodt (Berlin, New York: Walter de Gruyter, 2008), 205–27 and 'Politik' in the revised second edition of the *Nietzsche-Lexicon*, edited by Christian Niemeyer, published by the *Wissenschaftliche Buchgesellschaft* in (Darmstadt, 2010/2011). The lack of use of this chapter in studies of Nietzsche's political thought and philosophy becomes even more remarkable when we observe that almost all commentators regard *Götzen-Dämmerung* as giving a summary of his works and thought.
121 The letter or letters in which he sent in the rest of the additions is lost.
122 *Die fröhliche Wissenschaft*, V, 370. The text of this section is also republished by Nietzsche with some small changes in *Nietzsche contra Wagner* under the title 'We Antipodes'. There he adds to the earlier text: 'Regarding artists of all kinds, I now avail myself of this main distinction: is it the *hatred* against life or the *excess* of life which has here become creative? In Goethe, for example, the excess became creative; in Flaubert, hatred'. We can note that Nietzsche uses the same criterion also in ethics.
123 I mention in Section 4.4 how important, for example, Nietzsche's reading of the brothers Goncourt was for *Götzen-Dämmerung*.
124 Nietzsche was all along highly favourably disposed towards Emerson. His very first important encounter with philosophy (before both Plato and Schopenhauer) was with the American philosopher and writer Ralph Waldo Emerson, who probably stimulated both his break with Christianity and his discovery of philosophical thinking. Although Nietzsche rarely referred to Emerson in his published writings, he continued to read and be stimulated by Emerson almost every year of his life and he annotated books by him (in German translation) more heavily than perhaps any other books in his library. And in letters and notes he highly praised Emerson, with such comments as: 'the author richest in thought this century' (KSA 9, 12[151], autumn 1881).
125 *Götzen-Dämmerung*, 'Expeditions of an Untimely Man', 1 and 3.
126 D. D. Runes (ed.), *Dictionary of Philosophy* (Totowa, New Jersey, 1979).
127 I have discussed this aspect of his thought in much more detail in my *Nietzsche's Ethics of Character: A Study of Nietzsche's Ethics and its Place in the History of Moral Thinking* (Uppsala, 1995). This aspect has often also been discussed by Robert Solomon, in a similar sense.
128 UB, III, 8 for 'new Platos' and, for example, FW, 289 and JGB, 2, 44, 203, 210 and 229 for 'new philosophers'.
129 After having summarized in *Ecce homo* the contents of the three essays of *Zur Genealogie der Moral* Nietzsche writes: 'Three decisive preliminary studies by a psychologist for a revaluation of all values. – This book contains the first psychology of the priest'. EH, 'Why I Write such Good Books', 'GM'.
130 KSA 12, 2[95], also published as WM, 505. Note that in Nietzsche's view the fact/value distinction is not valid at this level. This and several other nearby notes are based on Nietzsche's reading of Nägeli, discussed earlier in Section 4.3.

131 'the thinking that rises to *consciousness* is only the smallest part of all this - the most superficial and worst part [. . .] the development of language and the development of consciousness [. . .] go hand in hand. [. . .] each of us will always succeed in becoming conscious only of that what is not individual but 'average''. FW, V, 354.
'We no longer have a sufficiently high estimate of ourselves when we communicate. Our true experiences are not garrulous. They could not communicate themselves if they wanted to: they lack words'. GD, 'Expeditions', 26.
132 According to, for example, *The Encyclopedia of Philosophy*: 'Aesthetics is the branch of philosophy that is concerned with the analysis of concepts and the solution of problems that arise when one contemplates aesthetic objects'.
133 *Nietzsche contra Wagner*, 'We Antipodes'.
134 Explicit references to this chapter or theme are even given in his published works *Zur Genealogie der Moral* and *Der Fall Wagner*.
135 *Die fröhliche Wissenschaft*, V, 370.
136 GD, 'Morality as Anti-Nature', 2.
137 Nietzsche criticizes, among others, Darwinism for having a view which was too passive. His own belief in 'will to power' can explain his view of inherent and spontaneous activity.
138 GD, 'Expeditions of an Untimely Man', 10.
139 See also *Die fröhliche Wissenschaft*, 299, where he seems to construct a dichotomy between art and life, where wisdom (and the philosopher) is higher than the artist whose skill is limited to art.
140 I have discussed the case of ethics in some detail in my *Nietzsche's Ethics of Character: A Study of Nietzsche's Ethics and its Place in the History of Moral Thinking* (Uppsala, 1995).
141 *On the Genealogy of Morals*, III, 8.
142 *Der Fall Wagner*, 7. Compare also KSA 13, 17[9].
143 However, it has not been much discussed in English-language studies of Nietzsche. For example, Julian Young does not seem to refer to it at all, neither in his *Nietzsche's Philosophy of Art* (Cambridge, 1992), nor in his biography *A Philosophical Biography: Friedrich Nietzsche* (Cambridge, 2010). Nor is it mentioned in Burnham's *The Nietzsche Dictionary*.
144 The absence of the expression in his notes before this is surprising, especially considering his promise to discuss it in the earlier *Zur Genealogie der Moral* and *Der Fall Wagner*. This may be a reflection of that some of Nietzsche's late notes have been lost.
145 KSA 13, 16[71, 72, 73 and 86]. It is true that it also occurs three times in the one year earlier note, KSA 12, 7[7], but that appears to have been due to additions Nietzsche made after 26 August 1888 (when he wrote his last detailed table of contents of the *Hauptwerk*), when he edited older notes and added titles to them to fit that outline.
146 KSA 13, 18[17].
147 This is true from the note KSA 13, 11[71] and onwards. Discussions of art thereafter may well have been planned to also be included in other chapters, with titles such as 'Philosophy as Décadence', 'Critique of Modernity', 'Problems of Modernity' and 'Modern Ideas are False'.
148 Such as, for example, 'the aesthetic misunderstanding', KSA 13, 16[70], several chapters in the outline KSA 13, 17[1] and 'Among Artists', KSA 13, 16[64].

149 KSA 12, 7[7] and KSA 13, 17[9].
150 And yet, surprisingly, this note appears not to have been translated into English and published previously. Unfortunately, it (and near-lying notes) seems not to have been included in the KGW IX volumes, at least not so far, that gives diplomatic and facsimile versions of Nietzsche's notes.
151 It is fairly common to realize that social utopias, if realized, would actually turn out to be rather nasty places. I believe that Nietzsche is unusual as pointing out the same thing for individual moral ideals, that the perfectly moral person would actually be life-denying, unwanted and negative.
152 KSA 14, 430f.
153 *Götzen-Dämmerung*, 'Expeditions of an Untimely Man', 36. Compare also the section 'Of Voluntary Death' in the first book of *Also sprach Zarathustra*.
154 'Besonders abstossend wirkt N.s unerbittliche 'Moral für Ärzte', die bedenkliche Einstellung der damaligen Psychiatrie radikalisiert', as Marco Brusotti writes in *Nietzsche-Handbuch* (2000), 152.
155 KSA 13, 14[9], also published as WM, 247.
156 The word Nietzsche uses is: 'der Kranke'.
157 See, for example, Tobias Dahlquist's *Nietzsche and the Philosophy of Pessimism* (Uppsala: Acta Universitatis Upsaliensis, 2007).
158 *Ecce homo*, 'Why I Am So Wise', 1 and 2.
159 See his draft of a letter to Paul Lanzky, end of April 1884, where he writes: 'What do I have to do with people who *have* no goal! My recommendation, by the way, in regard to those, is – suicide'.
160 In an earlier version, KSA 13, 14[9], Nietzsche writes: 'As I understand all the phenomena of Christianity and pessimism, they say: "we are ripe for non-existence; for us it is reasonable not to exist"'.
161 However, Nietzsche did not use the term *Übermensch* at all in *Jenseits von Gut und Böse*, and I have not found it used at all in the eleven reviews of that work that I have examined and that Nietzsche could have read before he wrote *Götzen-Dämmerung*. Only one of them refers to Cesare Borgia – and that is almost certainly the one Nietzsche is referring to, and the one which is the most interesting one, and the one he explicitly refers to in the next sentence (as the one who understands the book as 'a proposal to abolish all decent feeling' – Josef Viktor Widmann (who, was a friend of Peter Gast, and with whom Nietzsche had exchanged letters) – who wrote this review on 16 and 17 September 1888 in *Der Bund*, under the title: 'Nietzsche's Dangerous Book'. The review is largely very positive to Nietzsche, although also expressing some critique, and Nietzsche liked it at first and only later turned against it. Widmann writes concerning Cesare Borgia: 'Konsequenter Weise wird ein Cesare Borgia als ein "gesündester Mensch" gefeiert: "Man mißversteht das Raubthier und den Raubmenschen (z.B. Cesare Borgia) gründlich, man mißversteht die Natur, so lange man noch nach einer Krankhaftigkeit im Grunde dieser gesündesten aller tropischen Unthiere und Gewächse sucht, oder gar nach einer ihnen eingeborenen 'Hölle', wie es bischer fast alle Moralisten gethan haben". Solche Menschen sind ihm tropische Prachtexemplare, denen gegenüber man nicht zu Gunsten der gemäßigten Zone plädiren dürfe. Thue man es dennoch, so sei das nichts anderes als "*die Moral der Furchtsamkeit*"'.
162 This and several other themes are well discussed by Robert C. Holub in his *Nietzsche in the Nineteenth Century* (2018).

163 Goethe, Homer, Shakespeare, Beethoven, Napoleon, Voltaire, Sophocles, Aeschylus, Heraclitus, Byron, Horace, Raphael and Montaigne are the most often referred to and praised persons in Nietzsche's published books, in this order.
164 I have discussed this in much more detail in my study *Nietzsche's Ethics of Character: A Study of Nietzsche's Ethics and its Place in the History of Moral Thinking* (Uppsala, 1995).
165 *Jenseits von Gut und Böse*, 260.
166 'Du scheint mir Schlimmes im Schilde zu führen, man möchte glauben, du wolltest den Menschen zu Grunde richten?' – sagte ich einmal zu dem Gotte Dionysos. 'Vielleicht, antwortete der Gott, aber so, daß dabei Etwas für ihn heraus kommt'. – 'Was denn? fragte ich neugierig. - *Wer* denn? solltest du fragen'. Also sprach Dionysos'. KSA 12, 2[25] and 4[4], both from 1886.
167 *Der Antichrist*, 3.
168 KSA 12, 9[116]. In a later note, he confirms that this note concerns the whole *Hauptwerk* project, KSA 13, 12[1](76). Compare also the poem 'Ariadne' in *Dionysos-Dithyramben*.
169 KSA 13, 12[2].
170 KSA 13, 18[17], from 26 August 1888.
171 These themes are not explicitly discussed in *Götzen-Dämmerung*, but are referred to in *Ecce homo*, '*Morgonröthe*', 2 and in the last chapter 'Destiny', 7. They are also briefly alluded to in the epilogue to *Der Fall Wagner* and in *Der Antichrist*, 54.
172 See, for example, the note KSA 12, 10[168] with the title '*Aesthetica*' which includes a short discussion of the tragic artist, and which Nietzsche in a later note says belongs to those which he will use for the writing of volume 4 of the *Umwerthung aller Werthe*, KSA 13, 12[1](271).
173 KSA 13, 14[169] and 16[51].
174 In an early version of this text he also included Petronius, but he later decided to strike that out and use it in *Der Antichrist* 46 instead. See also KSA 13, 15[104].
175 Several late notes suggest that Nietzsche rejected things-in-themselves, and instead meant that we can only see things as relational. This is possibly a theme which he intended to discuss in the planned *Umwerthung aller Werthe*, as suggested by, for example, KSA 12, 10[202] and KSA 13, 11[145] and 14[93, 103 and 122].
176 Will to power is also briefly mentioned in sections 11, 14, 20 and 38 of the chapter 'Expeditions of an Untimely Man', but none of these four or five references do it justice in the sense that he had spoken of it earlier.
177 For example, in JGB 259, GM, II, 12 and in KSA 11, 38[12] (also published as WM 1067).
178 In both these books, its presence is much more apparent than in *Götzen-Dämmerung*, this is especially true for *Der Antichrist*, where will to power is much emphasized, and discussed in sections 2, 6, 9, 11 and 17. Will to power is also frequently referred to and discussed in late notes.
179 Nietzsche also did so in *Die fröhliche Wissenschaft*. The last sections of the first edition of *Die fröhliche Wissenschaft* (1882) foreshadow and point at his next book *Also sprach Zarathustra* (although the original readers could not possibly see or realize this).

In the epilogue to *Der Fall Wagner* Nietzsche explicitly discusses the two ways; of the ascending and the descending life.

180 *Götzen-Dämmerung*, 'Ancients', 4 and 5. The first part of this quotation shows us that it is indeed the Greeks, not the Romans, to whom Nietzsche owe thanks, and whom he had found a new way – in particular to the tragic and the Dionysian.
181 The last of these is closely related to the 'innocence of becoming' briefly discussed in Section 7.4.
182 Compare his statement in section 43 of 'Expeditions of an Untimely Man'.
183 *Der Fall Wagner*, Epilogue.
184 '*Ich habe das Griechenthum entdeckt*: sie glaubten an die *ewige Wiederkunft*! Das ist der *Mysterien-Glaube*! (Stelle des Cratylus) Plato meint, die Todten im Hades seien *rechte Philosophen, vom Leibe erlöst*'. KSA 10, 8[15], summer 1883.
185 Nietzsche, in this section, has Dionysos say: 'I often reflect how I might yet advance him [man] and make him stronger, more evil and more profound than he is'.
186 '*ich, der letzte Jünger und Eingeweihte des Gottes Dionysos: und ich dürfte wohl endlich einmal damit anfangen, euch, meinen Freunden, ein Wenig, so weit es mir erlaubt ist, von dieser Philosophie zu kosten zu geben?*' *Jenseits von Gut und Böse*, 295. It seems as if all earlier English translations have skipped or ignored the word 'einmal', which here surely has the meaning of 'one day', 'some day' or 'later on' and thus have made it look like Nietzsche is expounding on Dionysos' philosophy here, in 295, rather than it being a promise of doing so in the future, that is in the *Umwerthung aller Werthe*. That this is a promise, and a promise about disclosing more about Dionysos' philosophy in the future (i.e. in his planned four volume *magnum opus*) is still more visible in the early draft to this section, where he writes: 'and perhaps there will come a day with so much stillness and halcyon happiness [. . .] that I will tell you, my friends, the philosophy of Dionysos' ['vielleicht kommt mir auch ein Tag von so viel Stille und halkyonischem Glück [. . .] daß ich Euch, meine Freunde, die Philosophie des Dionysos erzähle'] (KSA 14, 374).

Nietzsche at this time, 1885/86 frequently uses Dionysos in titles, some of which are likely to be for the planned *Hauptwerk*.
187 See KSA 13, 23[8 and 13].
188 KSA 11, 26[259], summer/autumn 1884. This is Nietzsche's first use of the word 'revaluation', 'Umwerthung'.
189 In the commentary volume KSA 14, 454, Montinari writes: 'Zusammenfassend: der Titel "Der Hammer redet" bezieht sich zweimal auf § 29 im Kapitel "Von alten und neuen Tafeln" (Za III) und wurde sukzessive Schluss 1. von AC, 2. GD; er bezieht sich das dritte Mal auf § 30 desselben Kapitels, welcher bis 29. Dezember den Schluss von EH bildete'.
190 Letter to Peter Gast, 30 October 1888.
191 Zarathustra is described as such in Za, III, 'The Convalescent', 2, which follows immediately after 'Of Old and New Law-Tables'. Compare also the similar statement in *Ecce homo*, 'Zarathustra', 1 and 3.
192 See, for example, *Also sprach Zarathustra*, III, 'Der Genesende', 2 and KSA 11, 27[67].
193 Nietzsche here, as is evident in the text, instead of letting a man become a fate speaks of fate becoming a man, but in what is relevant here, they are equivalent. Most of this text from *Ecce homo* is a slightly modified quotation from *Also sprach Zarathustra*, II, 'On Self-Overcoming'.
194 This is closely related to Nietzsche's philosopheme of *amor fati* (not explicitly mentioned in *Götzen-Dämmerung*) but of paramount importance to the late Nietzsche and his thought.

195 Compare also Nietzsche's approval of Heraclitus' affirmation of that the whole existence is war and struggle. Compare also Heraclitus' view of great men with Nietzsche's in *Götzen-Dämmerung*, 'Expeditions', 44.
196 See also the discussion in Chapter 7.
197 Many of Nietzsche's later notes show that he intended to criticize 'the good and the just' in the third book of the *Umwerthung aller Werthe*.
198 See my *Nietzsche's Ecce Homo and the Revaluation of All Values: Dionysian versus Christian Values* in which I discuss the meaning of the symbol of Dionysos in Nietzsche's late writings.
199 *Ecce homo*, 'Good Books', 3.
200 *Ecce homo*, 'Wise', 2.
201 *Ecce homo*, '*Unzeitgemäße Betrachtungen*', 3.
202 *Götzen-Dämmerung*, 'Ancients', 2.
203 That is, until the last week before his mental collapse. During those last few weeks he is obviously partially incapacitated and has lost part of his sense of judgement. In my view, the *Ecce homo* which he finalized during early December (and then read proofs of), with this epilogue, is a more correct and suitable version of the text than the one which includes his final, in part confused and misjudged revisions, made during the last two weeks before his collapse on 3 January 1889.
204 Note the similarity with the last of the aphorisms (no 44) in the first chapter of *Götzen-Dämmerung*, entitled 'Maxims and *Arrows*' (my italics).
205 'A good wind? Alas, only he who knows *where* he is going knows which wind is a good and fair wind for him', *Also sprach Zarathustra*, IV, Der Schatten.
206 *Götzen-Dämmerung*, 'Maxims and Arrows', 44. The importance of having a goal is also a theme in *Ecce homo*, 'klug', 9. This is also visible in a draft to a letter to Paul Lanzky, end of April, 1884, where he writes: 'Einstweilen ist es noch lange nicht Zeit für Zarathustra – und ich will mich verwundern, wenn in dem Rest meines Lebens mir fünf, sechs Menschen begegnen, welche Augen für meine Ziele haben. "Einstweilen" – das heißt so lange noch alle diese Allemanderies und niaiseries von "Bejahung und Verneinung des Willens zum Leben" – Bemerken Sie doch: ich habe mich mit diesem übermenschlichen Bilde [i.e. *Also sprach Zarathustra*] ermuthigen wollen. Alle Menschen aber, die irgend einen heroischen Impuls in sich haben zu ihrem *eigenen Ziele* hin, werden sich eine große Kraft aus meinem Zarathustra herausnehmen. Was habe ich mit Denen zu thun, die kein Ziel *haben*! Mein Leibrezept, beiläufig bemerkt, ist, in Hinsicht auf Solche, – Selbstmord. Aber er mißräth gewöhnlich, aus Mangel an Zucht'. This draft of a letter was found late, and is placed out of order in the last volume, KSB8, 597f.
207 Notes in which 'great midday' is associated with eternal recurrence are: KSA 9, 11[148], KSA 10, 16[3], KSA 11, 25[6 and 323], 26[465], 27[82], 34[191], KSA 12, 2[71, 72, 74 and 129] and 6[26] and KSA 13, 13[2] and 18[17].
208 See Chapter 7 for a discussion of this idea, and also how it can be both destructive and constructive (or affirmative).
209 Nietzsche here plays with the title of his 'Hauptwerk', and immediately after the quoted text he will in a similar manner play with the title of his *Der Fall Wagner*. Nietzsche here writes 'Eine *Umwerthung aller Werthe*', which all four English translators have chosen: 'A *Revaluation of All Values*' (except that Hollingdale has falsely added italics also to the 'A', which I have corrected in the quotation earlier). The German here is ambivalent. It can both be an emphasized statement (which is what the translators have chosen, probably because of the indefinite particle before

it) and/or a title (then 'A *Revaluation of All Values*'). Both are correct, and I would argue that Nietzsche means both of them, but in English one has to choose. Nietzsche writes it identically the same way here and at the end of the foreword, where he obviously refers to the literary work.

210 I am quoting Hollingdale's translation here (and earlier). Nietzsche actually writes: 'das erst Buch der *Umwerthung aller Werthe*' (which is how one usually writes a book title in German). In English, it ought thus to be 'the *Revaluation of All Values*', which is also how W. Kaufmann, Duncan Large and Judith Norman has translated it in their translations.

211 *Götzen-Dämmerung*, 'The "Improvers" of Mankind', 2.

212 Nietzsche also refers to these dialogues or this theme in the notes KSA 11, 37[4], KSA 12, 9[115] as well as in *Jenseits von Gut und Böse*, 295 and in *Dionysos-Dithyramben*, 'Ariadne's Complaint'. In the long note, KSA 12, 9[115], from the autumn 1887 Nietzsche expresses plans for his *Hauptwerk* (which is further confirmed by the note KSA 13, 12[1]) and develops there these dialogues for about one page. He in this note intends to place them at the end of, or after, the fourth book: 'Satyrspiel am Schluss' (in line with that Greek tragedies were followed by a satyr-play). Also a year later, in his last detailed table of contents for the *Hauptwerk*, from 26 August 1888 (quoted earlier), he seems to have planned to have something lighter, which he then calls '*Psychologen-Kurzweil*' (approximately 'Entertainment for psychologists'), now placed between the third and the fourth book. This probably refers to either a collection of aphorism or to these Naxos dialogues.

213 *Ecce homo*, '*Götzen-Dämmerung*', 1.

214 *Ecce homo*, '*Jenseits von Gut und Böse*', 1. It seems reasonable to assume that what he meant was that *Götzen-Dämmerung* constituted the summit of this, together with the first three volumes of the *Umwerthung aller Werthe*, while the fourth volume would re-connect with *Also sprach Zarathustra*, but now discuss its and Nietzsche's affirmative philosophy in a less metaphorical and more philosophical manner.

215 *Ecce homo*, '*Götzen-Dämmerung*', 2.

216 These three notebooks have been published in facsimile and diplomatic text in KGW IX, volumes 6 and 7.

217 Letter to Karl Knortz, 21 June 1888. Compare also the interesting statement in a letter to Malwida von Meysenbug, 12 May 1887: 'In den langen "Vorreden" [to the new edition of *Menschliches, Allzumenschliches*] welche ich für die Neuherausgabe meiner sämmtlichen Schriften nöthig befunden habe, stehen kuriose Dinge von einer rücksichtslosen Aufrichtigkeit in Bezug auf mich selbst: damit halte ich mir "die Vielen" ein für alle Mal vom Leibe, denn nichts agacirt die Menschen so sehr als etwas von der Strenge und Härte merken zu lassen, mit der man *sich selbst*, unter der Zucht seines eigensten Ideals, behandelt und behandelt hat. Dafür habe ich meine Angel nach "den Wenigen" ausgeworfen, zuletzt auch dies ohne Ungeduld: denn es liegt in der unbeschreiblichen Fremdheit und Gefährlichkeit meiner Gedanken, daß erst sehr spät – und gewiß nicht vor 1901 – die Ohren sich für diese Gedanken aufschließen werden'.

218 Letter to Naumann, 20 December 1888.

219 Letter to Peter Gast, 14 October 1888: 'In der That hat man mich mit dieser Schrift *in nuce*: sehr Viel auf kleinem Raum' and to Georg Brandes, 20 October 1888: 'Diese Schrift ist meine Philosophie *in nuce* – radikal bis zum Verbrechen . . .'.

Chapter 6

1. I examine the relation between *Also sprach Zarathustra* and the planned *Hauptwerk* in my study *The Close Relationship Between Nietzsche's Two Most Important Books* (2023). *Götzen-Dämmerung* cannot be regarded as a summary of *Also sprach Zarathustra*, but the two works are nonetheless closely linked.
2. Wagner is only very briefly mentioned two times.
3. *Götzen-Dämmerung*, 'Four Errors', 7.
4. For an account of Nietzsche's inspiration for this, and that it was new at this time, see my article 'Nietzsche's Relation to the Greek Sophists', *Nietzsche-Studien* 34 (2005): 255–76, and references in this work.
5. This is also the view of the main editor of Nietzsche's collected works, Mazzino Montinari, as discussed in Section 2.2 earlier, and he also argues that this was not the case for *Jenseits von Gut und Böse* and *Zur Genealogie der Moral*.
6. We should also be aware that Nietzsche frequently went back and edited and used older notes, which supports this approach.
7. Montinari is very explicit: '*Nietzsche's collapse in Turin came when he literally was finished with everything*', Mazzoni Montinari's essay 'Nietzsches Nachlaß von 1885 bis 1888 oder Textkritik und Wille zur Macht' published in *Nietzsche lesen* (Berlin, New York, 1982), 118.
8. In the proofs for *Ecce homo*, which he, after examination, states are ready to publish. See my discussion in *Nietzsche's Ecce Homo and the Revaluation of All Values* (Bloomsbury, 2021), 92 ff, where this page of the proofs is also reproduced.
9. KSA 13, 16[86], from June to July 1888. In this note he explicitly states thirty-five or thirty-seven pages per chapter. Nietzsche apparently planned the books of the *Umwerthung aller Werthe* to be fairly short. He planned four chapters per book; that is, each book about 140 pages. Even more important is that the one volume that he did write, *Der Antichrist*, is just less than a hundred pages.
10. This is visible in many notes, see, for example, KSA 13, 12[1], 59, 60 and 170, 12[2] and the very late notes from October 1888 where he drafts the planned contents of *The Immoralist*, KSA 13, 23[4 and 5].
11. Letter to Overbeck, 4 January 1888. Compare also his letter to Paul Deussen, 3 January 1888. For Nietzsche's plans for a second volume of *Zur Genealogie der Moral* and its contents, see KSA 12, 9[83], autumn 1887, for later discussions and it being incorporated into his *magnum opus*, see, for example, KSA 12, 10[57 and 58], autumn 1887 and many further notes.
12. *Beyond Good and Evil*, 23.
13. *Beyond Good and Evil*, 6.
14. 'What is good? – All that heightens the feeling of power, the will to power, power itself in man. What is bad? – All that proceeds from weakness. What is happiness? – The feeling that power *increases* – that a resistance is overcome. *Not* contentment, but more power'. *The Antichrist*, 2.
15. *Beyond Good and Evil*, 259.
16. It occurs in sections 11, 20 and 38 of the 'Expedition' chapter and the third section of the last, 'Ancients' chapter. He there discusses it in relation to architecture, aesthetics, freedom and the psychology of the Greeks, respectively.
17. Perhaps not as generalized as in *Jenseits von Gut und Böse*, but much more so than in *Götzen-Dämmerung*.

18 Nihilism is discussed in section 10 and 208 of *Jenseits von Gut und Böse* (1886) and became a major motif in *Zur Genealogie der Moral* (1887). Later it is present but not emphasized in *Twilight of the Idols*, *The Antichrist* and *Ecce Homo*.
19 Many of his drafts for a *Hauptwerk* show that one of the projected four books of this planned work was going to deal with the problem of nihilism.
20 Prosper Mérimée's 'Lettre à l'éditeur' in Turgenev's *Pères et enfants* (1863).
21 KSA 12, 5[71], June 1887, 211–17. The last sentence in the note before this one, 5[70], is as follows: 'The eternal recurrence as hammer'.
22 The only full English translation which I am aware of (but it has probably been translated earlier) is in Rüdiger Bittner (ed.), *Friedrich Nietzsche: Writings from the Late Notebooks* (Cambridge: Cambridge University Press, 2003), 116–21.
23 The most important misreading occurs in section 6 of the '*European Nihilism*'. Nietzsche gives two reasons for why eternal recurrence should be regarded as 'the *most scientific* of all hypotheses' (and gives yet another one later on in section 13). The first one is in the new reading of KGW IX.3: 'Energie des Stoffes u der Kraft *zwingt* zu einem solchen Glauben' – where the older (KSA) reading had: 'Energie des Wissens und der Kraft *zwingt* zu einem solchen Glauben'. The latter (KSA) version is translated in the Bittner edition as: 'the energy of knowledge and of strength *compels* such a belief' – which now is better translated as: 'energy of matter a[nd] force *compels* such a belief', that is referring to the recently discovered law of conservation of energy. Compare KSA 12, 5[54].
24 It is not completely clear to me why Montinari's order (in KSA 12) is so different from that of the actual notebook, which is unfortunate for our conception of the importance of the '*European Nihilism*' essay. It may be that Montinari attempted to publish the notes in the notebook in chronological order (and had sufficient information for rearranging them), and this is in that case a very valuable service, but unfortunately not explicitly stated.
25 On pages 13–24 of the notebook N VII 3, published in diplomatic style in KGW IX.3. The pages before this (1–13) and immediately after (25–7) contain personal notes (what to buy, where to travel etc.) and drafts for letters, which almost certainly have been added later. If '*European Nihilism*' was written on 10 June 1887, as it is dated (but it is not impossible that the version in the notebook is a clean copy written a little later, but dated back to when it was first composed), the pages around it seems to have been empty – for several of the notes and drafts for letters can be dated as having been written near middle of June or later.
26 KSA 12, 5[75], also in KGW IX.3, 33. See also the following notes where '*European Nihilism*' is listed or referred to: KSA 12, 2[131], 5[50, 71, 75 and 97], 6[26], 7[31 and 64], 9[1], KSA 13, 11[150 and 328], 13[3], 14[114] and 18[17].
27 *Zur Genealogie der Moral*, III, 27.
   As a typical example of how Nietzsche's intention and work on this *Hauptwerk* is assumed to be irrelevant (since no such work was finished) and is associated with the problematic selection of Elisabeth and Gast, and thus, it is implied, is best ignored, see Maudemarie Clark and Alan Swensen's translation of and comments to this work, 167 (1998).
28 According to the text of *Zur Genealogie der Moral* and the note KSA 12, 5[75].
29 Possibly this rhetorical question was meant to be placed at the very end of the third book of the *Hauptwerk*, pointing towards the fourth book, which was meant to deal with eternal recurrence.
30 *The Gay Science*, 341. Kaufmann's translation.

31 KSA 13, 16[32], also published as WM, 1041: 'ich suchte nach den Ansätzen dieser umgekehrten Idealbildung in der Geschichte (die Begriffe 'heidnisch', 'klassisch', 'vornehm' neu entdeckt und hingestellt –)'.
32 We can note that relatively few persons are mentioned in the first seven chapters (the first philosophically more important part of the book), and that by far the most persons are mentioned in the long miscellaneous chapter 9.
33 Heraclitus, Goethe, Napoleon, Hegel, Heine, Burckhardt, Baudelaire, Raphael, Emerson, Caesar, C. Borgia, Dostoevsky, Stendhal, Sallust, (Corssen), Horace, Thucydides, Machiavelli and Fontanelle. Most of them, twelve, he only refers to once in the text, and combining this with examining what he says about them in other late books we can conclude that the more important ones are: Heraclitus, Goethe, Napoleon, Burckhardt, Emerson, Caesar, C. Borgia, Dostoevsky, Stendhal, Thucydides and Machiavelli.
34 It is not impossible that Nietzsche would regard Goethe, at least sometimes, as a sort of philosopher, but this is not the general view, and I have not included him in this group.
35 Emerson is probably the philosopher who has altogether influenced Nietzsche most in an affirmative sense, compare my brief discussion of his relation to him in Chapter 5. In some ways he can be regarded, from Nietzsche's perspective, as a somewhat more philosophical Goethe.
36 For Nietzsche as an historian, see my articles 'Nietzsche's View of the Value of Historical Studies and Methods', *Journal of the History of Ideas* 65 (2004): 301–22 and 'Nietzsche's Relation to Historical Methods and Nineteenth Century German Historiography', *History and Theory* 46 (May 2007): 155–79, and the several important studies by Christian Emden, *Friedrich Nietzsche and the Politics of History* (2011) and *An Interpretation of Nietzsche's On the Uses and Disadvantages of History for Life* (2018).

Several of the other persons mentioned with appreciation by Nietzsche, also wrote and thought on history, such as Caesar, Emerson, Hegel, Heraclitus, perhaps Horace, Napoleon and Stendahl, but that is not the primary reason why Nietzsche refers to them in this book (although it may have contributed).
37 In the chapter 'The Four Great Errors', 7 and 8.
38 The only reference to it in his late notes is in KSA 12, 9[91].

Chapter 7

1 *Ecce homo*, 'GT', 3.
2 KSA 11, 25[214], early 1884.
3 KSA 12, 5[71], also published in part as WM, 55.
4 The goal or purpose must not necessarily be egotistical or individualistic. Such a purpose can well go beyond one's own life – the important thing is that it is separate from grand purposes (of which the old Christian God and the idea of progress are good examples).
5 See, for example, Paul S. Loeb's interesting critique of many earlier discussions of this in 'Identity and Eternal Recurrence', in *A Companion to Nietzsche*, ed. Keith Ansell-Pearson (Blackwell Publishing, 2006).
6 Beginning with the important note KSA 9, 11[141] entitled 'The Recurrence of the Same' [*Die Wiederkehr des Gleichen*], and dated by him as 'early August 1881 in Sils-Maria'. It is thereafter a major theme in many of the following notes.

7 *Ecce homo*, 'Za', 1.
8 At Schulpforta Nietzsche had already encountered some Christian teachings similar to the idea of eternal recurrence. Nietzsche's personal tutor, professor Robert Buddensieg, published a scholarly work (published together with the Pforta *Jahresbericht* 1856), with the title *Gottes Wort und die Wiederbringung aller Dinge*. Since Nietzsche had a warm friendship with Buddensieg and often discussed religion with him, it is not unlikely that Nietzsche read this work. Although the 'Wiederbringung aller Dinge' does not have the same meaning as eternal recurrence, some of its meaning echoes in it, and Nietzsche himself used the expression 'Wiederbringung aller Dinge' a number of times in the early 1870s. Furthermore, in the *Old Testament* it is stated: 'The Earth is forever the same. What has been will be again, what has happened will happen again. There is nothing new under the sun.' One other later such distinctly religious 'stimulus' to the idea of eternal recurrence could have been the lecture by the Basel philosopher Karl Steffensen, which Nietzsche attended in October 1877. An eye-witness account of the occasion states: 'I looked over at him out of the corner of my eye, while the other man at the rostrum celebrated the Christian rebirth of Plato in Origen and revelled in the *pochaastasix*, the eternal bringing back of all things, that boldest thought of the Greek church father'. (Edgar Steiger's account of the incident is published in Sander L. Gilman's *Begegnungen mit Nietzsche* (Bonn, 1981), 346–8), 95–9 in the English translation of this work. An early religious inspiration to the thought of 'eternal recurrence' is not unlikely. Nietzsche himself states: 'I have found this idea in earlier thinkers: every time it was determined by other ulterior considerations (– mostly theological, in favor of the *creator spiritus*)' (KSA 13, 14[188]).
9 KSA 9, 11[163], written during the autumn of 1881.
10 Nietzsche also considered that something similar to his idea of eternal recurrence was part of early Greek religious mysteries, as one can see in the last chapter of *Götzen-Dämmerung*.
11 See my brief discussion of these influences in my study *Nietzsche's Philosophical Context: An Intellectual Biography* (Urbana and Chicago, 2008).
12 Nietzsche used the expression for the first time in two notes from the autumn of 1881, KSA 9, 15[20] och 16[22], and thereafter in *Die fröhliche Wissenschaft*, section 276 (1882). He also referred to it in a letter to Overbeck from 5 June 1882.
13 *Also sprach Zarathustra*, III, 'The Convalescent'.
14 This is shown in several letters from this time, for example, letter to Overbeck, 29 January 1882. The hesitation was due to the fact that he found the idea so fundamental and with such far-reaching consequences. He therefore, in the end, really only points at the idea.
15 The expression also occurs in section 285, but seemingly in a much less important sense.
16 *The Gay Science*, 341. Kaufmann's translation. Compare especially KSA 9, 11[143].
17 *Also sprach Zarathustra*, III, 'The Convalescent', 1 and 2.
18 Hammer is referred to in sections 62, 203, 211 and also 225. The first and third of these are likely to also contain a vague reference to the idea of eternal recurrence.
19 KSA 11, 26[325], with the draft title: 'Beyond Good and Evil: Foreword to a Philosophy of Eternal Recurrence'. Compare also KSA 11, 26[293, 297, 298] and 27[58].

20 See the discussion of the subtitle in Chapter 5 of this book. For example, KSA 12, 5[70]: 'The Eternal Recurrence as Hammer'.
21 It is possible to find yet further aphorisms which also are or can be associated to the idea of eternal recurrence – this is, for example, true for aphorisms 41–43, building up to the last one. In 41, the importance of having a goal is again referred to: 'One must know *what* one wants and *that* one wants'. Aphorisms 42 emphasizes continual change and evolution, and in 43, the importance of the here and now: 'And he who laughs best today will also laugh last.'
22 *Ecce homo*, 'Za', 1.
23 KSA 9, 11[141], from early August 1881. This expression 'eternal recurrence' occurs in the fifth section.
24 Compare also the somewhat later note, KSA 9, 12[21]: 'The first book as a *funeral oration* on the occasion of the death of *God*. –'
25 KSA 9, 11[195–197].
26 *Der Antichrist*, Foreword.
27 KSA 10, 1[70]. Maybe the slightly earlier note 1[43] is also an outline for the same book, but that is not certain.
28 KSA 10, 1[83].
29 See, for example, KSA 10, 4[39], draft for a title 'Midday and Eternity: Thus spoke Zarathustra'. See also KSA 10, 13[2 and 22] and 16[3], KSA 11, 31[30], 34[145].
30 See KSA 10, 24[4], from the winter 1883/84. See also KSA 11, 25[1, 6. 7. 214, 227, 290, 323, 410 and 500], and many later notes, for example, KSA 11, 26[284].
31 For example, KSA 11, 25[500] and 26[243].
32 KSA 11, 26[243]. Compare also 26[259, 283, 293, 297, 298, 325 and 465].
33 KSA 11, 26[259]. This is the very first time Nietzsche uses the expression 'revaluation of all values'.
34 Although, at this early stage, it was sometimes conceived in three or five parts or volumes. Furthermore, sometimes just the title is given, and we do not know how many parts it was meant to contain.
35 KSA 11, 26[465], 27[58, 80 and 82], 29[40 and 66], 34[33, 78, 188 and 191] and 35[39, 40 and 41].
36 KSA 11, 27[82], 34[188 and 191].
37 See, for example, KSA 10, 14[1].
38 See, for example, KSA 12, 2[70].
39 KSA 12, 2[73]. This note from the spring of 1886 is especially interesting for it lists ten future works, including *Jenseits von Gut und Böse* and *Der Wille zur Macht* (it is not completely clear if this constituted the whole *Hauptwerk*, which is most probable, or if that work would also incorporate a few of the other titles). In the notes 2[74] and 2[100] the contents of *Der Wille zur Macht* is specified in more detail. '*Midday and Eternity*' seems in this note to refer to a book of poems, while '*The Eternal Recurrence*' was used both as a draft title of the fourth part (or book) of *Der Wille zur Macht* and for a book of poems.
40 Montinari, 103, and also KSA 14, 345f.
41 This note is quoted in KSA 14, 345.
42 KSA 12, 5[54].
43 KSA 12, 5[71].
44 KSA 13, 18[17].
45 KSA 13, 19[8] and 22[14].

46 KSA 13, 14[14]. I am quoting Kaufmann's translation of this note as *Der Wille zur Macht*, 1050.
47 KSA 13, 14[24]. Compare also KSA 13, 14[33], 16[32] and 17[3]. Especially 16[32] is an important note, in which both *amor fati* and eternal recurrence is related to the Dionysian and to the revaluation of all values.
48 KSA 13, 16[32]. Also published as *Der Wille zur Macht*, 1041. I am here using Kaufmann and Hollingdale's translation of this text.
49 I discuss the close relation between the idea of eternal recurrence and revaluation of all values in my book *The Close Relation between Nietzsche's Two Most Important Books* (2023).

Chapter 8

1 In *Also sprach Zarathustra* Nietzsche expresses it as follows: 'God is a supposition: but I want your supposing to be bounded by conceivability. Could you *conceive* a god? – But may the will to truth mean this to you: that everything shall be transformed into the humanly-conceivable, the humanly-evident, the humanly-palpable! You should follow your own senses to the end!' Za, II, 'On the Blissful Island'. On the same theme Zarathustra already at the beginning of the prologue proclaims: 'I entreat you, my brothers, *remain true to the earth*, and do not believe those who speak to you of superterrestial hopes!' Za, Prologue, 3.
2 *Jenseits von Gut und Böse*, 23.
3 Letter to Karl Knortz, 21 June 1888.
4 EH, 'Why I Write such Good Books', 5.
5 EH, 'Why I am a Destiny', 6. In *Ecce homo*, his forward-looking 'autobiography', he refers to psychology and psychological more often (totally circa forty-two times) than to philosophy and philosophers (totally circa thirty-four times).
6 EH, 'Why I am a Destiny', 7.
7 To give just four examples of Nietzsche's emphasis on the importance of the unconscious (and instinctual) and the relative unimportance of the conscious are:

> 'our thinking is superficial and content with the surface; indeed, it does not notice that it is the surface' (M, 125).

> 'by far the greatest portion of our life actually takes place without this mirror effect [consciousness] [. . .] Man, like every living being, thinks continually without knowing it; the thinking that rises to consciousness is only the smallest part of all this – the most superficial and worst part – the growth of consciousness [. . .] it is a disease' (FW, V, 354).

> 'the greater part of conscious thought must still be counted among the instinctive activities [. . .] so, "being conscious" is in no decisive sense the *opposite* of the instinctive – most of a philosopher's conscious thought is secretly directed and compelled into definite channels by his instincts' (JGB, 3).

> 'The whole surface of consciousness – consciousness *is* a surface' (EH, 'Clever', 9).

8 Apart from often referring to man as an animal, he also calls us both 'the over-animal', MA, I, 40, 'the animal *whose nature has not yet been fixed*', JGB, 62, and as the sick animal, GM, III, 13 and AC, 3, and the most interesting animal.
9 GD, 'The Four Great Errors', 3.

10 The words 'physiology' and 'physiologist', as markers for Nietzsche's interest, are more prevalent in Nietzsche's writings than is commonly noted by commentators. The words occur half as often (totally circa sixty-two times) as the words 'psychology/psychologist' and only just less than half as often as the words 'philosophy/philosopher' in the last five short books by Nietzsche, all written in 1888.
11 GM, I, 17, Nietzsche's note. The physiological emphasis that the biological assumption leads to is well demonstrated by the large number of books in his library dealing with physiology and related fields as discussed in Chapter 4.
12 AC, 14.
13 JGB, 23.
14 See, for example, *Götzen-Dämmerung*, 'Expeditions of an Untimely Man', 14.
15 JGB, 6.
16 'What is good? – All that heightens the feeling of power, the will to power, power itself in man. What is bad? – All that proceeds from weakness. What is happiness? – The feeling that power *increases* – that a resistance is overcome. *Not* contentment, but more power'. AC, 2.
17 JGB, 259.
18 Although it has a long prehistory in Nietzsche's notes, from 1877 onwards, and an emphasis on power is clearly visible in *Morgonröthe* (1881), see, for example, section 262. Apart from a single mentioning in book 1 of *Also sprach Zarathustra*, it is introduced in the chapter 'On Self-Overcoming' in the second book of *Also sprach Zarathustra* (but is then not mentioned in books 3 and 4).
19 Will to power is mentioned in ten sections of *Jenseits von Gut und Böse* and ten in *Zur Genealogie der Moral*.
20 The concept of will to power only occurs three times in the 'Expeditions' chapter, sections 11, 20 and 38 (but power also occurs in section 9), and the expression 'Gefühl zur Macht', feeling for power, occurs in the chapter 'The Four Great Errors', 5 (as well as in 'Expeditions', 11 and 20).
21 See, for example, 'Expeditions of an Untimely Man', 14.
22 See, for example, Julian Young, *Friedrich Nietzsche* (2010): 546–8.
23 For example, in the draft for *Der Wille zur Macht* from late June or July 1888, KSA 13, 16[86] there is a planned chapter entitled 'der Wille zur Macht'. This seems to be the last time the expression is used in a draft for chapter title, although the main title continued to be *Der Wille zur Macht* for one or two further months.
24 'Willing seems to me to be above all something *complicated*, something that is a unity only as a word', JGB, 19.
25 JGB, 19.
26 GD, 'Errors', 7. Nietzsche also attempts to weaken the claims of free will and to explain how it arouse and came to be accepted by arguing that the purpose of free will is to make accountable, that 'the doctrine of will has been invented essentially for the purpose of punishment, that is of *finding guilty*'. It was the theologians and 'the priests at the head of the ancient communities' which invented and carried on this belief. GD, 'Errors', 7. It seems correct that the concept of free will has its origin in Hellenistic and early Christian writings. Compare the article 'Free will' in *Dictionary of the History of Ideas*. In Homer, for example, there seems to be no free will, selfhood or consciousness in the modern or Christian sense, see for example Bernard Williams' *Shame and Neccesity* (1993).
27 JGB, 17. See also, AC, 15; EH, 'Write', 5; GD, 'Errors', 3; JGB, 16–19.

28 Za, I, 'Of the Despisers of the Body'. See also: ' – As regards the animals, Descartes was the first who, with a boldness worthy of reverence, ventured to think of the animal as a *machine*: our whole science of physiology is devoted to proving this proposition. Nor, logically, do we exclude man, as even Descartes did: our knowledge of man today is real knowledge precisely to the extent that it is knowledge of him as a machine. Formerly man was presented with "free will" as a dowry from a higher order: today we have taken even will away from him, in the sense that will may no longer be understood as a faculty. The old word "will" only serves to designate a resultant.' AC, 14.
29 Za, I, 'Of the Despisers of the Body'.
30 MA, I, 57.
31 'For every drive is tyrannical', JGB, 6, and 'A German who would make bold to say 'two souls, alas' [...] would fall short of the truth by a large number of souls', JGB, 244. Compare also M, 119 and WM, 613.
32 'Daß die Katze Mensch immer wieder auf ihre vier Beine, ich wollte sagen ihr eines Bein "Ich" zurückfällt, ist nur ein Symptom seiner *psychologischen* "Einheit", richtiger "Vereinigung": kein Grund, an eine "seelische Einheit" zu glauben.' KSA 12, 1[72], from autumn 1885 to early 1886.
33 Z, I, 'Of the Despisers of the Body'.
34 JGB, 6.
35 *Der Antichrist*, 14, 15 and 38, and *Ecce homo*, 'Wise', 6, 'Morgenröthe', 2 and 'Destiny', 8.
36 JGB, 12.
37 In EH, 'Why I Write Such Excellent Books', 5, Nietzsche summarizes some of the consequences of these reinterpretations: 'The propositions over which everybody is in fundamental agreement [...] appear with me as naive blunders: for example that belief that "unegoistic" and "egoistic" are antitheses, while the *ego* itself is merely a "higher swindle", an "ideal". There are *neither* egoistic *nor* unegoistic actions: both concepts are psychologically nonsense. Or the proposition "man strives after happiness" ... Or the proposition "Happiness is the reward of virtue" ... Or the proposition "pleasure and displeasure are opposites" ... The Circe of mankind, morality, has falsified all *psychologica* to its very foundations – has *moralized* it – to the point of the frightful absurdity that love is supposed to be something "unegoistic" ....'
38 JGB, 20.
39 'What then are our experiences? Much *more* that which we put into them than that which they already contain! [...] to experience is to invent'. M, 119.
40 JGB, 20.
41 'I fear we are not getting rid of God because we still believe in grammar...', GD, 'Reason', 5. Nietzsche also points at many other instances of how language determines our view of the world.
42 MA, I, 228. See also FW, 290.
43 Nietzsche gives several examples of the influence of physiology on the 'spiritual' in GD, 'Error', 2.
44 JGB, 6. Compare also, JGB, 5: 'They pose as having discovered and attained their real opinions through the self-evolution of a cold, pure, divinely unperturbed dialectic [...] while what happens at bottom is that a prejudice, a notion, an "inspiration", generally a desire of the heart sifted and made abstract, is defended by them with reasons sought after the event – they are one and all advocates who do not want to be regarded as such, and for the most part no better than cunning pleaders for their prejudices, which they baptize "truths" – ' and JGB, 8: 'In every philosophy there is a point at which the philosopher's "conviction" appears on the scene'.
45 WM, 258.

46 FW, 'Preface', 2.
47 GD, 'Expeditions', 47.
48 See, for example, his critique of St. Augustine, which he discusses while reading his *Confessions* in a letter to Franz Overbeck, 31 March 1885.
49 *Götzen-Dämmerung*, 'The Problem of Socrates', 11. See also his severe critique of dialectics in the same chapter, 'Nothing is easier to expunge than the effect of a dialectician, as is proved by the experience of every speech-making assembly' (section 6).
50 *Götzen-Dämmerung*, 'The Four Great Errors', 2. Compare also 'Socrates', 11.
51 Nietzsche mentions instinct in thirty-nine sections in *Götzen-Dämmerung* (and in thirty-eight sections each of *Der Antichrist* and *Ecce homo*), while reason (Verstand, Vernunft, Vernünftig and denken) occurs in forty-four (with twenty-four and thirty-two respectively for *Der Antichrist* and *Ecce homo*).
52 *Also sprach Zarathustra*, I, 'Of the Despisers of the Body'.
53 *Jenseits von Gut und Böse*, 218.
54 *Götzen-Dämmerung*, 'Socrates', 5 and 6.
55 *Götzen-Dämmerung*, 'The Problem of Socrates', 4.
56 *Götzen-Dämmerung*, 'Ancients', 3–5.
57 *Götzen-Dämmerung*, 'What the Germans Lack', 4.
58 *Götzen-Dämmerung*, 'Morality as Anti-Nature', 2.
59 It is true that Nietzsche provocatively praises Cesare Borgia, as an immoral and 'primitive' man of action as compared to modern decadents and idealists, who have no healthy instincts to sublimate. However, Borgia is not one of Nietzsche's true ideals, only better than decadents.
60 *Götzen-Dämmerung*, 'Maxims and Arrows', 6.
61 See, for example, 'One is *fruitful* only at the cost of being rich in contradictions'. GD, 'Morality as Anti-Nature', 3.

Chapter 9

1 Some, like Michael Tanner, have argued that the critique of Christianity is the main point of the book: 'Though *Twilight of the Idols* ranges very widely, taking in every theme that Nietzsche ever dealt with, there can't be any question that at each point he is preparing the ground for his final attack on Christianity', in the 'Introduction' to the Penguin edition of *Twilight of the Idols* and *The Antichrist* (London, 1990), 14. There is some truth in such claims, but also a great danger of overemphasizing the importance of Christianity in the book at the cost of other major themes. As part of the argument I am making in this study, such claims are not surprising, since *Der Antichrist* was written, and the other planned books of the *Umwerthung aller Werthe* were not, and hence they and the implications they would have had have been ignored. For example, Nietzsche's critique of morality is not less prominent in *Götzen-Dämmerung* than that of his critique of Christianity.
2 In German, the connection between gods and idols are much more apparent than in English: *Götter* and *Götzen*. It is thus clear in German that he here, with 'in the most eminent case' refers to God.
3 In sections 11, 12, 32 and especially 50 in *Der Antichrist*.
4 Compare, for example, the preface to *Jenseits von Gut und Böse*, where he refers to Christianity as 'Platonism for the people'.

5   This is discussed more explicitly in *Der Antichrist*.
6   However, it is also noticeable that much of Nietzsche's critique of morality is not mentioned or discussed in *Götzen-Dämmerung*. This is true for his classification of it as slave- and master-morality, his critique of self-sacrificing morality (including a critique of altruism) and of pity as the essence of modern morality. It is likely, as seen in Nietzsche's late notes, that those would be discussed in the planned third volume of the *Umwerthung aller Werthe*.
7   Also discussed while reading it in a letter to the professor of theology, Franz Overbeck, 31 March 1885.
8   Letter to Overbeck, 10 April 1886: 'das viel von *meiner* Art, über Religion zu denken, und eine Menge suggestive Fakta enthält'. The only study of Nietzsche's reading of this work is that of Andrea Orsucci in his *Orient-Okzident* (Berlin, New York, 1996), 294–7. He there also is able to comment on the 'large number of suggestive facts' referred to by Nietzsche, by studying especially the note KSA 12, 1[5].
9   However, a fairly large number of other books and studies than those mentioned here are also relevant for Nietzsche's writing *Der Antichrist*, and for our understanding of it.
10 See my article '*The Antichrist* as the First Volume of Nietzsche's *magnum opus*', *Ideas in History* 3 (2008): 83–106, which discusses this question and these first fourteen sections.
11 *Der Antichrist*, 47. The Latin quotation reads: 'God, as Paul created him, is a denial of God'. Compare also Nietzsche's claim that Jesus' revolt was based on a '*disbelief* in "higher men"', *Der Antichrist*, 27.
12 The most significant exception to this is that in *Götzen-Dämmerung* Nietzsche seems completely reject the Laws of Manu as another faulty morality (although healthier than Christian morality), while in *Der Antichrist* the critique of Christianity is so hostile that the Laws of Manu can appear as a 'healthier' contrast.
13 A possible minor difference or contradiction is that in *Götzen-Dämmerung* Nietzsche claims that one should not want the destruction of Christianity, while that seems to be what he wants and argues for in *Der Antichrist*. Possibly this contradiction can be reduced by assuming that *Der Antichrist* was not meant to be read or understood by everyone, but only for the more select (and for them, Christianity should be destroyed).
14 In letters to Overbeck and to Gast, 13 February 1888: 'die erste Niederschrift meiner "Umwertung aller Werthe" ist fertig'.
15 These notes were collected into three large notebooks, meant only for this purpose, notebooks W II 1–3, totally of about 430 printed pages, and the 'index' (listing with a one-line summary of each of them) in the seventeen-page-long note KSA 13, 12[1 and 2], in notebook W II 4, from February 1888. These notebooks have been published in diplomatic and facsimile in volumes 6 and 7 of KGW IX.
16 KSA 13, 11[139–415], in notebook W II 3. Most of these were probably written down during the latter part of February and during March 1888. Nietzsche later, in the summer of 1888, went back and revised many of them.

Chapter 10

1   Letter to Gast, 12 September 1888.

Bibliography

The books Nietzsche read, discussed in Chapters 4 and 9, are not included in this bibliography.

Berti, Maria Christina, 'Beiträge zur Quellenforschung', *Nietzsche-Studien* 26 (1997): 580–1.
Bittner, Rüdiger (ed.), *Friedrich Nietzsche: Writings from the Late Notebooks*, Cambridge: Cambridge University Press, 2003.
Brobjer, Thomas, *Nietzsche's Ethics of Character: A Study of Nietzsche's Ethics and its Place in the History of Moral Thinking*, Uppsala: Acta Universitatis Upsaliensis, 1995.
Brobjer, Thomas, 'Beiträge zur Quellenforschung', *Nietzsche-Studien* 26 (1997): 574–9.
Brobjer, Thomas, 'The Absence of Political Ideals in Nietzsche's Writings: The Case of the Laws of Manu and the Associated Caste-Society', *Nietzsche-Studien* 27 (1998): 300–18.
Brobjer, Thomas, 'Götzen-Hammer: The Meaning of the Expression "To Philosophize with a Hammer"', *Nietzsche-Studien* 28 (1999): 38–41.
Brobjer, Thomas, 'Beiträge zur Quellenforschung mitgeteilt von Thomas H. Brobjer', *Nietzsche-Studien* 30 (2001): 418–21.
Brobjer, Thomas, 'Nietzsche's Disinterest and Ambivalence toward the Greek Sophists', *International Studies in Philosophy* 33 (Fall 2001): 5–23.
Brobjer, Thomas, 'Nietzsche's View of the Value of Historical Studies and Methods', *Journal of the History of Ideas* 65 (2004): 301–22.
Brobjer, Thomas, 'Nietzsche's Wrestling with Plato', in *Nietzsche and Antiquity: His Reaction and Response to the Classical Tradition*, edited by Paul Bishop, 241–59, Rochester: Camden House, 2004.
Brobjer, Thomas, 'Nietzsche's Relation to the Greek Sophists', *Nietzsche-Studien* 34 (2005): 255–76.
Brobjer, Thomas, 'Nietzsche's *magnum opus*', *History of European Ideas* 32 (2006): 278–94.
Brobjer, Thomas, 'Nietzsche's Relation to Historical Methods and Nineteenth Century German Historiography', *History and Theory* 46 (May 2007): 155–79.
Brobjer, Thomas, 'The Development of Nietzsche's Ethical Thinking', in *Nietzsche and Ethics*, edited by Gudrun von Tevenar, 283–310, Bern, Oxford, Berlin: Peter Lang, 2007.
Brobjer, Thomas, 'Critical Aspects of Nietzsche's Relation to Politics and Democracy', in *Nietzsche, Power and Politics*, edited by Herman Siemens och Vasti Roodt, 205–27, Berlin, New York: Walter de Gruyter, 2008.
Brobjer, Thomas, *Nietzsche and the 'English'*, New York: Humanity Books, 2008.
Brobjer, Thomas, *Nietzsche's Philosophical Context: An Intellectual Biography*, Urbana and Chicago: University of Illinois Press, 2008.
Brobjer, Thomas, 'The Late Nietzsche's Fundamental Critique of Historical Scholarship', in *Nietzsche on Time and History*, edited by Manuel Dries, 51–60, Berlin, New York: Walter de Gruyter, 2008.

Brobjer, Thomas, 'Politik' in the Revised Second Edition of the *Nietzsche-Lexikon*, edited by Christian Niemeyer, published by the *Wissenschaftliche Buchgesellschaft* in Darmstadt, 2011.

Brobjer, Thomas, 'The Place and Role of *Der Antichrist* in Nietzsche's Four Volume Project *Umwerthung aller Werthe*', *Nietzsche-Studien* 40 (2011): 244–55.

Brobjer, Thomas, 'Nietzsche's Last View of Science', in *Nietzsches Wissenschaftsphilosophie*, edited by H. Heit, G. Abel and M. Brusotti, 39–54, New York, Berlin: Walter de Gruyter, 2012.

Brown, Richard, 'Nietzsche: "That Profound Physiologist"', in *Nietzsche and Science*, edited by G. Moore and T. H. Brobjer, 51–70, Aldershot and Burlington: Ashgate, 2004.

Brusotti, Marco, 'Beiträge zur Quellenforschung mitgeteilt von Marco Brusotti', *Nietzsche-Studien* 21 (1992): 390f.

Brusotti, Marco, *Die Leidenschaft der Erkenntnis*, Berlin, New York: Walter de Gruyter, 1997.

Brusotti, Marco, *Grosses Werklexikon der Philosophie*, edited by Franco Volpi, Stuttgart: Kröner, 1999, 'Nietzsche'.

Brusotti, Marco, *Kindlers Neues Literatur Lexikon*, München: Kindler, 1999, 'Nietzsche'.

Burnham, Douglas, *The Nietzsche Dictionary*, London and New York: Bloomsbury, 2015.

Cate, Curtis, *Friedrich Nietzsche*, London: (Cate) Hutchison, 2002.

Dahlquist, Tobias, *Nietzsche and the Philosophy of Pessimism*, Uppsala: Acta Universitatis Upsaliensis, 2007.

Dictionary of the History of Ideas, 'Free Will'.

Diethe, Carol, 'Twilight of the Idols', in *A Companion to Friedrich Nietzsche*, edited by Paul Bishop, 315–38, Boydell & Brewer in their Camden House imprint 2011, 2012.

Etter, A., 'Nietzsche und das Gesetzbuch des Manu', *Nietzsche-Studien* 16 (1987): 340–52.

Georgsson, Peter, 'Nietzsche's Hammer Again', *Nietzsche-Studien* 29 (2000): 342–50.

Gilman, Sander L., 'Nietzsche's Reading on the Dionysian: From Nietzsche's Library', *Nietzsche-Studien* 6 (1977): 292–4.

Gilman, Sander L., 'Nietzsches Emerson-Lektüre: Eine unbekannte Quelle', *Nietzsche-Studien* 9 (1980): 406–31.

Gilman, Sander L. *Begegnungen mit Nietzsche*, Bonn: Bouvier Verlag, 1981.

Hayman, Ronald, *Nietzsche: A Critical Life*, London, Melbourne, New York: Quartet Books, 1980, 1981.

Heit, Helmut, 'Wahrheit', in *Nietzsche-Lexikon*, edited by Christian Niemeyer (Hrsg.), Darmstadt: Wissenschaftliche Buchgesellschaft, 2009.

Hollingdale, R. J., *Nietzsche: The Man and His Philosophy*, 1965, reprinted with additions 1999.

Hollingdale, R. J., 'Introduction' to his translation of *Götzen-Dämmerung and Der Antichrist*, Penguin Classics, 1968 and later editions until 1986.

Holub, Robert C., *Nietzsche in the Nineteenth Century*, Philadelphia: University of Pennsylvania Press, 2018.

Horn, Anette, *Nietzsches Begriff der décadence: Kritik and Analyse der Moderne*, Frankfurt, Oxford, Bern, Berlin: Peter Lang, 2000.

Hödl, H. G. *Der letzte Jünger des Philosophen Dionysos: Studien zur systematischen Bedeutung von Nietzsches Selbstthematisierungen im Kontext seiner Religionskritik*, Berlin, New York: Walter de Gruyter, 2009.

Janz, Curt Paul, *Friedrich Nietzsche: Biographie*, 3 vols. 1978, second revised edition 1993.

Kaufmann, Walter, Preface to his translation of *Götzen-Dämmerung* published in *The Portable Nietzsche*, New York, 1954.

Kaufmann's translation of *Ecce Homo* (New York, 1967), 314, footnote 1 and *The Will to Power* (London, 1967).

Large, Duncan, '"Introduction" to his Translation of *Götzen-Dämmerung*', in *Oxford World's Classics*, Oxford: Oxford University Press, 1998.

Loeb, Paul S., 'Identity and Eternal Recurrence', in *A Companion to Nietzsche*, edited by Keith Ansell-Pearson, Oxford: Maiden, 2006.

Magnus, Bernd, 'Nietzsche's Philosophy in 1888: *The will to power* and the *Übermensch*', *Journal of the History of Philosophy* 24 (1986): 79–98.

Magnus, Bernd, 'The Deification of the Commonplace: Twilight of the Idol', in *Reading Nietzsche*, edited by R. Solomon and K. Higgins, 152–81, New York, Oxford: Oxford University Press, 1988.

Middleton, Christopher, *Selected Letters of Friedrich Nietzsche*, Indianapolis, Cambridge: Hackett Publishing Company, 1969.

Montinari, Mazzino, 'Nietzsches Nachlaß von 1885 bis 1888 oder Textkritik und Wille zur Macht', in *Nietzsche lesen*, edited by M. Montinari, 92–119, 114f., Berlin, New York: Walter de Gruyter, 1982.

Montinari, Mazzino, 'Nietzsches Philosophie als "Leidenschaft der Erkenntnis"', in *Nietzsche lesen*, edited by M. Montinari, 64–78, Berlin, New York: Walter de Gruyter, 1982.

Montinari, Mazzino, *Nietzsche lesen*, Berlin, New York: Walter de Gruyter, 1982.

Montinari, Mazzino, 'Nietzsche lesen: Die Götzen-Dämmerung', *Nietzsche-Studien* 13 (1984): 69–79.

Moore, Gregory, 'Nietzsche, Medicine and Meteorology', in *Nietzsche and Science*, edited by Gregory Moore and Thomas H. Brobjer, Aldershot and Burlington: Ashgate, 2004.

Moore, Greg, *Nietzsche, Biology and Metaphor*, Cambridge: Cambridge University Press, 2002.

Nietzsche-Handbuch, Stuttgart: Weimar, 2000.

Nietzsche-Lexikon, edited by Christian Niemeyer, 112 and 114, Darmstadt, 2009.

Orsucci, Andrea, 'Beiträge zur Quellenforschung', *Nietzsche-Studien*, 22 (1992): 371–88.

Orsucci, Andrea, *Orient-Okzident*, Berlin, New York: Walter de Gruyter, 1996.

Prideaux, Sue, *I Am Dynamite*, London: Faber and Faber, 2018.

Rattner, Josef, *Nietzsche: Leben – Werk – Wirkung*, Würzburg: Königshausen und Neumann, 2000.

Ross, Werner, *Der ängsliche Adler*, Stuttgart, München: dtv, 1980.

Runes, D. D., (ed.), *Dictionary of Philosophy*, Totowa: Littlefield, 1979.

Safranski, Rüdiger, *Nietzsche: Biographie seines Denkens*, Hanser, München: Wien, 2000.

Schrift, Alan D., 'Nietzsche's *Nachlass*', in *A Companion to Friedrich Nietzsche*, edited by Paul Bishop (Hrsg.), Boydell & Brewer in their Camden House imprint 2011.

Sommer, Andreas Urs, *Friedrich Nietzsches 'Der Antichrist': Ein philosophisch-historischer Kommentar*, Basel: Schwabe, 2000.

Sommer, Andreas Urs, 'GD: *Götzen-Dämmerung*', in *Nietzsche-Lexikon*, edited by Christian Niemeyer, Darmstadt: WBG, 2009.

Sommer, Andreas Urs, *Nietzsche-Kommentar: 6/1. Der Fall Wagner und Götzen-Dämmerung*, Berlin, Boston: Walter de Gruyter, 2012.

Tanner, Michael, 'Introduction', in *Nietzsche, Götzen-Dämmerung and Der Antichrist*, London, New York: Penguin Classics, 1990 and later editions.

Thatcher, David, 'A Diagnosis of Idols: Percussions and Repercussions of a Distant Hammer', *Nietzsche-Studien* 14 (1985): 250–68.

Wahrig-Schmidt, B., '"Irgendwie – jedenfalls physiologisch". Friedrich Nietzsche, Alexandre Herzen (fils) und Charles Féré 1888', *Nietzsche-Studien* 17 (1988): 434–64.

Wilcox, John, *Truth and Value in Nietzsche*, Washington, DC: University Press of America, 1982.
Williams, Bernard, *Shame and Neccesity*, Berkeley, Los Angeles, London: University of California, 1993.
Winteler, Reto, 'Nietzsches *Antichrist* als (ganze) *Umwerthung aller Werthe*. Bemerkungen zum 'scheitern' eines "Hauptwerks"', *Nietzsche-Studien* 38 (2009): 229–45.
Young, Julian, *Nietzsche's Philosophy of Art*, Cambridge: Cambridge University Press, 1992.
Young, Julian, *A Philosophical Biography: Friedrich Nietzsche*, Cambridge: Cambridge University Press, 2010.
Zittel, Claus, 'Wissenschaft', in *Nietzsche-Handbuch*, edited by Henning Ottmann (Hrsg.), 355f, Stuttgart, Weimar: Verlag J.B. Metzler, 2000.

Index

Note: *Italicized* and **bold** page numbers refer to figures and tables. Page numbers followed by "n" refer to notes.

abstraction   90, 91, 175
  logical   70
  psychological   89, *90*
abstract thought   111, 137
ad hominem   48, 78, 88–9, 170
Adler, A.   168–9
aesthetics   9, 155
  bad *vs.* good   **94**
  critique of   205 n.15
  of *décadence*   111
  physiology of   4, 93, 205 n.29
affirmation of life   25, 111, 146, 148, 155, 156, 161
affirmative contents   140–4
afterlife   99
agnosticism   47, 181
agnostics   105
agon   110
Also sprach Zarathustra (*Thus Spoke Zarathustra*)   1, 5, 7, 37, 45, 104, 119, 121, 189, **195**, 202 n.16, 204 n.24, 218 nn.28, 30, 223 n.103, 226 n.153, 227 n.179, 228 n.193, 229 n.206, 230 n.214, 231 n.1, 236 n.1, 237 n.18
  aphorisms   67
  critique of philosophy   70, 72
  English-language discussions of   19, 23
  epilogue   112–16
  eternal recurrence   148–51, 154–60, 162–4
  German-language accounts of   15
  morality   73
  new content in   128
  subtitle   57, 61
  Übermensch   136
  will to power   134, 168
altruism   48, 49, 98, 108, 171, 240 n.6

amor fati   4, 6, 7, 20, 23, 47, 58, 77, 83, 104, 108, 110, 128, 148, 152–5, 161, 189, 192, **199**, 220 n.70, 228 n.194, 236 n.47
ancient values   25, 141
Antichrist, The   40
  aphorisms   65
  brief commentary to general contents   88
  laws of Manu   44
anti-Christianism   44
antiquity   64, 98, 109–12, 119, 141, 183, 185, 186
anti-Semitism   44
aphorisms   62–7, 83, 131
Apollinian   92, 96
art   89–93, *90*, 155
  bad *vs.* good   **94**
  physiology of   5, 86, 87, 92–6, **94**, 133, 205 n.29
  physiology of art, plans for and attempt to construct   93–6
atheism   182
atheist   182, 221 n.78
autobiography   2, 52, 71, 191, 236 n.5
axiology   192

Bain, A.   42, 46
Baudelaire   142, 212 n.32, 233 n.33
becoming   47, 70, 110, 111, 153, 157
  hard   115–17, 142
  innocence of   76, 118, 129, 143, 154, 159, 222 n.95, 228 n.181
behaviourism   168
Berti, M. C.   210 n.17
Beyond Good and Evil: Foreword to a Philosophy of Eternal Recurrence   150
Bildung   79, 83, 84, 110, 115, 141, 144, 165, 174

biographical studies   41
Birth of Tragedy   5
Bishop, P.
    Companion to Friedrich Nietzsche, A
        24
Bittner, R.   232 nn.22, 23
Blanqui, A.   148
Borgia, C.   142, 239 n.59
Bourdeau, J.   56
Bourget, P.
    Essais de psychologie
        contemporaine   43
Brandes, G.   63
Brobjer, T.   209 n.11, 210 n.22, 212 n.31
Brochard, V.
    Les sceptiques grecs   40
Brusotti, M.   17, 204 n.21, 226 n.154
Buckle, H. T.
    'De l'histoire de la civilisation en
        Angleterre, par Buckle'   49
    Essays   49
    role in *Götzen-Dämmerung*   49–51
Buddhism/Buddha   148, 183, 185–7
Bunge, G.
    Vitalismus und Mechanismus   41
Burckhardt, J.   45, 84, 142
Burnham, D.   225 n.43
    Nietzsche Dictionary, The   22

Caesar   142
Carlyle, T.   51
    On Heroes, Hero Worship and the
        Heroic in History   49
    role in *Götzen-Dämmerung*   49
Caspari, O.   148
Cate, C.   19
    Friedrich Nietzsche   18
Catholicism   44
Christian ideals   182
Christianity   9, 38, 39, 111, 119
    aphorisms   64, 65
    critique of   1, 21, 29, 39, 68, 71, 105,
        122, 128, 132, 177–88, **179–80**, 191
    eternal recurrence   148, 153, 155
    morality of taming   79
Christian morality   44, 51, 82, 83, 100,
    105, 126, 166, 178, 186, 240 n.12
Christian teaching   234 n.8
Christian values   39, 47, 64, 182

Christ/Jesus/the crucified   40, 112, 183,
    185–7
cognitive psychology   168
Colli, G.   215 n.3
conscience   64, 126, 152, 170, 178, 181,
    219 n.40
consciousness   75, 89, 90, 166, 169–73,
    202 n.22, 225 n.131, 236 n.7,
    237 n.26
consequentialism   49
courage   47, 63, 64, 67, 102, 109, 116,
    140, 152, 159, 219 n.40
creation/creativity   92, 110, 111, 114,
    161
cultural studies   41

Dahlquist, T.   226 n.157
Darwinism   41, 49, 99, 168, 225 n.137
death of God/God is dead   71, 72, 128,
    146, 182, 191, 219 n.40, 235 n.24
decadence/*décadence*   42, 43, 69, 91, 101,
    155, 212 n.32
    aesthetics of   111
    morality   98, 108
Delboeuf, J.
    La matière brute et la matière
        vivante   41
depersonalization
    (*Entpersönlichung*)   108
Der Antichrist   1, 2, 4, 6, 8, 9, 38, 104,
    119, 150, 177, 191, 205 n.3,
    218 n.28, 227 n.178, 240 n.13
    affirmative contents of   142, 143
    antiquity   109, 110, 112
    aphorisms   66–7
    critique of Christianity   177, 178,
        183–8
    critique of philosophy   68, 69
    English-language discussions of
        19–21, 23
    epilogue   112, 116
    eternal recurrence   152, 155, 163
    foreword   62
    free will, error of   75
    general and philosophical sources
        to   39
    general consequences and
        observations   53
    genesis of   28, 29

German-language accounts of
   13–17
and *Götzen-Dämmerung*, relatrion
   between **180**
history of   31
morality   73, 79–83
new content in   128
physiology   43
place and role of British philosophy
   and thinkers in   46
pointers and references in *Götzen-
   Dämmerung*   105–7
pre-empt or exhaust the
   contents   130–3
psychology   168
references   118
religion   79–81, 83
subtitle   59
Übermensch   136
will to power   134
Der Fall Wagner   1, 8, 54, 189, 190,
   225 n.144, 227 n.179
antiquity   110, 111
art and aesthetics   89, 91
English-language discussions of   18
eternal recurrence   150, 162
genesis of   28
German-language accounts of   16, 18
main title   56
morality   82
new content in   128
notes   30
physiology   43
religion   82
summary of   126
*Der Immoralist: Umwerthung aller
   Werthe*   118, 131, 208 n.32
de Roberty, C. E.
   *L'ancienne et la nouvelle philosophie:
   Essai sur les lois générales
   du développement de la
   philosophie*   40
Descartes, R.   238 n.28
dialectics   69
Die fröhliche Wissenschaft   5, 7, 227 n.179
   brief commentary to general
      contents   87
   eternal recurrence   146, 148–9, 152,
      157

German-language accounts of   12–13
new content in   128
subtitle   61
Die Geburt der Tragödie   12, 18
antiquity   109, 111, 112
art and aesthetics   89
critique of philosophy   70
eternal recurrence   156, 161
new content in   128
psychology   166
revaluation of all values   135
summary of   127
Diethe, C.   24, 25
Dionysian   9, 13, 20, 64, 71, 83, 87, 92,
   95, 96, 107–15, 119, 127, 135,
   143, 153, 155–7, 161, 162, 185,
   228 n.180, 236 n.47
Dionysos   25, 59, 104, 106, 112, 118, 144,
   161, 221 n.82
Dionysos (*Dionysos philosophos*)   7, 35,
   71, 107–9, 112, 143, 144, 156, 189
Dionysos-morality   31
Dionysus   5, 12–13
Dostoevsky, F.   142, 167, 233 n.33
   Les Possides (*Bési*)   184, 188
Druckmanuskript   29
Druscowitz, H.   51
Dühring, E.   148

Ecce homo (*EH*)   1, 3, 7, 9, 104, 191,
   220 n.70, 224 n.129, 229 n.203
affirmative contents of   142
antiquity   110, 112
art and aesthetics   89
critique of philosophy   68–72
English-language discussions of
   19–21, 23
epilogue   112–16
eternal recurrence   146, 147, 151, 154,
   160, 161, 163
foreword   62
general consequences and
   observations   55
German-language account of   13,
   15, 17
main title   56
morality   80, 83, 96, 101, 108
notes   31
physiology   43

place and role of British philosophy and thinkers in 46
pointers and references in *Götzen-Dämmerung* 106, 107
pre-empt or exhaust the contents 130
psychology 166, 168
references 118
self-portrait 103
subtitle 57, 58, 61
summary of 126, 127
will to power 135
ecstasy (*extasis*) 96, 161, 174
egoism 98, 108
egoistic 98, 238 n.37
EH, *see Ecce homo* (EH)
Eliot, G. 105
　Adam Bede 52
　Die Mühle am Fluss 51, 52
　Middlemarch 51, 52
　role in *Götzen-Dämmerung* 51–2
Emerson, R. W. 46, 88, 142, 224 n.124
empiricism 46
English-language discussions of *Götzen-Dämmerung* 18–25
enslavement 64
epilogue 112–17
epistemology 7, 21, 41, 93, 159, 178, 182, 203 n.4
equality 49, 58, 98, 100, 101
Espinas, A.
　Animal Societies 41
eternal recurrence 4–7, 9, 23, 25, 58–61, 72, 75–6, 83, 104, 110, 112, 113, 128, 129, 138–40, 145–64, **199–200**, 235 n.21
　discovery of, in 1881 147–8
　in *Götzen-Dämmerung*, presence of 151–7
　Hauptwerk 157–62
　as physical theory of the universe 147
　place and role of 148–51
eternity 63
ethics 49, 82, 83, 86, 88, 93, 96, 98, 102, 107, 133, 178, 224 n.122, 251 n.74
　deontological 51, 222 n.99
　evolutionary 41
　sublimation 78
　utilitarian 51

of virtue 51, 78, 214 n.54
Etter, A. 44
euphoria 92, 95, 96
Euripides 141
'European Nihilism, The' 137–9, 160, 232 n.25
existentialism 7, 63, 192
experimental psychology 168

false causality, error of 74, 178
Féré, C. 43
　Dégénérescence et criminalité: Essai physiologique 42
　Sensation et mouvment 42
Fischer, K.
　Geschichte der neuern Philosophie 40
Förster-Nietzsche, E. 15, 53
Foucauld, M. 169
Fouillée, A.
　La science sociale contemporaine 39, 208 n.5
freedom 20, 64, 100, 104, 174, 231 n.16
free-thinking 181
free will 43, 76, 169, 170, 237 n.26, 238 n.28
　error of 75, 181
Funke, G.
　Historisches Wörterbuch der Philosophie 174

Galton, F.
　Inquiries into Human Faculty and its Development 41
Gast, P. 28, 50, 52, 63, 109, 113, 137, 202 n.16
GD, *see Götzen-Dämmerung* (GD)
Gebhart, É.
　Etudes méridionales 39–40
Georgsson, P. 217 n.22
German-language accounts of *Götzen-Dämmerung* 12–18
Gilman, S. L. 213 n.37, 234 n.8
Goethe, J. W. von 38, 45–6, 78, 83, 87, 89, 93, 101–4, 107, 110, 136, 141, 142, 156, 165, 174, 182, 209 n.12, 224 n.122, 227 n.163, 233 n.33–5
　Conversations with Eckermann 103
　as *exemplum* 101–4, 156
　Faust 103–4

good, the/good human being/good man/
    the benevolent   6, 8, 15, 17, 21, 31,
    46, 49–52, 57, 59, 60, 73, 74, 76–9,
    81–4, 89, 92, **94**, 99, 102, 103, 110,
    113, 115, 126, 132, 133, 134, 136,
    141, 142, 144, 150, 155, 158, 161,
    166, 167, 173, 174, 181, 190
Götzen-Dämmerung (GD)
    ad hominem approach and
       method   88–9
    aesthetics   85–6, 89–93, *90*
    affirmative contents of   140–4
    antiquity   109–12
    aphorisms, first chapter of   62–7
    art   88–93, *90*
    brief commentary to general
       contents   87–8
    chronology of   27–9, **194**
    critique and affirmation   **196**
    critique of philosophy   67–72
    and *Der Antichrist*, relation
       between   **180**
    English-language discussions of   18–25
    epilogue   112–17
    eternal recurrence   145–64, **199–200**
    extracts of or excerpts from
       Hauptwerk   129
    foreword   61–2
    general and philosophical sources to
       38–40
    general consequences and
       observations   53–5
    genesis of   27–9
    German-language accounts of   12–18
    laws of Manu   44
    and *magnum opus* (*Hauptwerk*),
       relation between   3–6
    main title   55–6
    morality   72–84, 96–101, **97**
    new content in   128–9
    Nietzsche's own philosophemes
       in   133–40
    notes   29–31
    old preface   84–5
    physiology   42, 43
    physiology of art, plans for and attempt
       to construct   93–6
    place and role of British philosophy
       and thinkers in   46–52

pointers and references to *Umwerthung
    aller Werthe*   104–9, **197–8**
pre-empt or exhaust the contents of
    Hauptwerk   130–3
psychology   41–3
purpose of   1–9
reading and regarding   2–3
reason and instinct, status and role
    of   173–5
references to *Revaluation of All Values*
    in   117–18
religion   72–4
society   96–101, **97**
sources to 'The "Improvers" of
    Mankind'   43–4
sources to 'What the Germans
    Lack'   45–6
subtitle   56–61
summary of   125–44
as summary of Nietzsche's
    philosophy   6–9
themes, summary of   **195**
great/grand politics   13, 167
great men   101–4
guilt   75, 76, 126
Guyau, J. M.
    L'irréligion de l'avenir   184

hammer metaphor   56–61, 112–17, 146,
    152, 219 n.48
happiness   49
Hartmann, E. v.
    Philosophie des Unbewussten   40
Hauptwerk   1, 2, 8, 38, 104, 119–22, 188,
    190, 207 n.28, 214 n.2, 220 n.65,
    222 n.96, 232 nn.27, 29
    affirmative contents of   144
    antiquity   110
    aphorisms   63, 65–7
    art and aesthetics   91
    critique of philosophy   67–8, 72
    English-language discussions of   19,
       22–5
    eternal recurrence   140, 145, 150, 151,
       157–64
    evolution of   **32**
    extracts or excerpts in *Götzen-
       Dämmerung*   129
    general consequences and
       observations   53–5

genesis of 27–9
German-language accounts of 12–18
and *Götzen-Dämmerung*, relation between 3–6
history of 31–5, **34**
main title 56
morality 73
nihilism 137, 139
notes 29–31
physiology of art 93–5
place and role of British philosophy and thinkers in 46
pointers and references in *Götzen-Dämmerung* 105, 107, 108
pre-empt or exhaust the contents 130–3
preface 84–5
psychology 168
references 117, 118
revaluation of all values 135
subtitle 58–60
will to power 135
Hayman, R. 19
Nietzsche: A Critical Life 18
health/healthy/unhealthy/sick 43, 46, 47, 64, 77, 78, 81, 83, 89, 95, 96, 98, 111, 129, 138, 141, 142, 146, 154, 155, 165, 171, 182, 191, 240 n.12
Hegel, G. W. F. 45, 142, 233 nn.33, 36
Heraclitus 142
herd 133
herd-instincts 72, 73, 133, 174
Herzen, A. 43
Le cervau et l'activité cérébrale au point de vue psycho-physiologie [*The Brain and Cerebral Activity from a Psycho-Physiological Viewpoint*] 42
higher human being/higher men 4, 136, 240 n.11
Hödl, H. G. 204 n.23
Höffding, H.
Psychologie in Umrissen auf Grundlage der Erfahrung [*Outlines of Psychology on the Basis of Experience*] 41–2, 210 n.21
Holland, H. W.
'Heredity' 41
Hollingdale, R. J. 9, 21, 230 n.210, 236 n.48

Nietzsche: The Man and His Philosophy 18
Holub, R. C. 226 n.162
holy lie (*pius fraus*) 79
honesty 47, 102, 115
Horace 109, 174, 227 n.163, 233 nn.33, 36
Horn, A. 211 n.25
Houssaye, H.
Les hommes et les idées 42
Huang, J. 215 n.5
Human, All Too Human 18
new content in 128
human greatness 102–3
human ideals 107
humility 182

idealism 89, 91, 128, 141, 175
imaginary causality, error of 74–5, 76
immoralism 118
Immoralist, The 35, 66, 72, 75, 79, 86, 96, 118, 133, 143
immoralists 66, 75, 77, 78, 98, 118, 122, 142, 143, 154
improvers 13, 30, 38, 43–4, 73
innocence
of becoming 76, 118, 129, 143, 154, 159, 222 n.95, 228 n.181
of existence 76, 222 n.95
instinct
status and role of 173–5
intoxication 87, 92, 95, 96
Islam 186

Jacolliot, L., see also Manu, Laws of
'Laws of Manu, The' 13, 80
Les legislateurs religieux: Manou-Moise-Mahomet 44, 184
Janz, C. P. 13
Friedrich Nietzsche: Biographie 12
Jenseits von Gut und Böse (JGB) 4, 7–9, 32, 108, 121, 189
antiquity 112
aphorisms 64, 66
English-language discussions of 20
Entselbstungmoral 223 n.117
eternal recurrence 150, 151, 158, 160, 163
morality 82

new content in   128
notes   30
place and role of British philosophy and thinkers in   47
sublimation   171
subtitle   55–9
summary of   126, 127
Übermensch   100, 226 n.161
will to power   134, 168
JGB, *see Jenseits von Gut und Böse* (JGB)
Joly, H.
   Psychologie des grands hommes [*Psychology of Great Men*]   42, 211 n.23
Judaism   186
justice/the just   39, 43, 227 n.176

Kant, I.   40, 45, 52, 65, 88, 103, 136, 185
Kaufmann, W.   21, 57
Klages, L.   169
Krauss, A.
   Die Psychologie des Verbrechens: Ein Beitrag zur Erfahrungsseelenkunde [*The Psychology of Crime*]   42

Large, D.   9, 205 n.31, 230 n.210
   Oxford World's Classics   21–2
Leisure of a Psychologist, The   166
Letourneau, C.
   Physiologie des passions   43
liberalism   101
life, affirmation of   140–1
life-affirming   64, 78, 89, 98, 100, 103, 111, 146, 162–3, 182, 185, 191
life-denying   77, 81, 98–100, 110, 162, 181, 182, 185, 226 n.151
Littré, É.
   La science au point de vue philosophique   49
Loeb, P. S.   233 n.5
logic   21
Löwenfeld, L.
   Die moderne Behandlung der Nervenschwäche (*Neurasthenie*), *der Hysterie und verwandter Leiden*   43

Machiavelli, N.   110
   Prince, The   40

Magnus, B.   54
   'Deification of the Commonplace: Twilight of the Idol, The'   22–3
Manu, laws of   13, 44, 79, 80, 181, 240 n.12
   critique of   80–1
Manu-smrti   44
Menschliches, Allzumenschliches
   aphorisms   63
mental collapse/insane/insanity   6, 15, 17, 130, 162, 172, 229 n.203
metaphysics   9, 20, 21, 39, 58, 61, 70–2, 80, 89, 107, 108, 111, 113, 119, 127, 128, 133, 152, 159, 164, 168, 172, 178, 182, 188, 191, 219 n.40
   critique of   98, 110, 204 n.26, 217 n.22
   of language   70
Midday   20, 59, 71, 72, 143, 153, 154, 157, 158, 229 n.207
'Midday and Eternity'   59, 157, 158
Middle Ages   141
Mill, J. S.
   Autobiography   48
   On Liberty   49
   role in *Götzen-Dämmerung*   47–8
   Subjection of Women, The   48
mistaking cause for consequences, error of   74
modernity   85–7, 96, 98, 100, 101, 111, 128, 184, 206 n.15
   critique of   205 n.15
modern morality   78, 240 n.6
modern values   135, 162
Montinari, M.   2, 3, 14–16, 28–30, 215 n.3
Moore, G.   212 n.31
moralism   153, 155
moral/morality   4, 7, 44, 72–84, 86, 96–101, **97**, 119, 126, 128–9, 153, 155, 178, 190
   as anti-nature   12, 64, 76–7
   of breeding   79, 181
   Christian   82, 83, 178
   critique of   18, 43, 60, 79–80
   decadence   98, 108
   genealogy or origin of   48, 49
   master   82
   noble   82, 83
   of pure blood   79

self-sacrificing 240 n.6
spiritualization and 129
of taming 79, 80, 181
Morgonröthe 19, 87

Nägeli, C. v.
Mechanisch-physiologische Theorie der Abstammungslehre (*Mechanico-Physiological Theory of Descent*) 41
Napoleon 45, 103, 142, 174, 227
nationalism 84, 103
naturalism 46
Naumann, H. C. G. 54, 86
new values 114, 115
Nietzsche, C. 40
    illness 100
Nietzsche, F.
    Der Fall Wagner 1, 8
    Die fröhliche Wissenschaft (see *Die fröhliche Wissenschaft*)
    Die Geburt der Tragödie 12, 18
    Ecce homo (see *Ecce homo*)
    Hauptwerk (see *Hauptwerk*)
    Human, All Too Human 18
    Jenseits von Gut und Böse (see *Jenseits von Gut und Böse*)
    Menschliches, Allzumenschliches 63
    Portable Nietzsche, The 21
    On the Genealogy of Morals 43, 50, 52, 93, 211 n.27
    Twilight of the Idols (*Götzen-Dämmerung*) (see *Götzen-Dämmerung* (GD))
    view of sublimation 170-2
    Will to Power, The 24
    Zur Genealogie der Moral 8
Nietzsche contra Wagner 201 n.1, 224 n.122
    antiquity 111
nihilism 4-7, 23, 29, 67, 69, 71, 98, 101, 121, 136-9, 146, 189, 190
nihilists 99, 137, 152
noble/aristocratic/nobility 58, 82-5, 102, 103, 114, 126, 141, 189
noon-day 72
noontide 116
Norman, J. 22
no-saying 7, 113, 114, 119, 162, 189

Old Testament 40, 80
On the Genealogy of Morals 43, 50, 52, 93, 211 n.27
    physiology of art 93
ontology 93
optimism 56
order of rank 7, 80-1, 98, 107, 136, 170, 189
Orsucci, A. 240 n.8
over-human 107
overman 65

pagan 82, 141
paganism 103
pathos of distance (*Pathos der Distanz*) 98, 100, 118
Paulhan, F.
    Les phénomènes affectifs et les lois de leur apparition: Essai de psychologie générale 42
peace of soul 76-7, 101, 171
perspectivism 6, 7, 23, 189, 191
pessimism 7, 9, 42, 61, 69, 88, 99, 100, 111, 119, 150, 153, 171, 191
    critique of 152
    Schopenhauerian 127
pessimists 98-100, 111, 156
philosophy
    critique of 67-72, 121
    reason in 70
physiology 127, 167, 237 n.10
    of aesthetics 4, 93, 205 n.29
    of art 5, 86, 87, 92-6, **94**, 133, 205 n.29
    reading in and about 41-3
pity 58, 100, 186, 240 n.6
Plato 38, 39, 70, 89, 91, 109, 112, 136, 140, 141, 143, 169, 173, 175, 182
Platonism 109, 111
politics 13, 84, 96, 167
positivism 46
preparatory/prelude 2, 5, 6, 12, 16, 17, 22, 25, 27, 30, 62, 79, 110, 118, 122, 133, 158, 160, 177, 185, 189, 191, 214 n.2
Prideaux, S.
    I Am Dynamite 20
psychology 237 n.10
    cognitive 168

experimental   168
free will   75
new   166–70
old, critique of   166–70
reading in and about   41–3
social   40
punishment   75, 76

radicalization   94
rationalism/rationality   70, 73, 170
Rattner, J.   203 n.9
   Nietzsche: Leben–Werk–Wirkung   13
reality/realism   18, 25, 40–1, 44, 57, 58,
      61, 66, 70, 71, 74, 78, 79, 108–10,
      113–17, 120, 127, 128, 136, 137,
      139–41, 143, 146, 152–5, 161, 162,
      178, 181, 185, 190, 209 n.10
   affirmation of   110, 140–1
   in art   92–3
   denial of   110, 155
reason, status and role of   173–5
recuperation   5, 8, 14, 61–2, 77
relativism   23
religion   4, 19, 31, 40, 72–84, 93, 96,
      113, 117, 119, 122, 128, 135, 143,
      152, 155, 161, 165, 166, 171, 178,
      179, 181–4, 188, 189, 191
Renaissance   82, 98, 112, 141, 183, 185,
      186
Renan, E.   184
   Vie de Jésus   40, 188
resentment   13, 79, 108, 126, 134, 167,
      182
revaluation of all values   4, 5, 8, 9, 18,
      21, 24, 35, 39, 56, 63, 64, 66, 67,
      74, 106, 111–13, 117, 127, 131,
      134, 135, 141, 161, 162, 178, 182,
      189–91, 203 n.9, 205 n.35, 219 n.48,
      222 n.96, 224 n.129, 235 n.33,
      236 nn.47, 49
   brief commentary to general
      contents   88
   critique of Christianity   185–8
   foreword   61, 62
   genesis of   28
   references   117–18
   spiritualization of the passions and
      desires   77
revaluation of values   64–5

revenge   76
Richet, C.
   Essai de psychologie générale   42
   *L'homme et l'intelligence: Fragments de
      physiologie et de psychologie*   42
Ridley, A.   22
Robins, E.
   'Maenadism in Religion'   44
Rolph, W. H.
   *Biologische Probleme, zugleich als
      Versuch zur Entwicklung einer
      rationellen Ethik* (*Biological
      Problems, also an Attempt at
      an Elaboration of a Rational
      Ethics*)   41
romanticism   87
Ross, W.   13
   Der ängstliche Adler   12
Rousseau, J. J.   88, 89
Roux, W.
   *Struggle of the Parts in the Organism,
      The*   40–1
Runes, D. D.   224 n.126

Safranski, R.   203 n.7
   *Nietzsche: Biographie seines
      Denkens*   13
Sallust   109, 142, 233 n.33
Sand, G.   52
Schmidt, L.
   Die Ethik der alten Griechen   112
Schopenhauer, A.   38–40, 45, 71, 93, 100,
      127, 148, 181, 212 n.32, 224 n.124
Schrift, A. D.   202 n.8
science   40–1
   and philosophy, relation between   69
self-control   102, 115
self-defence   116
self-discipline   116
self-mockery   64
self-mutilation   64
self-sacrifice   182
Semper, K.
   *Natural Conditions of Existence as they
      Affect Animal Life, The*   41
sin   75, 181
socialization   90
social psychology   40
society   96–101, **97**

sociobiology   168
Socrates   30, 42, 68–70, 77, 81, 91, 100,
    107, 111, 127, 136, 137, 141, 143,
    152–3, 155, 169, 174, 178
Sommer, A. U.   6
    Nietzsche-Kommentar: Band 6/1   18
    Nietzsche-Lexikon   17
sophistic culture   109
sophists   40, 127, 128, 141, 142
soul   75–7, 101, 108, 169, 171, 172,
    238 n.31
Spencer, H.
    Data of Ethics, The   48
    Die Thatsachen der Ethik   48
    *Einleitung in das Studium der
        Sociologie*   48
    role in *Götzen-Dämmerung*   48–9
spirit   4, 21, 50, 54, 63, 75, 80, 85, 93, 106,
    108, 114, 122, 126, 133, 156, 171,
    178, 181
spirituality/spiritualization
    (*Vergeistigung*)   77, 81, 129, 175
    of enmity   76, 78
    and morality   129
    of sensuality   76
Stendhal   41, 142, 167, 212 n.32, 233 n.33
Strauss, D. F.
    Das Leben Jesu   51, 105
    Der alte und der neue Glaube   45
    magnum opus Das Leben Jesu   45
Stricker, S.
    Physiologie des Rechts   43
striving   110, 111, 115, 116, 168
sublimation   64, 78, 81–3, 90, 110, 129,
    141, 155, 170–3, 175
subtitle (to *Twilight of the Idols*)   56–61
suicide   98–9, 226 n.159
Sully, J.
    Le pessimisme (histoire et critique)
        [*Pessimism: A History and a
        Criticism*]   42
    Les illusions des sens et de l'esprit
        [*Illusions: A Psychological
        Study*]   42
superman   136, *see also* Übermensch

tabula rasa   170
Taine, H.   101

Geschichte des englischen Literatur   49,
    51
Tanner, M.   21, 239 n.1
telos   61, 139, 146, 152
Thatcher, D. S.   57, 205 n.32, 217 nn.21,
    22, 218 n.23
    'Diagnosis of Idols, A'   23–4
Thucydides   109, 110, 116, 140, 142,
    209 n.10, 233 n.33
Tolstoy, L.
    Ma religion   188
tragedy   25, 83, 108, 109, 127, 146, 148
tragic   9, 70, 71, 87, 108, 110–12, 119,
    135, 141, 143, 152, 153, 155–7, 161,
    162, 228 n.180
transvaluation   22
truth/truthfulness/honest/truthful   3,
    13, 23, 54, 56, 57, 62, 64, 69, 71, 85,
    100, 101, 115, 121, 126, 133, 134,
    147, 158, 167, 171–3, 181–3, 185,
    186, 189, 191, 238 n.44
Turgenev, I. S.
    Fathers and Sons   136
Twilight of the Idols (*Götzen-Dämmerung*),
    see Götzen-Dämmerung

Übermensch   6, 7, 23, 24, 65, 100, 102,
    106, 128, 134–6, 140, 192, 226 n.161
Überthier   65
Umwerthung aller Werthe   2–8, 27,
    38, 86, 104, 119–22, 129, 189,
    202 nn.19, 22, 203 n.4, 207 n.20,
    208 n.32, 214 n.2, 215 n.7, 220 n.65,
    224 n.118, 228 n.186
    affirmative contents of   143
    antiquity   109–12
    aphorisms   65–7
    brief commentary to general
        contents   88
    critique of Christianity   177, 184, 188
    critique of philosophy   67–9, 71, 72
    English-language discussions of   19–
        22, 24, 25
    epilogue   112, 114
    eternal recurrence   151, 154, 157, 158,
        161–3
    foreword   61, 62
    free will, error of   75

general consequences and
    observations 53, 54
genesis of 28–9
German-language accounts of 12–18
history of 31, 32, **34**
main title 55, 56
morality 72–5, 77–9, 81, 83, 96, 108
nihilism 138
pointers and references in *Götzen-
    Dämmerung* 104–9, **197–8**
pre-empt or exhaust the
    contents 130, 131, 133
preface 84, 85
psychology 166
religion 74, 75, 77–9, 81, 83
revaluation of all values 135
subtitle 58, 59
Übermensch 136
unegoistic 238 n.37
Unmensch 65
unselfing oneself (*Entselbstungsmoral*)
    108, 114, 223 n.117
Unthier 65
Unzeitgemäße Betrachtungen 115–16
utilitarianism 46, 51, 65, 213 n.38
utility 49

virtue/*virtù* 51, 66, 72–4, 78, 91, 102,
    104, 143, 156, 166, 174, 214 n.54,
    217 n.21
Vogt, J. G. 148
    Force 41

Wahrig-Schmidt, B. 211 n.25
Wellhausen, J. 184
    *Prolegomena zur Geschichte
        Isreals* 188
    Skizzen und Vorarbeiten 188
Weltanschauung 108, 184
Williams, B. 237 n.26
will to power 5–7, 13, 20, 24, 41, 43, 47,
    49, 73, 74, 76, 81, 82, 96, 110, 111,
    118, 134–5, 167, 168, 174, 189, 192,
    211 n.26, 225 n.137, 227 nn.176,
    178, 231 n.14, 237 nn.16, 19, 20

developmental theory of 167
Will to Power, The (*Der Wille zur
    Macht*) 2, 24, 29, 237 n.23
aphorisms 63
critique of philosophy 72
English-language discussions of 24
eternal recurrence 157, 160–1
general consequences and
    observations 54
German-language accounts of
    14, 15
history of 32, 33, 35
nihilism 137, 138
psychology 168
subtitle 59
Winteler, R. 203 n.14, 214 n.1
wisdom 161, 169, 173, 225 n.139

yes-saying 7, 113, 114, 119, 162
Young, J. 19–20
    *Philosophical Biography: Friedrich
        Nietzsche, A* 18, 71

Zarathustra 20, 71, 72, 88, 104, 105, 113,
    116, 143, 146, 149, 152–4, 162, 164,
    221 n.82
zenith of mankind 153–4
Zur Genealogie der Moral 8, 9, 23, 27,
    121, 189, 190, 204 n.24, 205 n.29,
    224 n.129, 225 n.144
aphorisms 66
art and aesthetics 89
Entselbstungmoral 223 n.117
eternal recurrence 150, 160, 163
morality 82
new content in 128
nihilism 138
notes 30
place and role of British philosophy
    and thinkers in 47
pre-empt or exhaust the
    contents 131, 133
psychology 42
summary of 126
will to power 168

www.ingramcontent.com/pod-product-compliance
Lightning Source LLC
Chambersburg PA
CBHW071819300426
44116CB00009B/1372